National Security

The seventh edition of this highly successful textbook analyzes the history, evolution, and processes of national security policies.

It examines national security from two fundamental fault lines—the end of the Cold War and the evolution of contemporary terrorism dating from the 9/11 terrorist attacks—and traces their path up to ISIS and beyond. The book considers how the resulting era of globalization and geopolitics guides policy. Placing these trends in conceptual and historical context and following them through military, semimilitary, and nonmilitary concerns, *National Security* treats its subject as a nuanced and subtle phenomenon that encompasses everything from the global to the individual with the nation at its core.

New to the Seventh Edition

- An assessment of the impact of the Trump presidency on national security and relevant domestic policies, including border security and energy security matters.
- The continuing impact and evolution of terrorism as a security problem, with notable emphasis on the decline of the Islamic State (IS) and what terrorist threats are likely to succeed it.
- A description of the cyber security problem with an emphasis on Russian efforts to interfere with the 2016 US presidential election and beyond.
- A revised delineation of the geographic and substantive challenges facing the United States in the form of a chapter on "lethal landscapes," emphasizing the rise of China as a global rival and opponent in Asia and an attempt to deal with state aspirants like the Kurds.

This book will continue to be highly beneficial to students and scholars working and studying in security studies, military and strategic studies, defense studies, foreign policy, US politics, and international relations.

Donald M. Snow is Professor Emeritus of Political Science at the University of Alabama, where he specialized in international relations, national security, and foreign policy. He has also served as visiting professor at the US Air, Army, and Naval War Colleges and the US Air Command and Staff College.

Donald Snow offers a compelling approach to understanding the complexities of US national security. By moving beyond worst-case threat analysis, he grounds foreign policy in American domestic politics to reinvigorate thinking on the future of national security.

—**Derek S. Reveron**, *Harvard University*

I recommend the new edition of *National Security* without reservation. It is a readable and informative text, and students find it useful and engaging. In addition, Donald Snow's use of contemporary as well as historic examples opens the door for many meaningful classroom discussions. I find the text essential in the discussion of the complexities surrounding the study of the politics of US national security issues and list it as required reading every semester.

—**Matthew Wahlert**, *Miami University*

Dr. Snow has once again delivered a text for its time. Rather than focusing on the institutional aspects of national security, he looks at the real issues of national security in a post–Cold War, post-9/11 world. The strong connection he makes between domestic politics and international threats goes beyond the normal "guns v. butter" debate. I am looking forward to the publication of this book so that I can adopt it for my courses.

—**Michael Kanner**, *University of Colorado Boulder*

This book offers readers an excellent introduction to national security. It skillfully combines a clear conceptual framework with thorough applications to both historical and contemporary security challenges. The book carefully guides readers through the abstract logic of interests, power, security and domestic politics, before examining the concrete manifestations of these concepts in the context of US national security from the early days of the nation to the post-9/11 world and the rise of the Islamic State.

—**Benjamin T. Jones**, *University of Mississippi*

National Security

Seventh edition

DONALD M. SNOW

Routledge
Taylor & Francis Group

NEW YORK AND LONDON

This edition published 2020
by Routledge
52 Vanderbilt Avenue, New York, NY 10017

and by Routledge
2 Park Square, Milton Park, Abingdon, Oxon, OX14 4RN

Routledge is an imprint of the Taylor & Francis Group, an informa business

© 2020 Taylor & Francis

First edition published by Pearson Education Inc. 2004
Sixth edition published by Routledge 2017

Library of Congress Cataloging in Publication Data
Names: Snow, Donald M., 1943– author. Title: National security/Donald M. Snow.
Other titles: National security for a new era.
Description: Seventh edition. | New York, NY : Routledge, [2019]
Identifiers: LCCN 2019012238|
Subjects: LCSH: National security—United States. | United States—Military
    policy. | World politics—21st century.
Classification: LCC UA23. S5253 2019 | DDC 355/.033073—dc23
LC record available at https://lccn.loc.gov/2019012238

ISBN: 978-1-138-37057-9 (hbk)
ISBN: 978-1-138-37058-6 (pbk)
ISBN: 978-0-429-42792-3 (ebk)

Typeset in Sabon
by Apex CoVantage, LLC

CONTENTS

PART II   The Historical Context   53

CHAPTER 3   Influences from the Past: The American Historical Experience   54

CHAPTER 4   The Post-1945 Challenge: The Nature and End of the Cold War   77

PREFACE

The last edition of this book (the sixth) was drafted in 2015, and it has a copyright date of 2017. In terms of the oddities of academic publication dates, that means the book was revised in 2015–2016 and "hit the streets" in 2016. A lot has gone on since then that is relevant to the substance and study of national security.

The changes for the new seventh edition are both domestic and international, and the two sources of that change are interactive (or intemestic, part international and part domestic). The most important domestic political event was, of course, the 2016 presidential election, which resulted in the election of the most unconventional chief executive in terms of foreign policy and national security since the period between the two world wars of the past century. President Trump has acted outside the mainstream of philosophical approaches to relations with the rest of the world, and the longer his incumbency has extended, the more distinct and pervasive the "Trump effect" has become.

One can think of the impact of the Trump presidency in three broad national security categories, not all of which he created and on which he has had varying effects. The first and most consequential elements are the direct result of Trump policies and attitudes toward the international environment and countries and areas. A suggestive list, some parts of which appear elsewhere in the text, includes his America First emphasis in unilateral, exclusionary nationalism; his retreat from globalism as a guiding principle; his rejection of internationalism and leadership in areas like NATO (North Atlantic Treaty Organization); his rejection of economic globalization and return to economic nationalism (through devices like tariffs); his embrace of authoritarian leaders like Vladimir Putin, Kim Jung Un, and Muhammad bin Salman (the notorious MBS); the reinstitution of a "bad neighbor" policy toward Central America; and a reemphasis on broad and extensive defense spending. The list could go on.

The second contribution is trends in which his actions and pronouncements have had an effect. Two stand out. The first is the notion of political tribalism. As noted in the text, loyalties to subnational groups, often tribally described and tribally based, have been a major source of political instability and violence in many developing world countries, and the concept has increasingly been employed to describe political cleavage in developed countries, including the United States. The basis of this extension has been President Trump and his spirited appeal to population segments in the United States, notably non–college graduate Whites who feel increasingly alienated in an increasingly multicultural society. The other trend has been the geopolitical assertiveness of American rivals. The Russians, notably in the areas contiguous to Russia with large Russian minorities (what was known as the "near abroad" during the Soviet era), are one ominous example, as are the Chinese in consolidating and expanding political repression in China proper and in minority enclaves in places like the Uighur lands of central Asia. Neither trend has elicited major objection from the Trump White House.

The third trend has been area specific. There are increasingly apparent shifts and conflicts surrounding the power struggle in the Middle East, a phenomenon that has elicited little activism in Washington. It has several aspects that individually or collectively could alter the power map of the region, over which the United States has been reluctant to attempt to influence. One aspect is the changing Israeli-Palestinian relationship, where the Trump administration has backed the Netanyahu government of Israel and its expansion of control through acts like moving the US Embassy to Israeli-controlled Jerusalem, an action that has effectively mortally wounded the peace process between the two parties. The Syrian government has effectively defeated the civil war against it over international objections, but Syria's remaining supporter, Russia, is in no position to make even a dent in the repatriation and rebuilding task facing the country. The enormous tragedy of Yemen illustrates the power struggle between Shiite, non-Arab Iran and Sunni Saudi Arabia for geopolitical advantage in the Persian Gulf region. The Trump contribution has been to continue to back Saudi Arabia and notably its rogue ruler-in-waiting, MBS, despite his apparent complicity in ordering the assassination of an American-based Saudi journalist. All this continues while the apparently never-ending war in Afghanistan goes on without realistic prospects of conclusion. The most positive aspect of the region has been the decline to insignificance of the Islamic State (IS), which has effectively imploded as a major threat.

One can make too much and too little of the atmospherics of national security concerns at any point in time. Specific situations, including threats, arise and require attention and action, but the differences between the situation "on the ground" at any two moments can easily be exaggerated in the heat of crises. The national security environment consists of both long-term conceptual and physical concerns—structural hierarchies of national interests, threats, risks and risk management at the conceptual level, and governmental dysfunction, for instance—that coexist with more transient challenges of the day. By deed and philosophy, President Trump has changed some of the parameters of discussion of the pattern, but the structure of challenges will continue to evolve and change regardless of how long he or someone else occupies the Oval Office.

This book has also evolved over the years. The original version of it, *National Security*, was published in 1985 by St. Martin's Press, and that version went through four editions before St. Martin's got out of the political science college textbook business at the end of the 1990s. The book was reborn shortly after the turn of the new century as *National Security for a New Era* under the Longman's and later the Pearson imprints, where it went through five editions. The book has found a new home at Routledge, which published the sixth edition and this current iteration, the seventh. It could as easily be labelled the eleventh edition of the original work.

The book has four discernible themes that dominate its concerns, all of which were part of the last edition and serve as parts of this effort. Part I is conceptual, dealing with the idea of national security and the concepts and dynamics that make national security a distinctive area of study. These distinctions endure to provide a framework for thinking about contemporary problems. Part II is historical, with chapters that examine the American military past, as well as its more recent history, to help frame how Americans feel about national security, the Cold War, its ending, and adjustment to a post–Cold War world.

Part III deals with the politics of national security, including the conceptual contributions of the Trump administration, one of the most unorthodox actors in recent national security evolution. It begins with a chapter on the basic structure of national security within the American political system. From there, it moves to the current malaise in which the political system exists, including themes of hyper-partisanship, dysfunction, and the inability to project a single national vision to the world during crises. All these factors affect national security adversely. The part ends with a review of current "legacy" American forces and priorities from the past and changes necessitated by a dynamic national security environment.

Part IV, the longest section of the book, with six chapters, examines the contemporary environment, the challenges that environment poses for the United States, how it can approach these problems, and what they may look like in the future. Chapters focus on such topics as asymmetrical warfare, holdover problems from the last decade (Iraq, Afghanistan, and terror), the current distribution of potential military threats to the United States ("lethal landscapes"), other forms of possible national security activism (such as peacekeeping, state building, and humanitarian intervention), and new sources of security concern (border security, environmental and natural-resource security, cyber security). Part V consists of two chapters that project some prominent influences on future policy development. One chapter looks at three specific policy areas (border protection, natural-resources policy, and cyber security). The final chapter looks at more general prospects and concepts for the future of national security policy.

NEW TO THIS EDITION

Like any book that has gone through multiple editions, new materials appear as the environment changes, and older concerns fade or reappear.

Early editions, for instance, gave significant attention to nuclear weapons and deterrence and to economic globalization. The threat of nuclear war has seemed increasingly remote (although not impossible), but has returned with North Korea's emergence as an active nuclear power. Much of the sheen has disappeared from the prospect of an increasingly globalized economy, in large measure because of policies pursued by Trump. Newer concerns have appeared or expanded, such as the increased use of special operations forces (SOFs) in American force utilization.

The table of contents of this edition is similar, but not identical, to the last edition because that iteration represented a major restructuring of the flow, analysis, and arguments that are emphasized here. Chapter titles have not changed, nor has the structure of the table of contents, but there have been important additions and deletions within chapters. New points of emphasis have been added or elaborated. The changes include:

- An assessment of the impact of the Trump presidency on national security and relevant domestic policies, a theme recurring throughout the text.
- An examination of the changing nature and content of threats in terms of the realist framework in Asia and places like Russia and the Middle East.
- A greater level of attention to the problems of the American system and how they represent difficulties for the conduct of national security policy and strategy, including the effects of policy-making gridlock and the extremely difficult problems hyper-partisanship poses for creating and sustaining effective policies and how the Trump presidency has affected that environment.
- The continuing difficulties of defense budgeting, with emphasis on the impact of the sequester.
- Changing material and manpower needs, including the decline of major European-style warfare scenarios and the increasing importance of developing world internal conflicts (DWICs) emphasizing SOFs rather than more traditional American forces.
- Increased attention to the threats posed by an expansionist Russia and the unique influence of Vladimir Putin on the problem.
- A revised delineation of the geographic and substantive challenges facing the United States in the form of a chapter on "lethal landscapes," emphasizing, among other things, the rise of China as a global rival and opponent in Asia and an attempt to deal with state aspirants like the Kurds.
- The delineation of DWICs as the primary source of violence and instability in the contemporary environment and its implications for US national security.

- The complex problem of conducting successful operations in DWICs, particularly in contrast to Cold War actions and the convoluted consequences of DWIC-based involvements, using US support for suppression of the Hauthis in Yemen as an example.
- The continuing impact and evolution of terrorism as a security problem, with notable emphasis on the decline of IS and what terrorist threats are likely to succeed it.
- The impact of the Trump presidency on the dimension of the US national security problem, including border security and energy security matters.
- A description of the cyber security problem, with an emphasis on Russian efforts to interfere with the 2016 US presidential election and beyond.
- A summary and prospectus of the impact of American unilateralism on the structure of the ongoing and future American national security environment.

FEATURES

The book retains the basic structure and features it had in the past. Each part of the book includes a brief description of the chapters that are a part of it, including some explanation of how they relate to one another. Each individual chapter begins with a summary of its contents to provide an indication of what follows. At the end of each chapter are two continuing features. The first is a series of Discussion/Study Questions that are intended to direct readers in their review of the chapters and as subjects for potential classroom discussion. The second is a Selected Bibliography. This listing includes two types of citations: the first is books, articles, and the like to which direct reference has been made in the chapter text; the second is other sources that may be of utility to readers who desire to pursue further information about topics raised in the chapter. An effort has been made to include items that are timely and not so technically sophisticated or jargonized that they confuse rather than enlighten the reader.

ACKNOWLEDGMENTS

The author would like to recognize the help provided by colleagues who read and reviewed all or parts of this work. These include Valentine J. Belfiglio, Texas Women's University; David Benjamin, University of Bridgeport; Lamont Colucci, Ripon College; Charles Cushman, George Washington University; Gary L. Guertner, University of Arizona; Joe D. Hagan, West Virginia University; Patrick Haney, Miami University; Christopher Jones,

Northern Illinois University; Michael Kanner, University of Colorado Boulder; Richard J. Kilroy Jr., East Carolina University; Lawrence Korb, Center for American Progress; William Lamkin, Glendale Community College; Eleonora Mattiacci, Amherst College; Gale Mattox, US Naval Academy; Edward G. Moore, University of Texas at Brownsville; Linda Petrou, High Point University; J. Patrick Plumlee, University of North Florida; Philip Schrodt, University of Kansas; Michael E. Smith, Georgia State University; Chris Van Aller, Winthrop University; and Matthew Wahlert, Miami University.

Thanks also to Jennifer Knerr, Ze'ev Sudry, and Olivia Hatt at Routledge. Any remaining errors are, of course, my own.

SELECTED BIBLIOGRAPHY

Snow, Donald M. *Thinking About National Security: Strategy, Policy, and Issues*. New York: Routledge, 2016.

The Conceptual Nexus

Debates about national security can seem confusing to the point of being off-putting to the newcomer to the subject. National security policy and its study occur within a framework of concepts and ideas that is not part of everyday political discourse. In addition, national security deals with life-and-death concerns about the safety, well-being, and even potentially the physical existence of the country and its citizens. Together, these factors set it apart from other areas of the policy process. As a result, national security and its study have evolved their own special language and ways of looking at their special policy area. Part I introduces the concepts and ways of thinking around which national security has been built and evolves.

It consists of two chapters that introduce the area and serve as an underpinning for the rest of the book. Chapter 1 addresses the question of how the idea of national security is changing in the contemporary world, with emphases both on the international environment and on the domestic political scene. The operative, and distinctive, idea of national security is the concept of threat, and thus the discussion of the international aspect of the "intermestic" policy area (partly *inter*national and partly *domestic*) looks at how the pattern of threats to the United States is changing, whereas the discussion of domestic concerns concentrates on the current debate about national security. Chapter 2 introduces and elaborates on the series of interrelated concepts around which national security policy matters are organized. It concludes with a discussion of the dominant pattern of thinking that has helped frame those discussions, the realist paradigm.

National Security for a New and Changing Era

American national security policy continues to evolve. Since the 2016 election, it has entered a new international and domestic political environment in which influences inside and outside the country have accentuated an "intermestic" situation to which the country must adapt. Internationally, the country is adjusting to a changed emphasis in terms of how it interacts both with friends and adversaries. Disagreements within the G-7 and tariff threats are examples of adverse dealings with allies while the country vies with North Korea and Iran globally. Domestically, political dysfunction, hyper-partisanship, and gridlock continue to dominate political and economic agendas and extend to the national security effort. The two environments intersect over both the impact on defense budgets. After reviewing and laying out some of the basic concerns associated with each factor and their intersection, the chapter concludes with an attempt to show how these influences are relevant to the current national security condition.

The United States is at or nearing one of its periodic crossroads in its national security orientation toward the world. Since 1945, the United States has been the leading power in the world, the country whose policies and actions have mattered everywhere. Much of this predominance has had a national security base, premised on and often enforced by the military strength of the United States, which has been the primary measure of national security. During this period, the United States has generally adopted an expansive, sometimes aggressive global role based on an abundance of resources that could be devoted to national security chores.

This period of American dominance, sometimes described in superlatives like "American hegemony," has eroded. It developed after World War II when the United States was virtually alone in the possession of great economic strength and military potential and thus stood astride the world system. This position was occasionally challenged, but until recently there has not been any systematic suggestion that the United States might have to dilute its role of world predominance. Domestic and international dynamics suggest that traditional American dominance may be becoming less tenable, possibly even untenable. Assessing these assertions produces important questions that form much of the core of what follows.

There are two major sources of contemporary challenge to the traditional American national security role. Neither is unprecedented. The first is weakness at home, a basically domestic concern caused by major difficulties in the operation of the American political system. The strongest manifestation of this weakness has been the slow growth of the American and global economies, which has further served to exacerbate underlying dysfunctions, and the political battle over domestic priorities, including national security posture and actions. One early 2000s outcome of internal developments was a determination to try to reduce federal spending, including the national security budget, to help balance the budget, a goal that has quietly been effectively abandoned. Another has been a reaction against US involvement in national security operations in the past decade that have been controversial and have raised questions about the wisdom of extrapolating future actions from traditional policies and levels of activism. Syria is a prime example.

Neither condition—economic stricture or policy reassessment—is unique to this time. The United States suffered a period of economic downturn in the 1970s and 1980s that some suggested might result in a permanent reduction in American economic prosperity and America's economic position in the world, and that crisis proved overblown. The popular negative reaction to the outcome of American efforts in Vietnam in the 1970s produced a far more severe demand for reassessing the level of American national security activism.

The period between the end of World War II (1945) and the present witnessed remarkable development and transformation in the idea and shape of national security in the American experience. National security was not a central and enduring concern in most of the previous 150+ years of American history, when American interests were more clearly focused on institutionalizing the independence won in 1783 and in developing the vast reaches of the North American continent.

World War II and the Cold War were watersheds in the American concern with national security as an ongoing, central American problem. World War II permanently ended any American delusions that it could remain politically aloof from the rest of the world. The peacetime politico-military threat posed by the Soviet Union and the growing communist world was also a transformational experience that produced, among other things, the first major sustained peacetime American concern with national security, the first coherent American security orientation toward the world, and the first sustained commitment of substantial American resources to the problem of national security.

The United States is now entering a new phase in its national security evolution. National security policy has always been quintessentially *intermestic*, a combination of *inter*national and do*mestic* influences. This term is more generally associated with national security's close conceptual cousin, foreign policy (it is, for instance, a central theme of Snow and Haney, *American Foreign Policy for a New Era*), but it applies equally well to national security policy. The heart of the intermestic dynamic is the belief that national security policies have both an international and a domestic content and impact and that those influences physically interact in making and implementing policy. An internationally based problem like terrorism also has domestic consequences that must be taken into consideration in making an international response and that will be affected by the international outcome of the issue. Similarly, many domestic issues, such as trade policy, have an international impact, and how they are resolved affects the international dimension of economic policy.

American national security policy and politics can be cast in intermestic terms. After World War II, for instance, the major international factor was the rise of a powerful, antagonistic Soviet bloc in political and military opposition to the United States and the rest of the noncommunist world, and it demanded a response in kind. The primarily military dimension of that change became the basis for the American national security policy and strategy of containment, a construct that evolved over time as the Soviet threat inflated and eventually deflated. Domestically, the threat was manifest in a parallel political demonization of communism with sharp domestic political impact and the first large-scale continuous commitment of sizable American resources to national security in times other than a major "hot" war.

This pregnant period of American national security development and physical resource commitment was not linear. The negative outcome of American involvement in Vietnam in 1973 brought with it a strong but temporary negative reaction to, and thus rethinking of, the national security commitments the country had made. At the same time, the late 1970s and early 1980s witnessed the American economy in an apparent crisis of competitiveness that raised questions about the affordability of America's ongoing global commitments and its willingness to bear those costs. The Vietnam "hangover" (the intense negative attitude toward security resulting from the outcome of the war) was largely over by the early 1980s, and by the end of that decade, the American economy had rebounded on the coattails of American preeminence in high technology, thus restoring the luster to both international and domestic aspects of national security policy. After the Cold War ended, the United States enjoyed a decade-long apparent respite from serious international threats during the 1990s while the American economy flourished in the early stages of economic globalization. The terrorist attacks on September 11, 2001, punctured the international tranquility in the new millennium and re-created a sense of threat and national security vitality that had receded during the 1990s. The second decade of the twenty-first century has already provided a new permutation that may mark another new era for American national security. The questioning of possible overextension and misapplication of American force in Vietnam has its parallel in similar questioning about the American wars in Iraq and Afghanistan.

That national security has been in a process of transition since 2016 is hard to deny, as is its intermestic nature. What may be different this time is that the national security debate of the latter twentieth century was driven primarily by international threats to which the domestic environment provided resources, whereas resource constraints in the current period may instead affect the extent and nature of national security responses to perceptions of international threats. The idea that the United States should pull back from a generous but expensive commitment to enforcing the global order has been a signature characteristic of the Trump administration's approach to America's role in the world.

Whether the complex of influences swirling around national security will represent a fundamental or transitory adjustment is uncertain. The motor that drove national security during the second half of the twentieth century was a clear, relatively unambiguous, and compelling challenge and threat driven by the international environment that could not be left unattended. The primary engine of the current reconsideration is more clearly domestic and surrounds the question of how much activism the American political system is willing to bear. A return to a period of national economic growth, the balm that has healed previous economically influenced crises, may provide the salve that reduces the sharp edges of the argument. In the meantime, there is little consensus about what the national security problem is or how much to commit to its amelioration.

While the idea that national security is inherently an interplay of domestic and international (in other words, intermestic) factors may have broad implications, the current sense of concern and priorities may be somewhat more ephemeral. Things change, and the circumstances that are currently of such great import may be among them. As the Greek philosopher Heraclitus said over 2,500 years ago, "Nothing endures but change. Nothing stays still." Change, in other words, is the real constant, and what it means in the current environment forms the national security problem. Abstract philosophy aside, adapting to change is the essence of the policy debate.

The sources, dynamics, and prospects for consequences of intermestic change in the traditional American national security equation provide the major theme of this volume. The discussion moves first to an introduction of the nature and sources of change in the international and domestic environments that underlay the current reexamination of how the United States approaches national security, themes that are elaborated and explained in subsequent chapters. The question is then phrased in terms of possible directions that change may take and the consequences and desirability of those possible changes.

THE NATURE OF CHANGE IN A HERACLITEAN WORLD

The analysis of national security is always conducted in an atmosphere of some controversy, emotion, and uncertainty. The major source of controversy is the subjective nature of the problem. National security's basis is in threats (promises to do harm in the absence of compliance with some condition demanded by the threatening party) and responses to them. Threats may or may not be overt and overwhelmingly obvious, but they are almost always subject to interpretations that allow reasonable people to disagree about them. Within the current debate about national security, one issue that encapsulates this subjectivity is the contentious matter of Chinese military expansion and its clear pretension to challenge the United States as a world power. By almost any measure, the Chinese are devoting considerable resources to military modernization and expansion. What this expansion means for the United States is not so clear. If one wants to inflate the threatening nature of Chinese expansion, one points to the ominous possibilities of a fleet of Chinese aircraft carriers with designs—and presumably capabilities—far more advanced than the current American carrier fleet. If one wants to downgrade that threat, one questions how or to what extent this capability directly threatens the United States. Alternatively, one can argue that modern missile technology leaves aircraft carriers exceedingly vulnerable and thus an anachronistic target, like capital surface battleships in World War II—a capability from which sensible countries should be divesting themselves. On the other hand, Chinese naval expansion can be seen ominously as a challenge to American naval hegemony in East Asian waters like the South China Sea that carry much of the world's trade.

National security matters are also highly emotional because of the potentially enormous impact and consequences of policy outcomes. The heart of national security is ultimately ensuring the physical survival of the state and protection against those who would encroach upon it. Prior to the Cold War, these were rarely prescient concerns for Americans, but the ever-present possibility of a civilization-ending nuclear Armageddon created a sense of urgency and emotion that has attached to the subject ever since. This has been revived in the new century by the threat of international terrorism and the danger posed if its actors could obtain these weapons. Threat—such as that posed by terrorism—particularly influences discussions on future policies because the failure to take adequate measures today could possibly jeopardize the ability to ensure security and even survival in an uncertain future. This dynamic gives a conservative bias to national security planning. One cannot afford to underestimate threats because being wrong could be catastrophic. The result is a proclivity for overpreparation and "tried and true" approaches that have succeeded in the past.

Uncertainty fuels both controversy and emotional anxiety. Much of that uncertainty arises from the volatile and largely uncontrollable nature of an international environment to which national security policy must respond. Who, for instance, foresaw in early 1990 that the United States would be at war with Iraq by early fall of that year? The action precipitating that involvement, of course, was Saddam Hussein's decision to invade and annex Kuwait, a decision US planners neither anticipated nor could influence effectively. Despite elaborate peacetime military planning, it is a soldier's axiom that no war plan survives first contact with the enemy intact. Since uncertainty is concentrated on events that have yet to (and may or may not) occur, there will be controversy over these futures, and the threat of dire consequences of "worst case" outcomes ensures a highly emotional content to these controversies.

During reasonably prosperous and tranquil times, these kinds of concerns remain abstract because the country is able to afford a robust national security response to the widest possible range of current and potential threats, thereby minimizing controversial risks in the national security environment. Such an approach is conservative because it covers the wide range of what Admiral Mike Mullen, the former chairman of the Joint Chiefs of Staff, called "the other very real and very serious threats we face around the world" in an August 2011 statement.

The International Dimension

The nature of the international threat that faces the United States should be thought of as a variable rather than as a constant. There are two basic reasons for this. The first is that threats change across time. Prior to World War II, for instance, the Soviet Union/Russia had never been considered a major threat to the United States (a claim some residents of the San Francisco area might contest based on Russian fur settlements penetrating the Bay Area early in the nineteenth century). After 1945, the two countries became direct and pervasive antagonists and the sources of the most serious threat to one another for the duration of the Cold War. After the dissolution of the Soviet Union, the relationship has vacillated and in some ways been ambiguous, but until recently no one would argue that Russia is a threat to the United States in the way the Soviet Union once was. Threatening conditions, in other words, change.

The other reason is that threats are subjective. This point is developed more elaborately in the next chapter, but different people are threatened by different sources of discomfort primarily to the extent that they feel frightened or insecure because of them. In some cases (e.g., the threat posed by the Soviet nuclear arsenal), there may be widespread agreement about the existence and severity of threat, but in other cases, reasonable people can disagree about what makes them insecure. The implications of Chinese military growth provide an example. One useful way to think about much of the debate over national security—including the commitment of public resources—is to consider whether some conditions are threatening enough to warrant different levels of national attention and the potential consequences of different commitment levels to the future status of these conditions. The threatening conditions that seem "very real" to Admiral Mullen may seem less real or dismissible to others. Those who believe in the cogency of individual threats and the consequent need to counteract them will naturally accentuate those threats and thus the need to devote resources to blunt them. Those who prefer smaller commitments to national security efforts tend to minimize the extent of threat generally or the cogency of those same threats.

The current international threat environment is difficult to assess. Current changes are not as cataclysmic as those associated with the outcomes of major wars like the Napoleonic Wars of the early nineteenth century, World War II, or the prospect of a nuclear World War III during the Cold War. Economic and military challenges are evident today, but they are not as dramatic as the major change points that produce seismic shifts in power relations. The position of the United States in the world order is not fundamentally threatened by international or domestic forces, but that order does contain enough troubling elements to demand continued engagement. Terrorism is the obvious source. Some reassessment of the American role in ordering the world may be appropriate. Internationally, that reassessment has two major facets.

The international dimension of the current national security debate is about both the nature of the future threat environment to the United States and the extent to which the United States must expend resources in the name of national security that could otherwise be devoted to other priorities. The first question is about how dangerous the threats are to the United States and thus the degree to which the United States can or should exert efforts to reshape conditions more to its liking. The second question is more about the availability of resources to deal with those threats and where such resources fit in the greater scheme of priorities for the United States.

The context for discussing the nature of the present threat environment is the experience of the United States since the terrorist attacks of September 11, 2001. Those attacks elevated perceptions of threat that had become torpid during the previous decade. It also raised national security concerns, to which the onus of a distinct effort in the area of homeland security was added. National security concerns languished during the 1990s; 9/11 revived them. Rectifying the wrongs done in those attacks and ensuring they did not reoccur became a central reality for government in ways reminiscent of the importance given to deflecting the communist threat a generation earlier.

The purity of this new consensus around the mission has been at least partially compromised by what now appear excessive or misguided actions taken in the name of combating the international terrorism associated with Al Qaeda (AQ). Three prominent examples are the botched attempt in December 2001 to capture and destroy AQ in the mountainous Tora Bora region of Afghanistan, the costly invasion and long occupation of Iraq, and the inconclusive and ongoing war in Afghanistan, the United States' longest military adventure. Many Americans have come to view the Iraq and Afghanistan experiences as unwarranted and inconclusive extravagances that would be questionable in good economic and political times but are increasingly intolerable as the burden of national security becomes a factor in domestic politics as well. Combined with the "failure" of both actions to achieve their goals, the inevitable concerns prompted by this reaction involve whether the level of national security activism that gave rise to them was wise, necessary, and/or sustainable, issues that easily extend into the debate about future policy.

There are two clear pivots to this debate, as there were before. Both can be introduced here. One is the nature and dangerousness of the threat the United States faces. Like most national security issues, it is a matter of disagreement. Since the attacks of September 11, 2001, the underlying premise of national security efforts has been the terrorist threat, and individual applications of American force have been justified and measured in terms of their contribution to containing and eradicating terrorism. Sometimes that connection proves to be far-fetched, as in the allegation of ties to terrorism (including possible supply of weapons of mass destruction to terrorists) against Iraq's Saddam Hussein, which formed a key rationale for the 2003 invasion. At other times, such as in the case of Afghanistan, the initial rationalization (the country was used as a safe haven by AQ) might have been quite strong and direct but has become diluted in the long involvement of American forces in a country that currently houses very few Al Qaeda terrorists. In other cases, such as US assistance in African countries to aid in their efforts to resist terrorist intrusion, the effort has been largely unnoticed.

The other pivot is the appropriateness of different responses to different aspects of the threat. The Soviet Cold War threat was concrete, recognizable, and called for responses that were physically and conceptually familiar. The most prominent element of that threat was nuclear weapons, and a conceptual framework based in deterrence became the accepted standard for managing that competition. The same level of clarity, however, does not hold as obviously for the current threat environment.

This second pivot has two aspects. One is whether individual situations are sufficiently threatening to require a forceful response, and if so, what kind of response. Many critics of the Iraq invasion of 2003, for instance, object that what happened in Iraq was simply not important enough for the United States to commit forces to change. That same concern arose again in 2015 as Iraq was being attacked by the Islamic State (IS), an assault they seemed unable or unwilling to repulse on their own.

The other aspect is whether appropriate and effective responses are available under any circumstances. Most global violent threats to world stability emanate from parts of the developing world, and that is particularly the case with terrorism. The United States (as well as the rest of the developed world) has been trying to implement strategies and programs in developing world countries to facilitate peaceful development for over half a century (see Latham for a particularly good overview), with spotted success at best. Attempts to devise military strategies have been particularly unsuccessful. In the American experience, that lack of success was first demonstrated in the postwar world in Vietnam (there is an equally unimpressive record that goes back much further in American history), and it once again reared its ugly head in Afghanistan. Most of these conflicts are asymmetrical in conduct, internal in nature, and in the developing world. They will be referred to as DWICs (developing world internal conflicts).

These two pivots interact to complicate dealing with the international threat environment. The first pivot suggests that not all threats are unambiguously important enough to merit vigorous responses, and the second pivot adds the concern that there may be no satisfactory way for the United States to meet the challenges that do exist effectively.

These distinctions are important because much of the possible national security agenda for likely future national security activity will consist of DWICs where the importance of favorable outcomes and the prospects of success for the United States are not overwhelmingly obvious. In times of manifestly compelling circumstances (consensual threats) or relative resource abundance (great enough prosperity for large national security investment not to strain available resources), a detailed examination of and accounting for national security concerns was not necessary. The situation is not so clear now, when the threats are debatably compelling and the prospects of success are uncertain.

The Domestic Dimension

The country went into the economic doldrums in 2008, a condition from which it has rebounded. The lightning rod of the 2008 economic malaise was an enormous growth in American budget deficits and accumulated indebtedness, a problem shared by many other countries. These deficits became the centerpiece of an ideologically powered political struggle in which both sides increasingly defined success in terms of their ability to keep the other side from exacting its preferred solution. Both sides have learned how to frustrate the other but not how to accomplish their own revisions. Government blocks things from happening but does not make things happen. Gridlock has become a seemingly permanent condition.

Political Gridlock The American political system has, in the gauzy euphemism of contemporary political jargon, "underperformed" since the turn of the new millennium. Translated into more recognizable terms, the political system has not worked in the sense of proposing and providing solutions to domestic political priorities, and this inability to act has extended to national security. Arguably, the political gridlock that is the most frequent expression of this problem is getting worse as time goes by—to the point that very few political disagreements are resolved in the interaction between the legislative and the executive branches of the federal government.

The reasons for the perpetual impasse in which the government finds itself are complex, extensive, and highly partisan. Both sides blame the other for the failure of the government to accomplish the country's business, and both sides are correct. In the words of Walt Kelly's cartoon character Pogo a half century ago, "We have met the enemy, and he is us." Why this situation has evolved and how one might try to alleviate it are also highly contentious questions described in Chapter 7. What is possible is to summarize the manifestations of the current malaise.

If the purpose of the political system is—as most civics instruction suggests—to resolve political differences among competing claimants, the current system is clearly dysfunctional. In historical times when political situations were confronted and resolved to the satisfaction of some—or preferably all—interested parties, one of two principles overrode partisan differences to allow resolution. One of these was compromise, the willingness to recognize that those with whom one might disagree have legitimate reasons for holding the preferences they do and that a satisfactory solution to a problem required accommodating all interests, if not necessarily in their purest forms. The political figures who crafted compromise solutions were generally political centrists whose philosophies were not mutually exclusive from the opposition and who viewed the effective operation of government as the greatest good: national priorities were more important than individual priorities. The compromisers were also pragmatists who believed the national interest was best served by finding ways in which everyone got some, but not necessarily all, of what they wanted. For many, being called a pragmatist was the highest form of accolade.

The other principle was that partisan differences should not extend to American interactions with foreign powers so that when disputes occurred with elements of the outside world, the country would unite behind its chosen leaders in opposition to foreign intrusion. The catchphrase for this determination is often associated with the late Senator Arthur Vandenburg (R-MI), who was chair of the Senate Foreign Relations Committee (SFRC) during the late 1940s as the Cold War was developing and Democrat Harry Truman was president: "Politics ends at the water's edge." At that time, public disagreement with the commander-in-chief on national security and other foreign policy matters was considered unthinkable.

Neither of these principles is adhered to in the contemporary environment. Being called a pragmatic compromiser is a term of derision, not respect, and the president can barely express any foreign policy statement before political opponents oppose it publicly. The pragmatic centrists have virtually disappeared from legislative chambers, replaced by ideological partisans from either extreme who extol gridlock as preferable outcomes when their side does not "win" unconditionally. In this atmosphere of hyper-partisanship, compromise is considered a dirty word, and elected politicians argue their success is measured by the extent to which they can frustrate their political opponents, a position that gets them reelected. In the absence of an overwhelmingly compelling outside threat like the imagery of 9/11, political partisans feel no need to rally their support behind the chief executive—politics virtually *begins* at the water's edge in contemporary practice. This form of dysfunction has become especially pervasive since the election of President Trump in 2016.

The result of dysfunction and hyper-partisanship is political gridlock. Its chief manifestation is that elected officials primarily block solutions with which they disagree rather than devising solutions to problems acceptable to a majority. This gridlock debilitates the ability of government to perform political tasks across the range of problems requiring some level of public action. This is especially pronounced in two policy areas. One is economic policy, since essentially all government activity requires some expenditure of public funds. The other is national security policy and strategy, which requires public support—normally provided by the political process—to underwrite its mission. The two areas are inextricably linked because national security is a major consumer of public resources.

Internal Economic Debate   There is an old saw in politics that says, "policy is what gets funded." It means that virtually everything the government does requires the expenditure of public monies and is thus critical to the political debate: if it does not involve appropriations, it is not very important. The major problem is that since the turn of the century, the government has routinely spent more money than it has collected. In domestic politics, deficits have come from the expansion of spending on government programs and decreases in taxes for at least some Americans. Internationally, the cause has largely been national security–justified overseas military actions in places like Afghanistan and Iraq.

National security crises have thus frequently been a source of budget deficits. The United States ran the first sizable deficits in its history paying for its conduct of World War II, and one of the consequences of Lyndon Johnson's determination to finance the expansion of entitlements and the Vietnam War simultaneously without raising taxes to pay for them led to a sizable increase in public indebtedness as well.

Both sources of deficits (war expenses and increased non-defense spending) are present in the current atmosphere. Budget deficits had more than quadrupled during the early 2000s as President George W. Bush pursued a variation of the LBJ strategy by pushing through tax cuts (thereby decreasing revenues) while simultaneously championing an unfunded addition to Medicare (subsidies for prescription drugs) and pursuing two wars for which no revenue provisions were made within the structure of the national budget (both were funded by so-called supplemental appropriations discussed in Chapter 7). President Trump has followed a similar strategy.

None of these events are unique in the American economic experience, but they are taking place in the politically poisonous, hyper-partisan atmosphere that currently exists in Washington. Budgetary deficit reduction has become the rhetorical mantra, if not concertedly pursued goal, of American politics. There is no agreement either on the ordering of priorities of the debt or on the sources of its solution.

The focus here is not on the solution to the domestic economic crisis, but to outline its general parameters because of their national security implications. Basically, there are three possible sources of enough economic adjustment to get a handle on the balance between government spending and revenues collected. Two are areas of government spending that are large enough that cuts would make a meaningful impression on the calculus of deficits: entitlements and defense spending. Amplification 1.1 examines this basic dynamic. The third, euphemistically called "revenue enhancements," deals with how much money the government collects to pay its expenses.

As might be expected in the current political climate, there is considerable disagreement about which of these sources should be the focus of deficit reduction. The arguments from all sides on all aspects of this issue are intricate and controversial, but they can be roughly described in partisan terms. One side of the argument emphasizes excessive government spending as the problem. Their mantra has been that the government does not have a taxing problem (how much it collects); it has a spending problem. This perspective is held particularly by fiscally conservative Republicans who are also historic supporters of robust spending for national security. As a result, they advocate cutting deficits primarily by reducing spending on entitlements, minimal if any cuts in national security, and few if any increases in revenue collection.

Why Entitlement and Defense Cuts?

The 1930s bank robber Willie Sutton was once asked in an interview why he robbed banks. His succinct answer was, "Because that's where the money is." In examining why entitlements and national security spending have become the object of attempts to reduce the deficit, the same rationale holds: these are the largest areas of government expenditure and thus the repository of the largest potential dollars to be saved.

In rough terms, maximum government spending occurs in three areas. Entitlements like social security, Medicare, and Medicaid are the largest recipient, accounting for about two-fifths of the budget, and this proportion is increasing as the aging population, who constitute the largest group of recipients, expands. Defense spending and servicing of the interest on federal debt vie for second place, with each having a share of about one-fifth of government dollars. Everything else the government does accounts for the other one-fifth of the budget, but it is not a large enough segment to cover the current deficits, and most of the "fat" in these budgets has already been excised in past reforms.

One of the three major components of government spending, interest on debt, is exempt from budget cutting. The United States owes interest payments on loans that cannot be denied without damaging its credit status, and most of this debt is owed to Americans and the US government itself anyway. That leaves entitlements and defense as the only budget areas with "deep enough pockets" for meaningful reduction.

Defense spending has both a unique claim and vulnerability in the funding fight. Cuts in defense spending can reduce the country's security, often in unpredictable ways that might prove difficult to rectify if needs are neglected, a potent source of resistance. At the same time, nearly two-thirds of the "discretionary spending" in the federal budget (money that must be appropriated annually by the Congress and simply disappears if not appropriated) is in defense, making it an inviting target. Entitlements, by contrast, are nondiscretionary, meaning they are automatically issued by the federal Treasury Department unless specific legislation alters or eliminates their mandate.

Since both budgets have sizable constituency support, any attempts to curb spending in either brings great resistance, generally along partisan lines. Republicans usually represent wealthier Americans who are less reliant on entitlements and thus are more prone to advocate savings there. Democrats have entitlement recipients as core constituents and have much less support among pro-defense advocates so are more likely to favor cuts in that spending. The result can be a virtually insurmountable impasse, as the ongoing debate continues. Politically, the least unpalatable solution is effectively to "kick the can" by proposing cuts in the future that have little immediate impact in the hope that general economic growth will absorb much of the deficit problem and thus not require implementation of draconian measures. ∎

The other side of the argument is more classically liberal and Keynesian. It covers a spectrum of advocacies. On the left, for instance, are social and economic liberals who oppose any reductions in entitlement spending; more toward the center are advocates, including President Obama, who favor a balanced approach in which all three sources are tapped: some modest cuts in entitlements, meaningful reductions in defense spending, and increased tax revenues, mostly accomplished by raising taxes on the wealthiest Americans. The major point of contention is over raising taxes. Conservatives are diametrically opposed to all revenue increases, arguing that the government will frivolously spend any increased revenue it receives and that added taxes dampen economic recovery. Liberals counter that actions adequate to shrink or do away with deficits are impossible without added taxes. The alternative is to reduce either politically popular entitlement programs on which millions of Americans rely or spending on defense. A secondary difference is on the extent of spending cuts that should be borne by entitlements as opposed to other priorities like national security. President Trump's 2017 tax cut reduced government revenues, increased defense spending, and vowed to reduce entitlement spending. Deficits are expected to increase with this set of emphases.

Politics and economics roil one another in this debate. Politically, the traditional solution for revenue "shortfalls" has been to stimulate economic growth. When growth occurs, there are more wage earners who contribute at least part of their earnings to tax coffers, thereby increasing revenues. All the budget balancing schemes put forward in the current debate make some assumption of economic growth as part of their path to the huge reduction in deficits/debt that are proposed. This solution, however, has its own built-in economic limitations. One of these is the most efficient way to create growth, and it divides the partisans along familiar lines. Liberals want more pump-priming through spending that creates jobs from public coffers until growth is ignited in the private sector, and conservatives want tax cuts or freezes so that investors (particularly the wealthy) will have more to invest. Both sides have a point, and both arguments are also debatable. A problem is that predictions of growth are classically difficult, and the tendency of politicians is to overestimate how much growth will occur and when. In purely economic terms, there is no consensual "best" solution—one that will most likely solve the physical problem—around which economists can rally political figures, so the correct path remains a matter of controversy. One source of this controversy is the most effective combination of budget cuts and additional revenues.

The magnitude of the problem—several trillions of dollars, depending on whose estimate one accepts—suggests that each element of the troika must contribute and that the question is what part comes from revenues and what part from cuts in existing budgets. These, of course, are politically divisive and poisonous ideological divisions. One area of concern is the impact of different levels of defense spending on America's place and security in the world.

The economic debate is inextricably intertwined with the toxic hyperpartisanship that pervades domestic politics. Purist ideologues on the right refuse to consider tax increases and insist upon savings from entitlement program "reforms." Leftist ideologues hold entitlements as sacrosanct, believe new programs in areas like education and infrastructure are necessary for a sound economy, and oppose expensive military activism. In an atmosphere where compromise is viewed as akin to sedition, the result is a dynamic in which national security is often the victim.

National Security Implications

Calls for budget tightening are by no means a new phenomenon, and awarding national security less than it wanted or felt it needed has deep historical roots. During the American Revolution, for instance, one of the least favorite aspects of command for General George Washington was the periodic need to plead with the Continental Congress to entreat their state legislatures to provide additional resources to support the war effort. When the war was over, the armed forces were essentially dissolved. During pre-1945 peacetime periods, commitments were generally minimal.

There have been two circumstances in which the American political system, regardless of its level of functionality otherwise, has been a generous supporter of military spending. One is times of general prosperity wherein there seemed adequate resources for both defense and non-defense priorities. The other is in times of consensus that a compelling threat requiring sacrifice existed. Neither of these conditions clearly holds in the current environment. There are residual sentiments for reining in government deficits to restore fiscal balance within the government, but bipartisanship and gridlock have prevented serious efforts that might endanger national security budgets.

The last serious effort to engage in deficit reduction occurred in 2011, and its fate is indicative of the problems faced by such attempts. In that year, the White House and Congress had characteristically deadlocked on the problem, and Congress responded by appointing a Joint Select Committee on Budget Reduction (nicknamed the Super Committee) composed of equal numbers of members from each house and from each party to reach a compromise solution. Their incentive was that if they failed, large cuts in both defense and non-defense spending would automatically go into effect to reach reduction goals to offset projected accumulating debt. The incentive was that the automatic reductions were considered so draconian that agreement would be achieved. The committee, however, failed, and the result was something called the "sequester." Under its provisions, reductions in budgets were mandated to begin in 2013 (which they did) and run until 2021. These reductions were particularly felt in the national security community, as noted in Amplification 1.1, and they were temporarily suspended by the 2018 budget agreement that reinstated much of the defense budget's losses (see Chapter 7). Congress has not seriously addressed the problem since.

While there is little argument within the defense structure about the negative effects of the sequester, there are stern warnings about its consequences for the country's ability to defend itself and about how to accommodate the losses. One obvious, and for present purposes exemplary, source of future savings, for instance, is in costs for manpower. Funding the active force (including funding for veterans) currently absorbs around 30 percent of defense dollars (like everything else about the defense budget, there is disagreement about the exact amount), largely because the all-volunteer, professional force is very expensive (the average wages and benefits for a service member are currently over $115,000). The result is a large personnel budget that can be reduced either by contracting the number of personnel (and thus salaries) or by reducing the costs of the individual soldier, sailor, or airman. One way to do this would be to reduce wages and benefits, but that would drive many of the best people out of the service. Another is an alternate form of recruitment like conscription since involuntary service members do not have to be paid as well as volunteers. These issues are further examined in Chapter 8.

Although President Trump advocates the reinstatement of robust defense budgets, the effects of austerity continue to be debated. As its advocates point out, national security spending is sui generis, and unless considerable care is exercised in what gets cut and how, the consequences could be far different than originally intended. As P. W. Singer pointed out in 2011, the dynamics of most of the pressure underlying deficit reductions have been fiscal, and "fiscal experts may know tax policy, but they do not know national security, and vice versa." Acknowledging this gap, proponents of defense spending cuts argue that turning over cuts to the military itself (and its allies in the defense industry) is likely to lead to the self-serving conclusion that meaningful participation is impossible without grievous dangers.

Force reductions will have consequences. The current force has been stretched to its arguable limits over the past decade of constant deployments in two wars, and all the costs (for instance, the mental health and medical consequences of repeated deployments) are not yet in and will provide a burden on future budgets. A smaller force, particularly if it is not to be stressed beyond reasonable limits (like those the present one has endured), can do less. If the implication is that American activism in shaping the world will be reduced, the degree to which that matters depends critically on a world environment that is unpredictable and difficult to manipulate—particularly if one has reduced capabilities with which to influence events. The national security implications of change are thus truly intermestic in nature.

Economics and politics also affect the ability of the defense community to engage in future planning. One of the frequent charges made against the Obama administration whenever a crisis arose was that it lacked a credible strategy for dealing with it. This criticism had truth value, but it was also unfair. Since the end of the Cold War, the United States has lacked a comprehensive national security worldview or paradigm to encompass coping with a very different environment, a shortcoming highlighted in Chapter 14. This means the country does not have a template of appropriate responses from which to choose whenever a crisis breaks out. The consequence is that all crises must be addressed as unique events and the consideration of alternatives must be considered virtually from scratch.

The criticism is unfair in that the formulation of a paradigm must be a national exercise in which all major parties participate. The Cold War paradigm was framed in such an atmosphere: virtually everyone agreed on the nature of the threat, its importance, the most efficacious ways to deal with it, and the need for economic sacrifice to achieve national goals. These characteristics are almost entirely missing today. The hyper-partisan political climate means there is no consensus on virtually anything, especially something as complex as national security strategy. Disagreement about a compelling threat further means there is no agreement on needed funding for defense. The result is that no national strategy has emerged, and there is little prospect the situation will change. As a result, all situations must be treated as discrete events outside any common frame of reference, as suggested in Amplification 1.2.

AMPLIFICATION 1.2

Ad Hoc Policy

Policymaking is greatly simplified if those who make or influence policy begin from a common framework. During the Cold War, for instance, whenever a conflict broke out in a developing world country and there was any hint of communist involvement (which there usually was), it was assumed that the Soviet Union or China was "behind it." This presumption has two consequences. Since such actions threatened the containment line, it meant there was an American interest in the outcome and the United States must take some action to thwart the communists. This framework did not always produce desirable results, but it did promote coherent policy.

Contrast this clarity with the contemporary environment. There is no shortage of conflict, instability, and violence in the world—primarily in the Middle East and Africa—and it has a common element in terrorism. There is not, however, any general agreement about what the United States should do about the kinds of problems that exist. How should the country decide in which problems to involve itself and what forms its action should take, for instance? Hyper-partisanship guarantees spirited, loud advocacy of all possible actions and equally shrill opposition to alternatives.

The result is that there is no common framework to help guide policy responses. Instead, each situation must be considered as unique, and policy must be fashioned ad hoc for each situation. This condition and the outcomes it produces please no one entirely, but this is the best a gridlocked, dysfunctional process seems capable of manifesting. ∎

THE INTERMESTIC INTERSECTION

In times of general economic tranquility and prosperity, the tensions between domestic and international politics are not as obvious in the national security era as they are today. The 1990s was a case in point. The end of the Cold War created a temporary respite from the high national security tensions and stakes that had preceded it and was matched by a decade of general and growing prosperity for most Americans. A widely advertised "peace dividend" from reduced defense spending disappeared like a wisp of smoke but was largely unlamented, except by the staunchest opponents of defense spending. Defense spending was more modest than it had been during the Cold War, but so were threats that required less resources to counter. A new equipoise was reached. It was temporary.

The positive intermestic intersection became a potential crash site after the turn of the century. The Bush tax cuts of 2001 produced smaller tax revenues (a domestic influence) than previously, and involvement in Afghanistan in late 2001 and in Iraq in 2003 created large, internationally focused expenditures for which spending priorities (e.g., consciously moving funding from other programs to pay for the wars) were not made. Regardless of who was to blame and how much impact these actions had on the present, they heightened the movement toward tension between domestic and international concerns at the intermestic intersection. International threats and domestic willingness to spend on defense got out of balance. The imbalance has persisted ever since.

There is no permanent solution to the relative priorities of domestic concerns (such as deficit reduction) and international concerns (such as threat levels), and necessary responses to them, because things change. The domestic environment is not as bleak as it was in 2008, and the nature and texture of the international threat environment could become more or less menacing in the future. The post-9/11 spate of defense activism coincided with domestic aversion to large-scale spending. Spending proceeded to finance two wars, but it was obscured by hiding the costs outside the regular budget through supplemental appropriations. That ruse could not be employed indefinitely, and as the United States considered an expensive campaign in Iraq against IS, the question of whether such an expenditure was affordable inevitably arose. This tension forms the basis of concern expressed in the *Challenge!*

CHALLENGE!

Is a Reduced Commitment to National Security Acceptable?

The arguments presented here have been preliminary and sketchy, not fully raising or analyzing all the complex issues surrounding the contribution of national security to the intermestic balance between domestic and international imperatives. Some of these complexities are explored in subsequent chapters, and by the time the reader finishes the book, he or she should have a much more complete and sophisticated array of information on which to base a judgment in individual situations. At this point, only general views and predilections are reasonable to assume.

With that in mind, what is your general view of including defense meaningfully in deficit reduction? Should the Pentagon "shoulder its share of the load," or is the national defense so important that it should be partially or wholly excluded? If defense spending is to be included, at what level should it be? The defense budget today is over $700 billion (depending on the accounting criteria employed), and that has not included most of the expense of Iraq and Afghanistan (collectively well over $100 billion a year). Spiraling medical and other assistance to returning veterans adds to this burden. What domestic costs are reasonable to deal with these internationally generated problems?

If you think national security should be exempt or only have a small role in domestic reductions, where should the mandated savings come from? A dollar not saved on defense, after all, must come from somewhere else. Should it come from entitlements? Before you answer, ask a grandparent what he or she thinks. Or should it come from "revenue enhancement"? If larger revenues are the answer, from whom should they come, and what do you think the consequences will be? None of these are easy questions with facile answers, or the issues probably would have been solved. If you feel a bit overwhelmed or underqualified to answer these questions, you have lots of company (including, arguably, many of those with responsibility for answering these questions). For now, a simple expression of how you feel is all that is reasonable to elicit, recognizing that you may change your mind. ■

CONCLUSION: THE WAY FORWARD

The reader will notice that the preceding pages of this introductory chapter raise numerous questions but few answers about national security and its role in the intermestic politics of the contemporary world. This lack of answers and recommendations was probably particularly apparent in the reader's attempt to sort through the concerns raised in the *Challenge!* immediately prior. Why?

There are at least three responses to this question. Numerous answers to all these questions have been raised and formulated by various analysts and political figures, but all the answers frequently advocated are to one degree or another suspect, based on ideological or methodological grounds that may or may not stand up under close examination, as well as along partisan political lines.

This problem abounds in the discussion of both domestic and international factors. Domestically, it is particularly sharply drawn over the issue of tax revenues, where both sides argue with equal fervor and selectively chosen supporting evidence that adding taxes—primarily to the wealthy— would be a "job killer" and depressant on the economy or that such additional revenues are necessary, fair, and will aid rather than depress the economy, an element in the 2017 tax cuts. Internationally, there is also the nature of threat and appropriate responses. How much of an actual threat, for instance, does IS pose to the United States? The major difference is that many of these arguments are couched in highly technical terms (especially those regarding weapons technologies) quite beyond the expertise of the average citizen to evaluate.

A second reason for caution is that most of the predictions deal with the future, in which uncertainty is a major constant. Political projections about the future are notoriously difficult and faulty, and this problem is worse the farther into the future one projects and the more complex and adversarial the situation. Singer, for instance, argues that "none of the conflicts facing the United States threaten its fundamental, core interests." That may be true now, but will it also be true five or ten years from now? How will what the United States does or fails to do today affect these problems? Future threat scenarios are almost infinite and can support entirely contradictory policies today, including spending levels necessary in the event one or more especially threatening visions materialize. But who knows? Similarly, the economic situation in the United States will almost certainly change in the coming years, probably for the better but conceivably for the worse. Which way will it go? Nobody knows for sure.

The third source of caution is the human factor. The individual US officials who make decisions change, and different people have and seek to implement different solutions to problems. That certainly has been an important factor since 2016.

STUDY/DISCUSSION QUESTIONS

1. How has the contemporary world environment placed the United States in a position where it is undergoing one of its periodic national security debates? What does it mean to describe the situation as Heraclitean?
2. What are the principal challenges to the traditional American national security role in the world? Contrast the Cold War period with the contemporary world in these terms.
3. What is the international dimension of change in national security? Describe important sources and examples of change, with emphasis on the changing nature of systemic violence and its effects on the United States.
4. What is the current domestic dimension of national security concern? Specifically, describe the problems of hyper-partisanship, dysfunction, and political gridlock and how domestic politics generally, and national security specifically, are affected by these conditions.
5. How do the domestic and international environments come together to form an "intermestic intersection" in the current debate over national security policy? Elaborate.
6. Is it true that, as many allege, the United States currently lacks a true national security strategy? If so, whose fault is it? What are its consequences?

SELECTED BIBLIOGRAPHY

Adams, Gordon, and Matthew Leatherman. "A Leaner and Meaner Defense." *Foreign Affairs* 90, 1 (January/February 2011), 139–153.

Altman, Roger C., and Richard N. Haass. "American Profligacy and American Power." *Foreign Affairs* 89, 6 (November/December 2010), 25–34.

Bacevich, Andrew C. *Washington Rules: America's Path to Permanent War*. New York: Metropolitan Books, 2010.

Bonner, William, and Addison Wiggin. *The New Empire of Debt: The Rise and Fall of an Epic Financial Bubble*. 2nd ed. New York: John Wiley and Sons, 2009.

Carafano, James J., and Paul Rosenzweig. *Winning the Long War: Lessons from the Cold War for Defeating Terrorism and Preserving Freedom*. Washington, DC: Heritage Books, 2005.

Christensen, Jane (ed.). *The National Debt: A Primer*. New York: Palgrave Macmillan, 2006.

Farrow, Ronan. *War on Peace: The End of Diplomacy and the Decline of American Influence*. New York: W. W. Norton, 2018.

Fishel, John T. *American National Security Policy: Authorities, Institutions, and Cases*. Lanham, MD: Rowman & Littlefield, 2017.

Gelb, Leslie H. "GDP Matters More Than Force." *Foreign Affairs* 89, 6 (November/December 2010), 35–43.

George, Roger, Harvey Rishikoff, and Brent Scowcroft (eds.). *The National Security Enterprise: Navigating the Labyrinth*. 2nd ed. Washington, DC: Georgetown University Press, 2017.

Hacker, Jacob S., and Paul Pierson. *Winner-Take-All Politics: How Washington Made the Rich Richer—and Turned Its Back on the Middle Class*. New York: Simon and Schuster, 2010.

Jarmon, Jack. *The New Era in U.S. National Security: An Introduction to Emerging Threats and Challenges*. Lanham, MD: Rowman & Littlefield, 2014.

Joyce, Philip. *The Congressional Budget Office: Honest Numbers, Power, and Policy Making*. Washington, DC: Georgetown University Press, 2011.

Kessler, Ronald. *The Trump White House: Changing the Rules of the Game*. New York: Crown Forum, 2018.

Mandelbaum, Michael. *The Frugal Superpower: America's Global Leadership in a Cash-Strapped Era*. New York: Public Affairs, 2010.

Meacham, Jon. *The Soul of America: The Battle for Our Better Angels*. New York: Random House, 2018.

Mead, Walter Russell. "The Tea Party and American Foreign Policy." *Foreign Affairs* 90, 2 (March/April 2011), 28–44.

Peck, Don. "Can the Middle Class Be Saved?" *The Atlantic* 308, 2 (September 2011), 60–78.

Preble, Christopher A., and John Mueller. *A Dangerous World: Threat Perception and U.S. National Security*. Washington, DC: Cato Institute, 2014.

Reveron, Derek S., and Nikolas Gvosdev. *The Oxford Handbook of U.S. National Security*. Oxford, UK: Oxford University Press, 2018.

Shultz, George, and Kenneth Dam. *Economic Policy Beyond the Headlines*. Chicago, IL: University of Chicago Press, 1998.

Sigal, Leon V. (ed.). *The Changing Dynamics of U.S. Defense Spending*. Westport, CT: Praeger Publishers, 1999.

Singer, P. W. "Think Before You Act." *Foreign Policy* (online), (August 11, 2011).

Snow, Donald M. *Thinking About National Security: Strategy, Policy, and Issues*. New York and London: Routledge, 2016.

——— and Patrick J. Haney. *U.S. Foreign Policy: Back to the Water's Edge*. 5th ed. Lanham, MD: Rowman & Littlefield, 2018.

The Concepts and Logic of National Security

National security is concerned with arguably the most basic purpose of the state: to provide for the physical safety—or security—of itself and its people. The state is the designated political unit for providing security in the international system organized around the principle of state sovereignty. The gravity of this responsibility sets national security apart from other policy areas where the potential failure of policy may be less catastrophic. This unique character leads those involved in national security analysis to view their subject through a specialized set of organizing concepts, and this chapter presents four basic conceptual categories of ongoing importance. First, what is the nature of security? Second, what is the nature and extent of risk in the national security arena? Third, what impact has change in that environment had on basic interests and approaches to security? Fourth, what is the challenge of effective power in the present and the future? This set of constructs is then applied to the realist paradigm and challenges to it, notably from China and Russia.

National security has not been the only or even the most prominent aspect of the ongoing political difficulties facing the United States, but there are strong national security implications implicit (and in some cases explicit) for non-security-based decisions in the gridlock that has immobilized politics. The economic argument lurks in the background of security questions, but the deep ideological divisions within the body politic extend to the national security arena. How to treat prominent traditional adversaries like China and Russia is part of this disagreement and is a matter of debate that requires clarification.

A fundamental problem is that the parties to the discussion do not share a conceptual common ground about problems and solutions. As suggested in the P. W. Singer quote in the last chapter, tax experts speak the language and follow the logic of accounting, but national security experts have a distinctly different worldview. For decisions made by politicians and their supporters to minimize the harmful fallout of decisions on each group, all interested parties need to appreciate the positions of the others. That journey begins by analyzing the concepts of national security as the fundamental building blocks for understanding the subject and then applying those concepts to the dominant intellectual mindset of much of the period, the realist paradigm.

National security analysis tries to determine what environmental threats may cause concern for the security and well-being of Americans and citizens of the world generally and what can be done to attenuate or eliminate sources of disturbance. The same questions are asked today as were asked fifty, or even a hundred, years ago; it is the answers that change to a greater or lesser extent, based on the flow of events and environmental transformations.

The United States is clearly still in the process of reassessing the national security problem for a new century. International terrorism introduced a force not previously confronted and certainly not resolved by the Afghanistan and Iraq wars. As responses unleashed by 9/11 have evolved, people have begun questioning the degree of effort that should be devoted to the national security enterprise and, at a more personal level, the extent of personal effort and sacrifice that should be expected from them. Commercial airliners slamming into their targets removed the complacency about security that had developed in the 1990s. "Everything has changed" became the mantra after September 11, 2001, "nothing will ever be the same again." Dormant security concerns were revived and now seem permanent parts of an environment that has been unalterably changed. Or has it?

Terrorism has not been erased, and whether focused, quasi-military actions will reduce the effective threat to some "tolerable" level is arguable. Iraq and Afghanistan have soured the American palate for large overseas interventions for a while, but for how long? Will something like the Islamic State (IS) take their place? If the result is a less activist stance in terms of the use of American force as a palliative, what does this mean for the defense sector?

The discussion in this chapter proceeds through sequential steps. Keeping the United States and Americans safe from harm—or secure—is the basic purpose of national security policy, so the discussion begins by exploring what makes people secure. Because safety is potentially endangered by a variety of sources that may exceed resources, it looks at the question of how to decide what to protect and what to accept as risk. Deciding where to nullify risk and where to accept it is a matter of what the country's most important interests are, so the discussion returns to the matter of determining levels of interest. The realist paradigm has provided the historic consensual answers to most of these questions, but its premises are under assault from individuals and groups of theoreticians with different perspectives.

THINKING ABOUT SECURITY

Security is a variable. One dictionary definition of security is what makes people safe or *feel* safe. This definition suggests that security has both a physical and a psychological dimension and that both dimensions assume different values, or vary. The most obvious source of variability is what threatens the things people value. The most obvious and objective of these are *physical threats*, such as the objective ability of the Soviet Union to destroy the United States with nuclear weapons during the Cold War. *Psychological threats*—what makes people *feel* secure or insecure—are often less tangible and are the subject of human interpretation: different people feel secure or insecure in the same situation. In either case, the degree of security experienced can vary depending on the individual and the situation.

This leads to the second variable quality of security, which is the interpretation of the environment. Does the environment make one feel secure or insecure? In case of the latter, what actions might be contemplated to change the environment and make it less threatening (increase a sense of security)? Clearly, a hostile physical environment will diminish the psychological feeling of security more than a benign environment and thus produce a greater feeling of insecurity in people.

The discussion about these aspects of security can be divided into two related concerns. The first is the changing balance between military and nonmilitary sources of concern about security. This leads to and is conditioned by the second concern: the differing levels of security enjoyed by different actors in international politics and how concepts of security may be changing.

MILITARY AND NONMILITARY ELEMENTS OF SECURITY

Historically, national security and military security have been largely synonymous. Although other matters might threaten the well-being of the country, those threats about which policymakers and analysts are principally worried and that fall most obviously into the category of national security are military threats, especially during the Cold War.

The inclusion of nonmilitary elements began during the Cold War in the area of economic security, but nonmilitary and semimilitary elements have more prominently been added to contemporary concepts of national security. Among the nonmilitary aspects, for instance, economic security has been broadened to encompass environmental security. Other added security concerns are partly military and partly nonmilitary. Terrorism is a prime example. These problems can have a clearly military component, but significant aspects of terrorism and its suppression are also political and law-enforcement concerns for which purely military responses are ineffective (see Chapter 12).

Nonmilitary and semimilitary elements of security have risen in relative importance as military threats have receded. One thing contemporary threats have in common, for instance, is that none provides a physical threat to the United States in the way that a potential Soviet nuclear attack did. The 2001 terrorist threat against the United States demonstrated that the American homeland has become vulnerable to attacks that can kill many Americans, but these attacks do not currently place the integrity of the United States at direct risk.

Beyond terrorism, the remaining security threats are at a lower level of urgency and importance, placing them squarely within the psychological dimension of security, where people can and do disagree about the importance of threats. That the proliferation of weapons of mass destruction (WMD) to additional countries like North Korea (see Chapter 8) is a problem is a matter of broad agreement; how much of a threat it poses is not.

The new military and nonmilitary elements of security come together in concrete ways. The situation between the United States and China is an example. China was, of course, a Cold War military adversary of the United States, even if the threat posed was somewhat ambiguous after the opening of Sino-American relations in 1972. In recent years, Chinese rivalry with the United States has become broader, extending to both economic and military concerns (see Amplification 2.1).

Levels of Security

The discussion to this point has concentrated on state security. This is the primary focus of concern in a system where state sovereignty predominates. This focus is one of the more controversial consequences of a realist paradigm worldview and has caused many reformers to argue there should be a more balanced approach to legitimate security concerns below and above the level of the state.

Competing levels of security arguments challenge traditional notions of sovereignty. The idea that there could be a source of superior authority to the state was, of course, a major issue in the Thirty Years' War (1618–48) in the clash between sectarian authorities claiming the primacy of the supranational church and secular authorities claiming the supremacy of territories ruled by secular regimes. There are parallels within the contemporary assertion that the security of subnational groups and individuals should be a primary consideration superior to the primacy of the state, reflecting the notion of popular sovereignty first put forward by political thinkers like Locke and Rousseau and that heavily influenced the writers of the American Declaration of Independence and Constitution.

One line of contrary reasoning questions the consequences of states acting principally out of their own security concerns while ignoring other levels. The most basic formulation of this concern is something known as the *security dilemma*. In this construct, states may act in ways to increase their security against real or potential adversaries, such as by building up levels of armaments, regardless of the effect on the larger international system. The response of those targeted by the original action may be to respond in kind by building up their own arms levels, which may result in an arms race spiral wherein, in the end, all parties are left feeling less secure than in the beginning. Security dilemma situations represent the perspective of *international security*, that is, the security of the overall system.

The American terrorism campaign raises some of these concerns. The American military response in Afghanistan has clearly been framed in terms of American state security—removing the source of a threat to the American homeland. When the United States threatened to widen the campaign to other sources of potential threat—notably Pakistan—the prospects were inevitably raised that such actions might increase Pakistani insecurity and thus detract from international security.

The other level of concern is with *individual security*, a primary orientation of security around individuals and groups. This emphasis is most often associated with the protection of the safety of people within states. The problem arises from the traditional interpretation of state sovereignty and a state's absolute power over its population. The consequences of this power have become an international concern in the post–Cold War environment of internal wars that involve atrocities against victim populations and groups within populations.

Traditional definitions of sovereignty give the state total control over its territorial base, including the treatment of individual citizens and groups, and make illegitimate any outside efforts to affect that treatment. In cases of particularly tyrannical regimes, the result has often been state-sponsored or state-conducted campaigns against their own citizens, which the international community technically cannot prevent or alleviate; it is nobody else's business how a state treats its people. The conditions in North Korean gulags are a stark example of this position taken to extremes.

An assertion of the validity of individual security challenges that assumption. It is related to the assertion of popular sovereignty since presumably no one would delegate to the state the right to abuse them. The history of individual security, however, is relatively recent and based in two post–World War II phenomena: reaction to the Holocaust and the emergence, particularly since the end of the Cold War, of notions of enforceable universal human rights.

RISK AND RISK MANAGEMENT

In an ideal world, means would be available to remove all sources of insecurity at all levels. In the real world, however, threats—or potential threats—always outnumber the resources available to negate those threats to safety. The gap between the threats and the resources to nullify those threats is *risk*, and it can be depicted in this suggestive formula: risk equals threat minus capability to nullify threats (risk = threat − capability).

Since risk is calculated based on threats to security, it is also a variable quantity. How much threat must be endured is, according to the formula, the result of two factors, each of which varies. The first and most elastic of these quantities is threat. The degree of threat experienced is the result of physical and psychological aspects of security. This means that the level of potential risk that people perceive is the result of what makes them *feel* secure or insecure, and people differ on what frightens them and thus on what must be countered to reduce insecurity. Almost everyone agrees that international terrorism threatens the United States, but people disagree on the degree and nature of that threat and what to do about it.

Threat is also interactive. A threat environment exists when the incompatible interests of two countries collide and one or both decide to pursue policies that reinforce their own security but threaten the security of the other if successful (a kind of security dilemma situation). The risks that arise from any outcome affect the threat perceptions of either or both. The developing Sino-American competition in East Asia reflects this interactive, dynamic relationship.

AMPLIFICATION 2.1

What Should the United States Do about China?

The 2017–18 conflict between the United States and North Korea has opened and accentuated differences between the United States and China that many argue could be the major international problem of a large part of this century. The basis of this developing conflict are the contrasting worldviews of the two countries in the East Asia/Pacific region, where both perceive their national

(continued)

interests and threats to them in very different ways. The current focus is on the Korean Peninsula, but it also extends to the waters of the South China Sea. Whether or how this conflict is resolved will vitally affect the national security concerns and efforts of both countries.

China's position is that it desires and plans to reassert itself as a world power and, more specifically, to restore its historical role as the effective suzerain of the East Asia mainland. To accomplish this, China desires and has worked to ensure that regional regimes are friendly to it and accept its influence. The American position, by contrast, has concentrated on its position in the Pacific region washing on East Asian shores. This means securing the safety of its allies like Japan, the Philippines, and South Korea, a mandate that requires freedom of the seas for the commerce of those countries.

There are two points at which the interests of the two countries collide. One is the Korean Peninsula, where the American presence in South Korea is a thorn in China's aspirations to control. The other is the South China Sea, which is both a strategic transportation waterway and contains considerable petroleum the Chinese covet.

These two interests affect the security equation for each. China will not fully accept that it has achieved East Asian hegemony while the United States is physically in South Korea, and it uses assistance in settling the North Korean nuclear threat as a lever to push the Americans militarily off the peninsula. The United States will not relinquish its claim that the South China Sea is an international waterway, and it refuses to cooperate with the People's Republic of China (PRC) on numerous economic issues while the PRC claims the sea is part of its territorial waters. Resolving these differences is difficult, but it is at the heart of reducing threat perceptions in both countries. ∎

The other variable in determining risk is capability—that is, the capacity to negate threats. Capability is generally defined in terms of various kinds of power available to ensure that threats cannot successfully be used against a threatened party. In the simplest terms, for instance, the existence and structure of the US armed forces are designed to make certain that any foreign invader will be repulsed, thereby nullifying the threat of invasion and conquest. The semimilitary threat posed by terrorists, on the other hand, is so diverse and diffuse that it is not clear what resources are needed to nullify efficiently the risks posed by terrorist threats to harm the country.

In general terms, it is almost always true that the volume and variety of threats will exceed the ability to nullify them all. This means that choices must be made about which threats to nullify and which targets to leave at risk. Since the potential list of what makes people feel safe or unsafe is subjective, it is always a lively process to determine which potential threats to neutralize. Those threats that one cannot nullify constitute risk.

Determining what risks will and will not be addressed is the job of policy-makers, who regularly engage in what amounts to a triage of risk reduction and risk management. Risk reduction consists of those actions that maximize the extent to which threats are countered. Determining which threats will be neutralized and which will remain risks is the realm of risk management.

THINKING ABOUT INTERESTS

Where risk is accepted and where it is not depends on the hierarchy of things countries value (i.e., their interests). Questions about the role and implications of interests mirror differences over what constitutes security in the contemporary order. The interplay of interests—whose are realized and whose are not—is central to the dynamics of international relations. The interests at the base of these calculations are invariably state interests. Interest-driven calculations remain the criteria by which states operate in the anarchical international system. When the interests of states come into conflict, the question of which states' interests will prevail also arises, and this leads to trying to determine how important interests are, where and how they are threatened, and thus what means will be employed to attempt to achieve them. Sino-American interests regarding the continuing US physical (and especially military) presence in South Korea exemplify this interaction. America believes its presence is crucial to the security of the Republic of Korea (ROK or South Korea). The Chinese world vision requires the absence of potentially hostile countries on the East Asian land mass, which requires an American withdrawal.

Levels of Interests

People and states value some things more than others and thus have greater interest in preserving some values (or interests) than others. In national security terms, the most important boundary is between vital interests and those that are deemed to be less than vital. The salience of that boundary is that it is theoretically the demarcation point at which the state will contemplate the use of military force to realize its goals. Interests failing the test of vitality imply the use of means of lesser intensity than for those that are vital. This conjunction between interests and security can be depicted in matrix form, as in Table 2.1.

In Table 2.1, Cells 1 and 6 are the easiest to describe. The heart of the realist formulation is that when vital interests are threatened, force may become an option if the situation is solvable by using military force (military security, as depicted in cell 1). At the same time, when less-than-vital

TABLE 2.1

Interest Levels and Security Means Dimensions

		Interest Level	
		Vital	Less Than Vital
Security	Military	Cell 1	Cell 2
Means	Semimilitary	Cell 3	Cell 4
Dimension	Nonmilitary	Cell 5	Cell 6

interests come into conflict, they are normally nonmilitary because military force is either inappropriate or more drastic than the situation's resolution dictates (cell 6). An imminent attack on one's territory would be a clear cell 1 situation; a dispute over tariff schedules would clearly fall in cell 6. When vital interests are involved, the first inclination is to try to use nonmilitary means to resolve the differences; force is a "means of last resort" if all other methods (cell 5) fail. Applying economic sanctions backed by military contingencies would be an example of this.

The real debate is over situations in which vital interests are not engaged but military aspects of security may be contemplated because they are the only means that may bring about a satisfactory resolution. Given the human and monetary consequences of applying force, the question raised in cell 2 is whether force is warranted to achieve less important ends. The traditional answer is negative, but in practice, the experience has been mixed. War in Iraq and Afghanistan raises this question.

The continued controversy over applying realist concepts for using force rages in cell 2, with strong national security implications. Because the United States possesses such an overwhelming amount of force, there is some temptation to apply it to a variety of situations perceived as threatening. As President Bill Clinton's secretary of state Madeleine Albright once said, "What is the point of having armed forces if you never use them?" The retort from the realist perspective is that one uses them only when the situation is important enough (vital interests) and when force can be effective. At what level, for instance, does Chinese-American disagreement over the Korean Peninsula enter into a discussion of ways either can achieve favorable resolution?

The role of force is more complicated in cells 3 and 4 (semimilitary dimensions). Where vital interests are at stake, force is justified to the extent it can be effective. The military aspects of the campaign against terrorism are a clear cell 3 application. The questions revolve around how much of a role force plays when it may be a necessary but not sufficient condition for success (force is needed but will not solve the problem by itself). The war on drugs and border security arguably represent cell 4 since both can be important but not system-threatening problems. In this case, questions can be raised about whether the problem is severe enough to invoke force and whether the use of force is appropriate for dealing with the problem.

The debate within cell 2 and in cells 3 and 4 can thus be viewed as a question about how much the change in the international environment of the post–Cold War world has moved the boundary surrounding what is and what is not vital and the extent and role of force in semimilitary situations. During the Cold War period, the location was relatively clear. The United States could and would use force when Soviet-inspired or Soviet-directed communist movements threatened to come to power at the expense of American friends or allies. The clearest cases were in Western Europe and Northeast Asia (Japan and Korea), cases in which the Soviets could threaten the United States directly with nuclear weapons. In cases that put the physical survival or independence of the American homeland or the territory of its closest friends at risk (the physical dimension of security), it was clear that military security was at stake and that force would be used (cell 1).

Even during the Cold War, the demarcation was a confidence interval, not a line, and this was most clearly seen in places that might be of interest to the United States in communist versus noncommunist terms but where otherwise the United States had few clear interests. Those situations occurred most often in developing world areas, such as Africa and much of Asia, and the American assessment became more debatable, falling within the psychological dimension of what makes the country feel secure, about which reasonable people can disagree. These are the instances that fall in cell 2 or surrounding the boundary between cells 1 and 2.

The American involvement in Vietnam offers an example of the ambiguity such situations represent. When the United States replaced France as the principal barrier to communist victory in that country after the Geneva Conference of 1954, there was relatively little debate about direct American interests in the outcome of that conflict. Rather, the prevailing criterion for some level of involvement was opposition to communist expansion globally. At the time, Southeast Asia happened to be the most current example. Opposition to communism as a general proposition led policymakers to conclude that the worst possible outcome (the unification of the country under communist rule) was sufficiently dire and dangerous to justify military intervention.

Why engage in a lengthy discussion of the relationship between security dimensions and interest levels? For one thing, it illustrates that in the real world such determinations are difficult and ambiguous. Were the world made up exclusively of clearly cell 1 or cell 6 situations, making and implementing national security policy would be simple. In fact, one source of nostalgia about the Cold War is that the central confrontation between the United States and the Soviet Union was precisely such a cell 1 instance. Building security policy from that construct was straightforward and relatively noncontroversial. Having said that, the United States never used military force during the Cold War in an unambiguously cell 1 situation (the closest possible exception may have been Korea); rather, it *deployed* force to deal with cell 1 contingencies (North Atlantic Treaty Organization [NATO] forces in Europe), but it *employed* forces in situations more closely associated with cell 2.

AMPLIFICATION 2.2

Vital and Less-than-Vital Interests in Russia

The United States and Russia have had a schizophrenic history. For much of early American history, their interaction was minimal. Russian fur traders in San Francisco Bay were an annoyance, and when Russia sold Alaska to the United States, they interacted. In World War II they were allies against Germany and Japan; after the war, they became the principal antagonists in the Cold War. Since the Union of Soviet Socialist Republics (USSR) collapsed, their relationship changed again as Russia moved from the doldrums of that collapse to a more assertive policy under Vladimir Putin. The constant in the Cold War and since is that both countries still maintain large nuclear arsenals aimed at one another.

The current state of Russo-American relations is dominated by Russian resurgence in the form of territorial expansion into former parts of the Soviet Union like Crimea (which became part of Ukraine within the USSR), as well as antagonistic Russian overtures toward former Soviet states like Ukraine. The Russian ploy is intended to re-create Russian status as a great power, but it is constrained by a Russian economy heavily dependent on oil exploitation and a negative demographic trend that is shrinking the Russian population. The long-term prospects for Russia are questionable, but they pose a current threat.

The American position has been to oppose Russian expansionism, although that preference has been quieted under the Trump administration. The United States is committed to freedom and self-determination in Europe, where expansionism is occurring. But how important is that opposition? The United States Congress has imposed economic sanctions on Russia congruent with an LTV evaluation, but the current administration has not even enforced those penalties. What is the Trump interest-driven evaluation of Russia and its international actions? Does it comport with a realist version of the world or some other worldview? An interest-driven analysis can help clarify these distinctions. Is it a cell 1 or a cell 2 situation? ▪

The post–Cold War world consists almost exclusively of situations that cause debate about where the boundary between vital and less-than-vital interests should be placed and what kinds of responses—military, semimilitary, or nonmilitary—are most appropriate. There are hardly any clear cell 1 situations for which to prepare and around which to ground planning. If international terrorism truly threatened the physical integrity of the United States and was a force appropriate for military eradication, it might rise to cell 1, but it is the exception, not the rule.

Security and Interests in the Contemporary Environment

It is an old saw that basic national interests rarely change but threats to those interests do change. A stable, free Western Europe, for instance, is just as important to the United States today as it was a half-century ago; what is different today is that there are no realistic threats to the fundamental security of the countries of Western Europe other than those posed by Russian expansionism. At the same time, new (or apparently new) threats to long-term interests may arise, as the terrorism threat to American territory exhibits.

The military dimensions of that security are especially challenging. While there may be a variety of situations that potentially engage American vital interests in the contemporary world, the only one that has activated American efforts has been the alleged vital interests in Iraq and Afghanistan. Saddam Hussein's invasion and conquest of Kuwait in 1990 threatened guaranteed US access to Middle Eastern oil, a clear American vital interest. His alleged stockpiling of WMD and consorting with terrorists in 2002 raised questions of vital interests again, which was a more debatable proposition.

The ongoing effort against terrorism most clearly represents a response to a threat to a vital American interest, but the questionable appropriateness and effectiveness of traditional military action to overcome it muddies the situation. What defines terrorist acts is their size and responses to them. Attacks against civilians in European cities are atrocious, but while these losses are tragic, they are not on a scale that threatens the basic integrity of the United States or Europe. It is also not clear how to respond to these kinds of acts. The United States retaliated for the embassy bombings by launching cruise missiles against suspected terrorist training camps in Afghanistan run by bin Laden, but they failed to either kill the Saudi expatriate (which officials later admitted was their intent) or slow down his activities. A major conceptual problem—part of the difficulty in the Afghanistan situation—arises because Al Qaeda lacks a territorial base that can be attacked, which is a main use of conventional force in normal military situations.

How to use armed forces when the kinds of situations for which they have traditionally been employed (securing vital interests) are basically missing is a major agenda item in the current debate about national security. Clearly, many of the actual threats to American national interests arguably fall on the less-than-vital side of the demarcation line. The clear implication is that there is not adequate guidance about what military forces, and especially conventional forces, can do in these situations.

POWER AND THE INSTRUMENTS OF POWER

The international system is anarchical, meaning there is no political authority superior to that of the individual states that are the basic units of that system. In such a situation, states must engage in self-help to realize their interests. A recourse to some superior source of authority before which they could adjudicate conflicts of interests with those of others purposely does not exist because states have vital interests that might not prevail if some outside authority decided the outcomes of conflicts of interest. Since, by definition, a state will not willingly accept denial of its most important interests, the solution is to avoid having anybody that can make adverse rulings that would probably have to be disobeyed.

This situation forms the heart of approaches deriving from the realist paradigm. In an anarchical system, states achieve their goals to the extent they can coerce or convince others to comply with their goals or interests (self-help). One can applaud or decry that situation, but it is the dynamic that energizes the system in the absence of some fundamental reform of a sovereignty-based world.

Power

The principal tool of self-help is power. Definitions of power are plentiful, but for present purposes it will be defined as the ability to get some other party to do something it would not otherwise willingly do. Power, in other words, is a relationship between two parties (in the international system, normally states) that have conflicting interests (situations that cannot simultaneously be realized in the way each prefers). Those parties interact to convince or compel the other to act in such a way that the party against which power is successfully applied will conform to the other's preference, which in turn requires it to do something or act in a manner it would not willingly do in the absence of power being applied against it. Put more simply, a person or entity that has power over you can cause you to do what you do not want to do. This distinction is developed more fully in the next section.

While most relations among states are not as "raw" and basic as a pure power model might suggest, the application of power remains a critical underlying part of the security calculations in which all states must engage. Threats, the most basic datum with which national security deals, are normally assertions of power trying to cause the United States (or whomever they are aimed at) to conform to someone else's interests, and risk management has as its basic goal trying to reduce American vulnerability to being forced to do things it does not want to do (have power exercised against it) or gaining the compliance of others to American preferences. The concrete debate over matters such as funding for national security is thus essentially over what national resources the political system must provide to maximize power to assert American interests and to protect those interests from power being applied against them.

Instruments of Power

The policy tools by which states exercise power are known as the instruments of power. They consist of an array of different kinds of capability states must possess to achieve their goals. To exercise power, of course, the state must be capable of carrying out threats. Doing this requires possessing the instruments of power. In traditional terms, these instruments are divided into three categories: diplomatic (or political), economic, and military power. Diplomatic power encompasses qualities such as the persuasiveness of a country's diplomatic corps, the attractiveness of the country's political profile, and the ability of the country to use other implements to back up its political rhetoric. Economic power is the use of economic rewards and deprivations to obtain compliance with a country's demands. Military power is the threat or actual use of military threats or applications to achieve a country's goals.

Some authors believe the list of instruments should be extended in the contemporary world. A leading candidate is informational power, the ability to control and manipulate the amount and quality of information an adversary has in a power situation (cyber security). Elements of this power include information-gathering capability (obtaining intelligence) and manipulation (interrupting information sources and transmission or distorting that flow). Information is so important that some analysts argue intelligence should be considered an independent instrument of power. An exotic form, cyberwar, attempts to disrupt and control computer systems and their ability to collect, analyze, disseminate, or even retain information.

In an anarchical system, power and politics are intimately related. Politics is about who gets what in terms of scarce resources, and scarcity means some parties will have to do what they would otherwise prefer not to do. In the absence of authorities who can resolve conflicts, the parties must help themselves by possessing and being ready to employ the various instruments of power in support of their country's national interests.

Power and Security

This section has raised and examined various aspects of international politics relative to understanding the problem of national security. The first concern was with security and how a changed environment affects American national security in both a physical and psychological sense. Is American security enhanced or diminished by changes that have occurred? Are Americans more secure than before, and do they feel more secure? The second concern was how the changed security environment affects the kinds and extent of risk the country must endure and the problem of risk management and risk reduction. Is the world a riskier place than during the Cold War, for instance? The third concern was with national interests, phrased particularly with an eye toward which of the most important interests of the United States might become endangered in the current environment.

These three concerns lead to the fourth, which is the power the United States needs to confront and compete in the world environment to realize its interests or see them frustrated. The way one answers questions about security, risks, and interests provides important criteria and guidelines for how much power the United States prudently needs to deal with its environment.

This calculation used to be more straightforward than it is today. It was straightforward in that the threats facing the United States were concrete and well understood, as was the kind and amount of power necessary to reduce risk associated with that threat. If, for instance, the Soviet Union built additional tanks with which to menace Western Europe, the United States would respond by building additional antitank weapons. Russia now poses a different kind of problem. It still has nuclear weapons, but its conventional forces are reduced so that they pose little danger outside the former communist world. How does this change American security calculations?

The threats facing the United States are more diverse and controversial (most reside in the psychological realm of security), and the appropriate means of confronting them (the correct instruments of power) are not so clear. Who would maintain, for instance, that the United States has devised an effective, efficient way to confront terrorism that maximizes results and minimizes resources expended in the effort? At the same time, the economic competition in which the United States operates challenges the resources available for all national priorities. What and how to configure resources to maximize power and how many resources are available are now variables in the national security equation.

Defining and clarifying the concepts and language of national security thus raises almost as many questions as it answers. When attempting to deal with a reality as complex, changing, and even bewildering as the setting of national security, it is necessary to adopt some intellectual framework to help order and understand the meaning and context of events, their causes and effects, and how one must respond to and influence those occurrences. The traditional framework for dealing with problems is clearly in transition. During the Cold War, the United States developed a kind of framework, the realist paradigm, and it remains the standard against which any changes can be measured.

THE REALIST PARADIGM

The realist paradigm is a tool to organize and define the "rules of the game" of international relations. The function of the framework can be understood by analogy. Imagine attending a baseball game with no idea of the rules and objectives of the game. In that situation, what one would see are two groups of people in contrasting uniforms on a field with odd markings alternately throwing, catching, or chasing a hard round ball they sometimes manage to hit with a wooden or aluminum stick, causing people to run around in some manner. Ultimately, one group is declared the winner and the other the loser for reasons that are not apparent. It is all utterly confusing—unless one knows the rules.

The baseball analogy may seem frivolous, but understanding the actions of states and groups within and across states can be equally incomprehensible and frustrating unless one understands the "rules" that underlay the "game" of international politics, especially those aspects that affect national security. The idea that has dominated the ways many practitioners and scholars have understood international relations for centuries is realism, and the framework it provides for organizing the "rules of the game" is the realist paradigm.

Realism emerged from World War II as the dominant explanation of and approach to international politics in reaction to the idealism of the interwar years. E.H. Carr's biting critique of interwar politics, *The Twenty Years Crisis, 1919–1939*, published as World War II began, was the opening salvo of this assault. In 1947, Hans Morgenthau published the first edition of his landmark exposition, *Politics among Nations*, in which he laid the realist position out in detail. Emphasizing concepts like power, self-interest, conflict, and war, the resulting realist paradigm seemed especially well suited for describing and organizing the policy response to the emerging Cold War competition.

Even at the height of the Cold War, realism never lacked for critics. Part of the criticism came from the conjunction of the academic and applied aspects of realism: it served both as an academic "theory" for understanding world politics and as a set of rules of the road for conducting international relations that reflected its basic values and principles. To many critics, the most objectionable aspect of the approach and its application was its recognition—even embrace—of military power as a central and enduring feature of the international system. To many observers who would have liked to see an evolution toward a more peaceful, less militarized international condition, realism and the realist paradigm were thus tainted.

Despite critiques and questions about its ongoing conceptual dominance, it is important to look at the basic tenets of realism and how they are woven into the realist paradigm that dominated understanding of national security from the 1940s into the new century. Many of the responses to the events of September 11, 2001, at least implicitly involved rejection of some of the tenets of the paradigm, and it is not clear whether the Trump administration embraces realism as its basic model, a determination that requires understanding the paradigm and examining policy for its conformance or rejection of its tenets.

Basic Concepts and Relationships

The basic dynamics of the realist paradigm can be reduced to a series of six propositions about the international system, which in turn can be arranged deductively in syllogistic order. Each individual statement contains one or more of the key concepts already introduced, and collectively they define the realist perspective. Because the paradigm has been such an important part of international reality, however, its content is important.

The six propositions composing the realist paradigm are:

1. The international system is composed of sovereign states as the primary units in a political and legal sense.
2. Sovereign states possess vital interests and are the only units in the system that can have vital interests.
3. Vital interests become matters of international concern when conditions of scarcity exist and are pressed by competing state actors.
4. When issues involving scarce resources are present in the relations between sovereign states, power must be used to resolve the differences.
5. The exercise of power is the political means of conflict resolution in realist international relations.
6. One instrument of power is military force, which is one option for resolving differences between sovereign states.

Following the syllogism from the first through the sixth proposition, a conclusion that must be reached is that in a system of sovereign states, those states must possess, and from time to time use, military force to resolve differences that arise between them. The realist paradigm therefore justifies a concern with national security defined, at least in part, in military terms. It is not surprising, then, that the realist paradigm finds more intellectual support from students and practitioners of military affairs and varying levels of disregard and disdain among people who are opposed to the use of military force as a "legitimate" tool for resolving differences among states. In addition, some military thinkers believe the paradigm's emphasis on *vital* interests is too restrictive and oppose it on that basis.

As stated in terms of these propositions, the realist paradigm is only a skeleton of concepts and relationships. It gains meaning when the basic concepts—especially sovereignty, vital interests, and power—of the paradigm are examined and placed in the logical sequence of their presentation in that set of propositions.

Sovereignty The most basic and critical principle of international relations and the building block of realism is *sovereignty*. The idea was originally articulated by a sixteenth-century Frenchman named Jean Bodin to justify concentrating the authority of the French monarch by asserting his sovereign authority over lesser French nobles. Sovereignty was enshrined as the basic operating principle of international relations through the series of agreements ending the Thirty Years' War (1618–48) known as the Peace of Westphalia.

Sovereignty means *supreme authority*. Within a system in which sovereignty is the basic value, no entity can have authority superior to that of the sovereign. When Bodin coined the term and it was adopted by others, such as the English philosopher Thomas Hobbes, sovereignty was thought to be a quality that primarily applied to domestic relations among individuals and groups within states rather than relations between states. In the early days of the modern state system, domestic sovereignty was considered to rest with the monarchy (which is why kings and queens are sometimes called sovereigns). In fact, Bodin never considered the effects on the relations between sovereign entities. The extension of the concept to the international level occurred over the next century and is usually associated with seventeenth-century Dutch legal scholar Hugo Grotius. It has been a principal operating rule of international politics ever since.

Both the domestic and international ramifications of sovereignty remain largely in force, although with quite opposite effects. Domestic sovereignty remains the basis of authority of the state over its territory, although sovereignty is now thought of as residing with the people (who delegate part of their sovereignty to the government) rather than with a person—the monarch. The domestic effect of sovereignty is to create the legal and philosophical basis for political *order* since authority rests with and can be enforced by the state.

The effect of sovereignty on international politics is to create *anarchy* (absence of government) as the basis for the relations among states because state sovereignty literally means no state can have any jurisdiction over what goes on in other states. Thus, all relations among states are among legal equals wherein no state has the authority to compel any other state to do anything, at least in a legal sense (which does not always conform to actual practice). Sovereignty in practice has never been as absolute as sovereignty in theory: states interfere with one another's internal business regularly, as Russian interference in the 2016 American election demonstrates. States cling tenaciously to the principle despite these practices. The reason for this is that states have matters of such importance that they are unwilling to leave them to the judgment of outsiders. As a result, states demand total control over matters they can enforce. This leads to the second major concept of the realist paradigm.

Vital Interests   The main reason sovereign states are generally unwilling to compromise on some matters is because states, unlike other entities in the Westphalian system, have vital interests. Indeed, Morgenthau argued the centrality of "vital interests defined as power" to the entire realist theory. Vital interests, of course, are properties or conditions on which states will not willingly compromise and are thus too important to be submitted to any superior authority. Such interests are to be guarded to the greatest extent the state can do so. Some analysts would add that a vital interest is an interest that is sufficiently important that the state will use force to ensure its realization. The critical point in national security terms is the boundary between vital and less-than-vital interests because it is generally agreed that this is the threshold for when the state will be willing to use force.

The location of the demarcation between vital and less-than-vital interests in any given situation will always be a matter of some disagreement in the domestic and international security debate. Looking at the basic interests at stake, for instance, there is little disagreement that defending the homeland from outside military incursion is vital to the state, and hence, challenges to that interest will be met by force. As one goes down any possible list of basic interests, the question of their vital nature becomes more debatable. In the Persian Gulf War of 1990–91, for instance, the primary American interests clearly involved were economic (access to petroleum that literally fuels the American economy). But were the issues surrounding the American invasion of Iraq in 2003 of the same order or importance?

Two final implications about vital interests and sovereignty bear mentioning. Because vital interests are so important, the state is unwilling to accept contrary judgments about its interests when it can avoid them. As a result, the state is unwilling to submit disputes to a higher authority (a sovereign above the state) for fear such an authority might rule against the state in an unacceptable manner that would have to be ignored or disobeyed to ensure an acceptable outcome. Vital interests, in other words, are matters that are too important to relinquish control over the outcomes. Having said that, the word *willingly* is part of the definition of vital interests because when vital interests come into conflict, somebody succeeds and somebody does not. Usually the weaker party must unwillingly accept an unacceptable outcome, with the upshot that the interplay of vital interests in a realist world is an exercise in power politics.

Power Politics International relations represent an inherently political enterprise in which the principal political actors are states seeking to maximize their advantage in an environment in which all cannot equally succeed. Who gets what is the essence of the political process in this, like any other, arena. For this purpose, a variation of the political scientist David Easton's definition of politics will be used: *Politics is the ways in which conflicts of interest over scarce resources are resolved.*

This definition contains two related elements. This first is procedural: "the ways in which conflicts . . . are resolved." The second is substantive: what "scarce resources" must be allocated and who gets those resources. The two dimensions are intimately related: the nature and importance of the resource may determine the procedures that are employed to decide the outcome, and the procedures may influence or prejudice the substantive outcome.

The unique possession of vital interests by states produces a political structure in which state sovereignty is the central feature in determining political outcomes. Since sovereignty precludes the imposition of political processes that can authoritatively allocate values in areas deemed vital by the sovereign states, the result is purposive international anarchy in dealing with matters vital to the state.

In the condition of anarchical international relations, states achieve their interests to the extent they can do so—through self-help. As already noted, the need to resolve important international political problems generally occurs when vital interests are involved and scarcity exists. In these circumstances, outcomes require some or all parties to accept less than they want. Determining outcomes becomes an exercise in the application of power.

Power is an elusive and highly controversial concept, but it is central to the realist paradigm. Its elusiveness comes from trying to operationalize and measure power to predict who will prevail when states clash in the international arena. Although the concept of power is pervasive for describing important elements of international relations, ways to measure it satisfactorily have remained largely elusive. Finding ways to measure and thus compare the power that different states possess would be highly desirable because this would make the outcomes of the interactions between states much more predictable than they are in fact.

There are two difficulties involved. The first is finding physical measures that adequately describe the ability of states to influence one another.

A concerted effort has been made to try to find concrete, physical measures, such as the size and sophistication of countries' armed forces or the productivity of industrial bases, to indicate which is the more powerful country in any head-to-head confrontation. The problem is that such measures only work part of the time. There is, for example, no physical measurement to compare physical capabilities that would lead to the conclusion that North Vietnam had any chance of defeating the United States in a war, but it certainly did.

The second problem is that concrete measures of capability have difficulty measuring the psychological dimension of will and commitment people may possess. How can an outside observer determine, for instance, when a clash of interests is clearly more important to one party in a dispute than it is to the other (at least before the fact)? Once again, the Vietnam War is illustrative. The outcome of that war—unification of the country—was clearly more important to the North Vietnamese and their southern allies than it was to the United States and the government and supporters of the South Vietnamese regime. This is clear in retrospect: it was not at all clear before and even during the conduct of hostilities. Being able to see clearly after the fact is of very little comfort to the policymaker.

Power is also a controversial concept because one of the most obvious and prominent forms that power takes in the international arena (and within some states) is military force. Those who oppose the use of military force find themselves in opposition to a system in which power, including military power, is a central, even normal, way to resolve differences. In this case, the key to a more tranquil, peaceful world lies in the abrogation of power as the basis of international politics.

Paradigm Summary and Implications

What does the paradigm mean for the actual operation of the international system and its national security aspects? Is an understanding of the basic concepts simply an intellectual enterprise without practical application to the real world, or is the paradigm a kind of rule book or road map that guides policymakers and thus allows students to understand how the system works? For better or worse, the latter is more clearly the case, and summarizing the paradigm's implications helps move the discussion forward.

The realist paradigm begins with state sovereignty as its basic value. The absence of a higher authority is the direct result of the possession of vital interests by states—but not other political entities. These vital interests are so important to the state that it will not willingly compromise on them and will use all means available, up to and including military force, to ensure they are achieved. The two concepts, sovereignty and vital interests, require and reinforce one another. The prosecution of vital interests in an anarchical system precludes the possibility that a superior authority could compromise the state's vital interests. Sovereignty provides the conceptual bedrock to deny that possibility. The government of the United States has been and continues to be among the world's staunchest defenders of state sovereignty, and at the bottom of almost all its defenses of the concept is its insistence that no outside power should be allowed to create conditions to which Americans do not want to or should not be subjected.

In a world of plenty, the state of international anarchy would not be a problem because states would rarely come into direct conflict with one another over who gets what. In the real world, of course, scarcity rather than abundance is more common, necessitating political processes to determine outcomes of disagreements. Sometimes conflicts can be resolved peacefully and cooperatively, and sometimes they cannot. Settlements in conditions of scarcity mean that some or all the parties to a given dispute must accept less than they would have preferred—in other words, do something they would prefer not to do. Because of this, international politics inevitably is power politics.

In a world of sovereign states interacting through power politics, the state succeeds to the extent it can through self-help. For one state to get others to do what it wants but the others do not, the state must possess the ability, in specific situations, to convince or compel other states to act in ways that serve its national interests, often at the expense of the interests of those other states. A state must, in other words, possess power to succeed.

Power comes in various guises, or instruments. The applicability of any form of power will vary depending on the situation and both the ability and the willingness of a state to use its power to gain compliance with its positions. For most purposes, the more power a state has, the more successful it will be in achieving its ends. In the anarchical situation of international relations, among the forms of power that must be available is military force. Thus, the international system ultimately is an environment in which the threat or recourse to force is a "normal" activity some of the time and in which states that succeed must possess, and sometimes use, armed forces.

Critiques, Examples, and Limits of the Realist Paradigm

The realist paradigm became the dominant way that policymakers came to look at the problems of national security/international relations during the period surrounding and especially after World War II. It became the dominant framework of the Cold War and especially the major actors in that confrontation, the United States, Russia, and China. Adherence to the application of the principles imbedded in the paradigm arguably allowed the competition to be ordered and modulated, but conditions have changed. The United States remains a great world geopolitical actor, many believe China has emerged as the chief challenger to American dominance, and Russians hold what are likely fading pretensions to something like their Cold War status. At the same time, new dynamics have entered the scene: the emergence of terrorism, whose adherents ignore realist "rules," and the movement of violence into DWICs raise questions about the continuing relevance of realist-based calculations. These combine with traditional assaults on realism to make it sensible to raise the question of whether realism is still the appropriate lens through which to observe and try to order national security.

There have always been critics who have disliked some of the implications of the paradigm. Some of these point out that the paradigm can also paralyze the application of force in the service of national interest. The central "villain" here is the paradigm restriction that force is only permissible when vital interests are threatened and that force is not justifiable when lesser interests are considered. The result is anomalous. In the contemporary environment, consensually agreed upon vital interests are rarely the objects of conflicts with other countries, and if a strict interpretation of the paradigm is applied, it is not clear how often and where the United States would be justifying force. Many traditional realists, including retired flag officers (generals and admirals), opposed the Iraq War on this ground, arguing essentially that the American interests involved in that country did not rise to the level of vitality and that, as a result, the use of force against Iraq was unjustified. Most contemporary situations are of this nature, and if applied strictly, the paradigm would reduce greatly the US employment, if not necessarily deployment, of force worldwide.

The critiques of realism thus come from both directions. Critics on the political left attack the paradigm because it justifies the maintenance and use of force as normal, whereas they see that use as pathological and its justification pernicious. More recent critics on the right attack the paradigm's insistence on the standard of vital interest engagement as too restrictive and ambiguous, particularly when it is raised in opposition to an action they espouse (such as the invasion of Iraq or maintaining forces in Afghanistan). It is restrictive because it can suggest a high bar that must be surmounted before force is invoked, and it is ambiguous due to the relative absence of clear vital interest involvement in most contemporary situations. During the Cold War, the realist paradigm was a construct embraced by conservatives seeking to justify robust commitments to national security. In the contemporary environment, it may have become more clearly the tool of political centrists seeking a more restrictive approach to national security. In other words, realism and the paradigm are blamed for creating a system in which the recourse to violence is both too easy and too hard.

The Realist Paradigm and Contemporary American Politics

Donald J. Trump is the first post–World War II US president who is not clearly a realist in his national security approach and conduct of national security policy. Rather than devising a comprehensive national security strategy, his approach has been more eclectic and transactional, based more on his assessment of individual situations and his personal ability to influence other leaders of his positions. His national security advisor, John Bolton, as an example, was one of the chief opponents of the paradigm during the early 2000s because adherence to realism unduly limited the justification for using force, in his view. Former Secretary of Defense Mattis, like most career military people, is a classic realist, but his influence on policymaking has been limited.

This decline represents a trend in the new century. Since 9/11, the realist paradigm has declined as a standard against which the country measures where and when it will use force. It is not clear, for instance, whether a strict application of the paradigm would have justified the Iraq invasion or the lengthy American involvement in Afghanistan. Applying the paradigm to places like China and North Korea changes the nature of that discussion, as suggested in the following.

Would a return to the realist paradigm as the standard that has to be met before force is employed help refocus American priorities in a period when US leadership in the world is being challenged? Would a conscious reinstatement of the paradigm help solve the problem by narrowing the number and kinds of situations where force is sustained? In other words, if force is only used in the service of agreed vital interests, could that reorder and even restrict the recourse to force? In the current geopolitical environment, would a disciplined application of the paradigm help refocus what many see as an undisciplined national security process? What do you think? Is the realist paradigm a benchmark whose time has returned? ■

Contemporary examples are mixed regarding the ongoing vitality of the paradigm. The ongoing crisis on the Korean Peninsula is a classic example of where phrasing the problem in realist terms refocuses the debate, arguably in ways that clarify the positions of each participant and thus form the basis of meaningful deliberation. There are two reasons for this. One is that the principal participants are all classic realists who think in realist terms, with the arguable exception of the current US administration (which may be part of the problem). The second is that the paradigm is driven by the concept of national interest, an explicit touchstone that has not been prominent in ongoing discussions.

There are four parties with different interests that must be reconciled. The United States has a strong interest in ROK independence and prosperity as part of its general vital interest in the Pacific region and its prominent role in it. China's motivation is an East Asian region where it is clearly supreme, which means the physical removal of competing powers like the United States from the Korean Peninsula—the US military in the ROK. North Korea is motivated by its own security and self-survival both physically and as an independent regime. South Korea has the protection of its sovereignty, physical survival, and economic prosperity as its major goals. Both Koreas also have interests in some form of reunification of the peninsula.

Casting the situation in this manner does not solve the problem, but it does clarify it so all parties understand the positions of the others and thus allows the possibility of negotiations where all parties start from common references and what are acceptable and unacceptable outcomes for the participants. The crisis on the Korean Peninsula is a classic twentieth-century geopolitical exercise the realist paradigm was designed to manage.

Not all current examples are positive. The major national security challenge for the United States in the twenty-first century has been terrorism, and the paradigm is of dubious value in dealing with the threat. Once again, the reasons are two-fold. First, it is not clear how to define the level and quality of interests that terrorists pose, and thus how to approach dealing with them (see Chapter 10). Second, the terrorist threat defies the structure of the paradigm. Terrorist organizations are not state actors with which one can interact, and they specifically reject or ignore basic values built into the paradigm like state sovereignty. Applying the paradigm to the terrorist problem is not unlike trying to drive a square peg into a round hole.

The terrorist problem exemplifies the broader problem of applying realism in a global environment very different from the environment in which it was devised. The principal sources of international violence, and thus the potential for American national security involvement, have shifted from the traditional European locus of world politics to the peripheries. Most violence and instability are in the developing world in the form of DWICs. Applying the realist paradigm to these situations is difficult. For one thing, most of these situations fall on the LTV side of the vital interest divide, meaning realist calculations downplay them. Second, the United States and others have not devised especially effective methods for dealing with the problems that do exist. American overt interventions in Vietnam, Iraq, and Afghanistan have not been enormous military successes, for instance, and they hardly support activism in realist ways, a problem similar in structure and effect to the terrorism problem.

The realist paradigm also had some anomalies in application. One of these is the gap between sovereignty in theory and in practice. An important example is the result of the rigid American adherence to the principle of something close to the idea of absolute state sovereignty. The source of anomalies is the strongly held American position that there must be no outside interference in the affairs of the United States—American national sovereignty is inviolate. The problems arise from this position in application. First, it sets the United States at odds with international efforts in the national security area, along with other places. Second, it creates a situation where the United States can only engage in certain acts it deems necessary in the pursuit of its national interests by ignoring the universal validity of a notion of sovereignty that it jealously guards for itself.

These objections amount to creating a basic hypocrisy in the application of American national security efforts. All states technically adhere to standards of absolute control, but many regularly relax or ignore purist applications of the principle. Border control is an example. Until recent years, Americans could freely cross the Canadian border merely by showing their driver's licenses, a privilege enjoyed by Canadians entering the United States (a similar standard was involved in traveling to Mexico). The practices represented a dilution of total border control and thus sovereign exercise, but they were simply part of practice. At the same time, the United States, like virtually all countries, regularly violates the sovereignty of others to influence events to their advantage. The United States has, for instance, regularly engaged in semi-overt efforts to influence elections in the Western Hemisphere, up to and allegedly assassinating candidates of whom it disapproves, and the US government was an unabashed supporter of Boris Yeltsin in Russia. Russian interference in the American electoral process may have been wrong, but Americans appalled at these acts must be tempered by similar American behavior.

CONCLUSION: REALISM AND THE REALIST PARADIGM

Realism and the realist paradigm have been venerable parts of the national security American experience for over a generation. The Cold War experience was the crucible within which the set of principles described in this chapter were honed into an enduring policy outlook toward the world. Even when the Cold War ended and many of the circumstances that helped shape the realist paradigm disappeared, it remained the largely unchallenged intellectual underpinning of American security policy.

The period of high American national security activism (a concept explored at length in Chapter 14) associated with the reaction to September 11, 2001, brought with it an implicit broadening of the permissible circumstances for employing armed forces, including a relaxation of the realist tenet that the recourse to force should only be a last resort when vital interests were clearly threatened. The so-called neoconservatives prominent in foreign and defense policy in the Bush White House sought to expand realist dictates, bringing with them an evangelical sense that basic political change, especially democratization, could be stimulated by applying force against antidemocratic governments, a notion first applied in Iraq and arguably still the basis of American activism. This broadening of circumstances did not include an open rejection of the realist rejoinder, even if it operationally proceeded as if the prohibition were not in force.

Three factors, two of which are closely related, have called this increased recourse to armed force into question. The first two deal with the wisdom of expanded deployment arising from the relaxation of the vital interest standard. First, the result has been an arguable overuse of the available force to a dangerous point of stress that is unsustainable unless capability is increased. Second, some critics argue that lowering the conceptual bar about when force could be employed has resulted in promiscuous use of American forces in places like Iraq and Afghanistan that could have been avoided or very different had the realist paradigm been enforced.

These questions become particularly important given the third factor, which is the rapidly changing definition of national security interests since 2016. The designation of friends and adversaries has been under assault: the United States fights publicly with its NATO allies, embraces Russian leadership, and engages in economic "warfare" in the form of tariffs against both historical adversaries and friends. One prominent characteristic of realism is the negotiation and attempt to settle differences through traditional diplomatic efforts and in traditional forums, both of which have been implicitly rejected by the current administration. Realist governments in other countries do not quite understand how to deal with these changes, and their heterodoxy challenges analysts as well.

A return to the principles underlying the realist paradigm provides a mechanism by which to rationalize and organize the transition to a changing national security future. At the heart of the guidance the paradigm provides is the limitation of force employment to situations where vital interests are engaged, which effectively raises the bar from standards of the 2000s. Where the boundary between vital and less-than-vital interests resides in any specific situation is, of course, always a matter of debate, but simply phrasing questions in these terms is likely to have some dampening effect on positive decisions to use force in the future.

Restraints on when the United States will and will not resort to the use of force—and the availability of adequate forces to leave maximum options available—are debatable propositions that will be particularly heated in the current crucible of hyper-partisan politics in the United States. The possibility that the United States will have less and will thus be able to do less is, however, a likely consequence of the Trump administration's emphasis on "America First." The ramifications and impacts of these dynamics will occupy much of the analysis in the rest of this volume. The realist paradigm will serve as a guideline to evaluate policy.

STUDY/DISCUSSION QUESTIONS

1. What major elements compose security? At what levels does security exist? How are conceptions changing relative to one another? Discuss.
2. What is risk? How does one deal with the problem of risk? What are the chief means by which risk can be managed? Elaborate.
3. Relate levels of interest, focusing on the distinction between vital and less-than-vital interests and means to realize them. Which kinds of interest are most relevant to national security? What kinds of interests are most threatened in the contemporary environment?
4. Define power and the instruments of power. Why does the nature of the international system require that states possess and sometimes employ the instruments?
5. What is realism? What is the realist paradigm, and how does it serve both as a theory of international relations and as an action guide for policymakers?
6. What are the key concepts of the realist paradigm? How do they form a syllogism that dictates that states must possess and occasionally employ armed forces? Particularly show the relationship between sovereignty, vital interests, and power. Why is the boundary between vital and less-than-vital interests so important a distinction? Cite relevant examples of the distinctions.
7. What are the principal objections to the realist paradigm? What limits and anomalies arise from applying the paradigm? Discuss.
8. Is the realist paradigm still a useful construct for dealing with the intermestic circumstances in the current national security environment? Why or why not?

SELECTED BIBLIOGRAPHY

Art, Robert A., and Kenneth N. Waltz (eds.). *The Uses of Force: Military Power and International Politics*. 7th ed. Latham, MD: Rowman & Littlefield, 2009.

Berkowitz, Bruce. *The New Face of War: How War Will be Fought in the 21st Century*. New York: Free Press, 2003.

Bodin, Jean. *Six Books on the Commonwealth*. Oxford, UK: Basil Blackwell, 1955.

Brodie, Bernard. *War and Politics*. New York: Palgrave Macmillan, 1973.

Carr, E. H. *The Twenty-Years Crisis, 1919–1939*. London: Palgrave Macmillan, 1939.

Cusimano, Maryann. *Beyond Sovereignty*. Boston: Bedford/St. Martin's Press, 1999.

Djerejian, Edward P. "From Conflict Management to Conflict Resolution." *Foreign Affairs* 85, 6 (November/December 2006), 41–48.

Drew, Dennis M., and Donald M. Snow. *Making Twenty-First Century Strategy: An Introduction to Modern National Security Processes and Problems*. Montgomery, AL: Air University Press, 2006.

Easton, David. *A Systems Analysis of Political Life*. New York: John Wiley and Sons, 1965.

Etzioni, Amatai. *Security First: For a Muscular, Moral Foreign Policy*. New Haven, CT: Yale University Press, 2007.

Fromkin, David. *The Independence of Nations*. New York: Praeger Publishers, 1981.

Goldstein, Joshua S. "Think Again: War." *Foreign Policy* 188 (September/October 2011), 53–58.

Grotius, Hugo. *The Rights of War and Peace: Including the Law of Nature and Nations.* New York: M. W. Dunne, 1981.

Hobbs, Thomas. *Leviathan.* Oxford, UK: Clarendon, 1989.

Kaplan, Robert D. "Center Stage for the 21st Century." *Foreign Affairs* 88, 2 (March/April 2009), 16–31.

———. *The Coming Anarchy: Shattering Dreams of the Post—Cold War.* New York: Random House, 2000.

Locke, John. *Two Treatises on Government.* New York: Cambridge University Press, 1988.

Lyons, Gene M., and Michael Mastanduno (eds.). *Beyond Westphalia: State Sovereignty and International Relations.* Baltimore, MD: Johns Hopkins University Press, 1995.

Machiavelli, Niccolo. *The Prince.* Irving, TX: University of Dallas Press, 1984.

Morgenthau, Hans J. *Politics among Nations.* 7th ed. Revised by Kenneth W. Thompson and W. David Clinton. New York: McGraw-Hill Education, 2005.

Nuechterlein, Donald. *America Recommitted: United States National Interests in a Reconstructed World.* Lexington, KY: University of Kentucky Press, 1991.

Rogov, Sergei. "International Security and the Collapse of the Soviet Union." *Washington Quarterly* 15, 2 (Spring 1992), 16–28.

Schelling, Thomas C. *Arms and Influence.* New Haven, CT: Yale University Press, 1966.

Smith, William Y. "U.S. National Security After the Cold War." *Washington Quarterly* 15, 4 (Winter 1992), 21–35.

Snow, Donald M. *Cases in U.S. National Security: Concepts and Processes.* Lanham, MD: Rowman & Littlefield, 2019.

———. *Thinking About National Security: Strategy, Policy, and Issues.* New York and London: Routledge, 2016.

Stares, Paul B. *Preventive Engagement: How America Can Avoid War, Stay Strong, and Keep the Peace.* New York: Columbia University Press, 2018.

Thucydides. *The History of the Peloponnesian Wars.* New York: Penguin Books, 1954.

Waltz, Kenneth N. *Realism and World Politics.* New York and London: Routledge, 2006.

———. *Man, the State, and War: A Theoretical Analysis.* New York: Columbia University Press, 1959.

Wolf, Martin. *Why Globalization Works.* New Haven, CT: Yale University Press, 2004.

The Historical Context

The past does not predetermine the present and future in any precise way. A country's historical experience and the ways it remembers the past clearly condition how people look at and interpret current events. Sometimes these influences are positive and nationally reinforcing, and at other times they are not. Nevertheless, trying to understand the national historical experience and how the "ghosts of the past" have affected the ways in which the present and future are contemplated is a necessary component in gaining a full grasp of national security.

The three chapters in Part II examine the American historical national security experience and how that experience colors the contemporary discussion of national security. Chapter 3 reaches back to the formation of the American Republic and how early and Cold War–era experiences created a series of predilections in the American mindset toward the subject. Chapter 4 concentrates on the Cold War from the end of World War II until the collapse of the effective communist threat at the end of 1991. During this period, national security threats gained a salience and importance they had not previously occupied and that catapulted the whole idea of national security to a level of prominence it had never before achieved. Chapter 5 describes and assesses the traumatic impacts of the end of the Cold War and the rise of international terrorism symbolized by the September 11, 2001, attacks on New York and Washington as more contemporary influences on the present. Individually and collectively, these three chapters create much of the "lens" through which Americans view the current national security scene.

Influences from the Past: The American Historical Experience

A country's orientation toward the world combines multiple influences that shape its domestic and international attitude and behavior. These influences include its generalized historical experience and other conditioning factors that help define how it perceives global realities. For most of American history, that experience has been primarily positive, marked especially by low levels and qualities of threat that make the current high-threat environment all the more dramatic. This chapter begins by identifying general influences on the American experience and then looks at the question historically, designating and describing three historical parts of the national security experience. It concludes with suggestions of how the past may influence the present and future and how recent experience may have affected the impact of historical patterns and legacies, including the impact of an unorthodox Trump administration that tends to view many of these elements differently than its predecessors.

The way different countries view the world, their place in it, and patterns of threat and opportunity is in part the result of unique national factors that affect a country's general orientations toward fundamental aspects of the domestic political scene. Historical experience and geographical accident inform attitudes on, among other things, national security. For some countries, the experience has been harsh. Citizens of any country on the northern European plain cannot avoid some historically based fear of a possible invasion of their territory from one direction or another and thus view national security threats very seriously. At the other end of the spectrum, a country like Japan that successfully isolated itself physically from the rest of the world for hundreds of years has an equally distinctive worldview and perception of what constitutes security.

The relatively benign American historical experience means the United States was relatively insulated from global power politics until the end of the nineteenth century and arguably until World War II. This tranquility allowed the United States to delay developing any kind of coherent, comprehensive view of its role in the world for over a century and a half. International political activism is thus a relatively new American phenomenon. Americans have simply not had to worry about traumatic national security threats for as long as other countries have.

Despite this national security respite, the United States is no exception to the effects of history. The American experience is not as lengthy as that of the traditional European and Asian powers, but it has been conditioned by a series of historical factors that influenced the American worldview. American history helped shape a generally positive view of the world and the security of the American place in it that did not require a great deal of sacrifice or continuing effort on matters of national security before World War II and its aftermath. Americans have felt secure for most of their history as a country. This sense of tranquility has certainly accentuated the sense of insecurity most Americans have experienced since September 11, 2001.

The American experience with national security concerns can be divided into three basic periods—the formative, Cold War, and contemporary periods. Following a discussion of basic, underlying conditioning factors that help shape the American worldview, the chapter introduces the formative period, from the eighteenth-century beginnings of the republic through World War II. It was a period of relatively low, episodic American involvement in international affairs, including concerns over national security. The second period encompasses the Cold War, when the United States was thrown figuratively into the middle of the geopolitical fray as one of the two major actors in the international system and had to learn to act in that environment. The chapter concludes with an introduction to the third period, the contemporary system.

CONDITIONING FACTORS IN THE AMERICAN TRADITION

At least three conditioning factors stand out as important influences on the way Americans have come to view questions of defense and national security. These influences are the essential American lack of a sense of shared history, the unique and essentially benign and bountiful American geographical endowment, and the country's Anglo-Saxon heritage, which affected Americans' earliest and some ongoing political attitudes.

American Ahistoricism

It is fair to typify the American people as lacking basic, shared historical views of the United States and its place in the world. This ahistoricism has several bases. One is that the American experience is brief compared to the historical experience of major European and Asian counterparts. The territory occupied by the United States was inhabited for thousands of years by Native Americans, most of whom did not maintain a systematic recorded history, and most Americans do not share a sense of ethnicity or history with them. American history, as perceived by most Americans, is little more than four hundred years old (dating to the English arrival in Virginia in 1607), and it is not even a history shared by most current Americans or their ancestors.

The pattern of American population settlement has been in immigrant waves since the 1600s, and this means relatively few Americans can trace their own roots back to the beginnings of the American experience. It is, for instance, no coincidence that there are no Vietnamese Americans who are members of the Daughters of the American Revolution, and the same can be said for many other Americans whose ancestors had not immigrated to these shores when the "shot heard round the world" was fired in Massachusetts in April 1775.

This lack of historical experience and interaction has not been an altogether bad thing. Most Americans came to the United States either to escape some form of tyranny or calamity in their native lands or with the hope of becoming part of the greater prosperity the country appeared to offer, a trend that continues to this day. As Fareed Zakaria noted in a 2007 *Newsweek* analysis, more people immigrate annually to the United States than to all other countries in the world combined, generally because they view the United States as a place of hope and opportunity. As a result, there has been a greater sense of optimism in this country than in many more-established cultures where the historical record offers a greater balance of positive and negative legacies. Except for some aspects of the Civil War, the United States has no national tragedy that mars the national consciousness and tempers American optimism in the way, for instance, that the Battle of Kosovo in 1389 has tainted Serbian history (after losing the battle to the Ottoman Turks, Serbia fell under foreign control until the early twentieth century). While there is a certain irony in the descendants of past immigrant waves raising emotional objections against ongoing immigrant movements (e.g., the current opposition to "illegal" immigrants from Central America), the general proposition holds: the United States is a polyglot of immigrants. There have been anti-immigrant phases in American history before, and they all have passed. Presumably the contemporary "nativism" will pass as well.

American ahistoricism contributes to the American sense of exceptionalism and thus to American attitudes toward national security. When combined with American physical isolation from the world, the result has been a positive self-image about the United States that has extended to its military experience. Americans have historically viewed themselves as winners both at war and at peace. The general national ahistoricism allows Americans to ignore less glorious aspects of its military experiences, such as its performance in the War of 1812 (in which the United States decisively won exactly one land battle, at New Orleans, fought two weeks after the peace treaty had been signed). This general attitude of success has made acceptance of the outcomes of the Vietnam, Iraq, and Afghanistan conflicts more difficult than they might otherwise have been.

Americans have also liked to portray themselves as an essentially pacific people, slow to anger but capable of vanquishing any foe once aroused. The premises underlying this belief are the ideas that peace is the normal and preferred condition and war is an abnormality that is thrust upon Americans when they are attacked by hostile others. The Japanese sneak attack at Pearl Harbor that dragged a reluctant United States into World War II is a talisman of this conviction, as is contemporary terrorism.

Many outsiders, as well as Native Americans, would, of course, contest both the notion of American passivity and the need to be provoked into violence. It is hard, for instance, to argue that most of the wars against the Native Americans of the Great Plains and the American West were "thrust" upon the United States, and the Spanish, who had already agreed to all the American terms when the United States declared war on them in 1898, would certainly question the reactive nature of Americans in that situation, as have many Iraqis and Afghans during the current conflicts. The self-proclaimed notion of American passivity can thus be maintained only with a very selective view of the American experience.

ACCIDENT OF GEOGRAPHY

Geography blessed the United States in at least two distinctly benign ways. First, the physical location of the United States between two of the world's great oceans made it virtually an island, at least as far as potential foreign incursions from Europe or Asia were concerned. When combined with comparatively weak or friendly countries on its northern and southern borders, the result has been effective physical invulnerability for much of American history. With the exception of Pancho Villa's raids into the Southwest in the second decade of the twentieth century and a few submarine incursions during World War II along the West Coast, the forty-eight contiguous states (the continental United States, or CONUS) were safe from the danger of physical harm from 1814, when the British left at the end of the War of 1812, until 1957, when the successful testing of a Soviet intercontinental ballistic missile (ICBM) made the United States vulnerable to nuclear missile attacks. The only other sources of American physical vulnerability have come when the United States has expanded beyond the continental mass (e.g., Hawaii) or added foreign colonies (e.g., the Philippines).

The other part of the geographic legacy is resource abundance. The American continental land mass was blessed in two highly beneficial ways. First, the farmland in the central United States is some of the best in the world and has allowed the country to produce enough food for itself and surpluses for export. Second, the United States also possessed adequate supplies of both mineral wealth (e.g., iron ore, copper, etc.) and energy (e.g., coal, petroleum, natural gas) to allow it to proceed through most of the industrialization process without relying on foreign sources for natural resources.

The result of both these geographic factors was to produce an essential independence and sense of invulnerability that set the country apart from most other countries of the world, the majority of which were physically vulnerable, dependent on foreign resources, or both. The United States thus had to spend little time or effort meeting its basic needs in national security terms.

A sense of American dependence on the rest of the world for its well-being is a comparatively recent phenomenon. Absent the need to defend American territory from invading enemies or to secure scarce resources, most uses of American force have been expeditionary, sending the military overseas either to defend some American interest like US colonies or to aid a besieged country somewhere in the world. At the same time, there was no need to guard access to natural resources or food supplies from invading or otherwise intruding foreign sources. Effectively, the result was that the United States had, for most of its history, no compelling need to form a national security strategy to protect itself from the vagaries of a world it could largely ignore if it chose to do so.

These unique geographic advantages began to diminish by the middle of the twentieth century. The Pearl Harbor attack and the Japanese conquest of the Philippines demonstrated that an extended United States was no longer physically invulnerable. Soviet missile capability made that vulnerability more dramatic, and advances in telecommunications and transportation have produced arguable American vulnerabilities to threatening events, such as terrorist attacks. The North Korean nuclear arsenal is the most recent example.

American resource independence has also eroded dramatically. Increased demand for energy resources, such as petroleum, at low prices made the United States dependent on foreign supplies after World War II, with strong and controversial national security consequences in places like the Persian Gulf (see Amplification 3.1). At the same time, the development and use of more exotic materials unavailable in the United States, such as titanium for jet engines, has also reduced resource independence. The desire for exotic foodstuffs, such as year-round access to fresh fruits and vegetables, has made the United States an agricultural importer as well.

The Odyssey of American Petroleum Dependence

The Persian Gulf littoral, under which as much as two-thirds of the world's known reserves of petroleum are located, has been a major concern and problem for the United States since 1979. Prior to 1979, American interests in the region—almost exclusively based in uninterrupted access to reasonably priced oil—were ensured by the United States' closest regional ally, and the strongest power in the region, Shah Reza Pahlevi's Iran. In 1979, the shah was overthrown by a violently anti-American revolution that catapulted Ayatollah Ruhollah Khomeini into effective power, removed from authority the enforcer of American policy in the region, and raised unhindered American access to the region's oil as a national security concern.

The Persian Gulf crisis has been a source of major foreign and national security concern ever since. In 1980, President Jimmy Carter issued the Carter Doctrine, declaring access to Gulf oil to be a vital American interest. In 1990 and 1991, the United States led the coalition that evicted Iraq from Kuwait, an action taken in part to prevent Iraq's Saddam Hussein from gaining a stranglehold on Gulf petroleum reserves.

American national security policy in the Middle East has, as a result, been effectively held hostage to its addiction to Persian Gulf oil, greatly limiting the options it can contemplate or execute in that part of the world. Given the crucial importance of petroleum energy both for transportation and fundamental economic activity, petroleum dependency has put a considerable burden on US policy. (This dependency is discussed at length in Snow, *The Middle East, Oil, and the U.S. National Security Policy*).

Technological forces are reducing that dependence. The vehicle for this transformation has been the exploitation of shale gas and oil through hydraulic fracturing (commonly known as fracking). This process allows the extraction of petroleum resources from shale formations as opposed to traditional methods. The United States and Canada are the world leaders in this technology, which has greatly reduced the American need for Persian Gulf oil and virtually made the United States energy independent again, especially reducing its dependence on Middle East sources. Some controversies—largely environmental—surround fracking. The shale revolution and its implications are discussed in more detail in Chapter 13. ■

THE ANGLO-SAXON HERITAGE

Although the country has greatly diversified ethnically and nationally and much of the original American culture has changed as a result, the original United States was a British colony. Most of the original settlers in the eastern United States were of British extraction, and they brought with them many of the customs and predilections of the mother country.

This Anglo-Saxon heritage affected the early American national security experience in a couple of obvious and enduring ways. First, it created an aversion to and suspicion of the military, and more specifically the army, in peacetime. This dynamic was largely the result of the British experience during the Cromwellian period in the 1640s and beyond, when British forces were used to suppress political opposition to the regime at home. The British insistence on stationing elements of the British army in the American colonies after the French and Indian War became a serious issue that contributed to causing the American Revolution: Americans resented being subjected to a condition that citizens of the mother country would have found intolerable. This aversion manifested itself throughout the formative period of the American national security experience (see the next section) in the tendency essentially to disarm after major wars and to rely disproportionately on part-time citizen soldiers for the country's defense. The prohibition on the use of American armed forces in a law enforcement role on American soil, which was enacted in 1868 (known as *posse comitatus*), further reflects the fear of military abuse that has been invoked, for instance, when some officials have since 2016 proposed an expanded military role in patrolling the Mexican border. This aversion also creeps into domestic politics as part of the recurring theme of limited central government.

This influence affects broad American attitudes both toward government and governance and toward the specifics of national security. One of the themes that runs through the formative American period was the fear of government accumulation and abuse of power against the citizenry and is one of the reasons for the separation of powers within the federal government and the division of jurisdictions and authorities between the federal and state levels of government. One frequent expression of this legacy is a libertarian reaction to the power of central government and a desire for greater restraint on governance, a theme echoed by Tea Party/Freedom Caucus activists.

The theme also has a specific national security aspect that sometimes recurs in contradictory ways. The current all-volunteer, professional US military force structure was, in large measure, the direct result of resistance to infringements on individual liberties due to the involuntary, conscription-based manpower system in the Vietnam War. At the other extreme, fear arising from the threat of terrorism allowed passage of the

Patriot Act (Uniting and Strengthening America by Providing Appropriate Tools Required to Intercept and Obstruct Terrorism) in 2001 during the George W. Bush administration.

EVOLUTION OF THE AMERICAN EXPERIENCE

The American military tradition has evolved over time and with the different experiences the country has undergone. This evolution generally conforms to the three historical periods identified earlier. The two historical periods were distinct from one another in two clear ways. In terms of the level of threats and the American role in the world, the longer, formative period was one of low security threats and commitments, and the Cold War featured high threats and commitments. Neither historical combination fits the contemporary environment perfectly. On the one hand, the level of American involvement in the world since 1991 has never been higher. At the same time, the degree of threat to the United States was greatly reduced during the period between 1991 and 2001, but threats appear to have intensified greatly after September 11, 2001. Because history includes adaptation to changing circumstances, a major question is how changes in the environment have altered or amended fundamental American attitudes toward national security.

THE FORMATIVE PERIOD, 1789–1945

The period following the birth of the American republic was obviously formative for what would become the American military tradition and how Americans look at military force. The period was heavily influenced by the events surrounding the Revolution itself and why it had come about. In comparison to the nature of modern revolutions, the American Revolution was a rather low-key affair in terms of both its motivations and its conduct. As Dennis Drew and I have argued in *From Lexington to Baghdad and Beyond*, it might not have occurred at all had the British government acceded to the demands by Americans to be treated as full British citizens rather than colonial subjects. After the fighting began more or less accidentally at Lexington and Concord in April 1775, it took the colonials almost fifteen months to declare they were, in fact, revolting by issuing the Declaration of Independence on July 4, 1776. The war itself was, by current standards, a fairly low-intensity conflict fought between relatively small armed forces, mostly when the weather was good.

A series of "lessons" about military force arose from the revolutionary experience and were, by and large, reinforced during the next century and a half before the United States was thrust into World War II and could no longer remain aloof from world politics. Five elements of the American military tradition were born during this formative period. The first four—an antimilitary bias, the belief in the efficacy of the citizen soldier, the myth of invincibility, and the preference for rapid mobilization and demobilization—can be directly attributed to the revolutionary experience. The fifth, a preference for total war, was more a product of the Civil War and subsequent events in the international system generally. These elements collectively reinforced a general sort of disdain for military affairs that manifested itself, until the Korean War, in an American military establishment that was, except during wartime, small, physically isolated, and generally held in low regard.

At first glance, one may wonder whether these influences remain important in the contemporary world. Clearly, the antimilitary bias has faded (largely the result of the greater status accorded to the military due to its central role in the Cold War), and the demobilization preference was deflated by the near disaster of Korea (where demobilization after World War II had left the ranks so depleted that only the remobilization of World War II veterans in the US Reserves prevented the complete conquest of the Korean Peninsula by North Korea). At the same time, the role of reservist citizen soldiers was raised by Iraq and Afghanistan, the myth of US military invincibility has once again been questioned, and appropriate force levels in the 2010s (an aspect of mobilization) are part of the debate as well.

Two broad factors limit the applicability of these formative-period influences on contemporary perceptions. One has been the increasing salience of military forces in confronting the world since 1945. Put simply, a heightened threat environment has meant Americans need military force more than they did in the early days of the republic and have come to accept its contribution more than previously. The other has been the transformation of the military itself since the Vietnam War from a true citizen force composed of some members who were products of conscription to an all-volunteer, professional force. The result is a military that is both more professional and more competent but also smaller, more expensive, and arguably more removed from its popular roots.

Antimilitary Bias

It may sound strange to assert, when public opinion polls regularly rate military service as one of the more prestigious professions, but prior to the Cold War, military service was not universally held in high regard in the United States. The peacetime military was generally a small, skeletal body whose purpose was to be ready to train a civilian conscript force for military duty when the need arose. For the most part, the professional military (especially the Army) was consigned to military posts in remote areas of the country where the general population's day-to-day exposure to it was fairly limited. Moreover, outside the ranks of the professional military itself, soldiering was not thought of as a particularly prestigious occupation.

Much of this sentiment has its origins in the Anglo-Saxon tradition and the issue of British military presence in the colonies prior to the American Revolution. As in England under Cromwell, Crown forces had acted to suppress colonists, and many new Americans wanted to protect against the same possible fate in the new republic.

In addition to creating a predilection toward keeping the military as small and nonthreatening as possible, this antimilitary bias favored keeping the military apolitical and hence politically nonthreatening, as well. The US Military Academy at West Point, for instance, was designed essentially as an engineering school to teach the science of war but not the reasons for war (a precedent primarily followed in the other service academies). The leading work detailing the relationship between war and its political purposes, Carl von Clausewitz's *On War*, was originally published in 1832 but was not translated into English and did not enter into the West Point curriculum until 1876. Moreover, professional members of the military were effectively disenfranchised until 1944, when legislation permitting absentee balloting was enacted. Prior to that, military personnel could vote only if they happened to be physically in their hometowns on Election Day, which rarely happened.

The Citizen Soldier

How could a disdain and distrust for the military be reconciled with the occasional need for military forces to prosecute the wars of the United States? Part of the answer, of course, was to keep the military as small and unthreatening as possible during peacetime. The other element was to develop a part-time military whose members were also integral parts of the civilian society from which they came, citizen soldiers who were more citizens than soldiers. The result was to reinforce and glorify the militia tradition that was part of the colonial experience.

Militia members, the lineal forefathers of the National Guard and Reserves, were part-time soldiers. Members served for fixed terms and with limited commitments. Just as contemporary Guard and Reserve units have historically served actively for limited periods each year (e.g., one weekend a month, two weeks in summer camp), militia units would drill periodically, often for short periods (some as little as a few days per year). The idea was that such limited commitment would not "infect" these citizen soldiers with military values to the point they would lose their primary attachment to the civilian community. The activation of Guard and Reserve units for extended (including involuntarily extended) deployments in Iraq and Afghanistan is a temporary violation of this tradition that has been reduced considerably as American commitments in those two countries have shrunk.

The militia arrangement was satisfactory if one could assume militias were competent to carry out the country's military needs. From the Revolutionary period, a myth was developed that this was indeed the case. To some measure, this belief was little more than wishful thinking, but militia units were involved in enough successful operations during the Revolution (Lexington and Concord, Breed's Hill, Saratoga, Cowpens) that their performance could be embellished, and instances when militia units dissolved and ran when confronted with regular British Army opponents (Camden) could be ignored. When the country was not at war, the question was largely moot because militias were rarely called upon to demonstrate their strictly military competence.

The argument over the efficacy of the militia has never disappeared and remains part of the debate over current and future forces. Reserve and Guard units remain integral parts of the US armed forces. Reserve units have been increasingly placed in combat roles in recent years due to shortages of full-time, active-duty personnel, a consequence of the all-volunteer principle discussed in Chapter 8. Reservists are less expensive than active-duty soldiers and represent an additional reservoir of personnel when active-duty members are inadequate for a given task. These forces are also useful for other purposes such as disaster relief, but become controversial when proposals arise for other missions such as border patrol.

The Myth of Invincibility

The indomitable nature of the American military is the third legacy of the early period of American military history. The resulting myth of invincibility is the idea that regardless of the circumstances, when the United States is forced to fight, it prevails. The truth of this belief is factually debatable. It is true that the United States has generally been successful in war, but American triumphs are liberally interspersed with episodes in which the country was less successful than the myth implies. More precisely, the truth generally is that when the United States becomes involved in long, total wars where superior American physical resources can be brought to bear to wear out an opponent, the country generally prevails. That generalization does not apply to all warfare; in Vietnam, the opponent refused to wear out or to fight according to established norms, and the result was certainly not victory. The same has arguably proven true in Iraq and Afghanistan.

This generally positive assessment of the American military experience has two corollaries. The first is the "can do" syndrome, the idea that no military task is too difficult to overcome if Americans truly apply themselves to surmounting it. The syndrome can be a major impediment to objective assessment of potential missions for which American military forces might be employed, suggesting the possibility of prevailing in situations where a more sober assessment might counsel otherwise. There is, for instance, little on the public record to suggest that any appropriate military officials considered in advance the prospect that the United States might not be able to prevail in Vietnam; no one in the appropriate position to do so effectively said "*can't* do," an assessment held by many midlevel professional military and outside civilian analysts at the time. This failure regarding Vietnam is described in former Trump national security advisor H.R. McMaster's *Dereliction of Duty* and with regard to Iraq in Yingling's "A Failure in Generalship."

The other corollary is that Americans prevail because of the brilliance and skill with which they fight. The facts largely fly in the face of such an assertion. The United States has, for instance, produced no major strategist of land warfare, although it has produced exceptional battlefield generals like George S. Patton and strategists who have contributed in other media (sea and air). Moreover, although American fighting forces have acquitted themselves well, the United States entered all its wars prior to Vietnam almost absolutely unprepared to fight them, meaning that in the early stages of those wars, American forces did not excel.

Mobilization and Demobilization

Through most of American history, the pattern of mobilization and demobilization has dominated the American military experience: when war seemed imminent or was thrust upon the country, it would raise and train a force to fight it, but as soon as the fighting ended, it would decommission that force and return it to the normalcy of civilian life. This preference reflected numerous elements of the American culture, from a belief in the abnormality of war to the fear of a standing military in peacetime. It also meant that after every major war until Korea, the United States returned its armed forces to the skeletal form that had existed before the outbreak of hostilities.

The tradition was sustainable throughout the formative period because the United States was never confronted with an enemy that could pose a direct and immediate threat to American territory. The accident of American geography historically created the luxury of forming a force after war because no hostile force could menace American territory quickly. The experience in World War II and the Cold War that followed changed that conclusion. In the attack on Pearl Harbor, American forces in the Pacific were nearly overrun by Japan to the extent that it would have been difficult to regain the initiative, and only the heroic efforts of Americans at places like the Battle of Midway and Guadalcanal allowed the United States to recover while it rapidly mobilized an adequate force to meet the emergency. The North Koreans almost conquered South Korea in 1950, and after that near debacle, the tradition of demobilization was abandoned. Today, the all-volunteer force (AVF) carries the banner of readiness (see Amplification 3.2).

AMPLIFICATION 3.2

Readiness and the All-Volunteer Force

Pearl Harbor and Korea taught the United States that there was a potentially steep price to be paid by demobilization. The Cold War reinforced that realization as the country faced a heavily armed Soviet opponent. Should war have broken out between the Americans and the Soviets, it would have been fought by the "force in being"—those troops that existed when war was declared. Given the severe potential consequences, Americans dropped their historical opposition to large forces during peacetime and agreed to be conscripted during times when a war was not ongoing, an unprecedented concession.

The Vietnam War broke Americans' willingness to do involuntary military service, but the Soviet threat remained for nearly another twenty years. The solution to the resulting dilemma was the AVF, a military establishment composed entirely of members who volunteered to do the country's military business as their profession. In the process, what amounted to demobilization was reinstated for all those Americans who chose not to serve since they were no longer subject to involuntary service.

This compromise has endured since 1972. It has taken several generations of Americans "off the hook" of military service, but the AVF is an inherently small and manpower-constrained force, is quite expensive to maintain, and has been pushed nearly to its limits in long wars in Iraq and Afghanistan. If the United States wishes to continue a militarily activist policy in the future, at some point this demobilization trade-off may have to be revisited. ■

Total War Preference

The first four elements of the American tradition are in contrast with a preference for involvement in total wars that stands in apparent contradiction to the rest of the tradition. At one level, this development reflected changes in the international environment between the eighteenth and the middle of the twentieth centuries regarding the purposes of war. It was also the result of an American perception that if the United States were to go to war, it should be for grand, righteous purposes that made the effort and sacrifice worthwhile.

The period between the mid-nineteenth and mid-twentieth centuries witnessed an expansion in both the means and the purposes for which war was conducted. The expansion of means was largely the result of the progressive application of the innovations of the Industrial Revolution to warfare. Gradually, it became possible to expand the extent of warfare by increasing the deadly effects of weapons and by increasing the places in which war could be fought. In 1789, warfare was largely limited to the surface of the ocean and to ground combat where armies could march and organize their linear formations on large, open fields; by 1945, the only place war could not be conducted was in space (a deficiency overcome since then).

This expansion in means coincided with and reinforced an expansion in the reasons for fighting. The triggering events in the expansion of purposes were the American and (especially) French Revolutions, which reintroduced political ideology into the causes of war. In the period after the end of the Thirty Years' War in 1648, the system had been dominated by monarchies that did not disagree on political matters and generally limited their fighting to small purposes. The French Revolution's evangelical period, when it spread its ideas across Europe, erased those limits, and as the means to conduct war expanded, so too did the reasons for fighting.

The purpose of war became the overthrow of enemy governments, which is the definition of total war. Although it was scarcely realized as such at the time, the prototype was probably the latter stages of the American Civil War, when the destruction of the Confederate Army and the overthrow of the government of the Confederacy were accepted as the necessary preconditions for reunion. The overthrow of the German government became the ultimate goal in World War I, and the epitome of total war was reached in the commitment to the unconditional surrender of Germany and Japan in World War II.

Total war fit the American worldview. The American self-image has always contained an evangelical component that suggests the virtue of sharing the American ideal with others, and that evangelism could be extended to provide an adequate moral justification to breach the normalcy of peace and go to war. The epitome of this zeal is captured in Woodrow Wilson's address to Congress proposing an American declaration of war in 1917: "The day has come when America is privileged to spend her blood and her might for the principles that gave her birth and happiness. God helping her, she can do no other."

Total wars are much simpler to understand than the limited wars that have been the norm since 1945. In total war, the enemy are viewed as totally reprehensible to the point that only overthrowing the enemy government is acceptable, and military force is raised and employed to crush resistance to that end. Once this goal is achieved, however, the war is over and normalcy (peace) is restored. Because the enemy has been depicted as evil, its toppling is morally satisfying as well.

Modern war is not so simple. Because the ultimate contemporary total interstate war is an all-out nuclear exchange, interstate wars must be limited to avoid that possibility. The object is not to overthrow the opponent's government (Iraq is an exception) but rather to force the government to stop doing something (supporting terrorists, for instance). The opposition often consists of so-called non-state actors lacking territory or a population to attack, and there is no sharp and definitive point at which war ends and peace is restored (a particularly painful lesson in Iraq). Such ambiguity is typical of internal wars so prevalent in the developing world (the DWICs), where total goals of government overthrow are the norm but the danger of escalation to general nuclear war is minimal. Contemporary war simply does not conform to traditional concepts of violent conflict as developed in American culture, and the result is, in Yingling's words, "a crisis in an entire institution."

THE COLD WAR, 1945–91

The end of World War II radically changed the place of the United States in the world and the way in which it had to consider matters of national security. As the wartime collaboration with the Soviet Union gradually deteriorated into the confrontation that would define the Cold War, national security moved to center stage in the political constellation. When North Korea invaded South Korea on June 25, 1950, and the United States responded (through the United Nations) by coming to the aid of the southerners, any doubt about the changed nature of international politics and the American role in it disappeared.

The Cold War made military affairs—national security defined in largely military terms—a central reality of American peacetime life. Geopolitics were clearly dominant for the first time in US history. The Korean experience demonstrated that a demobilized United States could not compete with a heavily armed Soviet opponent. Thus, the traditional practices of the formative period could no longer be afforded.

New Influences

The Cold War presented the United States with an apparently permanent military enemy for the first time since its rivalry with Great Britain abated after the War of 1812. The Soviets posed primarily a military threat of expansionist communism, and American policy had to respond militarily. The result was the emergence of a *national security state* in which matters of national defense took on a coequal footing with other foreign policy considerations. A large, permanent military establishment became an equally permanent part of the landscape.

The military culture changed because of several new conditioning factors in the environment, especially after the Korean conflict. Each factor represented a direct change and even, in some cases, a contradiction to the previous American experience, yet the nature of the Cold War caused these changes to be accepted without fundamental challenges from most Americans.

The nearly disastrous Korean War experience created the recognition that the Cold War would require a large American active-duty force all the time. The Soviets did not demobilize after World War II, and they and their allies maintained large offensive forces. Should the Soviets have decided to invade Western Europe, as was widely feared, there would be no time to mobilize, train, and transport a force to the war zone. The "force in being," comprising both volunteers and conscripts, would have to be available on the scene at all times, in effect creating a permanent state of mobilization. A large peacetime force of this size could be sustained only by the existence of a national conscription system, the first time an involuntary draft system had actually been used in peacetime in American history. As well, the defense budget had to be greatly expanded to support the defense effort.

This expanded role and prominence of the military resulted in much greater prestige for members of the military profession. With a constant threat against which it was necessary to protect the country, the work of the military now seemed more vital. The respect Americans had bestowed on the World War II military was extended to the Cold Warriors. Military service and even military careers now became attractive to growing numbers of Americans who before would probably not have considered such a career.

The advent and expansion of thermonuclear weapons and the development and deployment of intercontinental range missiles by both sides elevated the importance of military concerns by making the consequences of war potentially personally devastating to all Americans. At the height of the Cold War competition, the two sides faced one another with arsenals of between ten thousand and twelve thousand thermonuclear warheads capable of attacking targets in the other country and against which there were no defenses. The successful management of the nuclear balance to avoid nuclear war—nuclear deterrence—became the country's most crucial business (a literal survival interest). The Cold War world was a potentially very deadly place.

The Cold War confrontation was also a protracted competition from which no one could confidently project a peaceful ending. Most analysts agreed the only alternatives were Cold War and hot war, and since the latter would probably be nuclear, it had to be avoided at virtually all costs.

These factors directly contradicted previous American experience. The idea of permanent mobilization of large standing forces would have absolutely appalled the Founding Fathers, many of whom equated standing armed forces with tyranny. A world of perpetual and potentially disastrous military conflict requiring constant vigilance and extensive preparation and spending was entirely foreign to a country whose broad oceans had provided a barrier that permitted the leisure and luxury of a general mobilization. The idea that a military career would bring great prestige would never have occurred to most of the champions of the militia tradition.

Given the historical precedent, it is remarkable how readily these changes were accepted. Americans who had never been willing to (or had the need to) allow themselves to be taxed specifically to support a large standing peacetime military and who would previously have been fundamentally opposed to the existence of a draft during peacetime accepted both with virtually no complaint. The main reason was a threat that was real and ominous enough to justify greater sacrifices.

During this period, three new elements of the American military tradition became prominent parts of the military environment. Both the news media and democratic institutions had, of course, been present throughout American history. In the period surrounding the Vietnam conflict, however, their roles became more defined and influential. At the same time, the "seed" was sown for another influence: professionalization of the military. The media influence has greatly increased as democratic institutions have produced a more partisan political environment, whereas increased emphasis on military professionalism has provided some insulation from the toxicity of modern politics for the national security sector.

The Role of the Media

The relationship between the media and the military has changed. At times, the media have championed acts of war (e.g., the Spanish-American War); at other times, they have opposed it (e.g., Vietnam). It has always been a complex and contentious relationship, with the two institutions eyeing one another with some distrust and occasional disdain that was worsened by the very sour experience of the Vietnam conflict and media coverage of it. The relationship has become even more complex since the end of the Cold War.

A major manifestation of tensions between the two institutions has to do with what is reportedly a concern that centers especially but not exclusively on combat operations. The press believes coverage should be as complete and unfettered as possible, including access to combat operations and the right to report what they observe. The media's position is based on the public's right to know what its government's representatives (in this case its military) are doing, and this claim is based in the First Amendment.

The military disagrees in some cases, arguing unfettered coverage can provide the enemy with information that could compromise the integrity of military operations and even put soldiers at additional risk. At the same time, reportage of less-than-successful military actions can have a negative impact on morale and give solace to the enemy.

The interaction between the media and the military in Vietnam transformed the relationship to one of much greater animosity. Early in the war, the relationship was supportive because reportage was passive: the military would tell the press its version of what happened in the fighting, and the press would dutifully report that interpretation as fact. The picture portrayed was uniformly positive and suggested not only that progress was occurring but also that victory was imminent.

The Tet Offensive by the North Vietnamese and Viet Cong in January 1968 destroyed that symbiosis. The enemy launched a general attack throughout the country, especially against cities including the South Vietnamese capital of Saigon. The attacks were much larger than American casualty figures provided by the US military made possible. Members of the media concluded that they had been lied to, that both they and their audiences had been duped, and that they should be much more critical in the future. Trust between the military and the media was the victim.

The existence of electronic media and twenty-four-hour-a-day cable television news networks has changed the role of the media in another way. The coverage of war is much more public now than it was in years past. Not only does one know the status of fighting and American casualty figures, one is relentlessly exposed to the horrors, deprivations, and atrocities associated with war. Often even small military events seem blown out of proportion as "breaking news" by cable outlets. From studios in the United States, "talking head" experts on military affairs and area specialists offer detailed and often critical instant analyses of events and trends.

In important ways, the effect of the media on national security reflects the impact modern media has on society and politics generally. The relentless coverage now provided by media activity certainly exposes the application of force in far more detail. In the current vituperative relationship between the media and the Trump administration, the military has remained neutral and non-partisan. As a result, it has avoided getting caught up in the partisan web.

The Impact of Democratic Institutions

Within a political democracy, popular will and opinion are always a matter of concern in national security since the ultimate expression of that policy can be war that places citizens at physical risk. The "democratization" of national security affairs is largely a post–World War II phenomenon. Like so many other influences on contemporary affairs, it was accentuated by American participation in Vietnam. During most of the formative period of the American republic, there was little concern with military affairs, and most wars either were highly popular (the world wars, the Spanish-American War) or affected relatively few Americans because of their small size or length. A partial exception to this was selective Northern resistance to the Union cause in the American Civil War, which was the first massive American war and the first to involve large-scale involuntary service—the draft.

The sour taste of the Vietnam experience helped elevate the role of popular control over the democratic institutions making decisions about war and peace. After that experience, the military itself engaged in a good deal of self-examination of what went wrong, and a large part of its conclusion was that the war effort was undermined by public support and opinion that evaporated around them as the war dragged on. (Vietnam was the longest war in American history at the time, a distinction eclipsed by Afghanistan.) To the military, the war violated the Clausewitzian trinity, which posited that war may be successfully waged only when there is a bond among the people, the military, and the government. Reasoning that the political authority had never explicitly solicited popular support for the Vietnam conflict (for a discussion, see Snow and Drew), the armed forces (especially the Army) vowed this would not happen again.

A major consequence of public unhappiness with the Vietnam War was suspension of the draft at the end of 1972, and no American has faced involuntary military service since then. The draft system was replaced by the AVF, mostly to alleviate criticism of Vietnam based on sending the sons of American voters to fight and die in that unpopular war. The concept of an entirely voluntary, and thus professional, force has become the accepted standard for organizing American arms and American forces. It has been perceived as a successful experiment to the point that it is now imbedded in the American military tradition. The endurance of this concept given strains caused by multiple deployments of this force in the 2000s has resulted in problems introduced in the *Challenge!* box.

Professionalism of the Military

The AVF responded to dissonance arising from Vietnam and the breached Clausewitzian link between the military and the people. Once the war was over, it also provided an avenue to staff the "force in being" with soldiers, sailors, marines, and airmen who chose to perform that role rather than with reluctant conscripts. As time has passed, the effect has been to create a more professional, competent military force but one not as intimately tied to its civilian base or as expandable as before.

The professional military heartily endorses the change because it has produced a much more disciplined, proficient force than its predecessor, and the military itself is among the strongest detractors of returning to any other manpower system. The professional military of the 2000s performs at substantially higher levels of proficiency than did the Vietnam-era military, has substantially fewer disciplinary problems, can be deployed in a wide variety of situations without member dissent, and presents few political problems for civilian authorities.

Iraq and Afghanistan have raised questions about the future. A professional military must compete for members with other employers. As a result, it is expensive because military service is only attractive to a very small percentage of Americans, and this is smaller than a conscript force can be. When military commitments are small, as they generally have been since 1972, these smaller resources are not overly stressed. Iraq and Afghanistan, however, stretched them to their near breaking point and have raised questions about whether the concept is sustainable in the face of larger-scale demands.

CHALLENGE!

The Paradigm of the Professional Soldier

The AVF concept has become so imbedded in thinking about the American military as to seem immutable and unchallengeable. The professional soldier, an idea that was so abhorrent, even unthinkable, earlier in American history, is now accepted as a virtuous part of national life. This elevation in status certainly reflects an assessment of the admirable role and proficiency of modern military members. It also reflects a political element: as long as the AVF concept is in place, no American who does not want to serve in the military is in any danger of being forced to do so. A major virtue of the AVF-driven paradigm is that it insulates virtually all Americans from military service.

There are objections to this very popular condition that arise from the past and will be developed in the pages that follow. One is that the professional military is necessarily limited in size since military service is only attractive to a small part of the population. Is the AVF sustainable in the event of a major conflict? A second is that a professional force may be too "easy" to use since committing it does not have the same potentially negative effects of a decision to go to war that entails drafting voters. The endurance of the professional soldier paradigm is not as unquestionable as it might seem at first glance. ■

Professionalization also brings the citizen soldier concept into question. The modern American military member is still a citizen, but have contemporary soldiers become "more" soldier and less civilian than the country's past citizens would have countenanced? Americans who do not wish to serve are no longer troubled by the prospect of forced service. But has there been a price for that convenience that has yet to be paid?

CONCLUSION: THE CONTEMPORARY PERIOD, 1991 TO PRESENT

The end of the Cold War represented a major change in the environment and thus in the ways Americans think about matters of national security. This change was not immediately recognized, and there was not a great initial effort to test the nature and implications of the collapse of the Soviet empire. The response to September 11, 2001, provided another jolt to conventional wisdom, the implications of which are still being sorted out.

With more than a quarter century of the new environment and the threat of terrorism revealed as context, how will the American experience be shaped by the contemporary situation? Key elements in the past have included the role of the United States in the international system and the level of threat the environment provided, as noted earlier. American historical experience reveals a contrast of these two variables, as shown in Table 3.1. As the table displays, the two historical periods show that the United States has exemplified both "pure" combinations: high threat and a large international role during the Cold War and low threat and a small role during most of the formative period.

The contemporary period represents a hybrid. Clearly the American role in the world is large, and with the collapse of the Cold War, it arguably became larger than it had ever been before. The question was and still is: which part of the American tradition will dominate the contemporary view of the world? Particularly given the not entirely satisfactory outcomes in Iraq and Afghanistan, some Americans might want to reduce the United States' assertive presence and role, effectively promoting a return to the legacy of

TABLE 3.1		
American Roles and Threats		
	Threat	
Role	High	Low
Large	Cold War	?
Small	?	Formative

the formative period's preference for basically being left alone. The general approach of President Trump reflects this approach. The cutback in active-duty troop strength and the disappearance of conscription as part of the potential political agenda suggest that all the elements from the formative period have not disappeared and may reassert themselves as the United States returns from the "abnormality" of the Cold War to a more comfortable past.

The role of the United States, however, has not receded to where it was in the formative period but has remained roughly as prominent as it was during the Cold War. Does this mean the internationalism that dominated the Cold War approach of the United States toward the world has become such a permanent part of the landscape as to be inescapable? The Bush administration entered office in 2001 with the stated intention of trimming back the United States' commitments in areas such as peacekeeping, but it was mere months before the terrorist attack caused it to quietly jettison that rhetoric and adopt the aggressive military posture toward the international environment that was advocated by the neoconservatives. In 2001 it committed US forces to Afghanistan, and in 2003 it invaded and occupied Iraq. The outcomes of these adventures have not been unquestionably positive and have encouraged reluctance to engage in other activism in places like Syria. The Trump approach has some of the appearance of a conceptual retreat to an earlier era, but whether that is possible and with what consequences remains to be seen.

STUDY/DISCUSSION QUESTIONS

1. What are the three conditioning factors affecting the American view of national security? Discuss each, including how each has changed.
2. What is the formative period of the American national security experience? What principles did it produce? Which have been the most enduring, and which have changed the most? Why?
3. How did the Cold War represent a major change in how the United States views national security? Discuss.
4. What are the major influences on national security that came out of the Cold War? Discuss each, including how each influence has evolved.
5. The US military experience has moved from great restraint to great activism over time and with varying circumstances. In which direction do you think it is headed now? Why?

SELECTED BIBLIOGRAPHY

Ackerman, Bruce. *Before the Next Attack: Preserving Civil Liberties in an Age of Terrorism.* New Haven, CT: Yale University Press, 2006.

Allison, William T., and Jeffrey Grey. *American Military History: A Survey from Colonial Times to the Present.* New York and London: Routledge, 2016.

Boot, Max. *The Savage Wars of Peace: Small Wars and the Rise of American Power.* New York: Basic Books, 2014.

————. *War Made New: Technology, Warfare, and the Course of History: 1500-Today*. New York: Avery, 2007.

Brodie, Bernard. *War and Politics*. New York: Palgrave Macmillan, 1973.

Carroll, John M., and Colin F. Baxter. *The American Military Tradition: From Colonial Times to the Present*. Lanham, MD: Rowman & Littlefield, 2006.

Clausewitz, Carl von. *On War*. Rev. ed. Translated and edited by Michael Howard and Peter Paret. Princeton, NJ: Princeton University Press, 1984.

Cole, David, and James X. Dempsey. *Terrorism and the Constitution: Sacrificing Civil Liberties in the Name of National Security*. New York: New Press, 2002.

Dupuy, D. Ernest, and Trevor N. Dupuy. *The Encyclopedia of Military History*. New York: Harper and Row, 1972.

Gaddis, John Lewis. *Strategies of Containment: A Critical Appraisal of Postwar American National Security Policy*. Oxford, UK: Oxford University Press, 1982.

Haass, Richard. *Wars of Necessity, Wars of Choice: A Memoir of Two Iraq Wars*. New York: Simon and Schuster, 2009.

Hassler, Warren W., Jr. *With Shield and Sword: American Military Affairs, Colonial Times to the Present*. Ames, IA: Iowa State University Press, 1984.

Heymann, Philip B., and Juliette Kayyem. *Protecting Liberty in an Age of Terror*. Cambridge, MA: MIT Press, 2005.

Isikoff, Michael, and David Corn. *Hubris: The Inside Story of Spin*. New York: Crown Publishers, 2005.

Leckie, Robert. *The Wars of America*. Rev. and updated ed. New York: Harper and Row, 1981.

McMaster, Herbert R. *Dereliction of Duty: Lyndon Johnson, Robert McNamara, the Joint Chiefs of Staff, and the Lies That Led to Vietnam*. New York: Harper Perennial, 1997.

Millett, Allan R., and Peter Maslowski. *For the Common Defense: A Military History of the United States of America*. New York: Free Press, 1984.

Nye, Joseph Jr. *Bound to Lead: The Changing Nature of American Power*. New York: Basic Books, 2016.

Snow, Donald M. *Cases in U.S. National Security: Principles and Applications*. Lanham, MD: Rowman & Littlefield, 2019.

————. *When America Fights: The Uses of U.S. Military Force*. Washington, DC: CQ Press, 2000.

———— and Dennis M. Drew. *From Lexington to Baghdad and Beyond: War and Politics in the American Experience*. 3rd ed. Armonk, NY: M. E. Sharpe, 2009.

Tucker, Robert W., and Donald C. Hendrickson. "The Sources of American Legitimacy." *Foreign Affairs* 83, 6 (November/December 2004), 18–32.

Weigley, Russell F. *The American Way of War*. New York: Palgrave Macmillan, 1973.

Williams, T. Harry. *A History of American Wars: From Colonial Times to World War II*. New York: Alfred A. Knopf, 1981.

Yingling, Paul (Lt. Col.). "A Failure in Generalship." *Armed Forces Journal* (online), (May 2009).

The Post-1945 Challenge: The Nature and End of the Cold War

The Cold War has been over for nearly three decades, but the international and domestic structures and attitudes it produced continue to affect the contemporary world. A distinctly American form of geopolitics, roughly based in the form of the realist paradigm, was one product of the long confrontation; additionally, the American military structure still reflects preparation to fight World War III against a Soviet-style opponent despite evidence that warfare has changed in ways that negate the effectiveness of that form of fighting. Understanding how the Cold War occurred and evolved and what traces remain in places like Russia is crucial to understanding how the United States is predisposed to respond to the future.

The Cold War is, of course, history. It began in the aftermath of World War II as the remaining major powers from that conflagration, the United States and the Soviet Union, came to realize they could not agree on a common postwar vision for the world order. The revelation occurred gradually during the latter 1940s as relations between them deteriorated; the punctuation mark was the Korean War. It lasted until the end of 1991, when the Soviet Union formally dissolved itself.

The Cold War was a national baptism for the United States into world geopolitics. In the country's formative period, the United States was not a consistent major player in international relations for several reasons, including a relative tranquility in international relations between 1815 and 1914 and a general preference to be left alone to realize American manifest destiny. America remained on the periphery of a European-centric international system for most of its first century and a half.

The end of World War II made a return to isolation from the world impossible and thrust a reluctant, inexperienced United States onto the center stage of world events. When the last guns of the war were stilled, only the United States and the Soviet Union retained enough power to influence international events and to reorganize an international system laid prostrate by the war. The implications of this bipolar balance of power—and especially its adversarial content—were not clear immediately but took shape in the five-year period that climaxed in the Korean conflict. The United States was propelled into the vortex of the *realpolitik* of international relations for the first time.

The changed configuration of the international system was especially dramatic. Through most of American history, the international system was *multipolar*, a condition in which several countries of importance competed for positions of power but no single state predominated (although Germany arguably came close twice in the twentieth century). In this system, the United States gradually rose from being a weak, peripheral power to major member.

The post–World War II world was different. Except for the United States and the Soviet Union, all the traditional powers were so weakened by the war effort that they were unable or unwilling to remain central players. In these circumstances, the system became *bipolar*, with the United States and the Soviet Union as the major forces (or poles) around which other states more or less willingly congregated. With the end of the Cold War, the Soviet pole disappeared, and the system has been undergoing a process of reconfiguration ever since.

Understanding and managing the Cold War became the central task for the generations of American policymakers, strategists, and scholars who had to administer and explain this dramatic change and then had to adapt to the Cold War system for another forty years. Lurking constantly over their shoulders was the shadow cast by the possibility of the Cold War turning very hot in a totally ruinous nuclear war.

The major organizing construct they adopted was the realist paradigm introduced in Chapter 2. Its central feature was a harsh, confrontational relationship. It became a very *conservative* construct in the pure sense of that term: it sought to conserve the system below the level of general war, which both sides quite rightly feared. In the end, that construct and the fear it produced helped contribute to the end of the Cold War. But while it lasted, the Cold War provided an encompassing geopolitical worldview. Those analysts who challenged it were dismissed as dreamers and visionaries whose suggestions were too risky or foolhardy to be considered seriously.

It is important to emphasize the pervasive nature of the Cold War because it affects the way many people continue to look at the world.

Some of the military people who have flag rank (generals or admirals) in the services today were educated or influenced by the events and dynamics of that period, which remain the implicit underpinning of how they view the world—and the same is true of the many civilians in the foreign and national security community. Many nonmilitary analysts have, with varying degrees of success, sought to shed some of the now inapplicable aspects of the Cold War mentality, but they remain at least partly Cold Warriors nonetheless. The equation of the US response to terrorism with a war between good and evil, for instance, has antecedents in the Cold War against "godless communism." President Bush's "axis of evil" and President Reagan's "evil empire" come from the same intellectual cloth. The continuing influence of the Cold War experience on many ongoing national security debates like dealing with Russia is subtle and even subliminal, but it is impossible to understand the positions people take without acknowledging their Cold War roots.

The Cold War and its demise may be history, but it is important history that is relevant to understanding the present. Because of this, the chapter is devoted to the Cold War. It begins by looking briefly at the essence of the Cold War relationship as a distinct international system. It then turns to the military competition that was at the core of the US-Soviet conflict and that, in the end, helped contribute to the end of the Cold War. Some residues of the Cold War remain part of the current reality. For instance, Russia strains to reassert its preeminent position in the global community. At the same time, many ongoing problems, notably violence in the developing world, have roots in the Cold War period.

THE COLD WAR SYSTEM

At the end of World War II, the international system was confronted with two fundamental dynamics, the consequences of which would evolve and dominate international relations for most of the rest of the twentieth century. One question focused on nuclear weapons. The use of atomic bombs against Hiroshima and Nagasaki, Japan, by the United States helped break Japan's will to continue the war and meant these novel and enormously deadly weapons would be part of the calculation of future military affairs. Hence, a fundamental question facing planners was what difference these weapons would make in the future.

The other question was about the future of the wartime collaboration between the United States and the Soviet Union. Would friendship continue, or would the deep ideological differences between them result in a future of conflict and confrontation? In retrospect, the answer seems stunningly obvious, and most observers at the time suspected the collaboration could not be sustained. Continued cooperation, however, might have resulted in a much more tranquil international environment, and this hopeful possibility could not be dismissed out of hand.

Postwar contingency planning had gone on in the United States throughout the war, especially in collaboration with the British. Uncertainty about what kind of relationship would exist among what became the superpowers of the Cold War system dominated this deliberative process. In the face of this uncertainty, the planners devised a structure to accommodate either outcome—collaboration or confrontation.

The principal instrument for organizing the postwar world was the United Nations (UN) Charter. The primary purpose of the UN was to create a viable mechanism to organize the peace to avoid a repetition of the slide into World War II. Critical to crafting a viable, working system was whether the United States and the Soviet Union could agree upon a form of peace they were willing to enforce. In the end, they could not.

The two powers had very opposing worldviews, so finding a mutually acceptable peace to defend was not going to be easy. The United States preferred a world of Western-style political democracies and capitalist-based economies like its own, and the Soviets wanted to promote the expansion of communism in the world. Both sides were evangelical, and the secular "religions" they promoted were incompatible. Thus, the prospects of peace and cooperation were prejudiced from the beginning.

Collaboration was not sustainable because the two sides could not agree on a world order both could support. Thus, the UN mechanisms for organizing the peace through cooperation remained disabled and disengaged for the duration of the Cold War. The UN was able to act on Korea in 1950 because the Soviets were boycotting the organization in protest of the American-led refusal to seat the new communist government of China rather than the Nationalist government of Chiang Kai-Shek in Taiwan and thus did not veto the action. After Korea, the mechanisms for enforcing peace essentially went into a veto-induced hibernation for forty years.

By 1950, both wartime questions had been answered. The North Korean invasion removed any lingering doubt that confrontation rather than collaboration would be the central feature of the Soviet-American relationship. After the Soviets exploded their first atomic bomb in 1949, the question of the role of nuclear weapons was added to the calculus of what became the Cold War international system. This system had at least three prominent characteristics that helped define the period.

Characteristics

First, during the Cold War *political and military competition dominated international politics*. Only the United States and the Soviet Union emerged from World War II with enough residual power to organize and influence international events, but their power bases differed. The heart of American power was economic and military. The American industrial system was strengthened by the war and towered above those of everyone else (for a period in the 1940s, the American economy accounted for nearly 40 percent of world productivity, over twice what it is today). Military power rested on the sole possession of nuclear weapons by the United States. The much weaker Soviet economy had virtually been destroyed by the war, but the Soviets kept a force of close to twelve million under arms (the United States demobilized to around one million in 1946).

This distribution of power defined the international system as *bipolar* in nature: the United States and the Soviet Union stood as the two remaining powers (or poles) around which other states congregated and could be controlled or influenced. The American lever of power was economic; everyone in the West needed American money and goods for recovery. The Red Army occupation in Eastern Europe was able to impose friendly regimes in the occupied countries that became reluctant parts of the Soviet orbit.

The Cold War's pervasive nature took root first in a Europe divided by what British statesman Winston Churchill first called the Iron Curtain in a speech in Fulton, Missouri, in 1947. The relationship became formally militarized through the formation of NATO (North Atlantic Treaty Organization) in 1949 and its communist counterpart, the Warsaw Treaty Organization (WTO, or the Warsaw Pact), in 1955. The ideological struggle spread to the developing world as countries emerged from colonial rule, principally in Asia and Africa, during the 1950s and 1960s.

Nothing symbolized the intensity of the Cold War more dramatically than the superpower nuclear competition. At one level, the competition was incongruous as both sides constructed arsenals for potential use against one another so large and excessive that a war between them would almost certainly destroy both. It became popular to depict the relationship as two scorpions in a bottle: each scorpion was ready to kill the other and itself in a conflict both feared the other might be tempted to initiate if they showed weakness or vulnerability. Each superpower gradually came to dread the prospect of that conflict enough that nuclear weapons contributed to defusing the Cold War.

Second, the conflict was viewed as *protracted*, a long-term competition for which only great patience would suffice and the management of which required great vigilance. The Cold War was a battle between two diametrically opposed systems of political belief that was enduring and had no certain outcome. It was broadly assumed that the only means by which closure could come was through a massive nuclear clash, World War III, that would likely destroy both sides.

This protracted competition became both a prediction of the future and a prime value given its extremely destructive alternative. There was always something curious in this assessment. It was a matter of firm belief in the West that the communist philosophy was inherently inferior to its capitalist economic and democratic political ideals. This conviction was hardly ever translated into the conclusion that communism might collapse on its own as those flaws became manifest (which, of course, is exactly what happened). Instead, the operating assumption was that the Cold War was both immutable and fatalistically preferable to its believed alternative, hot war. One particularly fatalistic expression at the time is captured in Amplification 4.1.

The perceived communist strength was the totalitarian nature of Soviet rule. Soviet communism, the argument went, could not fail because its coercive strength was so great that any opposition would be crushed mercilessly. Thus, even if the regime lacked broad popular support, as it did, its power could not be challenged effectively.

AMPLIFICATION 4.1

Better Red than Dead? Better Dead than Red?

The Cold War was most intense and assessments of the future most pessimistic during the 1950s. The Korean War, which had become intensely unpopular after it stalemated in 1951 but dragged on until 1953, was a recent memory of apparent failure. The liberation of North Korea had not been accomplished, and the communist Viet Minh of Ho Chi Minh had prevailed in French Indochina, another victory for expanding communism. When the Soviet Union beat the United States into space by launching Sputnik into the heavens first and Americans peered into the night sky and saw it blink by overhead, there seemed reason to suspect the wrong side was prevailing in the competition. The flaws of operational communism had not become obvious to anyone.

In this atmosphere, despair emerged about how the Cold War might end. One possibility was that the Soviet Union might actually prevail, in which case the debate was whether it would be preferable to accept Soviet domination or to go down fighting in a cataclysmic nuclear war: better Red than dead? The second possibility was that war between the two systems was inevitable. It was not a question of whether there would be war but when. The debate was turned around to ask if perishing in such a conflict was preferable to communist overlordship: better dead than Red? Hardly anyone could imagine the outcome that eventually prevailed: neither dead nor Red. ■

This fatalism meant there was much less consideration about ending the Cold War than if participants had begun with the proposition that the competition was instead intellectually tilted in favor of the democracies. Over the years, a few observers had seen this, but their prophecies were largely ignored. George F. Kennan, the American diplomat who was the intellectual father of the American foreign policy of containment, argued that a policy of diligence could contain communism within the boundaries it had achieved. If containment was applied consistently, the inherent inferiority of the communist system would eventually cause it to implode. He was proven correct.

Third, another characteristic of the Cold War system was that it became *global*. Originally, it was geographically limited to the boundary between Western and Eastern Europe and, after 1949, the area surrounding China. As independence movements produced new states in Asia and Africa during the 1950s, 1960s, and early 1970s (decolonization was effectively over in 1975 when Portugal granted independence to the last members of its empire), both sides scrambled to gain advantage, even allegiance, from newly installed governments in new states.

Most of these new states were desperately poor and in need of developmental assistance, which was generally not available in adequate supply, to facilitate the economic progress they all desired. Their new governments often proved to be inept or corrupt (or both), leading to a spiral of instability and unconventional violence that remains the core of contemporary global conflict.

The nature and tenor of the Cold War competition changed over time. The presumption of an intractable, encompassing, negative relationship in the 1950s softened with experience to the point that, at the time the Cold War ended, Soviet political leader Mikhail Gorbachev was one of the most popular politicians in the West and adorned the cover of *Time* magazine as its Man of the Year.

Sources of Change

Cold War dynamics gradually changed in two ways. The first, not widely recognized at the time, was that the two superpowers began to lose some control over their individual blocs. The early postwar system had been known as one of *tight* bipolarity, meaning the major powers could control events within these blocs effectively. The system evolved, however, to one of *loose* bipolarity, wherein the ability to control events within their spheres of influence slipped.

Two events in 1956 started the change from tight to loose bipolarity. First, Great Britain joined France and Israel in an attack on Egypt to occupy the Suez Canal zone (which Egyptian President Gamal Abdul

Nasser had nationalized the previous year). The action was taken without prior consultation with the US government, which opposed it. The United States subsequently joined the Soviet Union in sponsoring a UN Security Council resolution condemning the invasion. The French concluded the United States could no longer be trusted and began the process of establishing a more independent position in international affairs.

The second event was the brutal suppression of the Hungarian rebellion by Soviet forces later in that same year. Initially seen as proof of Soviet iron-handed control over its bloc, the longer-term lesson was quite different. The United States led an anti-Soviet publicity campaign that included widely disseminating pictures throughout the developing world of Soviet tanks rumbling through Budapest. The Soviets suffered an enormous propaganda black eye in a developing world where they had portrayed themselves as peace-loving champions of freedom and self-determination, and they were clearly lying. The Soviets and their client states realized they needed to avoid another similar embarrassment. Most important, Eastern European countries learned that as long as they did not threaten Soviet security, they could act more independently than before.

The second great change was in the quality of the competition. The symbolic event was the Cuban missile crisis of 1962. The impetus was a Soviet attempt to deploy nuclear-tipped missiles on Cuba aimed at the United States, and it created a military standoff that almost all observers believed was the closest the two sides had come to nuclear war. That realization convinced both powers they had a joint interest in avoiding destroying one another and possibly the world.

FORMS OF MILITARY COMPETITION

The Cold War was both a military and a political competition, with the emphasis on one aspect or the other at different times and places. Originally, it was both. The communization of the occupied Eastern European countries was accomplished almost exclusively by the Red Army rather than through the political interplay of communist and noncommunist political elements. From 1950 until 1991, the Cold War in Europe was almost exclusively a military competition between NATO and the Warsaw Pact (after the latter became operational in 1956).

The political dimension of the Cold War was limited to the peripheries—Africa, Asia, and, to a lesser extent, Latin America. The process of decolonization and the subsequent emergence of inexperienced governments after independence created considerable political ferment into which both sides plunged, hoping either to gain influence or, more modestly, to deny influence for the other side. One of the means of currying support was providing military aid to various governments or factions within countries.

Occasionally, involvement would devolve into military intervention, as it did for the United States in 1965 in the Dominican Republic and Vietnam and for the Soviets in Afghanistan a decade and a half later.

The perceived nature of the Cold War military threat was influenced by the time and place in which it occurred. The fact that the competition emerged in Europe on the heels of history's largest conventional war affects the shape and purposes of military forces to this day, when the military situation is quite different. Militarily, the Cold War began as an extension of World War II. The military dimension of the Cold War mirrored this inherited reality in terms of both how it would be fought and with what kinds of forces. Even though the weapons became more sophisticated and deadly across time and would have produced a much bloodier result, in Europe. Since the military and political leaders on both sides were mostly veterans of that conflict, this was not an unsurprising projection and basis for preparation. Hidden within the assumptions about preparing for World War III was the notion that the forces and doctrines would also be effective against smaller, unconventional (asymmetrical) foes. That assumption has proven dubious, as Amplification 4.2 suggests.

AMPLIFICATION 4.2

Cold War (Symmetrical) Forces in a Non–Cold War (Asymmetrical) World

The Cold War military competition was largely an extension of the forces, means of fighting, types of contestants, and political purposes that marked World War II. This is unremarkable because the major Cold War powers had been major participants in the European-based and European-style warfare of that conflict. Extending World War II thinking to the new Cold War came naturally and reinforced how political and military leaders viewed military force. The World War II/Cold War tradition is still deeply embedded in how the United States thinks about military force to this day.

The forces and how they fight are different. The Cold War forces were European-style mass armies (and other forces) designed for massive clashes with similarly armed forces in large-scale positional warfare. The forces one encounters today are differently oriented and fight in different ways, which is developed later in this book. Traditional forces engage in what is called symmetrical warfare; modern war is asymmetrical.

(continued)

> The contestants are different and fight for different purposes. Traditional forces are the highly organized instruments of national governments; asymmetrical forces are the much more loosely based instrument of groups within states most of the time, and their purposes and means of fighting are usually not as clear or predictable as in conventional warfare.
>
> These distinctions are important because the dynamics of asymmetrical warfare upset and often frustrate the symmetrical warrior. The enemy seems weak and disorganized but also impossible to defeat decisively, and he disobeys the rules of "civilized" warfare to accomplish his goals. The symmetrical warrior must adapt how he organizes and fights against unconventional foes. This adaptation has not been easy or entirely successful. ■

The wild card, of course, was nuclear weapons. The Cold War provided the first occasion when a war could be fought by two opponents both armed with these remarkably destructive weapons. Whether a war in Europe could be fought without releasing the nuclear genie was a hotly debated issue in military, political, and academic circles around which no real consensus ever emerged. A second lively question was whether their employment could be restricted to the immediate theater of operations (a possibility about which the Europeans who would experience a nuclear defense understandably had little enthusiasm) or whether their use would somehow inexorably spread beyond the battlefield to society at large. Whether conventional war in Europe would escalate into a general nuclear exchange engulfing the homelands of the superpowers was the ultimate concern for American, and presumably Soviet, planners.

These concerns have not entirely disappeared. The nuclear balance remains intact, if at reduced levels, even if Russia and the United States lack the realistic motivation to attack one another. American conventional armed forces are still largely structured basically the same way as during the Cold War. A host of reformers have tried to reshape that force, but such efforts have been resisted by military and civilian leaderships at least implicitly clinging to traditional perceptions of military reality. Understanding those forces and why they are constructed the way they are is a necessary preface to dealing with contemporary forces for contemporary problems.

Conventional Forces

Militarily, the Cold War was primarily a confrontation between conventional (nonnuclear) forces facing one another across the no-man's-land that comprised the Iron Curtain. The focus was especially the so-called inter-German border dividing East and West Germany that was widely expected to be the initial battleground in a NATO–Warsaw Pact war. For NATO planning purposes, a heavily armored Soviet breakout at the Fulda Gap in Germany seemed the most likely way that war would begin.

World War II and the military predilections of the leaders of the two coalitions heavily influenced how they conceptualized the problem. Virtually everyone assumed the battlefield would be somewhere on the northern European plain, relatively flat terrain that gave the advantage to mobile yet heavily armed forces, such as the tank armies that leaders like General George S. Patton had popularized in World War II.

Both the Americans and the Soviets embraced this style of warfare in which huge forces would have slugged it out in an orgy of incredible violence until one side collapsed. For the Americans, this had historically meant committing the superior American productive system to building so much sophisticated equipment that the enemy eventually was beaten down by the sheer weight of arms. The Soviet experience on the Eastern Front had taught them that overwhelming numbers of troops could eventually carry the day, if at terrible human costs. The prospect of these two behemoths colliding on the battlefield created a nightmare scenario of unprecedented carnage and destruction.

This vision affected the politics of war preparation. The focus for NATO was to provide such a sufficiently daunting prospect to the Soviets that they would be deterred from starting a war. But politics got in the way. Since the Soviets always had a quantitatively much larger force than NATO and would have the advantage of choosing when and where to attack, how was NATO to provide such an inhibiting presence? The domestic politics of the NATO democracies made it politically suicidal to suggest conscripting a force that could match the Soviets soldier for soldier. Moreover, the longer that war was avoided, the less support there was for the sacrifice of military service.

The major concern was the force with which NATO fought, and this concern was influenced by perceptions of the conventional military balance that heavily favored the communists. In 1985, for instance, the Red Army was nearly two and a half times the size of its American counterpart and had four times the number of tanks and other armored vehicles and one and a half times the number of combat aircraft. The United States had the advantage in helicopters and naval vessels, but their direct applicability to the central front in Germany was questionable. Numbers were on the Soviet side.

Most quantitative comparisons suggested the very real prospect that a Soviet-led assault in Germany might succeed *if the war remained strictly conventional.* What the NATO allies needed were so-called force multipliers, ways in which to enhance the comparative capability of the NATO forces (multiply their effectiveness). The most obvious candidates for this enhancement were battlefield and theater nuclear weapons (TNWs), and analysts debated whether it would be better to accept conventional defeat or to escalate to nuclear exchange, with all the uncertainties such a shift would create for possible escalation to a general homeland confrontation between the two superpowers.

These strategies produced a distinctive force structure and a mindset that continue to this day. To many military planners, the plans were vindicated in the Persian Gulf War of 1990–91, where the basic blueprint for engaging and defeating the Iraqis was the highly mobile air-land battle concept designed for Europe, made easier to implement because there were no natural or man-made obstacles to rapid mobility in the Kuwaiti desert. That very success reinforced the continuing adherence in the Army to a heavily armored concept and in the Navy to forces based on aircraft carriers, which carried out a large part of the air mission in Desert Storm. Russian forces moving into eastern Ukraine in 2015 offered an eerie memory of this style of warfare.

Nuclear Forces

Nuclear weapons were the second legacy of World War II. A number of countries were studying the weapons potential of nuclear physics when the war began, and Albert Einstein convinced President Franklin D. Roosevelt to engage in research on the weapons potential of nuclear power to hedge against the success of the German research program. The American Manhattan Project succeeded in producing a bomb in early 1945, and the United States emerged from the war as the only nuclear power.

The US nuclear monopoly did not last long. The Soviet Union exploded its first atomic (fission) device in 1949, and both countries successfully developed far deadlier nuclear explosives in the early 1950s. These thermonuclear (fission-fusion) devices replicate the energy production methods of the sun and produce explosions measurable in the equivalents of *millions of tons (megatons) of TNT*; by contrast, the atomic bombs of the 1940s produced explosions the equivalent of thousands of tons, or kilotons, of TNT. For a real-world comparison, the explosion of Mount St. Helens in Oregon in the 1980s was estimated at forty megatons.

Parallel research was conducted on delivering nuclear and other weapons to their targets. Advances in rocketry produced the first successful Soviet intercontinental ballistic missile (ICBM) in 1957, a feat rapidly duplicated by the United States. Combined with similar work on shorter-range missiles, both sides had missile-borne nuclear bombs aimed at one another by the time of the Cuban crisis, and the weapons could be delivered against their targets with a reasonable expectation they would not be intercepted or neutralized. During the 1960s and 1970s, the arsenals grew enormously on both sides, with strategic inventories (those aimed at one another's homelands) numbering over ten thousand apiece and shorter-range missiles dedicated to the support of military forces in the European or other theaters numbering in the tens of thousands.

With these dynamics, the thrust in nuclear weapons thinking and planning shifted to *deterrence*, the development and maintenance of weaponry to convince the opponent not to use its weapons against you. Since neither side could defend itself against an attack by nuclear-tipped missiles, the threat had to be based in retaliation and punishment of a nuclear transgressor. The idea was that a potential aggressor would realize that the victim of the attack would retain such a large surviving force as to be able to launch a devastating retaliatory strike, making the initial attack in effect suicidal. One concept used to describe this dynamic and the strategy to implement it in the 1960s was *assured destruction*, to which a detractor added the prefix *mutual*, thereby creating an acronym reflecting his assessment of the idea: MAD.

It required the mindset of the Cold War for this nuclear balance to make sense, especially as the arsenals grew to the point that an all-out attack by either side (or especially both sides) could effectively immolate the enemy several times over—to "make the rubble bounce," in Winston Churchill's phrase. Both sides aggressively continued to research and deploy yet more deadly weapons out of the fear that failing to do so would create some advantage the other might feel it could exploit in a nuclear attack. Lamenting this aspect of the nuclear arms race, President Jimmy Carter's secretary of defense Harold Brown summarized it as: "We build, they build; we stop, they build."

DEADLOCK OF THE COMPETITION

Even as the Cold War competition proceeded most vigorously, the seeds of its demise were being sown. By the 1970s two trends, unrecognized at the time, began to congeal that would militate the end of the Cold War. One trend was the weakening of the Soviet economy, both absolutely and in comparison to the United States. The other was a growing recognition of a deadlock in the military competition between the superpower blocs. By the 1980s, these trends coalesced; both remain part of the contemporary landscape.

The Economic Dimension

The economic implosion that eventually engulfed the Soviet state had its roots in the 1970s or even before. Economic growth slowed in the early

1970s, and by the end of the decade the economy had stopped growing altogether, what Soviet economists would later call the "era of stagnation." This problem was known to some Soviet academic economists, but they lacked access to the leadership cadre associated with Soviet leader Leonid Brezhnev (known as the *nomenklatura*), who benefited from the system and were uninterested in seeing change that might adversely affect their privilege. Instead, the academic economists allied themselves with a rising star within the Communist Party, Mikhail S. Gorbachev, whose wife, Raisa, was their colleague at Moscow State University. When Gorbachev achieved power in 1985, this cadre was ready to roll out the mechanisms of reform. Unfortunately for them, their efforts were too little and too late.

A good bit of the Soviet decline was in science and technology. The Soviets were largely excluded from the high-technology revolution in the West that underlay the economic expansion in the 1980s and 1990s. Part of this exclusion was self-imposed—to shield a shaky economy from outside competition. Two additional dynamics exacerbated this technological gap. First, the problem was progressive. The motor of technological growth was the development of more-sophisticated generations of computers, a progressive process because the major tool for designing the next generation of computers is the current generation. Operationally that means the farther a country is behind (the more generations it is removed from the cutting edge), the farther behind it gets in the future. By the early 1980s, the Soviet Union was approximately three generations behind the United States, and the gap was widening. Beyond theft, the Soviets could not narrow the gap.

The second dynamic was that the Soviets could not collaborate with the West in technology. Almost all the technologies in which the Soviets were behind were *dual use*, meaning they had both civilian and military applications. For instance, a computer designed for research in theoretical physics could be converted to applying physics principles to weapons design. As long as the Soviet Union remained the avowed enemy, the United States and the rest of the West were not going to provide the Soviets with knowledge that might produce weapons with which to menace them.

Most of these dynamics went largely unnoticed in the West at the time. Soviet economists were rarely allowed to communicate with their Western counterparts, the Soviet government doctored economic statistics that were notoriously inaccurate anyway, and the military production system, on which attention was concentrated, seemed to be working well. The failure to recognize Russian weakness has carried over to the present.

The Military Dimension

By the end of the 1970s, the military competition was also undergoing change to the ultimate disadvantage of the Soviet Union. The competition had essentially deadlocked into a very deadly but ritualistic confrontation. This competition was enormously burdensome to a Soviet economy that was much smaller than its American counterpart and that needed to divert resources to economic priorities if the Soviets hoped to compete at that level. The military competition became a millstone around the neck of the Soviet future. The weight became unbearable in the late 1980s, when their ill-fated, expensive, unpopular, and failed intervention in Afghanistan contributed to the demise of the Soviet state.

Nuclear weapons played a major role. As the potential deadliness of the nuclear balance expanded, the danger of nuclear war declined, even if this was mostly unrecognized. The prospect of nuclear war with the levels of arms available in 1962 was sobering, but the prospect of such a war fought with the arsenals of the 1980s was positively catastrophic. Leaders on both sides, going back to President Dwight D. Eisenhower in the 1950s and Soviet Premier Nikita Khrushchev in the early 1960s, had publicly proclaimed the unacceptability of nuclear war as a means to resolve East-West differences.

The necessary step to reduce the danger—or likelihood—of war between the two sides was to add the unacceptability of conventional war to the equation. The key element in accomplishing this was the uncertainty of the escalatory process. Escalation could transform a conventional war into a nuclear war, and there was no empirical basis on which to predict confidently whether, when, or how that escalation would occur. In that circumstance, the only certain way to avoid nuclear war between the superpowers was to avoid *any* war between them.

This "necessary peace," as I described it in a 1987 book with that title, reduced the Cold War military competition to ritual status. Both sides developed and deployed weapons and conducted war games with them for the precise reason of avoiding their use in war. The old military axiom of "preparing for and fighting the country's wars" became twisted to "preparing to avoid fighting the country's wars."

Convergence

These two dimensions converged when Gorbachev succeeded Konstantin Chernenko as the Soviet leader in 1985. Gorbachev was a new kind of Soviet opponent. He was the first chief executive of the Soviet Union with a college degree, he was a lawyer by training, and he was clearly more urbane and sophisticated than his predecessors. His professor wife, Raisa, was also a handsome, urbane, and very public figure—in contrast to the dowager images of Gorbachev's predecessors' wives (some of whom were never seen in public). Gorbachev faced a daunting set of problems. He knew about the economic problems from the Soviet professors, and he sought to reform the economic system. As a believing Marxist, his initial approach was to fine-tune the existing system, but that system itself was beyond repair, and he was slow to recognize that the assumptions on which it rested were the problem.

What was Gorbachev to do? The choices were not attractive. The status quo was unsustainable, and trying to tinker with the system through the economic and political reforms known as *perestroika* was not working. The Soviet Union was sinking fast as a state and as a power. A radical solution was needed.

The answer was to end the Cold War. The logic of the Soviet situation dictated the decision. Economic stagnation was eroding its standing in the world and was progressively reducing the standard of living of Soviet citizens. The Soviet Union was becoming, as many critics described it, "a third-world country with nuclear weapons." Only access to Western technology and capital could change the situation, and their only hope was to cease being the enemy and to join the community of states as a normal rather than a rogue member. The same logic held for the military dimension. The military competition had also become an unsustainable loser. Cancelling the unwinnable competition of the Cold War was an increasingly attractive option.

The world stood by in stunned silence as the Soviet leader began to unravel the forty-year-long confrontation. Gorbachev published a blueprint of the changes he proposed in a 1987 book, *Perestroika: New Thinking for Our Country and the World*, in which he laid out a detailed internal reform plan. In the international realm, he detailed the transformation of the Soviet Union into a "normal" state by policy changes, such as non-interference in the affairs of other states and renunciation of the so-called Brezhnev Doctrine, which had justified Soviet intervention in the socialist states and had been used as the rationale for Soviet invasions of Hungary, Czechoslovakia, and Afghanistan.

Perestroika was initially greeted with skepticism in the West, but Gorbachev began to act in accordance with the book's proposals. In 1989, the Soviet Union completed its military withdrawal from Afghanistan, despite having accomplished none of its goals. That same year it stood by idly when the Polish parliament seated a non-communist government, an act that opened the floodgates for the rapid decommunization of Eastern Europe and, in 1991, the formal dissolution of the Warsaw Pact.

Domestic reform was not dramatic or attractive enough to avoid the breakup of the Soviet Union itself. Led by the Baltic States (Lithuania, Latvia, and Estonia), the constituent Soviet republics withdrew from the union and established themselves as independent states. On the last tick of the clock of 1991, the red Soviet flag came down from the Kremlin for the last time, replaced the next day by the Russian tricolor of red, white, and blue.

The peaceful implosion of the Soviet state was—and is—an unprecedented political act in world history. States, including major powers, have from time to time ceased to exist through Carthaginian peaces or partition at the ends of wars, but for one of the world's two most powerful countries simply to vote itself out of existence was absolutely and entirely unprecedented and unanticipated both within and outside Russia. Ultimately, the outcome hardly anyone had considered adequately—a peaceful end of the Cold War—occurred.

So why did Gorbachev do what he did? The short answer is that he had no choice. The old system was broken, if not exactly in the way he and his advisors thought at the time. Knowing the system could not be revived without considerable outside assistance, Gorbachev understood that the *sine qua non* for assistance was to end the Cold War and to remove its most obviously annoying symbols: the Iron Curtain, the Berlin Wall, and, most important, the structure of military confrontation. He and those around him did not foresee that the cost would be the destruction of the edifice they had sought to strengthen.

COLD WAR RESIDUES

The end of the Cold War left a geopolitical void in the international system. The most gaping hole was in Europe and featured two axes. The first was what succeeded a former Soviet Union now divided into fifteen independent states, of which the Russian Federation is the pivot, and the disposition of the old Soviet "empire" in Eastern Europe. Second, the resurgence of Russia as a world power under Vladimir Putin has become a cause for concern regarding the shape of the evolving world order.

Russian Retreat and Resurgence

Dealing with Russia has always been a difficult, problematic enterprise. Russia is a unique country. It has always been at the periphery of the European system, a giant, backward Eurasian power that was, as described by Winston Churchill in an October 1, 1939, radio broadcast, "a riddle wrapped in a mystery inside an enigma." Its exotic, secretive difference has always been central to confronting it. It is emblematic that it was Russian count Grigory Potemkin who fashioned the Potemkin Village, a series of false building fronts on the route to Crimea to deceive his lover, Empress Catherine II, into believing the country was more prosperous that it was. When assessing Russia, the Potemkin influence should always be remembered.

Russia was the largest single state that emerged from the breakup of the Soviet Union, containing roughly half the population and three-quarters of the land mass of the old Union of Soviet Socialist Republics (USSR). Russia maintained most Soviet military power, notably the thermonuclear arsenal. Although beset by enormous and debilitating political and economic problems that unquestionably diminished its place in the world in the 1990s, Russia's growing oil wealth reversed that fate, and Russia and its future remain an important international concern on economic/demographic, political, and security grounds.

The Russian economic and demographic profiles are not encouraging. The Russian economy was boosted in the early 2000s by gearing the economy to petroleum. During good times of high energy prices, this increased Russian prosperity and GDP to about $2 trillion. When the oil market collapsed in 2013, Russian GDP fell to $1.2 trillion with it.

The demographics are even worse. The breakup of the Soviet Union cut the Russian population by more than half. In 1990, the Soviet population was 291 million; in 2015, Russia's population was 142 million. By contrast, US figures were 249 million for 1990 and 321 million for 2015. Due to negative growth rates, Russia's 2050 population is estimated to be 128 million compared to an American estimate of 438 million. Demographics are not on Russia's side.

The political and economic transformation of Russia has moved forward in interrelated fits and starts. The political system appeared to be moving toward limited democracy under Boris Yeltsin in the 1990s, but that change has been arrested by Putin. Economically, an attempt to institute market practices was grafted onto an inherited institutional framework woefully inappropriate and inadequate for the market to take hold and prosper. When the Soviet Union became Russia, the country had essentially no banking or other financial laws or institutions, making it virtually impossible to regulate financial dealings. It lacked mechanisms to collect taxes to run the government. The breakdown of the communist levers of state coercion left the country with inadequate policing capacity, which resulted in the ascendancy of the *Mafioso* and other forms of lawlessness.

Russia has held several relatively free elections for president, and in the third one, in 2000, power was peacefully passed from Yeltsin to Putin, a momentous occasion in Russian history. Putin was reelected in 2004 and, after a four-year hiatus required by the Russian constitution (his handpicked ally, Dmitry Medvedev, was president from 2008–12), again in 2012. He ran successfully for a six-year term in 2018 that, according to the Constitution, is his last. He will be 78 years old in 2024.

Russia also has serious military and security problems. One of the major themes of Russian history has been a concern with—some argue paranoia about—military security that has been reinforced by invaders as diverse as the Mongol hordes, Napoleon Bonaparte, and Adolf Hitler. A major reason for constructing the communist empire in Eastern Europe after World War II was to provide a *cordon sanitaire* (buffer) against invasion.

The end of the Cold War meant Russia lost its Warsaw Pact allies; the breakup of the Soviet Union meant Ukrainians, Moldavians, and others were no longer part of the Russian security scheme and might even become part of the new security problem. It is sometimes said that Russia is surrounded by richly earned enemies; it is not an altogether inaccurate description.

Russian military problems prominently include relations with the "near abroad," the way Russians view the former states of the old Soviet Union, and the "internal abroad," parts of the Russian Federation with a significant non-Russian population. The Russians assert a kind of spheres of influence relationship with the old Soviet republics, referring to them as their "sphere of privileged influence" to indicate that other countries should defer to Russian dominance and interference in these areas. Russian military actions in support of ethnic Russians in Ukraine is an example of near abroad policy. Most of the problems of the internal abroad with military implications are in the Caucasus region, where non-ethnic Russians predominate and seek autonomy or independence; Chechnya and Dagestan are primary examples.

Further Russian actions in Ukraine in 2015 illustrate the Russian resurgence problem. Russian incursions were largely into Ukrainian areas where there was a Russian ethnic majority or sizable minority, making the actions a "near abroad" response from a Russian perspective. Outsiders saw the moves more ominously as evidence of Russian expansionism into former parts of the USSR.

Putin and the New "Cool" War

Russia is a very old and proud country that has striven for centuries to be seen and treated as one of the world's major powers. The Russian Empire was a member of the European-dominated Balance of Power from the seventeenth into the twentieth centuries, but it was widely regarded as the most backward, even marginal, member of that system. It ascended to superpower status as the Soviet Union after World War II, assuming the kind of lofty status Russian nationalists had always dreamed for it. When the Soviet Union disintegrated, that status declined, leaving many Russians discontented with their diminished status and yearning to reassert Russian greatness. Vladimir Putin was among those who most rued Russian decline, calling the collapse of the USSR the greatest geopolitical disaster of the twentieth century.

The period since the Soviet Union dissolved has been problematic for Russia. The Soviet superpower that Russia had dominated has shrunk physically and geopolitically. A mixture of often antagonistic regimes arose in the successor states, and many of these regimes viewed Russia with defiant distrust. Despite Russia's maintenance of Soviet nuclear weapons, its conventional power has receded to the point that many who had feared the Soviets ceased fearing Russia. As the 1990s progressed, the Russian economy declined into a state of chaos that left many wondering if the non-authoritarian regime could maintain power. Russian political democracy hung in the balance.

Oil wealth revived Russia for a time. The result was a resurgent Russian economy and Russia's emergence as the second leading exporter of petroleum in the world. The economic results were striking. Economic prosperity came—albeit selectively—to Russia and Russians. It also boosted the political appeal and fortunes of Vladimir Putin, who used oil wealth to effectively bribe the population to support him and to fund increased Russian assertiveness in world politics.

The political dynamics associated with this resurgence have been more potentially troublesome, both domestically and internationally. Domestically there has been a gradual accumulation of power in the presidency under Putin at the expense of the Russian parliament (the Duma), and that trend has been particularly pronounced the longer Putin remains in office. The concentration of power in the presidency has been accompanied by a more aggressive, even occasionally confrontational, policy toward its near abroad areas like Crimea and Ukraine proper, which seems to suggest Russia's attempt to reemerge as a major world power. What fuels this resurgence?

There are two basic answers, one largely domestic and the other international and at the heart of international concerns. Thomas L. Friedman describes the domestic side in terms of Russia's emergence as a *petrolist* state. In states that have great petroleum wealth but lack firm democratic traditions, governments can sometimes strike a kind of Faustian bargain with their populations wherein petroleum wealth is distributed to the citizenry to improve their material conditions, and in return the citizens cede some political rights to the government. The dynamic is what Friedman calls the first law of petropolitics: "the price of oil and the pace of freedom always move in opposite directions in oil-rich petrolist states."

This movement toward authoritarian politics has potentially troubling international ramifications. During the 1990s, Russia was a passive, compliant member of the international order, at least in part because its increasingly desperate economic condition left it in no position to act in any other way, a change that was humiliating to Russians like Putin seeking a return to Russian status as a major world power.

Hardly anyone is confidently projecting where Russian resurgence will lead. The worst-case scenario is that Russia will be transformed into a new authoritarian state that could become as antagonistic as the fascist states of the 1930s and reinstate something like a new Cold War. As Putin has consolidated power, the return to a diluted form of Russian-American relations—a "cool" war—seems increasingly likely. The tone of the American assessment has been contentious. The national security establishment sees Russian meddling in the 2016 election and expansionism as a threat to be countered by means like sanctions against the Putin regime. President Trump has sought to befriend Putin, even suggesting Russian reinstatement into the G-7 group of economic powers. No one knows exactly what form a new competition could take, but the shadow of a Putin-led challenge to the existing order is joining terrorism as a major international concern, a problem the *Challenge!* box explores.

CONCLUSION: THE LEGACY AND END OF THE COLD WAR

The Cold War is not part of the personal experience of most readers of this volume, who were either not born or were in their very early youth when the Cold War dissolved in 1991. As such, it is part of a receding history, the current relevance of which may seem suspect. The parents of student readers may recall the Russian tricolor rising over Red Square, and grandparents can remember the tense atmosphere of the "thirteen days" (the title of Robert K. Kennedy's account of the event) of the Cuban missile crisis, but what relevance does that have today?

CHALLENGE!

Dealing with the New Russia

The United States would like to see Russia evolve into a nonthreatening, democratic country that participates in international relations as a helpful partner rather than as an antagonist. For that kind of Russia to emerge, the country will have to evolve and strengthen its democratic institutions, but doing so must occur within the specific context of a Russian mentality where resurgent Russian nationalism competes for support with democracy. Under Putin in the 2010s, Russia seems to be leaning more toward being a great power rather than being a democracy.

How can the United States help redefine and influence that choice? There are two major points of contention. The first is Russian expansionism in the near abroad (Crimea, Ukraine) but also extending to Putin's support for the government of Syria's Bashar al-Assad. Russian actions in Western Europe threaten the European balance, which is at the heart of US security concerns; in

(continued)

Syria, they affront the Middle East balance and standards of human behavior (using poison gas against civilians). The second is Russian interference in the 2016 US election and similar Russian cyber behavior in Europe. From a US national security perspective, the Russians must cease those activities. Putin, denying wrongdoing, refuses.

What can the United States do? Most American national security experts favor sanctions to force Russian acquiescence to create positive change. In 2017, the US Congress passed legislation including strong sanctions, but President Trump had not, as of mid-2018, chosen to enforce those sanctions, preferring to try to convince Putin personally to change course through encounters like his July 2018 Helsinki meeting with the Russian leader.

The Russians do not operate from a strong position in these matters. Until oil prices rebound, the Russian economy is very vulnerable. Further, it needs American technology to exploit its energy abundance, a significant lever for the United States not dissimilar to the problem Gorbachev faced regarding computer technology in the 1980s.

The demographic time bomb facing Russia also affects the calculation of dealing with the Russians. Due to very low birth rates, the Russian population is gradually declining, and its size is sinking below the status of a major power, certainly well less than the size of the United States. The Russian population will no longer be among the world's largest, and it is not clear what impact this will have on Russian pretensions about being a world power. The Russians have been largely unsuccessful in reversing this decline, which, if it continues, threatens Russia as a competitor with the United States and other countries. How they will deal with this problem is a matter of speculation but of potentially great importance. ■

The answer, to reiterate the point made at the beginning of the chapter, is that the Cold War was the temporal and physical setting in which the framework for the national security state that remains largely intact today was crafted. The Cold War may no longer exist, but the ways of thinking it created still influence how the United States views national security in the world. An assessment of the applicability of current constructs and how they need changing begins by understanding what those constructs are and how and why they got there.

Examples of the residues abound and affect current policy debates. One of the canons of the Cold War national security state was the exalted position it conferred on the national security establishment. That meant, among other things, that national security concerns were above partisan political disagreements most of the time, and especially that the national security claim on national resources was virtually sacrosanct. That basic canonical construct remains part of the contemporary setting and is one of the major reasons there is greater advocacy for military activism in places like the Middle East than there might otherwise be. This holdover cannot be ignored when viewing the role of force in a world where the old Cold War framework no longer applies.

Russia has a unique position in this evolution. Russia is clearly and probably irrevocably in a condition of decline, and this realization creates a kind of obsession with the return of the country to its Cold War glory as a major power. It is difficult to interpret the actions of the Russians in any other manner than as an attempt to avoid the throes of incipient decline. It creates a perceived need to act aggressively to reassert Russia's place in the world while it still can, knowing the demographic window is closing in on their desires and pretensions. Putin epitomizes this Russian dilemma, and he and his country are probably more dangerous than they would be if they felt more confident and secure about their future. The United States has a vested interest in frustrating some of the more egregious examples of Russian behavior, but that does not mean it wants Russia to fail. The result is a balance in concern: how does the United States influence the positive transition of a Russia with grand pretensions into being a positive member of the international system?

STUDY/DISCUSSION QUESTIONS

1. How and why did the dissolution of the Soviet Union and the end of the Cold War represent a traumatic event for the international system? Discus.
2. Discuss the Cold War system. What were its major characteristics, and how did they help define how the system operated? What were the sources of change that occurred over time?
3. The heart of the Cold War system was the military competition between the United States and the Soviet Union. Discuss the dimensions of that competition.
4. How did the East-West competition deadlock? Discuss the economic and military dimensions of that deadlock and how they led Soviet leader Mikhail S. Gorbachev to conclude the competition had to be ended.
5. What are the major residues of the end of the Cold War? How is the problem of Russian resurgence under Putin part of that residue?
6. How should the United States try to deal with the problems created by Russia? What are those problems? What does Russia hope to accomplish in its foreign policy, what disadvantages does it face in doing so, and how should the United States approach the problem? Discuss the dilemmas involved.

SELECTED BIBLIOGRAPHY

Allison, Graham T. *The Essence of Decision: Explaining the Cuban Missile Crisis*. New York: Harper Collins, 1972.

Aslund, Anders. "The Hunt for Russia's Riches." *Foreign Policy* (January/February 2006): 42–49.

Biden, Joseph S., Jr., and Michael Carpenter. "How to Stand Up to the Kremlin: Defending Democracy Against Its Enemies." *Foreign Affairs* 97, 1 (January/February 2018), 44–57.

Bremmer, Ian. "Putin Won. But Russia Is Losing." *Time* 191, 13 (April 2, 2018), 41.

Brzezinski, Zbigniew. "The Cold War and Its Aftermath." *Foreign Affairs* 71, 4 (Fall 1992), 31–49.

Clark, Ronald W. *The Greatest Power on Earth: The International Race for Nuclear Supremacy, Earliest Theory to Three Mile Island.* New York: Harper and Row, 1980.

Claude, Inis L. *The Changing United Nations.* New York: Random House, 1967.

Committee on Foreign Relations, United States Senate. *Strategic Assessment of US-Russian Relations.* New York: CreateSpace, 2018.

DaVargo, Julie, and Clifton A. Grammich. *Dire Demographics: Population Trends in the Russian Federation.* Santa Monica, CA: RAND Corporation, 2007.

Dawisha, Karen. *Putin's Kleptocracy: Who Owns Russia?* New York: Simon and Schuster, 2014.

Friedman, Thomas L. "The First Law of Petropolitics." *Foreign Policy* (May/June 2006), 28–36.

Fukuyama, Francis. *The End of History and the Last Man.* New York: Free Press, 1992.

Gaddis, John Lewis. *The United States and the End of the Cold War: Implications, Reconsiderations, Provocations.* New York: Oxford University Press, 1992.

Gat, Azar. "The Return of Authoritarian Great Powers." *Foreign Affairs* 86, 4 (July/August 2007), 59–69.

Gorbachev, Mikhail S. *The New Russia.* Cambridge, MA: Polity Press, 2016.

———. *Perestroika: New Thinking for Our Country and the World.* New York: Harper and Row, 1987.

Isikoff, Michael, and David Korn. *Russian Roulette: The Inside Story of Putin's War on America and the Election of Donald Trump.* New York: Twelve Books, 2018.

Joffe, Julia. "Putin's Game." *The Atlantic* 321, 1 (January/February 2018), 68–85.

Kennan, George F. *Memoirs, 1925–1950.* Boston: Little Brown, 1967.

Kennedy, Robert F., and Arthur Schlesinger Jr. *The Thirteen Days: A Memoir of the Cuban Missile Crisis.* New York: W. W. Norton, 1999.

King, Charles, and Rajon Menon. "Prisoners of the Caucasus: Russia's Invisible Civil War." *Foreign Affairs* 89, 4 (July/August 2010), 20–34.

Kotkin, Stephen. "Russia's Perpetual Geopolitics: Putin Returns to the Historical Pattern." *Foreign Affairs* 95, 3 (May/June 2016), 2–9.

Lukyanov, Fyodor. "Putin's Foreign Policy: The Quest to Restore Russia's Rightful Place." *Foreign Affairs* 95, 3 (May/June 2016), 30–38.

Mearsheimer, John J. "Why We Shall Soon Miss the Cold War." *Atlantic Monthly* 262, 2 (August 1990), 35–50.

Rumer, Eugene, Richard Sokolsky, and Andrew S. Weiss. "Trump and Russia: The Right Way to Manage Relations." *Foreign Affairs* 96, 2 (March/April 2017), 12–19.

Shevtsova, Lilia. "Russia's Ersatz Democracy." *Current History* 105, 693 (October 2006), 307–314.

Snow, Donald M. *Cases in US National Security: Principles and Applications.* Lanham, MD: Rowman & Littlefield, 2019.

———. *The Shape of the Future: The Post—Cold War World.* 3rd ed. Armonk, NY: M. E. Sharpe, 1999.

———. *The Necessary Peace: Nuclear Weapons and Superpower Relations.* Lexington, MA: Lexington Books, 1987.

Toal, Bernard. *Near Abroad: Putin, the West, and the Contest over Ukraine and the Caucasus.* Oxford, UK: Oxford University Press, 2017.

Trenin, Dmitri. *Should We Fear Russia?* Cambridge, MA: Polity Press, 2016.

Tymoshenko, Yuliya. "Containing Russia." *Foreign Affairs* 86, 3 (May/June 2007), 69–82.

Moving to the Present: The Post– Cold War World

The end of the Cold War reduced the potential deadliness of US national security problems by making the prospect of nuclear war remote, but it did not remove all the dangers faced by the country. Since the Cold War ended, international politics generally, and the United States specifically, has experienced two major changes, called fault lines in the text, that have altered, sometimes in subtle ways, the nature of the international system and how the United States operates in it. The first was the end of the Cold War itself, which triggered a decade-long process of adjustment and relative national security tranquility. The second was September 11, 2001, and the subsequent spate of activity associated with combating international terrorism and adjusting to the rise of new powers like China. Individually and collectively, these fault lines and reactions to them help form the contemporary context within which the debate over national security occurs.

The United States has been on an intellectual roller coaster over matters of national security for the last quarter century. When the Cold War ended, it left a conceptual void regarding how to think about and conduct national security policy. The 1990s provided a physical and intellectual respite of sorts from the militarily dominated competition, and new influences like economic globalization arose in a system where the United States was the sole remaining superpower. After 9/11, the global war on terror (GWOT) returned military power to a more central role in international relations, and shifts in global power changed the strategic landscape.

This chapter examines the post–Cold War period from two perspectives. The first is the impact of the fundamental change events (called fault lines) on the operation of world politics. The second is the contrasting views of how the United States should deal with these changes based on differing perceptions about the nature and degree of change.

The distinguished Harvard political scientist Graham T. Allison Jr., analogized the end of the Cold War to an earthquake, a "tectonic shift" such as he views the current crisis between China and the United States. The collapse of communism and September 11 were such shifts. Put another way, 1989 and 2001 revealed major shifts in the evolution of the international environment. Before they were revealed, the world looked one way; afterward, in both instances it looked very different. Before the end of the Cold War, bipolar geopolitics was the large concern in a hostile world environment. The period between the two major events was, arguably, a less tumultuous time. The second trauma returned military force and violence to the center stage of world politics after a decade's respite.

The first fault line was revealed between 1989 and the 1991 end of the Cold War. The end of the Cold War traumatized policymakers mostly because it was so unanticipated. A few observers like George F. Kennan and Daniel Patrick Moynihan saw it coming, but most did not. Kennan prophesied in 1948 that vigilant containment could cause communism's implosion, and New York senator Moynihan consistently suggested its demise—but they were lonely beacons whose message was largely ignored. The Soviet Union crumbled as Soviet republics withdrew from the union throughout 1991, but the policy of the American administration of George H. W. Bush tried to keep that mortal enemy of forty years intact nearly to the end, fearful and suspicious of the alternatives to a known enemy. The end of the Cold War was a major surprise to almost everyone on both sides of the Iron Curtain.

Then the Cold War ended, and observers and policymakers struggled for a decade to describe and understand how the world was different conceptually and practically. During the 1990s, the forces of economic globalization slowly overshadowed the forces of geopolitics within the American administration and raised questions about something like a paradigm shift from geopolitics to globalization. When George W. Bush entered the White House in 2001, he brought with him a foreign and national security team of Cold Warriors. Like the Clinton administration that preceded them, they struggled during their early months in office to find a basis upon which to orient national security policy until responding to the terrorist attacks provided that focus for them. Like the end of the Cold War, the shocking introduction of international terrorism caught virtually everyone outside the small fraternity of students of terrorism more off guard than did the collapse of the communist threat.

The 1990s was largely devoted to reconciling policy and strategy to a new environment from which the primary threat had been removed but where no clear successor threat had emerged. That process of reconciliation was by no means complete when terrorist-abducted airplanes flew into New York's World Trade towers and the Pentagon, thereby providing Americans with an apparently worthy successor to the communist threat. International terrorism became the major focus of security concerns and policy, prompting a series of actions like the wars in Iraq and Afghanistan justified in its name.

More quietly, the world power map was shifting geographically. During the 1990s, it became popular to talk about the new century as the "Asian century." The chief engine in this transformation was the growth of China to the status of an economic superpower, and the apparent desire of China to reclaim its historic position as one of the world's great powers is an increasing trend in the 2010s.

None of these matters have been resolved entirely. The Cold War will not return in its old form, despite recent Russian provocations, nor will a structure of threat resembling it likely emerge. The new threat of terrorism has not proven analogous to communism, although it remains a nagging, changing problem the ultimate resolution to which remains elusive. China's forceful emergence as a geopolitical world force is still evolving, and it is not clear how American national security policy will respond to it.

THE FIRST FAULT LINE: THE WORLD AFTER THE COLD WAR

It is difficult to capture—or even to exaggerate—the trauma that began in 1989. In 1990 and 1991, breathtaking political change was virtually the norm; the central feature was the death of communism as country after country peacefully (except in isolated cases like Romania) abandoned Marxism/Leninism. The Soviet Union stood by idly. In 1991 constituent parts of the Soviet Union began the process of secession; ultimately, the Soviet empire (and it was, in many important respects, the last European empire since much of the territory had been acquired by force by Russia) broke into fifteen independent states, all of which officially disavowed communism. By the end of the decade, only four states in the world remained nominally communist. Two of those states, Cuba and North Korea, entered the twenty-first century professing a continued dedication to the principles of communism. The other communist states, China and Vietnam, retain the dictatorship of the Communist Party politically but have openly rejected Marxist economics and are enthusiastic participants in the world economy. As a competitive political ideology, the belief system articulated by Karl Marx and Friedrich Engels has essentially been consigned to the intellectual dust pile of history. It is hardly missed by anyone.

The implosion of communism was the most obvious, dramatic, and important change of the last decade of the twentieth century and was arguably the most important international event since World War II. It was unique in the sense that a major global power source simply vacated the playing field without a shot being fired. The same Soviet Union that had, for the most part, brutally imposed communist systems on most of what was known as the Second (or Socialist) World simply watched those systems dissolving with scarcely a shrug of its national shoulders. The virtually peaceful implosion of the Soviet Union itself was, as noted in the last chapter, an act of nonviolence without precedent.

The end of "operational communism" (communism as the official political organizing system for a country) has had major systemic impacts to which the world is still adjusting. The Cold War international system of bipolarity simply collapsed, and the result was a power vacuum. With one pole gone, the system could no longer be described as bipolar. There was only one pole left because Russia, despite Putin's pretensions, has lacked the stature and resources to be a "superpower" in the Cold War sense beyond its continued possession of a large but, thanks to arms control agreements, shrinking arsenal of nuclear weapons. China is arguably replacing Russia as the major challenger to superpower status.

Hardly anyone was willing to designate the resulting system *unipolar* because that would imply a level of American control that did not exist and that most other states would have opposed. The United States remained the central power, but defining that centrality has been a critical and evolving part of defining the new system. It is probably of some symbolic importance that a consensus never formed on what to call the new system and that the most common name describes what it is not—the post–Cold War world.

The Cold War had the major physical and intellectual advantage of developing a very orderly set of rules of interaction. The competition between the communist and noncommunist worlds was well defined, as were its rules of conduct. It was conceptually a *zero-sum game* in which the gains of one side were assumed to be the losses of the other and the possibility of *positive-sum* outcomes in which both sides gained were infrequent and considered unlikely in any specific situation. The lingua franca of this competition ultimately was the enormous military machine each side maintained, capped by the possession of enormous arsenals of thermonuclear weapons.

The end of the Cold War shattered that order. As Georgi Arbatov, director of the Soviet USA and Canada Institute and a member of the Central Committee of the Communist Party of the Soviet Union, put it to the Americans in mid-1991, "We have done a terrible thing. We have deprived you of an enemy." The terrible thing was that national security thinking, clearly grounded in the Soviet threat, suddenly lost most, if not all, of its relevance. The result was both physical and intellectual disorder in how to think about the world. No institution was more affected by this change than the US military, as suggested in Amplification 5.1. As it evolved, the emerging order provided both benefits and drawbacks, many of which remain part of the national security landscape.

Undeniable Benefits

The most obvious and most dangerous aspect of the Cold War was the military confrontation between the competing blocs led by the United States and the Soviet Union. Managing that confrontation short of hot war was a serious mandate that, given the possible consequences of a misstep, had to be taken very seriously. The prospect of general war employing nuclear weapons even produced a political culture that was fatalistic about the future, resulting in the expenditure of large amounts of resources in its possibility. Keeping the Cold War cold was the preeminent international responsibility beside which other priorities paled by comparison. The Cold War was a very deadly environment.

AMPLIFICATION 5.1

The End of the Cold War and the US Military

The end of the Cold War brought major changes to the American military. It was, in some fortuitous sense, a boon for American arms. After the Vietnam War, the military suffered serious setbacks in its self-perception and in the view of Americans. For well over a decade, there was a hemorrhage of some of the ablest members as a result of a decline in institutional self-esteem and morale, and the military battled to maintain a quality all-volunteer force. The public, freed of the dark cloud of Vietnam-era conscription, by and large did not care one way or the other.

The collapse of the Cold War enigmatically boosted the military from its doldrums. The enigma is that the military lost its major mission of combating communism and consequently some of its funding but rebounded to a robustness by the end of the decade that restored its self-confidence and prestige. One of the major reasons for this turnabout was that the force was reduced in size ("downsized"), and this allowed the military to strip away some of its more marginal members. The remaining core were the "best and the brightest" of the old force, and they used the purging of their ranks as an

(continued)

opportunity to professionalize the remaining force into a highly capable and respected part of society.

This downsizing, however, became a problem in the 2000s, when the military had to undertake simultaneous major deployments in Iraq and Afghanistan that tested its reduced numbers of combat personnel. The military responded with multiple deployments of the active duty forces it had, reliance on Reserve forces to carry out its missions, and even the controversial use of private contractors to perform its military tasks. Each of these actions was controversial and have had longer-term effects (such as post-traumatic stress disorder [PTSD]). ■

The immediate post–Cold War world produced no equivalent of the East-West military confrontation, and this fact had two obvious and overwhelming benefits for the citizenry of the 1990s. Both benefits condition how to think about the problem of national security in the contemporary world, even after the second fault line of terrorism was revealed.

The first positive change was the virtual disappearance of any real concern about the possibility of a general systemic war that could threaten national and international survival. Within the context of the Cold War, the possibility—thought by some to be a probability—of a global nuclear World War III was ever present, a problem suspended over mankind like a Sword of Damocles. The two sides were certainly politically opposed enough to find adequate cause for war; managing the competition in such a way to reduce the likelihood of such a war was a major task. That intensity is gone; Russian resurgence is a problem, but nowhere near its previous dimension.

This changed dynamic enormously relaxed the security environment because it downgraded the "worst case" planning problem of nuclear holocaust from the heart of concern to a lower order of likelihood and thus lower concern. All the realistic military contingencies for the present and foreseeable future are more limited in conduct and potential for expansion to general war. It is virtually impossible to conjure a realistic scenario that would lead the world to a general nuclear conflagration. Terrorism reminds mankind that the world can still be a dangerous place; the unlikelihood of nuclear escalation makes the widespread prospects less deadly.

The second change flows from the first. During the Cold War confrontation, both potential adversaries and their major allies maintained large and expensive military machines that could be quickly inserted into the fray should war somehow break out. Given the destructiveness such a war could rapidly produce, it was assumed that it would be fought and completed with the forces on hand when it began—the "force in being"—and both sides maintained large conventional forces for that possibility. It was a very expensive proposition.

The end of the Cold War was accompanied by a sizable demilitarization among the major players and especially the leaders of the Cold War coalitions. Troop strength for the United States went from 2.15 million active-duty troops in 1988 to 1.4 million in 1998, and NATO allies slashed their forces even more deeply. The Russians reduced their forces even more. On both sides, these cuts were more quantitative than qualitative. American forces may have been reduced by one-third, but the result was basically a smaller version of the Cold War, heavy European-style force that has not proven especially effective in contemporary asymmetrical warfare scenarios. In any case, force sizes and expenditure levels went down substantially for all the major powers as the perceived threats they faced faded.

Debatable Impacts

The danger of global war and the need to prepare for it undeniably were receding, but the effects of other changes in the environment were more controversial. Three interrelated changes with some impact on the security equation have arisen or intensified in the process.

One change, from which the others partially follow, was a greater emphasis on the developing world. In one sense, this emphasis did not represent much of a change at all in national security terms. Although national security during the Cold War focused on the major power competition, virtually all the actual fighting by American forces occurred in the developing world. The United States *deployed* forces worldwide, including in the developed world (Europe, Japan); it *employed* force exclusively in the developing world (Korea, Vietnam, and Grenada, for example). The reasons are complex, of course, but the fact that most of the actual violence and international instability was in the developing world had something to do with this pattern of employment. In Cold War terms, in most instances violent confrontations between clients of the two sides could be waged without a real danger of escalation to direct superpower confrontation. Since many of these conflicts had communists battling anticommunists, the use of force could be argued to have constituted a proxy war that avoided shifting the geopolitical balance between the East and the West (the Vietnam War is a prominently cited example).

During the Cold War, the uses of American armed forces in the developing world tended to be conventional in terms of purpose and methods of employment: the reason to use *American* military might was to thwart communist takeovers that might occur in the absence of American assistance, a direct extension of the central geopolitical competition. Whether that force was warranted or wise in specific places such as Vietnam was a matter of disagreement, but the central purpose was not. In those circumstances, the way forces were used—strategically if not always tactically—was conventional: the idea was military victory over a well-defined enemy. That enemy might fight unconventionally (asymmetrically) and thus create the need for tactical adjustment to bring about enemy defeat, as was the case in Vietnam, but the goal was long established—fighting to support traditional governments. American interests were *instrumental* (thwarting global communism), not *intrinsic* (responding to perceived needs of people in countries of the developing world as they saw their needs).

Opportunities to employ force in the period between the fault lines were different. The disappearance of communism meant that such involvement could no longer be justified in terms of the kinds of geopolitics that underlay Cold War actions. More typically, justifications became "softer," framed in terms of arresting and reversing humanitarian disasters where clearly military conflict between defined military forces was not present. The purpose was more often framed in terms of reinstituting peace and protecting civilian populations from the return of atrocity. As a result, military victory in a traditional sense gave way to an open-ended commitment to imposing, enforcing, and keeping a fragile peace.

When the new Bush administration entered office in 2001, it clearly demonstrated ambivalence over how and when to use force. During the 2000 campaign, Bush had come out strongly in opposition to future uses of American force for peacekeeping when American interests were not clearly engaged. Condoleezza Rice, who became national security advisor in the first Bush term and secretary of state in the second, was the point spokesperson for this position, arguing that the United States should not act as the "world's 911," that it was an improper role for elite American troops like the 82nd Airborne to be used to escort children to kindergarten in places like Kosovo, and that endless deployments were eroding troop morale. The Bush team even suggested the desirability of terminating American involvement in Kosovo and Bosnia.

These positions did not long survive Bush's oath of office. The United States' European allies quickly informed the Bush administration of the necessity of maintaining the missions in the Balkans and of the vital nature of the American presence in those missions. The rhetoric of noninvolvement was quietly cooled, and Secretary of Defense Donald Rumsfeld quickly announced a comprehensive review of American military strategy and missions.

Globalization is the other 1990s trend with a significant developing world element, and disagreement exists about what it does and how or whether it should be promoted. Bursting upon the scene and coinciding with or stimulating (there is disagreement about which) the worldwide economic expansion and prosperity of the global economy in the most developed states, globalization spread to selected parts of the developing world during the 1990s. During the first half of the decade and beyond, the results appeared overwhelmingly positive and formed the core of the Clinton administration foreign policy of engagement and enlargement (engaging those countries most capable of joining the global economy and thereby enlarging what he called the circle of market democracies). In its purest form, the expansion of the globalizing economy would be accompanied by political democratization and contribute to a spreading *democratic peace* around the globe. In this scenario, as democracies increasingly came into power, peace would follow since it was asserted that political democracies do not fight one another. Moreover, as the global economy reached out and encompassed more and more countries, the motivation to fight would give way to economic interdependence.

In this happy scenario, a geopolitical perspective that sought to minimize violence and instability in the world appeared to coincide with and reinforce globalization since they were both aimed at the same ends. Unfortunately, the rosy outlook of the 1990s began to fade as the twentieth century wound to an end. As the international system faced the new century, the desirability and contribution of globalization became more debatable. A "democratic peace" might be a lofty goal toward which to strive; its achievement became less certain and linear.

THE SECOND FAULT LINE: THE WORLD AFTER SEPTEMBER 11

September 11 was that traumatic event. Not unlike the end of the Cold War in effect, describing the distinctive characteristics of the resulting world has been difficult and often confusing. Like the post–Cold War world it superseded, it did not have a universally accepted name: the closest anyone has come in the immediate wake of the traumatic events is to proclaim it as the global war on terror, but it is not clear if that label is descriptively adequate. The response to the terrorist acts was not a war in the literal sense (although the same can be said of the Cold War), and the lasting endurance of the changes wrought by international terrorism has not been established. At the same time, the geopolitical map of world power has shifted eastward toward Asia, the most dramatic example of which has been the emergence of China as an economic superpower and competitor of the United States.

If it is difficult to agree on all aspects of the new environment in any detail, it is possible to discern differences on the post–September 11 side of the second fault line. The balance between traditional geopolitical and the more benevolent influences like globalization has clearly shifted from the latter back to the former. Geopolitics and its concomitant assertion of the relevance of force have had a rebirth that is clear and undeniable as the search continues for adequate ways to cope with the new geopolitical reality. One of the new forces that clearly entered the public international calculus is the emergence of non-state actors in the form of international terrorists whose base and loyalties do not coincide with any country. One result is an enemy hard to classify in national terms and hard to attack without alienating the government and people of the countries in which the terrorists reside. The relative power and prominence of East Asia requires a rethinking of balances of power and clashes of national interests different from those of the Cold War. Both phenomena, terrorism and the rise of China, are hallmarks of the post-9/11 world.

The Rise of New Forces: Terrorism

The revealed vulnerability of American soil to attack on 9/11 quickly revived interest in the more prominent tool of geopolitics—military forces—in the American debate after a decade when force received much less attention. In the patriotic outpouring following the terrorist attacks, this shift to an almost obsessive emphasis on national security went virtually unchallenged. As the threat has evolved and new non-state actors have emerged, much of the American debate has turned to the question of the degree and nature of American military activism appropriate to this hydra-headed opponent. Where, when, and how should the United States use formal military force against its new and constantly changing enemies? The answer is not as clear as some advocates would suggest.

The ascendancy of terrorism has been accompanied by the realization that the United States is locked in a new and different kind of war, a theme raised shortly after September 11 by the Bush administration and dutifully adopted by the media. It was never quite clear what was new about terrorism per se, but it was widely advertised that the new and amorphous enemy engaged in *asymmetrical warfare*. Calling such approaches "new" strained credulity to the breaking point. The adoption of methods to negate the advantages of a larger and superior force is as old as the first time a weaker foe outdid a superior enemy, and the United States tactically confronted—unsuccessfully—this kind of enemy in Vietnam a third of a century earlier. There is certainly nothing new about the use of terrorism—only the instruments have changed. What *is* new in the contemporary context is the relative emphasis now placed on combating unconventional opponents, an area of importance largely ignored during the Cold War by the mainstream military. Although terrorism as a method dates to biblical times, its scale is larger (or at least more publicized), deadlier, and more adaptive than before. Terrorism has become the most gruesome aspect of the post-9/11 landscape.

It is not the only challenge. The new geopolitical order has required an increased emphasis on non-state actors, organizations with neither a permanent territorial base nor loyalty to any country but that engage in activities that cross state borders. In a generic sense, such actors are also nothing new; the most prominent traditional examples of non-state actors are nongovernmental organizations (NGOs)—non-state-based international organizations that perform a variety of useful functions within the system, from providing humanitarian assistance (CARE, Doctors without Borders) to monitoring human rights violations (Amnesty International, Human Rights Watch), for example.

The terrorist attacks riveted attention on the most violent subcategory of non-state actors. Once again, violent transnational groups are not a novel feature of the post–Cold War world and beyond. In contemporary terms, the international drug cartels have been a prototype of sorts, and international terrorist organizations have operated for years. What is different is that modern terrorist organizations have attained a central position in national security attention.

This rise in importance of non-state opponents and threats coincides with the decline in traditional, state-based threats. One of the major phenomena of the post–Cold War period is that the United States clearly established itself as the preeminent traditional military power in the world. At the level of conventional military force, this meant no country could challenge the United States in traditional military terms.

The result has been a kind of self-fulfilling prophecy. No traditional state actors had either the will or the wherewithal to challenge American dominance. The collapse of Soviet power indeed deprived the United States both of an enemy and of a traditional mission, and no one yet has arisen to challenge American military dominance, although China may be trying to do so.

One effect is a curious anomaly examined in more detail in Chapter 8. American conventional military might has become so overwhelming that no one could possibly challenge it, and so others (especially other states) quit trying to do so. American military prowess, in effect, rendered itself obsolete since it became apparent that a direct challenge to American force was suicidal.

Grievances for which force is one possible remedy remained, however, and the question was how the aggrieved could pursue their interests in the face of overwhelming American force. Many of these grievances were held by non-state actors, and the answer they found was to adopt nontraditional, asymmetrical methods. This combination of kinds of actors and methods of fighting has become the major structural national security distinction of the post-9/11 world.

Dealing with international terrorist organizations poses some unique problems for national security policymakers beyond the fact that they were not given high priority in the past. The United States' historical experience has been combating the agents of state-based government conventional forces. Armed forces, doctrines for warfare, and the whole legal and ethical framework for warfare are geared to fighting such foes. International terrorism stands these concepts and rules on their head in several ways. Non-state organizations with terrorist ambitions but no accepted sovereign territorial base like the Islamic State (IS) complicate the problem.

One problem is depicting efforts to combat international terrorists. Calling it "war" is at least a partial misnomer given customary uses of that term. The analogy of "war" has its roots and designations in conventional interstate war and classic internal war over control of governments, but this does not clearly fit an opponent that has no territorial base or loyalty and is apparently uninterested in gaining and exercising authority over territory. Who does one attack in this war? Historically, acts of war are committed against states and their agencies. In the case of international terrorists, such distinctions are infrequent. The designation of the IS caliphate as a state is an extreme exception. That aspiration, it will be argued, helped lead to the decline of IS. It is relatively easy to assign blame when actions can clearly be identified with a state (and especially when that state acts overtly); it is more difficult when dealing with a non-state-based opponent, especially one that does not obey conventional rules of war, as examined in Amplification 5.2. This applies to terrorists, as discussed in Chapter 10, and to groups that use terror as part of their rules of engagement (ROEs).

AMPLIFICATION 5.2

Terrorists and the "Rules of the Game"

Especially from the viewpoint of traditional military organizations like the United States armed forces, dealing with opponents that employ terror has always created difficult ethical and physical problems for several reasons.

Those who employ terror do not "fight fair." Western-style armed forces are organized and trained to fight within boundaries that are prescribed within the various Geneva Conventions on War. These "rules of war" describe permissible and impermissible methods of combat that may be undertaken by armed forces, and Western military members are trained to obey these rules and to expect their opponents to do so as well. Terrorists normally reject these restrictions and routinely disobey the rules. The actions they undertake are outrageous by Western standards and lead Western military officials to hold terrorists in disdain and contempt, even as cowardly. Two examples are illustrative.

The first deals with distinguishing between civilian and military targets. The Geneva Accords sharply distinguish between civilian (noncombatant) and military (combatant) targets in war, and terrorists reject this distinction. It violates the rules of war to attack noncombatant targets, and purposely doing so constitutes a prosecutable crime against humanity. Terrorists maintain that their wars are against enemy societies as a whole and that attacking any enemy object is a legitimate act of war. To Americans, the 9/11 attacks were atrocious, despicable, and thoroughly punishable breaches of the laws of war. To the perpetrators, they were simply acts of war.

The second example deals with international legal norms about how enemy combatants must be treated if they are captured as prisoners of war (POWs). In essence, these rules require humane treatment during the period of incarceration, and these conditions are monitored by organizations like the International Red Cross. The details of these rules are not always honored during war, but there is the general expectation that they will in general be enforced. Terrorists often ignore these rules as irrelevant and commit atrocities against those whom they capture, presumably to strike fear in others who might try to penetrate their whereabouts. The gruesome beheadings of captives by IS in 2015 illustrate these actions at their worst. ■

Source: *Convention III: Relative to the Treatment of Prisoners of War*. Geneva, August 12, 1949. (Text available from the Society of Professional Journalists at www.spj.org/gc-text3.asp.)

Non-state actors such as international terrorists are thus difficult to combat in conventional military terms. These groups do indeed engage in asymmetrical forms of combat, in the process not obeying traditional rules of engagement or conventional laws of states. Terrorist acts invariably break laws and are considered criminal by the targets, just as these same acts are considered acts of war by the terrorists.

Another characteristic of the new form of conflict is the open-endedness of conflicts. Asymmetrical wars do not normally end dramatically or definitively. There are no formal surrenders or suits for peace that end these wars, and thus no clear-cut closures. Rather, asymmetrical wars tend to drag on seemingly endlessly. To an American military culture more accustomed to World War II–like endings, the result has been frustrating.

An outgrowth of the post-9/11 period has, of course, been American intervention in two countries, Afghanistan and Iraq. Both were justified as extensions of the "war" against terrorists, and both dragged on largely inconclusively with no definitive end. The last American forces left Iraq at the end of 2011, but the future of Iraq remains in doubt. United States forces remain in Afghanistan, but no one has surrendered, and the fighting goes on interminably and seems likely to continue indefinitely.

The United States experienced a similar outcome in Vietnam, and the result was disappointing, to say the least. Americans (and citizens of other democracies) do not like long, indeterminate wars, but these are the kinds of wars that distinguish the post-9/11 world. How to adjust to this dilemma is a major point of contention and disagreement.

The same kind of dynamics applies to terrorism itself. In the years since 9/11, the effort against international terrorism has ebbed and flowed with successful operations against some terrorists, juxtaposed by the emergence of new groups and threats. American emotional heat has cooled somewhat but has not disappeared. Emotional intensity tends to dissipate with time and the fading of memories. The absence of subsequent attacks on US soil has dampened the sense of immediacy, even if it has sparked an ongoing debate about what has kept the country free from attack since 2001. The successful killing of bin Laden brought a visceral satisfaction to Americans, but it has changed, not erased, the threat. Al Qaeda (AQ) remains a viable, if transformed, threat as it continues to commit acts of terror elsewhere in the world and threatens to bring these miseries back to American territory. The question is how best to deal with that threat.

The Asian/Chinese Challenge?

Power within the international system has shifted as well. Since the Middle Ages, effective international power has been Eurocentric, with a series of European countries acting in a kind of competitive balance and dominating the rest of the world. This system, formalized after the Thirty Years' War of 1618–48, survived until the middle of the twentieth century, when the outcomes of World War II so exhausted the traditional powers that they were forced to cede control to the two remaining powers, the United States and the Soviet Union, a relationship that ended when the Soviet Union dissolved. Between 1991 and the early twenty-first century, the United States was the sole remaining superpower. China has arisen to challenge that status.

China had been the world's sleeping giant. It is the world's oldest continuous civilization, was at one time the most advanced society in the world, and boasted the world's largest population. It considered itself so far superior that it turned introspective, believing outside influences would desecrate it, and withdrew from processes of modernization occurring elsewhere that eventually surpassed China. The Great Wall of China, built to exclude the barbarian outsiders (a symbol of racism that has not entirely disappeared), epitomized China's attitude toward the outside world. China's place in the world bottomed out in the nineteenth century—known as the Century of Humiliation in the country—when China was so weak it could not prevent effective European colonization.

China's rise effectively began when Deng Xiaoping succeeded Mao Tse Tung, the leader of the Communist Revolution that had governed the People's Republic of China (PRC) since 1949. The PRC was effectively the junior member of the communist side in the Cold War, largely fettered by its socialist economic system and the ideological dogmatism of Mao. Deng sought to make China competitive in the world by announcing the Four Modernizations of Chinese society: agriculture, science and technology, economics, and the military. Early emphasis was placed on adopting Western economic policies and attitudes, what Deng called "socialism with Chinese characteristics." The heart of the reforms was to open the country to Western investment and the influx of Western economic practices. The major example of progress was the opening of the Special Economic Zones (SEZs) in eastern China, which allowed Western investment and collaboration and fueled the Chinese economic miracle that has made the PRC an economic competitor of the United States and is moving in the direction of making China a geopolitical equal as well. This trend has been intensified since Xi Jinping assumed power.

The change has been striking and noted by numerous observers. The idea of this century as an "Asian Century" began to gain supporters in the 1990s, and during his presidency, Barack Obama talked about a tilt in foreign and national security policy away from traditional concerns toward Asia. In a 2016 interview in the *Atlantic*, Henry Kissinger (who played a major role in the opening of relations between the United States and the PRC), opined, "Our relations with China will shape the international order in the long term. The United States and China are the world's most consequential countries."

The question is how will they get along? They have had a mixed relationship as "frenemies"—part friends and part enemies. The friendly part of the relationship is based in the intertwining of their economies to the point they would both be hurt terribly by a deteriorated turn in their relationship. Former Obama economic advisor Lawrence Summers (quoted in Beeson) refers to it as the "balance of financial terror," wherein adversarial actions by one threaten the prosperity of both, which leads Shirk to conclude, "Both countries would suffer if one provoked a trade war, an arms race, or a military confrontation." There is, however, a lingering thread of animosity between the two that dates to their early postwar relationship. The United States backed the Republic of China (ROC) in the Chinese Civil War, fought against Chinese "volunteers" in Korea, and did not admit the existence of the PRC from 1949 to 1972. They also have lingering sources of disagreement on national security matters that are important to both. How these disagreements are dealt with will depend on how these two superpowers get along with one another and restructure the international system.

Describing the sources of their disagreement requires examining how each country views itself and its place in the world. Americans have become accustomed to their role as the world superpower, although the burdens of maintaining global leadership troubled some in the middle 2010s.

Americans are basically comfortable with the world as it is and seek to retain its parameters. China, on the other hand, is rebounding and seeks basic change that will allow it to reclaim its traditional role as one of the world's great—if not its greatest—powers. China wants to regain its role as the suzerain power in Asia and acknowledgment of its status as a superpower. The American and Chinese worldviews are not mutually exclusive, but they are also not entirely compatible either.

The heart of geopolitical differences between the two countries are based in different images and aspirations regarding East Asia. China considers itself the dominant East Asian power, a position with historical and substantive merit. It believes it should occupy a position of primacy among Asian states. This position is more popular among Han Chinese than the residents of other continental states, but it is considered a virtual obsession with President Xi Jinping. The primary American interest, on the other hand, is Pacific: its closest allies and friends are all situated along the Pacific Rim—Japan, the Philippines, Taiwan, and South Korea, for instance. Its interest is served by American naval supremacy in the Western Pacific that assures its associates cannot be attacked or coerced. These contrary positions clash at the Pacific shore, but they are not so mutually exclusive that they cannot be reconciled.

Two flashpoints illustrate the situation. The Chinese would like to see an end to a physical American presence on the continent, an interest that comes to a head over American military presence in South Korea (and to a lesser degree, offshore nuclear weapons). The American security guarantee to the Republic of Korea (ROK) includes American forces in that country, particularly given that a heavily armed North Korea with nuclear weapons menaces the ROK. China will not be happy until or unless the Americans leave South Korea; the Americans will not leave until the Democratic People's Republic of Korea (DPRK) no longer menaces the South. A mutually acceptable settlement of the DPRK situation is the clear prerequisite for settlement.

The current American interest conflict with the PRC is over the South China Sea, a body of water that laps the Chinese coast and the shores of American friends in the Western Pacific. China claims the sea as its territorial waters and has erected artificial islands to reinforce its claim (which includes the petroleum beneath the sea's floor). The United States rejects the Chinese claim because, if honored, it allows Chinese control of naval traffic through the sea and reinforces Chinese disputed claims to petroleum rights.

Both issues are resolvable if handled together. If the United States can get sufficient concessions about South Korea to erase the possibility of another 1950s-style DPRK invasion that are satisfactory to the South Koreans, and the PRC can be convinced to accept a compromise solution regarding the South China Sea (e.g., restricted territorial control of oil), some condominium may be possible.

Where does the relationship go? The two countries are so economically tied together that overt military conflict seems unlikely, but there is not consensus on this position. To cite the title of his 2017 book, distinguished Harvard political scientist Graham T. Allison argues the two countries are "destined for war." That judgment may be premature, but how they manage the transition in their relationship and in shaping the post-9/11 world will have a great deal to say about the prospects. The current and future American presidents will play a role in the outcome; so will Xi Jinping.

TOWARD THE NEW INTERNATIONAL SYSTEM?

The end of the Cold War and 9/11 both had major impacts on the nature of the international system and on how to think about the American place in that system. Three aspects of these changes are explored in this section, including how they may have shaped the dynamics of the post-9/11 world.

Paradigm Choices

During the 1990s, two quite opposite forces were at play and created an exaggerated view of the post–Cold War world. One of these was the apparently receding importance of the most visible manifestation of geopolitics: military forces. The demise of the superpower military confrontation clearly devalued traditional military force within the major power conglomerate of important countries, and this devaluation led many states to sharply reduce their forces. Following the apparent last hurrah of twentieth century–style warfare in the Persian Gulf War of 1990–91, military concerns shrank to considering smaller tasks, such as peacekeeping.

At the same time, globalization was making enormous headway as the leading edge of the great and spreading prosperity of the 1990s. During the first two-thirds of the decade, economic growth and prosperity seemed inexorable at the very same time that major systemic instability and the prevalence of violence faded from the world stage. The result was a euphoria that would prove with time to be partially false.

At one level, the rise of globalization and other concerns in the 1990s was nothing more than the latest conceptual and physical reaction to the realism represented by the geopolitically dominated Cold War period. Realism and geopolitics represent the conflictual side of international relations—the dark side, or yin, of politics. Globalization and other dynamics, on the other hand, emphasize the cooperative side of the international equation, the idealist assault on the worst outcomes of a realist-dominated world war. This assault has known many names, from interwar idealism and its attachment to international organization to the functionalism of the early post–World War II emphasis on the United Nations (UN) system as a means to make war practically impossible. The more direct lineage attaches to the idea of complex interdependence popularized by Robert Keohane and Joseph S. Nye Jr., in the 1970s. Globalization emerged as the yang to the geopolitical yin.

In some ways, economic aspects of globalization replaced—at least part of the time and in some instances—the military aspects of geopolitics during the 1990s. The growing economic prosperity of the decade fed this change of emphasis, as did a decline in major conflicts for which force was an option. Globalization and geopolitics even became interdependent: globalization became the servant of geopolitics, in some cases like the complex motivations and debates about the use of economic incentives to China to entangle that country in a spiderlike web designed to draw it toward the economic and political values of the Western-dominated system. These dynamics were new and complex and are still evolving. Their roots, however, are firmly planted in the 1990s. Increased economic competition and disagreement between the United States and China may be blurring the distinction between yin and yang.

The American Role in the New World System

One of the ways the new international order is clearly different from the Cold War era is in the distribution of power and influence among states. The language of bipolarity and multipolarity was shelved during the 1990s, but it has returned in the mid-2010s in the form of China's geopolitical challenge and the Trump-era retreat by the United States of a strong geopolitical role.

Politically, the United States emerged in the 1990s as "the indispensable nation," to use former secretary of state Madeleine Albright's phrase. The basis of American political advantage was at least twofold. The power and appeal of the American system and its political ideals (the core of Joseph S. Nye's concept of "soft power") made the United States the model many states and peoples worldwide sought to emulate. At the same time, the United States was the only country with truly global interests. Thus whenever situations arose almost anywhere, the United States was affected and had an interest in influencing the outcome. Because of American power in the other dimensions, American preferences were highly consequential and had to be dealt with by rivals regardless of the location.

The economic dimension was similar. After nearly two decades of economic doldrums during the 1970s and 1980s, the American economy revived and led the expansion of the globalizing economy during the 1990s and into the 2000s. The United States had remained the world's largest economy even during the down years, but as expansion occurred and the globalization system became ultimately a trading system, the United States also blossomed as the world's great market, which everyone sought to enter. At the same time, the Chinese challenge was only beginning in the 1990s, and its ultimate nature and direction were not clear, adding to the aura of American preeminence.

American military advantage increased the most. One obvious reason for this was the decline of the United States' military rivals. Russian forces were far inferior in size and quality to the old Soviet military machine, and the burdensome retention of a nuclear arsenal comparable to that of the United States, which the Russians could not afford to maintain adequately, was about the only way in which the United States' past rival posed any threat. Similarly, the People's Republic of China retained the world's largest army but had no way to project it far from its borders and spent much less proportionately on national security than the United States did despite a major commitment to defending itself.

This decline was not limited to America's traditional communist opponents. Freed of the danger of having to repulse a Soviet assault on their territory, America's NATO allies also sharply reduced their military forces to, in some cases, skeletal levels incapable of sustaining major participation in combat missions. American forces shrunk, but the military capabilities of former enemies and ongoing allies declined even more. The result was to exaggerate the degree of American military superiority in the post–Cold War environment. It also fueled mid-2010s criticism that the European allies were not contributing adequately to the common defense.

After 9/11, this position began to change. American political leadership was, ironically, temporarily enhanced by the world's sympathetic reaction to the terrorist attacks and the American display of resolution in mounting a retributive "war on terror." Much of this willingness to follow the American lead dissipated, however, when the United States invaded and conquered Iraq—an action justified on antiterrorism grounds but opposed by most other countries, both as a breach of international law and as being of questionable relevance to the campaign against terrorism. American involvement in Iraq and Afghanistan tied down the bulk of American forces during the rest of the decade, reducing the American ability to wield military influence elsewhere.

The economic calamity that emerged on Wall Street in the summer of 2008 completed the transformation of the 1990s decade of American predominance into something else. The trauma of the Wall Street banking community spread to the international economy, where American woes interacted with those of other countries and made matters worse for everyone. The economic system has, of course, rebounded from the 2008 recession, but its fragility has become an ongoing concern as periodic economic crises continue to interrupt global prosperity.

As Americans and the rest of the world survey the national security landscape for the remaining years of the second decade of the new millennium, the environment is very different than in the past. The dark, dividing tension of the Cold War is gone, but so is the bright, sunny optimism of the 1990s. International terrorism provided a clarifying focus for the first decade of the new century, but the clarity of its influence is changing as well. Osama bin Laden is, after all, dead, but he has been replaced by other, sometimes more vexing, terrorist challenges. What is clear is that the United States lacks a clear vision to confront the new era.

The Post-9/11 Era?

The national security environment has changed significantly since the eve of the end of the Cold War in 1989 in both the international and domestic arenas. Internationally, the change has been from a context in which very real and deadly threats to national existence dominated the scene to a still dangerous, yet not so deadly or all-inclusive, threat environment. The dictates of the Cold War demanded a high level of physical commitment to national security and a political consensus behind the national security effort. That unanimity of support for the national security problem has dissipated in the venom of partisan politics and strongly held differences about how best to respond to a changing national security environment.

The international and domestic environments have, of course, changed in interactive, intermestic ways. The perceived life-and-death struggle with communism overrode partisan bickering as disloyal and unpatriotic, and that restraint returned in the immediate response to international terrorism after 9/11. As the last decade evolved, some of the emotional impact of the "war against terror" has abated, partisanship has returned to the national security arena, and disagreement about military responses in places like Iraq and proposed actions against IS have all contributed to a lack of consensus.

The national security environment has clearly changed. The international environment has gone from the high-threat dominance of the Cold War to the comparatively relaxed national security environment of the 1990s and the highly charged response to 9/11. Along the way, new and nonmilitary influences like globalization have challenged the virtually exclusively military content of the Cold War national security environment, adding to change. The idea of a "post"-9/11 era suggests the terrorist threat may be changing as well as new terrorist groups emerge on a regular basis and novel changes and new challenges in Asia affect the world power map.

The challenge of internal political disagreement is the major domestic change in the environment affecting national security. It has occurred during a period when no monumental international catastrophes required unanimity of national effort. Unfortunately, the paralysis of the American political system has thus extended itself to the national security arena, where there is little consensus beyond the sheer rhetorical and hortatory level about what America should be doing in the world to ensure its continuing security.

The domestic malaise has, of course, been manifest in one concrete way that is central to this volume. For the first time since World War II, the level of resources that should be made available to the national security enterprise has come into serious question. As the movement toward budget deficit reduction grew to the proportions of an ineluctable force in the 2000s, the question, "Should national security participate in budgetary austerity?" has been replaced by the more ominous question, "*How much* should national security participate in austerity?" The Trump presidency has reduced the demands for defense spending austerity, but the questions remain.

CONCLUSION: THE CONTINUING ROLE OF FORCE

There are two broad interpretations of the extent to which the recourse to force has changed in the post–Cold War world. If one begins from an emphasis on the potential applications of force, then change has been dramatic since the most notable potential use was the ultimate employment of necessity, a military confrontation with the Soviet Union. That contingency has obviously disappeared, and much of the potential use of force in conventional interstate warfare has virtually disappeared in the general tranquility among those countries with conventional militaries, notably the most developed countries. It has become a simple fact since 1991 that the recourse to violence between the governments of states—traditional wars fought by conventional warring parties—has essentially ceased for now. This condition could, of course, change. The developing political relationship between the United States and China raised in the *Challenge!* box illustrates this change. Combating terrorism has replaced large-scale warfare at the pinnacle of national security priorities. This assessment, of course, has major implications for the kinds of forces the United States develops and the missions for which they are prepared.

The other way to look at the problem is how and where force was actually employed in the past and how it is employed in the present or will be in the future. From this vantage point, change is not very dramatic at all. As noted, the United States employed force exclusively in the old third world during the Cold War, and the current pattern also emphasizes deployments in the less developed countries of the world. In both periods, the conflicts were and are generally internal affairs, civil wars of one kind or another. The difference is in the motivation underlying involvement: during the Cold War, the United States was primarily motivated by ideological, proxy reasons, whereas now the temptations to intervene are either to relieve human-induced chaos and suffering, in effect to save countries from themselves, or to root out sources of international terrorism. It is a crucial difference that will be developed in the chapters that follow.

CHALLENGE!

Dealing with China

China is the wild card in the evolving international order. It is clearly the tip of the spear of the Asian challenge to the old order captured in the idea of the "Asian Century." It was not a major player in the international order for the first quarter century of its existence as it struggled with how to implement its revolution and its secondary role to the Soviet Union in the Cold War competition. Chinese leader Mao Tse Tung may have opined that China was the only country that could survive a nuclear war, but other than interfering in places like Southeast Asia, Chinese influence was not great.

The rise of Deng Xiaoping and his Four Modernizations started the change that is so evident today. China is now a major player in Asia, as its critical role in the North Korean–American nuclear confrontation has clearly demonstrated, and it is increasingly using its considerable economic assets to assert political influence elsewhere in the developing world. Since he was declared president for life, a tough Xi Jinping promises to move forward and to demonstrate that Chinese assertiveness is not a temporary factor. China is an expanding world power, and Xi is clearly dedicated both to sustaining and expanding that role.

The clear geopolitical challenge of the next decades is how to accommodate China without critically upsetting the settled order. There are three major elements in that process of adjustment. The first is to avoid antagonizing China so that it turns into a rogue, rather than a constructive, member of the evolving order. China wants and plans to expand its role in areas like the environment; how can that initiative be accommodated, for instance? Second, the United States and others must cooperate with China on drawing a new geopolitical map of Asia and the Pacific that accommodates the Chinese while not risking geopolitical military competition and instability. The evolving balance between American dominance in the Western Pacific and Chinese dominance on the continent is the key issue. Third, this process means the United States will have to adapt its traditionally superior role in Asia to something that is less pervasive but still accommodates American economic and military policy in that part of the world. None of these are easy tasks; all are vital. ■

This distinction regarding motivation for using force is not insignificant for at least three reasons. One is the relative importance attached to potential involvement. In the Cold War context, one could, and some did, make the argument that the United States was impelled to act in the developing world because of geopolitical dictates. Should our side lose, it would be yet one more instance of the "victory" of communism in the global struggle. Thus, intervention could arguably be a matter of necessity. Such geopolitical motivations are generally missing in many contemporary situations, where the goal often is either to restore order after some humanitarian disaster, promote democracy, eradicate terrorism, or some combination thereof. In any geopolitical sense, these are clearly employments of choice (efforts to combat terrorism are at least a partial exception). The activist argument regarding terrorism, and especially Middle Eastern terrorist groups, is that if the United States does not eradicate the threat at its source, one will eventually have to confront it here.

Whether the contemporary environment will prove to be more difficult and intractable than preceding periods, of course, remains to be seen. Both the international threat environment and domestic politics came together to provide distinct and combined intermestic influences on the assessment of the national security condition. How this adaptation occurs requires looking at both the setting and dynamics of the current situation, which is the thrust of Part III, and at the contemporary and projected problems to be confronted, which is the subject of Part IV.

STUDY/DISCUSSION QUESTIONS

1. Describe the first fault line (the end of the Cold War) and the impact it had on the structure of the international system and the problems affecting American security policy. What were the major benefits and debatable impacts of that change?
2. Describe the second fault line (September 11) and the impact it had on the structure of the international system and the problems affecting American security policy. What might it mean to describe Iraq as an "aftershock" of this fault line?
3. China has arisen as a prime competitor to the United States. Describe the Chinese challenge, its dimensions, and how they can be dealt with.
4. Geopolitics and globalization have been described in the text as the yin and yang of the contemporary international system. What does that mean? Discuss.
5. What is the United States' role in the contemporary international system? What does it mean that the United States is the only remaining superpower?
6. Is the international system moving toward a post-9/11 phase, where the fight against terrorism is a less central, compelling characteristic? If so, how? If not, why not?

SELECTED BIBLIOGRAPHY

Allison, Graham T. *Destined for War: Can America and China Escape Thucydides's Trap?* Boston: Houghton Mifflin Harcourt, 2017.

Brown, Kerry. *CEO China: The Rise of Ji Xinping.* London: I.B. Tauris, 2016.

Campbell, Charles. "China Steps Closer to Despotism as Xi Becomes Leader for Life." *Time* 191, 10 (March 12, 2018), 5–6.

Campbell, Kurt M., and Ely Ratner. "The China Reckoning: How Beijing Defied American Expectations." *Foreign Affairs* 97, 2 (March/April 2018), 60–70.

Economy, Elizabeth. *The Third Revolution: Xi Jinping and the New Chinese State.* New York and Oxford, UK: Oxford University Press,2018.

Fallows, James. "China's Great Leap Backward." *The Atlantic* 318, 5 (December 2016), 150–156.

Ferguson, Niall. "The Axis of Upheaval." *Foreign Policy*, March/April 2009, 56–60.

French, Howard W. *Everything Under the Heavens: How the Past Shapes China's Push for Global Power.* New York: Vintage, 2018.

Fukuyama, Francis. *The End of History and the Last Man.* New York: Free Press, 1992.

Gates, Robert M. "A Balanced Strategy." *Foreign Affairs* 88, 1 (January/February 2009), 28–40.

Goldberg, Jeffrey. "The Lessons of Henry Kissinger." *The Atlantic* 318, 5 (December 2016), 50–56.

Haass, Richard N. "The Age of Nonpolarity." *Foreign Affairs* 87, 3 (May/June 2008), 44–56.

Hill, Fiona, and Clifford G. Gaddy. *Mr. Putin: Operative in the Kremlin.* Washington, DC: Brookings Institution Press, 2015.

Keohane, Robert O., and Joseph S. Nye, Jr. *Power and Interdependence.* 2nd ed. Glenview, IL: Scott Foresman/Little Brown, 1989.

Laqueur, Walter. *Putinism: Russia and the Future of the West.* New York: Thomas Dunne Books, 2015.

McGregor, Richard. *Asia's Reckoning: China, Japan, and the Fate of U.S. Power in the Pacific.* New York: Viking, 2017.

Mearsheimer, John J. "Why We Shall Soon Miss the Cold War." *Atlantic Monthly* 266, 2 (August 1990), 35–50.

Menon, Rajan, and Eugene B. Rumer. *Conflict in Ukraine: The Unwinding of the Post-Cold War Order.* Cambridge, MA: MIT Press, 2015.

Nye, Joseph S., Jr. *Is the American Century Over?* New York: Polity Press, 2015.

Pei, Minxin. *China's Gang Capitalism: The Dynamics of Regime Decay.* Cambridge, MA: Harvard University Press, 2016.

Peters, Ralph. *New Glory: Expanding America's Global Supremacy.* New York: Sentinel, 2005.

Sarotte, Mary Elise. *1989: The Struggle to Create Post-Cold War Europe.* Princeton, NJ: Princeton University Press, 2014.

Shevtsova, Lilia. "Russia's Ersatz Democracy." *Current History* 105, 693 (October 2006), 307–314.

Shirk, Susan. "Getting to Yes with China." *Foreign Affairs* 96, 2 (March/April 2017), 20–27.

Slaughter, Anne-Marie. "America's Edge." *Foreign Affairs* 88, 1 (January/February 2009), 94–118.

Snow, Donald M. *Cases in U.S. National Security: Principles and Applications.* Lanham, MD: Rowman & Littlefield, 2019.

———. *When America Fights: The Uses of U.S. Military Force.* Washington, DC: CQ Press, 2000.

Zenko, Micah. *Between Threats and War: U.S. Discrete Military Operations in the Post-Cold War World.* Palo Alto, CA: Stanford University Press, 2010.

Intermestic Environments and Change

The contemporary national security environment operates within an institutional and political framework prescribed by the US Constitution and statutory actions to respond to the international environment. Internal and external forces often intersect and interact and are thus intermestic in both content and effect.

The three chapters of Part III introduce the major domestic influences and their interplay as they affect and are affected by the contemporary national security environment. The first two chapters examine the primarily domestic influences. Chapter 6 focuses primarily on those formal and institutional elements of the American political system that deal with national security matters, including homeland security responses to 9/11 and the budgetary sequester mandated by Congress on defense spending. Chapter 7 examines the parallel emergence in the early twenty-first century of the deep fissure within the American political system that has created the hyper-partisan gridlock in doing public business and how that dysfunction has and may continue to affect national security. Chapter 8 looks at the "legacies" of the recent past, notably the roles and missions of forces and ways of thinking that are ongoing holdovers—legacies—of the Cold War and beyond.

The Domestic Environment

National security policy is made within the constitutional and political frameworks that define the domestic environment. This chapter examines how the domestic political environment has an impact on political processes and outcomes. It begins by looking at the domestic context as it developed after World War II. It moves on to the executive branch of government, including constitutional powers and limitations and politically based structures, including the National Security Council and the interagency process, as well as the influence of outside actors— the hard men. The discussion then moves to formal factors, such as the effect of the congressional role and how Congress operates in this area. It concludes with extended discussions of two political examples, homeland security and the budgetary sequester.

National security policy is the result of the interplay of domestic and international factors. This interaction works in both directions. In one direction, forces in the international environment define the threats with which the country must cope, and domestic perceptions rank those threats as more or less dangerous and poignant. International religious terrorism, for instance, emanates from the international environment, but actions taken by the United States to deal with that threat can make the environment more or less troubling and hostile.

National security responses form the other direction. To a large degree, what threatens the United States and the extent to which those threats require different levels of response are subjective determinations arising from the psychological dimension of what constitutes security. People can and do disagree at this level, particularly when decisions require the expenditure of scarce resources (which they inevitably do) that reduce or eliminate risk in one area while potentially neglecting other priorities. The politics involved in such situations can often be quite intense, sometimes in ways not always directly connected to national security.

Disagreement about national security is reflected in domestic politics. The debate is partly a philosophical difference about the extent of American activism in the world that reflects an assessment of how threatening the world really is and the degree to which the United States has some role, obligation, or ability to affect the environment. The pendulum of opinion swings on the issue. The Clinton years, for instance, were marked by a high degree of international activism expressed in joint actions with other countries in an atmosphere of low and high threat and the formal and informal cooperation. The terror-driven atmosphere impacting the Bush years was typified by a much more confrontational, unilateralist view of the American role. The Obama years were generally internationalist and activist. The Trump presidency has been less internationalist and more introverted.

National security problems and their resolution can be fully analyzed and understood only in their political setting. Defending the country is arguably the ultimate purpose of the state and its government. No one questions the importance of security among state purposes, and for this reason, there is a tendency to elevate the processes by which national security policy is made as being above the "rough and tumble" of "politics as usual." But politics intrudes in ways that show that "the messiness" of domestic politics infects national security policy, and the formal and informal processes of government permit this intrusion, as illustrated in Amplification 6.1.

AMPLIFICATION 6.1

Executive Agreements and Congressional Oversight

President Trump's abrogation of American participation in the Joint Comprehensive Plan of Action (JCPOA) with Iran, in addition to denouncing the 2015 multilateral agreement harnessing Iran's nuclear weapons program, also illustrates the ease by which an American chief executive can change the parameters of security policy in controversial areas. Acting much as he had when he withdrew the United States from the Paris climate accord in 2017, he had no formal interactions with Congress about his decision, and neither house of Congress had any direct role in approving his decision. In this case, it was virtually as if the Congress did not exist or had no formal role in major national security decisions. It was politics in action.

How and why did this occur? Both the JCPOA and Paris accords were executive agreements (EAs) negotiated by the Obama administration that

(continued)

created international obligations for the United States. EAs have been part of American foreign policy since the 1930s and were originally created (and upheld by the Supreme Court) because the Senate simply did not have the time to act on all foreign exchanges. It thus allowed the president to create these treaty-like arrangements while avoiding the treaty ratification process. As the international agenda became more extensive, the use of EAs grew, and now over 90 percent of all US deals with other countries are in this form. At the same time, increased congressional partisanship has meant it is virtually impossible to muster the two-thirds Senate votes to ratify even the most mundane agreement by treaty. EAs avoid that problem.

They do so at a cost. EAs, like domestic executive orders, can be rescinded by the president without permission from Congress (treaties are arguably the same in this regard). This means that if a president disapproves of an obligation created by his predecessor, the chief executive can simply rescind the obligation by proclamation. ■

Too much can be—and often is—made about the life-and-death nature of national security policy. The worst-case possibility always lurks in the background of national security decisions as a rejoinder against precipitous change—and especially reductions in defense efforts. The logic behind being "better safe than sorry" is particularly powerful when the potential outcome is catastrophic. The result is a process that is weighted toward maximum risk reduction, where the response to additional threats is to expand the resources available to reduce risk (i.e., to spend more). These dynamics guarantee a very expensive, highly conservative national security process and make the current assault on the sacrosanctity of the defense budget more difficult.

To understand how this process operates, the discussion begins by looking at the historical context, including the attitudes of the Founding Fathers and the framework created for the Cold War through the National Security Act of 1947. This context leads to the institutional framework for the national security process within and between the executive and legislative branches of government. The chapter then moves to applications of the process in action, institutionally through the homeland security reaction to September 11 and the sequester of 2011.

THE POST–WORLD WAR II DOMESTIC RESPONSE

When the Founding Fathers were designing the American political system, matters that are now considered national security problems were not major concerns. The American Revolution had expelled foreign forces from American soil, and the major priorities of the country concentrated on devising and developing a new polity in a largely virgin, undeveloped land. Most of the "security" problems facing Americans were peripheral and marginally threatening (e.g., subduing and replacing Native Americans on the frontier) or aberrational (the self-infliction of the Civil War). As a result, the Founding Fathers were particularly spare in creating a constitutional framework in this area, and their modest rules sufficed until the end of World War II.

The National Security Act of 1947 created an enlarged institutional framework that has defined the national security policy process to this day. Signed into law on July 26, 1947, the act transformed a highly fragmented and inefficient governmental structure that had developed during World War II into the highly durable structure that managed the Cold War successfully and has remained the basic framework to this day.

The National Security Act created five institutions, each of which remains a vital part of the domestic national security effort. The first was the *Department of Defense (DOD)*. Prior to 1947, each of the independent military services (the Army and the Navy) was a cabinet-level agency, and this independence had proven an impediment to the most efficient conduct of World War II. There was thus great pressure to create a unified military department to supersede the old prewar structure to force greater cooperation and coordination among the military services in the areas of planning, war fighting, and budgets, as well as to establish more firmly the principle of civilian control of the military. The new structure was originally called the National Military Establishment and was changed to the current DOD by the amending National Security Act of 1949. At the time, this merger of military assets into one department was generally preferred by the Army and what would become the Air Force (which had been the Army Air Corps, a part of the Army) and opposed by the Navy. As partial compensation for the Navy, Admiral James Forrestal was named the first secretary of defense (SECDEF).

The act created a second institution, the *Joint Chiefs of Staff (JCS)*, to form a cadre of senior officers from the various services who would work together to coordinate and cooperate on military problems facing the country and provide military advice directly to the president. The chief of staff of each branch serves as a member, with the chairmanship of the body (the chairman of the JCS, or CJCS) chosen from the services basically on a rotating basis. By statute, the CJCS is the chief *military* advisor to the president, as opposed to the SECDEF, who is the chief *defense* advisor to the president. A postwar review of the Vietnam War experience suggested this structure had not produced a maximally integrated effort, so Congress passed the *Goldwater-Nichols Act of 1986* mandating much greater and more meaningful cooperation and coordination (known as *jointness*), a policy that has resulted in much more inter-service cooperation.

The third institution was the *Central Intelligence Agency (CIA)*. Prior to World War II, the United States had possessed no peacetime civilian organization for gathering and analyzing intelligence. To remedy that situation, President Franklin D. Roosevelt had created the Office of Strategic Services (OSS) under the leadership of Colonel (retired) William Donovan to provide intelligence to the government during the war, but the OSS mandate ended with the conclusion of hostilities. Recognizing the emerging threat posed by an increasingly hostile communist bloc led by the Soviet Union, this condition was deemed intolerable and resulted in the creation of the CIA as the country's first permanent peacetime intelligence agency.

Even at the time of its inception, the new CIA was plagued with two problems that continue to be part of the contemporary debate about the agency. The first was its place within the community of intelligence assets of the country. In addition to the CIA, there are major intelligence capabilities in several other areas of government. The most notable of these are within the DOD—the National Security Agency, the Defense Intelligence Agency, and the intelligence assets of the various services (which cumulatively make up about four-fifths of the country's intelligence assets). The CIA was designated as the lead agency for intelligence (with the responsibility of providing intelligence information and advice to the president). Its head, the director of central intelligence (DCI), was also designated as the chair of the intelligence community. This arrangement put the DCI in the awkward position of being both the head of one intelligence agency (CIA) and the official designated to oversee and coordinate the activities of all agencies, including his own. The result was a conflict of interest that was part of the reason for creating the position of director of national intelligence (DNI) in 2004.

There has also been some controversy about what the CIA does or should do. The gathering, compilation, and reporting of information (intelligence) is its basic mission, but there has always been debate about what the CIA should be able to do in addition to intelligence collection. The controversy has focused on the area known as "operations," which refers to active efforts the CIA may clandestinely undertake to influence international events (known as covert actions). Within the original legislation creating the CIA is a provision for the agency to carry out "other functions and duties related to intelligence." Russian meddling in the 2016 American election would qualify as an operations function.

The fourth institution was an independent *United States Air Force (USAF)*. During World War II, American air assets were divided among the Navy (including the Marines) and the Army (the Army Air Corps). Proponents of airpower had long lobbied for an independent air force to consolidate the various air roles and missions assigned to airpower. They were successful to the extent of extricating themselves from the Army and being established as an independent USAF. They failed in that the Navy and Marines maintained control of their own air forces, and the Army managed to get back into the air business through the application of helicopters for military purposes. Rationalizing the military uses of the atmosphere (and beyond) has been a recurring theme in attempts at military reform.

The fifth, and in many ways the most important, accomplishment of the National Security Act was the creation of the *National Security Council (NSC)*. The NSC was enormously symbolically important in defining the American role in the postwar world. At its most basic level, it recognized the new and growing importance of the United States and the consequent need for some formal mechanism to assist in how the United States would react in the world. It also implied and boosted the centrality of defense matters within the hierarchy of foreign policy concerns. The statutory members of the NSC are the president, the vice president, the secretary of state, and the new SECDEF (the president can add other members as he or she chooses, and subsequent legislation and practice have increased the normal membership to include the DCI, the CJCS, and others). The symbolism of the composition was the placement of the SECDEF as the lineal equivalent of the secretary of state on the NSC, indicating that the line between foreign policy (with diplomacy at its heart) and national security policy (with the military at its core) would be less clear than in the past and that much of foreign policy would indeed be virtually indistinguishable from national security policy. The fact that the Cold War emerged as a political competition largely framed in military terms reinforced this placement of the SECDEF within the structure. The NSC has proven an exceptionally durable institution and has been further elaborated through a system of executive branch mechanisms known collectively as the interagency process.

THE POLITICAL CONTEXT AND STRUCTURE OF DOMESTIC POLITICS

National security policy occupies a special place within the American federal system because its content includes decisions that can affect the very physical survival of the country, a unique role. This position gives the national security area an advantage in claims for funding against other priorities, tilting the debate between guns (national security) and butter (social programs) toward guns.

National security policy is also highly political because it involves the expenditure of very large amounts of money. Defense spending is historically the second-largest category in the federal budget, behind spending on entitlements (Social Security, Medicare, and the like) and just ahead of service (paying interest) on the national debt. During the Cold War, it involved roughly a quarter of the federal budget and 5 to 6 percent of the gross national product (GNP).

Defense spending is highly political for several reasons. One is that it is the largest discretionary element within the federal budget. One way to distinguish items in the federal budget is to divide them into discretionary (or controllable) and nondiscretionary (or uncontrollable) elements. A discretionary element is one that must be appropriated annually; thus, the Congress exercises maximum discretion over whether that element will be funded. A nondiscretionary element is one that is automatically appropriated unless there is specific legislation altering or rescinding the appropriation (Social Security is the best example). Nearly two-thirds of the discretionary money in the federal budget goes toward defense, meaning that attempts to increase, decrease, or alter the pattern of federal spending often begin with the defense budget. The infamous "sequester" that went into effect on March 1, 2013, came exclusively from discretionary, controllable budget elements, which explains why defense spending bore the large burden it did in this budget reduction exercise and why most defense advocates oppose the sequester (discussed below).

The political nature also reflects the impact of national security spending on Americans in two ways. Not only is a lot of money spent on defense, but those expenditures are made in many physical locales, wherever concentrations of military installations and defense industries are found. The competition for defense contracts and for the locations of bases or posts is a highly charged process wherein the financial health and prosperity of communities can be vitally affected by the effectiveness of congressional delegations in winning federal contracts for their states and districts.

The other impact is in the competition between defense and non-defense sectors for funding. It is an old saw of politics that "policy is what gets funded," and given the competition between national security and other priorities for funding (a subject elaborated on in Chapter 7), defense spending is highly politicized. The most familiar catchphrase by which this competition is depicted is in the "guns versus butter" debate about the advisability of allocating funds for either national security or social purposes.

The politics of national security is played out at various levels that come together in the budgetary process. One level is within the executive branch of government, where the representatives of various government agencies and functions compete for priority within federal policy, including the budget. This competition extends to the legislative branch, where the same kind of competition occurs within the various layers of the committee system in hammering out what budget the executive will ultimately have to spend. Ultimately, decisions involve the interaction of both branches of the government (a process in which the judiciary is rarely involved).

The Executive Branch

National security policy within the executive branch of the government operates on two separate tracks that are, in some ways, paralleled conceptually within the Congress. The day-to-day conduct of national security (as part of overall foreign policy) occurs within the federal agencies with authority in the field—such as the Department of State, the DOD, and the CIA—at the direction of the president. Policy decisions are coordinated and implemented through the *interagency process*, the chief vehicle of which has been the NSC and its subordinate bodies. New institutional actors, such as the Department of Homeland Security (DHS) and the DNI, are being integrated into this system. This process of policy development and implementation is conceptually similar to the role of the authorizing committees of the Congress. The other track is the competition for funding, which is at the heart of the budgetary process, and it pits parts of the national security community against one another and against competing functions of the government (see Amplification 6.2).

AMPLIFICATION 6.2

The President, the Constitution, and National Security

The US Constitution does not lay out an elaborate list of powers for the president in the area of national security or foreign policy, as noted. Specific powers are found in Article II of the Constitution, and essentially all are counterbalanced by contrary powers given to the Congress as part of the "checks and balances" system that characterizes the entire document. The result is an "invitation to struggle" (see Crabb and Holt) intended to make the two branches coequal in this area.

Chief Executive

In this capacity, the president is designated as the major presider over the executive agencies of the government, all of which report directly to the president. In the area of foreign and national security policy, these agencies include the Departments of State and Defense, the CIA, and the various economic agencies, including the Departments of the Treasury and Commerce and the US Trade Representative. These agencies collectively are the chief repositories of the expertise of the federal government on foreign matters, and the president's access to them provides an important advantage in dealing with foreign and national security matters.

Head of State

In this largely symbolic role, the president is designated as the chief representative of the US government to all foreign governments. This means, for

(*continued*)

instance, that officials of foreign governments (ambassadors, for example) are accredited to the president, and when the heads of other states interact with the US government, it is with the president or a representative of the president.

Commander in Chief

The president is designated as the commander in chief of the armed forces of the United States. This means, among other things, that he or she is the highest military official of the government to whom all members of the armed forces are subsidiary and that it is the president's authority to employ the armed forces in support of various public policies, including the commitment of force in combat (although this power is circumscribed by congressional limitation).

Treaty Negotiator

Only the president of the United States or his or her specified representative (known as plenipotentiary) is authorized to enter into negotiations with foreign governments leading to formal relationships and obligations on behalf of the US government. Although only a small percentage of agreements between the United States and foreign governments come in the form of formal treaties, this nonetheless sets the precedent for presidential leadership in all arrangements with foreign governments.

Nominator of Key Personnel

The president alone has the power to name key officials of his or her administration. The most important appointments are the cabinet members (the various secretaries of executive agencies), the members of the NSC, and the deputy and assistant secretaries, such as those who serve on the various committees of the NSC system.

Recognizer of Foreign Governments

Only the president has the authority to extend or remove formal recognition of foreign governments by the US government. This is one of the few powers of the president that does not require some form of formal supporting action by the Congress. ■

The Interagency Process

The interagency process has evolved since the Eisenhower administration in the 1950s implemented the National Security Act of 1947. The act was not specific about how the NSC would function, and both its structure and its operations have changed over time. Dwight Eisenhower used it extensively as a kind of military advisory board, and John F. Kennedy used it much less often. Lyndon Johnson expanded its use during the Vietnam War, and it began to take on its present form during the Nixon and Ford years. How it works at any time is largely a matter of presidential preference rather than legislative mandate. It has been a staple part of the national security process ever since, although President Trump has tended not to invoke it formally when making decisions. There is, for instance, no provision for a national security advisor (NSA) in the legislation, and that position has expanded from being a coordinator and office manager to being a major presidential advisor on foreign affairs. Similarly, there is no provision for a system of committees and subcommittees within the NSC structure, but that is what has evolved.

The modern NSC system began to congeal during the Eisenhower administration of the 1950s. Its present form as an interagency process came into being during the 1980s, and it is a fairly elaborate system. In addition to the four permanent members designated by the National Security Act, the White House chief of staff is normally always included in its deliberations, and on military matters, so are the CJCS and the NSA. The purpose of the NSC is purely advisory. The members offer advice to the president that he or she is free to accept or reject. No votes are ever taken, ensuring that the president will not feel obligated by what the majority may favor.

Directly below the NSC is the *Principals Committee (PC)*. This group has the same membership as the NSC itself, except that the president does not attend. There are two basic occasions when the NSC meets as the PC. If there are matters that do not require direct presidential involvement, the others may meet without him or her. At the same time, the president might occasionally absent himself or herself to facilitate a more frank exchange of views than might occur otherwise and when he or she feels the other members are unwilling to champion views they think the president might oppose. John F. Kennedy did not attend meetings during portions of the Cuban missile crisis when the PC was known as the ExComm (Executive Committee) because of fear his presence might dampen the range of debate over what to do in this crisis.

The next layer in the system is the *Deputies Committee (DC)*. As the name suggests, this group is comprised of the principal deputies of the members of the NSC. The meetings are traditionally chaired by the president's principal deputy for national security, the NSA. The DC is more of a working-level body, and its roles include formulating policy proposals for action by the NSC or PC and figuring out how to implement decisions made in those bodies. Other members of the DC include the undersecretary of state for political affairs, the undersecretary of defense for policy, the deputy director of national intelligence, and the vice chairman of the JCS.

The bottom layer of the process is the Interagency Policy Committees (IPCs). Formerly known as the *Policy Coordinating Committees (PCCs)*, this level was designated as the IPCs by the Obama administration. The dual purposes of the IPCs include oversight of the implementation of policy decisions made at higher levels in the process and formulation of proposals on policy as directed by the NSC, PC, or DC. Depending on the content under discussion, the IPCs are chaired by the NSA or the chair of the National Economic Council (NEC).

President Bill Clinton created the NEC by executive order in January 1993. It differed from the NSC in that it was not the product of legislation and thus could be dismantled without congressional action. Clinton gave it four charges that parallel the duties of the NSC: (1) to coordinate the economic policymaking process with respect to domestic and international economic issues; (2) to coordinate economic policy advice to the president; (3) to ensure that economic policy decisions and programs are consistent with the president's goals; and (4) to monitor implementation of the president's economic agenda.

The NEC was a prominent and important part of national security policy during the Clinton years and reflected the paramount importance of economic policy during the 1990s. The NEC was chaired personally by Clinton, and in addition, it had its own DC and staff capability through the Trade Policy Review Group and the Trade Policy Staff Committee. The first task assigned to the first director of the NEC, Robert Rubin (later secretary of the treasury), was Clinton's comprehensive budget reduction plan, which succeeded in balancing the budget in 1998, and the NEC was prominent in trade policy and multilateral negotiations on trade promotion. When he came to office in 2001, President George W. Bush threatened to do away with the NEC, but he retained it at a much lower level of visibility and with much less personal involvement.

The NEC became prominent again under President Obama as one of the two principal advisory groups to the president (along with the NSC). The spearhead of the NEC was Dr. Lawrence Summers, a prominent economic advisor from the Clinton years and former president of Harvard University, who was named director of the White House—based Council of Economic Advisors until he stepped down in 2011. It has retained prominence under President Trump.

The interagency process works largely the way the president wants it to operate. The NSC is assisted by the NSC staff, all of whom are members of the president's personal staff and thus not subject to congressional confirmation, review, or scrutiny. Because they serve at the president's pleasure, they are highly loyal to the chief executive and generally closely reflect the president's views. The degree to which the president utilizes this asset depends on presidential prerogative. Richard Nixon, for instance, had a long and deep-seated distrust of the State Department, which generally opposed Nixon's policies. As a result, he enlarged the NSC staff and used it in effect as an alternate State Department to ensure his policy preferences would be implemented. Presidents who are highly activist in foreign affairs, such as George H. W. Bush and Bill Clinton in his second term, relied heavily upon the NSC to carry out their desires, whereas those with less interest (such as Gerald Ford and George W. Bush) used the NSC less and relied more on the executive agencies to conduct policy on their own. The Obama administration's active engagement with the NSC system is symbolized by the level of his personal involvement in the killing of Osama bin Laden. The famous photograph of the president awaiting news of the success of the bin Laden attack includes all the important members of the NSC and the top NSC staff.

The Faceless Bureaucracy: The Hard Men

The constitutional and statutory bases of national security policy provide the parameters within which policymaking and implementation occur, but knowing them is insufficient for a full understanding of the politics that underlay that policy. Particularly in an area that can be arcane in content and that requires specialized knowledge and experience to navigate, much of the advice that shapes policy comes from individuals and groups that do not appear on any governmental organization chart but that are often the most important determiners of what policy actions the United States undertakes.

The people and institutions who compose the "faceless bureaucracy" of policy influencers are shadowy, amorphous, and controversial, and they have produced a growing interest among some largely revisionist analysts. Michael Glennon, borrowing from the work of Walter Bagehot, defines this group, which he designates the "double government," as "the shadow government of bureaucracy and a support network of think tanks, media insiders, and ambitious policy wonks." Some analysts add a more conspiratorial motive to the membership by including self-interested "experts" who personally benefit from governmental policy (see Bacevich and Kinzer, for example). Glennon defines this group as a "cohort of several hundred senior military, diplomatic, and intelligence officials who run the daily business of national security." Peter Dale Scott adds that they form a "second level of secret government" that lacks public accountability for their actions. More ominously, some refer to them as the "deep state."

One need not pass judgment about the motives of this group of people to acknowledge their existence and their level of influence. Washington is permeated with people who consider themselves—often with good reason—to be the real experts on national security and who believe the country is best off if it follows their advice. These experts are embedded in government agencies, on congressional staffs, in the national print and electronic media, as employees of corporations doing overseas business, as lobbyists, and as analysts in the think tanks. They are such a diverse collection that describing them as a "group" probably overstates reality. They share a philosophy that is staunchly realist and that deeply believes in the need for American resolution and forceful leadership. They are the hard men (and women) of national security decision making (a term the author introduced in *The Middle East, Oil, and the U.S. National Security Policy*).

This group is important to note for at least three reasons. The first is their origins. Demographics are changing gradually to alter their composition, but their senior leaders are by and large Cold Warriors whose education and formative experiences were as junior officials during the waning years of the Cold War. The second point is that this orientation, however implicitly it may be manifested in individual situations, makes them fundamentally conservative and prone to military solutions—an orientation that derives from their intellectual roots.

The third point is that these individuals do provide a useful and necessary role in the policy process. Their most fundamental value is the expertise they possess. Whether they were military officers doing tours of duty, government officials assigned to foreign posts, academics with area specializations, or businesspeople active in particular foreign settings, they bring a knowledge of foreign situations that elected officials often lack and without which policy would be more poorly informed.

These hard men and women are often veterans of the policy process who know how to influence and manipulate that process to get things they want done. They are the veterans who have "been there and done that" over a long period of time. They are the wise elders to whom many others defer, and when their advice is appropriate, they provide a real and necessary service.

They are also controversial. Their vantage point is one that cannot and should not be discounted, but it is also not the only perspective that may have merit in individual situations where the Cold War analogy is relevant. However, many areas where the United States is active (the Middle East, for instance) are not so clearly amenable to that framework. To provide the kind of advice relevant to these conditions, it may be necessary to nurture the development of a new generation of advisors—twenty-first century hard men—to counterbalance the current generation.

The Congress

The Constitution establishes the executive, legislative, and judicial branches as coequals in governing the country. As a matter of practice, the judicial branch does not involve itself in the national security policy process except in limited areas, such as the parameters of executive authority during times of war. In the area of national security, the "invitation to struggle" is largely between the president and the Congress. The basic principle involved in modulating this competition is checks and balances: for every executive power, there is a countervailing congressional power. Formal provisions specifically related to national security are summarized in Amplification 6.3.

AMPLIFICATION **6.3**

The Congress, the Constitution, and National Security

The US Constitution is also brief in its enumeration of congressional responsibility over foreign and national security affairs. The congressional powers are enumerated in Article I of the Constitution. Some of these are direct responses to and limitations upon presidential powers and others derive from the application of more general congressional authority to the national security arena.

Power of the Purse

The Constitution specifies that all authorization of the expenditure of public funds must be initiated in the House of Representatives and have the specific concurrence of both houses of the Congress. Particularly in the area of national security, this is a significant power because of the large amounts of money that are spent on national security and because most of those funds are controllable.

War-Making Power

The president is the commander in chief of the armed forces, but the Congress has important countervailing powers. The Congress sets the size and composition of the armed forces. The president can have no larger armed forces than the Congress authorizes. Moreover, the Congress is the only agency of government that can declare war. While this provision has been used only five times in the country's history, it remains a strong limitation on the president's practical ability to place American armed forces into combat or potential combat situations.

Confirmation of Officials

Presidential appointees to high offices in the administration (with the exception of the NSC staff, who are considered part of the president's personal staff and thus are exempt) are subject to confirmation by the US Senate. The purpose of this provision is to ensure the president does not appoint personnel who are personally obnoxious or politically objectionable in a policy sense. The president may, however, dismiss officials approved by the Senate without senatorial acquiescence.

(continued)

Ratification of Treaties

The president is the only official who can negotiate agreements with foreign governments, but treaties cannot take force until they have the positive advice and consent of two-thirds of the US Senate. This limitation is necessary because a ratified treaty is coequal to laws passed by the Congress. Because of the sheer volume of the relations between the United States and other governments, only a small portion of the dealings with other governments takes the form of treaties (executive agreements, which do not require senatorial ratification, are more common); however, most of the more important relationships are in the form of treaties. ■

The formal political process within the US Congress is theoretically simpler and more compact than that within the executive branch. The structure for considering the administration's budget request is more direct, for instance, consisting of three prescribed steps rather than the multiple steps in the formulation process within the executive branch. Compactness is also facilitated because the Congress does not have to develop a budget on its own. It theoretically only responds to a presidential request, which it can accept, reject, or modify. In practice, congressional groups often propose alternative budgets.

Other factors also influence this process. For instance, the two houses of Congress are in fact two large and often unruly committees, consisting of 100 highly independent senators and 435 equally independent members of the House of Representatives. Unlike the politically appointed officials of the executive branch, they are divided politically by party and by political philosophy. Moreover, the disposition of the defense budget is particularly important to individual members because defense dollars are spent in individual congressional districts and states. Members of Congress thus have an acute built-in self-interest in the outcomes. The result is quintessential politics.

The heart of congressional action in national security occurs largely through two mechanisms: the committee system and the budget process. The budget process is important because it produces the resources that fund efforts to ensure national security and thus provides much of the shape and nature of the national security effort. Because policy is so often what gets funded, the budget process is also intensely political, and control over power of the national security purse has become actively intense in recent years. It has become a central aspect of the "domestic battleground" that is explored in Chapter 7. Institutionally, much of the "action" within Congress has been on the committee system, although its role and dominance have been in decline in recent years.

The Committee System

Because of its size and consequent unwieldiness, the Congress does relatively little of its most important business acting as overall houses of Congress. The real, detailed business of the Congress is performed by the committee system, wherein smaller groups of senators and representatives, who have volunteered for the committees on which they serve, are supposed to hammer out congressional positions, draft and vote on legislation, oversee the activities of the executive agencies they parallel, and respond to presidential budgetary and policy initiatives. When the Congress is working properly (which it rarely has in recent years), the agreements that are reached by the committee are ratified by the overall memberships and, depending on concurrence between the houses and the president, become law.

One might reasonably ask why committees have been so important and powerful within the Congress. For one thing, the various committees (including their staffs) are the major repositories of congressional expertise in their areas of focus. Congressional members typically volunteer for committee assignments in which they or their constituents are interested or in which they have expertise. Thus, a congressional district with a large concentration of military facilities or defense contractors will produce congressional members who will develop an interest in and knowledge of defense matters because the outcomes of defense issues may affect their constituents. The longer members of Congress stay in the Senate or House and remain on the Armed Services Committees, for instance, the more expertise and seniority they acquire and the more influence they develop. The most prominent and knowledgeable members attain the status of congressional leaders in their area of expertise.

These experts—especially the chairs and the ranking members of the minority party (who become chairs if their party attains a majority)—become chief congressional spokespeople in their area of expertise. Members with less expertise than the experts have historically deferred to the judgments of these leaders (especially members of the same party) and have generally voted the way the chairs or ranking members recommend. The same is true of the major subcommittees of the major committees, where the chairs develop great expertise in their narrower subject area (military manpower, for instance). The key element in this process is the willingness of congressional rank-and-file to defer to their senior colleagues.

Another reason the committee system is so powerful is because of the smaller and more manageable size of committees compared to the full houses of Congress. It has often been said of the houses of Congress themselves that their size and organization make them great debating forums for the discussion of public policy but that they are so large and unwieldy as to be terrible places to frame and enact legislation. The major committees of Congress, normally with memberships of twenty or fewer members, are more compact and can give more thorough and knowledgeable consideration to matters of legislative review, including such things as calling for and considering the views of expert witnesses. The recommendations of the appropriate committees thus have a considerable impact on how the whole Congress acts on matters that come before it. To get a sense of what the Congress thinks about a given issue, the persons to listen to have historically been the appropriate committee's chair and its ranking member of the minority party.

Being the majority or minority party in Congress has particular importance in establishing control of the Congress. At the beginning of each congressional session, members of each house are assigned to committees in numbers reflecting their majority or minority status. In turn, the committees elect their chairs, almost invariably from the majority party or its allies. Barack Obama, the first sitting member of Congress to be elected president since John F. Kennedy in 1960, showed early deference to this system in his initial attempts to create bipartisanship for his ambitious reform package, but that spirit quickly dissipated as overwhelming levels of partisanship negated the collegiality on which the system has historically rested. President Trump largely ignores the system.

Challenges to Committee Dominance

The committee-dominated operation of Congress has been increasingly challenged in recent years. Part of the reason for this has been the rise in ideological partisanship within the electorate as reflected by its elected representatives. Younger and more ideologically distinct members have been increasingly unwilling to accept without question the direction of senior members, including chairs of their own and the opposing parties and even the top leadership of their respective parties. Some of the consequences of this rebellion on national security are explored in the next chapter.

All the factors contributing to this breakdown of traditional ways of operating within Congress are complex and often idiosyncratic. One reason junior members are generally less deferential than in the past, for instance, is because newer members are better educated than their predecessors and thus feel they know enough about issues to decide for themselves rather than needing to defer to others. This feeling is reinforced by the deluge of electronic information and punditry available on all sides of most issues.

The result has been to make the unruliness and unpredictability of Congress even greater than it was previously. Knowing which party has controlled each house of Congress and what the relevant committee chairs believed used to allow for a confident prediction of how Congress would act on different matters. The assault on the old order has reduced greatly that sense of orderliness and predictability, in the process reducing public perceptions of the governability of the country. A consensus on national security used to insulate this area of policy from much of the rough-and-tumble, but even that consensus has decreased.

WHY THEY CALL IT POLITICS: INSTITUTIONAL RESPONSES TO NATIONAL SECURITY CHALLENGES

National security, like all areas of governance, is quintessentially political. Because of its special importance and the large amounts of money spent on it, national security is one of the most important, revered areas of governance. That said, national security is also subject to all the foibles, missteps, and even misdeeds of other areas of public policy. Important parts of national security are handled inelegantly, and even if they are dealt with satisfactorily, they should be considered as products of an imprecise, messy process—what Robert Sherill captured in an evocative phrase a half century ago to evoke its nature—"why they call it politics." The homeland security debate of the immediate post-9/11 period and the budget process of 2011 that ended with the infamous sequester are examples of why the process is called politics.

Homeland Security

One of the most important questions raised after September 11, 2001, was the apparent institutional inadequacy of the US government to confront terrorism. After the attacks information became available that intimations of the impending assault had circulated at lower levels of the government before the actual events, and a planning document held over from the Clinton administration specifically warned about Al Qaeda (AQ). Despite this activity, the attacks came as an awful surprise, and it was reasonable both to ask why the United States government had failed to anticipate and act in advance and to raise questions about whether relevant parts of the government should be reorganized to prevent a recurrence.

The idea of homeland security arose from this examination to describe the problem and efforts to alleviate it. The problem is complex and ongoing. To frame it, three aspects of homeland security are examined: the historical evolution of concern with homeland security, its institutionalization as DHS through the Homeland Security Act of 2002, and ongoing problems of the effort.

Background and Evolution of the Problem

Although the term *homeland security* appeared abruptly after September 11 and seemed to be a very new kind of phenomenon, it is not. If homeland security is defined as that part of the national security effort focusing primarily on the protection of the physical territory and citizens of the United States, homeland security has been the major cornerstone of

American national security policy since the formation of the republic. The name may have been new; the function it describes is not.

The modern evolution of homeland security has proceeded along two policy tracks. The first is emergency management. Largely associated at the federal level with agencies like the Federal Emergency Management Agency (FEMA) and at the state and local levels with first responders like police and fire departments, it has had two major emphases: protection against and reaction to natural disasters (hurricanes, tornados, earthquakes, etc.) and man-made disasters. Emergency management problems were vividly illustrated by responses to Hurricanes Katrina and Rita in 2005.

Suppressing terrorism was added to the homeland security portfolio during the 1980s. During that decade the federal government undertook several actions to create federal antiterrorism and counterterrorism capabilities and to elevate and attempt to coordinate the efforts of the principal federal agencies with responsibility for terrorism: the CIA, the Federal Bureau of Investigation (FBI), and the Immigration and Naturalization Service (INS). INS functions are now assigned to DHS, and specifically to Immigration and Customs Enforcement (ICE). Operational responsibility for dealing with on-site efforts has remained at the state and local levels.

The two efforts remain parallel. Terrorism suppression is primarily a federal function, whereas emergency management is mostly state and local in execution. Operationally, the federal government is more interested in preventing disasters like terrorist attacks than in dealing with the consequences of natural disasters; the order of emphasis is reversed for the emergency managers.

The process of trying to organize the government to deal with homeland security matters began during the Reagan administration. In 1986, President Reagan issued National Security Directive (NSD) 207, which created the Interagency Working Group (IWG) under the NSC, designated the IWG as the mechanism to coordinate responses to terrorism, and established the lead agency designation (the federal agency with primary responsibility) of the State Department in international terrorism and the FBI for domestic terrorism.

During the 1990s, President Clinton issued Presidential Decision Directive (PDD) 39, with three emphases: preventing terrorist acts, responding to terrorist acts and provocations, and managing the consequences of terrorist attacks. The FBI was given broader responsibility domestically, including the formation of domestic emergency support teams (DESTs) to act in the event of significant problems. Clinton also authorized the suspension of *posse comitatus* (an 1869 law that prevents the use of the military for domestic police functions) during emergencies and designated FEMA to lead "consequence management" efforts.

The point of this discussion is that there was governmental activity in the area that has become homeland security for at least a decade and a half before September 11, 2001. Terrorism efforts were low-key and generally low priority as terrorism remained, for the most part, a peripheral concern for most Americans despite overseas instances of terrorist attacks against Americans and American facilities (the African embassy bombings of 1998, the attack on the USS *Cole* in Yemen in 2000) and domestically the partially successful 1993 attack on the World Trade towers (later linked to AQ) in New York.

The Homeland Security Response to September 11

The AQ attacks against New York and Washington instantly elevated homeland security to the heart of the national political process. The initial institutional reactions included the creation of a Homeland Security Council parallel in structure to the NSC, the establishment of an Office of Homeland Security, and the appointment of a director for the effort. Militarily, the DOD established a Northern Command (from the old Force Command) to coordinate military responses to threats against the American homeland. This process ultimately resulted in the passage of the Homeland Security Act of 2002, which President Bush lauded as the single most important and sweeping reorganization of government in fifty years (a comparison with the National Security Act of 1947). The DHS came into existence in 2003.

The initial response began with the creation of the Office of Homeland Security within the White House and the appointment of former Pennsylvania governor Tom Ridge as its director. Ridge was given a position conceptually based on that of the NSA. He was charged with rationalizing and coordinating improved government capabilities for dealing with terrorism.

In June 2002, the administration proposed a stronger institutional effort—the creation of the DHS. The new department, with full cabinet status, was legislated into being in November 2002 to perform four functions: border and transportation security; emergency preparedness and response; chemical, biological, radiological, and nuclear countermeasures; and information analysis and infrastructure protection. To accomplish its tasks, the president proposed pulling resources from several existing agencies and putting them under the control of the new department.

Virtually no one opposed either the general proposition of this effort or its implementation in principle. As is often the case, however, the devil proved to be in the details of implementation. The reorganization authorized by the act moved over 170,000 employees from twenty-two major federal agencies under the umbrella of DHS. Such a transfer is daunting, as many agencies, individuals, and organizations with contrasting work cultures and methods of operation and little or no tradition of interaction and coordination were suddenly thrust into positions in which they were expected to work as a team acting in a common effort. At the same time, there were significant "turf wars" over which agencies (and their budgets) found their way into DHS and which remained within their traditional homes. These political problems significantly spilled over into the oversight relationship between DHS and the Congress.

The first and most difficult problem was determining which agencies would become part of the new department and which would not. Three federal agencies have primary operational responsibility in the terrorism field, forming a kind of golden triangle of federal efforts. Ideally, the CIA had primary responsibility for discovering and monitoring the existence and activities of overseas terrorists; the INS (originally part of the Department of Justice, now ICE in DHS) had responsibility for monitoring and intercepting aliens entering the country; and the FBI (also part of Justice) monitored and arrested terrorists within the country. Within this relationship, the CIA would tell the INS who was attempting to enter the country, and the INS would then inform the FBI so it could begin its monitoring role. To maximize the likelihood for this relationship to be seamless and effective, it followed that all three agencies should have been included in DHS.

They are not. The INS and the Customs Service were made part of DHS, mostly because INS had so many political problems that Justice was glad to get rid of it, and designated it as ICE. The CIA and the FBI remain independent of DHS, directed only to coordinate with DHS. Why? Both the CIA and the FBI effectively argued that terrorism was only one part of their responsibilities. Virtually all the agencies that have been included in the new department could make the same argument, but the FBI and the CIA were sufficiently powerful that their arguments succeeded while others failed. In the process, of course, the traditional budgets of the FBI and the CIA were protected within the Justice Department. FEMA, also an independent agency created in 1979, was included in DHS, mostly because it lacked enough powerful supporters to block its inclusion.

The amalgamation of agencies into DHS has been analogized to a similar process that created the Department of Energy (DOE) in 1977. Both agencies share three major commonalities. First, they were both created as responses to national emergencies: the oil shocks of the 1970s led to a DOE and the terrorist attacks of 2001 to a DHS. Second, both departments represent attempts at government reform by rearranging the federal organization chart, pulling agencies and responsibilities out of existing structures and putting them under the umbrella of the new agency. Third, both agencies were created "on the cheap." The Bush administration initially argued that the DHS would require no added funding because resources would be made available by agencies contributing people and other assets to the DHS (which proved largely false). Underfunding remains a problem.

The oversight problem has proven especially arcane. Each function of the executive branch of government is overseen for programmatic and budgetary purposes by committees and subcommittees of the two houses of

Congress. The oversight function is a significant part of the power base of the members of Congress because it provides real clout in determining who receives and does not receive funding under whatever function they may control. As a result, members of Congress are quite jealous of their prerogatives with regard to oversight and resist the idea that a function over which they have some control might move to a committee created to oversee a new department like DOE or DHS, on whose committee they do not serve. Reform, in other words, threatened the power of members of Congress.

The result was a political fight at the expense of creating an effective and efficient DHS. The responsibilities of no fewer than eighty-eight committees and subcommittees in the two houses were affected by transfers into the new agency. When the DHS came into being in 2003, a survey showed that *all one hundred* senators and all but twenty members of the House were on committees whose jurisdictions were potentially affected by the reorganization. Everyone agreed in abstract principle that the new DHS would face the smoothest possible sailing if there was a single authorizing committee and a single appropriating committee in each house (which is the case for traditional departments) to which it reported, but the potential consequence of moving toward that ideal end would have been to erode the power of virtually every member of Congress by removing some power from a committee or subcommittee. This potential erosion of power has caused sufficient opposition to reform of the congressional part of the relationship that there is no committee in the Senate with homeland security as its sole responsibility and only a Committee on Homeland Security with largely symbolic value in the House of Representatives.

This problem extended to funding DHS. The Homeland Security Act was passed when President George W. Bush was pushing for additional tax cuts, and one consequence of this emphasis was that he did not want to appear to be increasing funding in other areas of the federal budget at a time when he was reducing revenues. The new mandates given DHS clearly required newly appropriated funds. The precedent, however, was set, and DHS attempts to gain additional resources have suffered from the albatross created by the original fiction that no new funds were needed.

Ongoing Problems and Controversies

Several ongoing questions and controversies have surrounded DHS. Two stand out: the tension within the agency between the federal and the state and local levels, with special attention to budgetary and political concerns, and the division of responsibilities between DHS and other agencies, of which Katrina relief was an example.

The first problem centers on the mission and political emphases of DHS terrorism efforts. The stated intention of the homeland security legislation was to elevate this function above the political fray, but it has not been altogether successful. The reason is that setting priorities and emphases has budgetary implications, and that means politics inevitably intrudes.

This question of emphasis has come to center on the debate over relative emphasis on combating and preventing attacks against the United States (the federal emphasis) and on emergency management by first responders (the state and local emphasis). Originally, the pattern was for the federal government to mandate actions by the states and localities, for which they were to find funds on their own (unfunded mandates). As concern with avoiding new spending ebbed, however, funding became available for the first responders, mostly in the form of equipment grants and funding for emergency plans. The availability of these kinds of funds provided opportunities for members of Congress to endear themselves to their constituencies by gaining funding for new ambulances, fire trucks with hazardous materials (hazmat) capabilities, and police capabilities.

Conflicting DHS mandates have also been a problem. Responding to natural disasters at the federal level has been the chief responsibility of FEMA since its creation in 1979 (it was created in response to inadequate responses that year to hurricanes). When it was folded into DHS, that first-responder role was redefined as response to terrorist attacks, such as coordinating efforts for catastrophes like biological or chemical attacks. In the process, emergency relief for natural disasters was deemphasized, leaving the agency deficient in supplies and personnel to deal with an event like Hurricane Katrina or the 2017 hurricanes in Puerto Rico.

Despite its problems, the DHS effort continues and has enjoyed considerable apparent success. There have not been any successful foreign terrorist attacks against American soil since 9/11, and at least some of the credit must go to DHS. Ironically, the very secrecy in which it operates makes a public evaluation of its success impossible since one cannot assess whether it has foiled plots and attacks that failed and were not reported in detail.

The Sequester

The national security establishment prides itself in being non-political, and yet it is at the heart of the most intensely political activity of government, the budget. Funding defense is expensive and currently consumes directly around one-fifth of federal spending (it is more if items not listed in the Department of Defense budget are included). Its vulnerability is increased because so much of its funds are discretionary, making it more vulnerable to manipulation than items like entitlements, which are part of the uncontrollable budget.

Those involved in national security have an inherent ambivalence about defense budgets. On the one hand, they uniformly support a robust defense posture to reduce risks to the country, which suggests the need for large amounts of funding for defense. At the same time, it is classically conservative, meaning it also advocates fiscal responsibility. Former President Dwight D. Eisenhower was a very strong advocate of this position in the 1950s (see *Challenge!* box); his basic message was that a balanced budget was the key element in a secure condition for the country. At the same time, national security practitioners, like other Americans, enjoy the benefits of entitlement programs. Ambivalence is built into the situation.

The result of this interaction can sometimes reach bizarre proportions, as it did in 2011. In that year, the Congress was concerned about mounting government deficits, many of which were the result of government stimulus spending to reverse the 2008 recession. To try to align government revenues and expenditures more closely, it passed something called the Budget Control Act, the heart of which was to create lower spending that would reduce the growth in the deficit by $1.2 trillion during the decade of its existence. Congress enthusiastically approved the principle; they could not agree on what should be cut from the budget to achieve it.

The legislation anticipated this gridlock with a provision to force the two houses and parties to find a solution in the form of a committee composed of equal members from each party from the House and Senate, something that came to be known as the Super Committee. Its composition meant that if members from both parties voted along strictly partisan lines, the result would be a tie that would produce no agreement, and that is exactly what they did.

The bizarre aspect of this episode was that the Budget Control Act anticipated this possibility and made provision for it. The provision was that if agreement proved elusive, the amounts necessary to meet deficit reduction goals would automatically be taken out of the discretionary items in the budget, a formula that meant defense and non-defense budgets would have to absorb about half the reductions each. This consequence was deemed to be so odious and unacceptable by both the congressional leadership and the Obama White House that it would certainly force the government to agree to a formula acceptable to all. The most unacceptable part of the automatic provision was the amount national security spending would be cut. Since it did not produce an agreement, defense suffered, even though no one particularly wanted it to do so. These automatic cuts were nicknamed the sequester. They went into effect in 2013 and are scheduled to continue until 2021. Under the guidelines, defense budgets have been or will be cut by a little under 10 percent annually.

The sequester was suspended for 2018 and 2019 by a budget agreement between the Trump administration and Congress as part of an agreement to keep the government open until September 2018. Under sequestered appropriations, the Department of Defense was set to receive $651 billion.

Was President Eisenhower Right?

Much of President Eisenhower's conviction that national security requires a balanced budget demonstrates the difference between the 1950s and today. The idea of balanced budgets and their importance to national health was a hallmark of the traditional conservatism of the Republican Party, an emphasis that is now only consistently advocated by a few members of the GOP. The Republican Party still argues for limited government, but its emphasis is on tax reductions, even if they produce deficit.

The change also reflects the national security environments then and now. The Cold War was at its zenith when Eisenhower was in office, and it was both a nuclear military and an economic battle between contrasting economic philosophies. Winning the economic battle was important and reflected basic economic beliefs. Eisenhower had decided to base US military strategy on the threat of nuclear weapons: the United States would retain the option to execute a nuclear response for a wide variety of provocations. The New Look, as it was called, had the added virtue in Ike's mind of being far cheaper than maintaining large manpower-intensive conventional forces. These positions made sense in the 1950s. Would they again? ■

At Trump's insistence, that appropriation was increased to $700 billion, as a result effectively (but not officially) rescinding the guidelines established in 2011. This action increased the ability to cover more security contingencies; it also increased the deficit and the accumulated national debt.

CONCLUSION: THE CONTEMPORARY ENVIRONMENT

Through constitutional provisions and evolved practice, the American political system has developed ways of dealing with national security problems that are part of the context within which the country views these concerns. The institutions and views have evolved and changed as the national condition has changed, but the bedrock institutions of the American political system remain as conceptual pillars within which the adaptation to a changing environment occurs.

Thinking about and dealing with the national security environment was set on its head by the events of September 11, 2001. Suddenly, a mostly benign and tranquil environment was revealed to have a very dark and hostile side that had heretofore been an abstract concern but was suddenly very real. Before the attacks on major symbols of American military and financial power, the only instances of foreign-inspired and foreign-committed acts had been small and relatively primitive. The scale of the 2001 attacks and the enormous loss of life revealed a level and quality of vulnerability that few Americans had imagined in their worst nightmares. The body politic was thrown into convulsion about how it could have happened, how it could be avoided in the future, and how to punish those behind the atrocity. How and to what extent this shock has reshaped the national security equation and how government has responded to it are explored in the pages that follow.

STUDY/DISCUSSION QUESTIONS

1. What is the National Security Act of 1947? Why was it necessary? What are its principal provisions? Why are they important today?
2. What are the constitutional powers provided to the executive branch in the area of national security? What are the congressional powers? Compare and contrast them.
3. What is the interagency process? Discuss its structure and its role in the national security decision-making process.
4. Why has the relationship between Congress and the executive changed since the 2006 election? Do you think divided government (different parties controlling the legislative and executive branches) or unified government (one party controlling both branches) better serves the national security of the country? Why?
5. The major political response to September 11 domestically has been the creation of the Department of Homeland Security. Discuss the process leading to the formation of the DHS, its structures (including those agencies included and excluded), and the difficulties associated with the new agency.
6. What are the major ongoing controversies surrounding homeland security? Discuss each.
7. What is the sequester? How and why did it come about? What is its status? What does it say about national security politics?

SELECTED BIBLIOGRAPHY

9/11 Commission. *The 9/11 Commission Report: Final Report of the National Commission on Terrorist Attacks upon the United States.* Authorized ed. New York: W. W. Norton, 2004.

9/11 Public Discourse Project. *Report on 9/11 Commission Recommendations.* Washington, DC: Public Discourse Project, December 5, 2005.

Ackerman, Bruce. *Before the Next Attack: Preserving Civil Liberties in an Age of Terrorism.* New Haven, CT: Yale University Press, 2006.

Bacevich, Andrew C. *Washington Rules: America's Path to Permanent War.* New York: Metropolitan Booms, 2010.

Berkowitz, Peter (ed.). *The Future of American Intelligence.* Palo Alto, CA: Stanford University Press, 2006.

Clarke, Richard. *Against All Enemies: Inside America's War on Terror.* New York: Free Press, 2004.

Crabb, Cecil V., Jr., and Pat Holt. *Invitation to Struggle: Congress, the President, and Foreign Policy.* 2nd ed. Washington, DC: CQ Press, 1984.

Englehart, Tom. *Shadow Government: Surveillance, Secret Wars, and a Global Security State in a Single Superpower World.* Chicago, IL: Haymarket Books, 2014.

Fishel, John T. *American National Security Policy: Authorities, Institutions, and Cases.* Lanham, MD: Rowman & Littlefield, 2017.

Flynn, Stephen. *America the Vulnerable: How Our Government Is Failing to Protect Us from Terrorism.* New York: Harper Perennial, 2005.

———. "The Neglected Home Front." *Foreign Affairs* 83, 5 (September/October 2004), 20–33.

Fullilove, Michael. "All the President's Men." *Foreign Affairs* 94, 2 (March/April 2005), 13–18.

Glennon, Michael J. *National Security and Double Government.* New York: Oxford University Press, 2014.

Hillyard, Michael J. "Organizing for Homeland Security." *Parameters* 32, 1 (Spring 2002), 75–85.

Hilsman, Roger. *The Politics of Policy Making in Defense and Foreign Affairs: Conceptual Models and Bureaucratic Politics.* 3rd ed. Englewood Cliffs, NJ: Prentice-Hall, 1993.

Irwin, Paul M., and Larry Nowels. *FY 2006 Supplemental Appropriations: Iraq and Other International Activities, Additional Katrina Hurricane Relief.* Washington, DC: Congressional Research Service, March 10, 2006.

Johnson, Loch. *Bombs, Bugs, Drugs, and Thugs: Intelligence and America's Quest for Security.* New York: New York University Press, 2000.

Kettl, Donald L. *System under Stress: Homeland Security and American Politics.* Washington, DC: CQ Press, 2004.

Kinzer, Stephen. *The Brothers: John Foster Dulles, Allen Dulles, and Their Secret World War.* New York: Times Books, 2013.

Lehrer, Eli. "The Homeland Security Bureaucracy." *Public Interest* 256 (Summer 2004), 71–85.

Maxwell, Bruce (ed.). *Homeland Security: A Documentary History.* Washington, DC: CQ Press, 2004.

McMaster, Herbert R. *Dereliction of Duty: Lyndon Johnson, Robert McNamara, the Joint Chiefs of Staff, and the Lies That Led to Vietnam.* New York: Harper Perennial, 1997.

Mulligan, Stephen P. *Withdrawal from International Agreements: Legal Framework, the Paris Agreement, and the Iran Nuclear Agreement.* Washington, DC: Congressional Research Service, February 9, 2017.

Nakayama, Andrea C. (ed.). *Homeland Security.* Detroit, MI: Greenhaven Press, 2005.

Rothkopf, David J. "Inside the Committee That Rules the World." *Foreign Policy* (March/April 2005), 30–41.

Scott, Peter Dale. *The American Deep State: Big Money, Big Oil, and the Struggle for U.S. Democracy.* Lanham, MD: Rowman & Littlefield, 2017.

Sherrill, Robert. *Why They Call It Politics: A Guide to American Government.* 6th ed. Boston: Wadsworth, 1999.

Smyrl, Marc E. *Conflict or Codetermination? Congress, the President, and the Power to Make War.* Cambridge, MA: Ballinger, 1988.

Snow, Donald M. *Cases in International Relations: Principles and Applications.* 7th ed. Lanham, MD: Rowman & Littlefield, 2018.

———. *The Middle East, Oil, and the U.S. National Security Policy: Intractable Conflicts, Impossible Solutions.* Lanham, MD: Rowman & Littlefield, 2016.

——— and Patrick J. Haney. *American Foreign Policy.* 2nd ed. Lanham, MD: Rowman & Littlefield, 2017.

Spar, Karen. *Budget "Sequestration" and Selected Program Exceptions and Special Rules.* Washington, DC: Congressional Research Service, March 22, 2013.

Stuart, Douglas T. *Creating the National Security State: The Law That Transformed America.* Princeton, NJ: Princeton University Press, 2008.

Thornberry, Mac, and Andrew A. Krepinevich, Jr. "Preserving Primacy: A Defense Strategy for a New Administration." *Foreign Affairs* 95, 5 (September/October 2017), 26–35.

Turner, Robert F. *The War Powers Resolution: Its Implementation in Theory and Practice.* Philadelphia, PA: Foreign Policy Research Institute, 1983.

Yingling, Paul (Lt. Col.). "A Failure in Generalship." *Armed Forces Journal* (online), (May 2007).

Domestic Battlegrounds and National Security

National security policy has become controversial in recent years to an extent not seen since the end of the Cold War. The unifying effect of 9/11 has faded, the impact of the 2008 recession has largely been absorbed, and the Trump presidency has added confusion to the definitions of what policies and actions enhance or detract from the country's safety while residues like Iraq and Afghanistan, both of which have been very expensive and yielded very marginal returns, continue. This crisis and reexamination are occurring in a particularly difficult domestic environment of political deadlock on all government priorities, including those surrounding national security. The dynamics of domestic politics, combined with changes in the international threat environment, will affect the shape and direction of American national security policy in the upcoming years.

National security became intimately entwined in the hyper-partisan domestic political debate over deficit reduction during the summer of 2011. Questions about national security policy were part of the overall political dialogue before that date, mainly centering on issues such as the wisdom, desirability, and timing of American withdrawal from the wars in Iraq and Afghanistan (and indirectly about whether the United States should have undertaken either). To a smaller extent, it was also over matters connected to defense budgeting, such as the desirability of additional large expenditures for new, expensive weapons systems. Such disagreements were moderated by the continuing consensus in support of national security that developed during the Cold War and that was accentuated by the national reaction to the terrorist attacks of 2001.

The 2011 political tsunami that washed over the defense area was the partisan debate over budget deficit reduction that swept through Washington and became the lightning rod for the very basic differences dividing Democrats and Republicans. The flashpoint of this flood of concern was the large budget deficits that began during the Bush administration and were accelerated by the Obama response to the "Great Recession of 2008." All political factions agreed (with varying enthusiasm) that reducing the deficit was the major priority of the political system, a sentiment with which a majority of the public concurred. The politicians and the public were not in such basic agreement on how to accomplish this reduction, however.

The ensuing debate can be traced to very basic questions about the role of government in society. The Preamble of the Constitution sets the parameters of debate, stating that two of the most basic purposes of the US government are the "pursuit of the common defense" and "the promotion of the general welfare." In programmatic terms, most of the national budget is devoted to one or another of these functions. Of the two, expenditures on programs designed for and justified as promoting the general welfare have expanded the most both in concept and in appropriations, largely driven by increases in the expense of so-called entitlements, such as Social Security and medical care (i.e., Medicare and Medicaid).

The crisis that has come to dominate the political system is that the government currently does not have enough revenue to pay for the cost of all the services it purchases. In 2011, for instance, government revenues (receipts derived from one form of taxation or another) were adequate to cover only about sixty cents on the dollar of government expenses. To meet its obligations, the government had to borrow the other forty cents. The political unacceptability of this situation became virtually universal, and widespread agreement grew that something had to be done to halt the continuing dependence of the government on deficit spending. The basic question was where to find the other forty cents so the government can pay for all its obligations. A chasm of political disagreement developed on that question.

National security emerged as a derivative, not a central, concern within the general deficit reducing/budget balancing battle between the two major American political parties. In military terms, the national defense arena became *collateral damage* (an unintended and unintentional consequence of the broader battle). Both parties agree on the centrality of the national security enterprise and pledge an unfailingly strong defense against the country's enemies. There are partisan differences between them, but their basic fealty to national security is not a point of contention.

The question that draws national security onto the partisan battlefield is from what sources must reductions in the national budget be found in order to reach the grail of deficit reduction or elimination: where does the missing forty cents come from? More specifically, the question is the extent to which national defense spending will participate in the more general austerity necessary to bring national accounts more closely into balance.

National security enters the debate and proposed solutions obliquely. National security was not the root cause of the current malaise. It can be argued that expenditures taken in the name of national defense—notably the commitment to fight wars in Iraq and Afghanistan without accompanying increases in taxation or reduction in other programs—helped turn the budget surpluses of the last years of the Clinton administration into the large and burgeoning deficits that have accumulated since, but these were contributory and not basic causes. Moreover, one can argue that the current indebtedness the United States is building with former adversaries like China may compromise national defense in the future or even, as President Dwight D. Eisenhower argued forcefully in the 1950s, that a balanced budget is the foundation of a truly secure country. Each of these assertions has some merit.

DYSFUNCTIONAL DOMESTIC POLITICS

The current domestic crisis is largely the result of the breakdown of the domestic political consensus over how and toward what ends to govern the United States and how to pay for what government does. One of the major manifestations of this change is the large-scale disappearance of the moderate political middle within the spectrum and its replacement by increasingly ideological political parties of both the right and the left, neither of which is willing to engage in significant political compromise in the name of the governmental consensus on what forms the greater good. The political center, the "moderates" within the political spectrum, have virtually disappeared as the critical element that could broker disagreements from the more ideologically committed and diametrically opposed actors within both political parties and within large segments of the electorate.

The victim has been the ability to compromise on important issues, which has historically been at the heart of successful reconciliation of the competing interests found in the population and among its representatives. The refusal to countenance compromise has become a virtual badge of honor within the so-called base of the Republican Party. Its symbol has been the refusal to even consider so-called revenue enhancements mostly in the form of new taxes to attack the size of budgetary deficits and thus accumulated government indebtedness (debt).

The outcomes of this political warfare are familiar. One is *hyperpartisanship*, the pursuit and loyalty to political ideas expressed along partisan political lines to the virtual exclusion of the vigorous exploration of policy solutions across party lines. Party discipline has increasingly congealed along ideological, liberal/conservative lines in which the willingness even to consider ideologically impure ideas is considered disloyal, even heretical. In the process, compromise has become a virtual dirty word that engenders the scorn of true believers.

The result has been *gridlock* in conducting the country's business. The US government has not passed and implemented a full national budget since 2009, instead being forced to finance governmental operations by a series of continuing resolutions that fund operations at existing levels for short, defined periods that must periodically be renewed and extended during the year. The consequence is government. This dynamic is discussed in Amplification 7.1.

AMPLIFICATION 7.1

Policy by Continuing Resolution and Supplemental Appropriation

In the gridlocked political environment, two historical methods have come to dominate how the government funds itself. One is the use of continuing resolutions that evade the need to compromise inherent in adopting federal budgets. The other is supplemental appropriations to create the illusion of spending money but not adding to deficits.

Continuing resolutions are a device by which the Congress agrees to go on funding the federal government without passing a new budget to do so. These resolutions typically extend for a short period of time. The temporary budget of 2018 that effectively suspended the sequester is an example. It is an exercise that must be repeated frequently, but it avoids disagreements over possible changes in spending priorities. It also means that very few basic changes in priorities can occur since these would require a new budget with new priorities.

Supplemental appropriations allow the spending of federal funds outside the federal budget. It is a venerable practice long employed and intended to allow federal responses to national disasters requiring an immediate federal response (e.g., Hurricane Katrina relief). These expenditures do not appear in the federal budget and thus do not become an official part of the deficit when funds are not appropriated to pay for them (which they have not been in recent years). The use of supplemental appropriations for the "normal" operation of government became prominent in financing the wars in Iraq and Afghanistan. This "off budget" method allows Congress to respond to national security concerns without appearing to add to deficits or having to find ways to add revenues to pay for these expenses. Additionally, however, the need for supplemental appropriations several times a year means the Congress can use this necessity to threaten to shut down the government by refusing to pass the supplemental appropriations that allow it to continue spending public monies. ■

Hyper-partisan Politics: Everything Is Contentious

The evolution of the sequester introduced in Chapter 6 exemplifies the state of domestic politics. There was not great optimism or enthusiasm for the committee's charge or prospects at the time it was formed. The committee's charge was arguably unduly modest since projected revenue shortfalls (deficits) were predicted to accumulate to a much larger debt over the decade of the implementation of its targeted goal of $1.2 trillion (most deficit estimates were in the range of $4–6 trillion for the period). Thus, the conceptual task of the Super Committee was arguably more symbolic than substantive in terms of solving the national problem. At that, there was not great optimism that a compromise could be obtained to allow even a minimal majority (the six members of one party plus one member from the other party) behind any specific proposals supported by one party or the other. Indeed, the language used to describe such possibilities tended to be phrased in poisonous terms, such as whether there would be a "defection" from the solid ranks of each party's contingent. In the end, there were no partisan "traitors," and the membership remained steadfast behind an ideological impasse that resulted in failure.

The failure of the Super Committee clearly demonstrated that Congress and the president both bore responsibility for the public disapproval for the ongoing state of political affairs, and leadership from either side had not been exemplary in attacking and solving the problem. Fairness dictates, however, that the responsibility also lies with the greater public, which is also noticeably divided on the same issues that define the hyper-partisan gridlock in Washington. As numerous observers have pointed out, the country elected both the president and the current members of Congress, presumably because it is as conflicted as its representatives about national policy direction.

Two points of context should be made. The first is that the contemporary trend in government deficits really goes back to the earliest years of the Bush administration, where a combination of reductions in taxes and the costs of the wars in Iraq and Afghanistan transformed the government budget surpluses of the end of the Clinton presidency into large and growing off-budget deficits. This situation is conceptually similar to the mid-1960s, when a Democratic president (Lyndon Johnson) and the Democratic Party–controlled Congress chose to fund the entitlement programs of the Great Society like Medicare and the Vietnam War without raising taxes to pay for them. In the 2000s, the witches' brew was tax reductions, greater entitlement spending (notably Medicare drug benefits), and two wars. The Democrats, of course, emphasize this root cause of the problem, and Republicans argue subsequent Democratic actions have made it far worse. The other point is that the current crisis also has deeper roots in philosophical divisions between the parties that predate the current situation. The movement of both parties away from the center goes back more than a decade, and although the current impasse accentuates those differences, it has not caused them so much as reflected them. It is probably worth noting, however, that American involvement in major military conflicts and budget deficits has tended to coincide since the end of World War II, and this coincidence is probably in some measure the result of wartime administrations not wanting to draw special attention to the military adventures by proposing to raise taxes or reduce spending on other programs to pay for these commitments.

Political Gridlock and the Entrapment of National Security

The current debate that has ensnared the national security enterprise in its web centers on the general gridlock that pervades politics generally, not on inherent disagreements about national security or even funding for it (although these do exist at the margins). The national security establishment per se is not a central player in this malaise. Rather, its contribution is indirect. The wars in Afghanistan and Iraq have been extremely costly, and thus national security is a part of the problem. At the same time, the parameters of economies necessary to reduce deficits is so enormous that it is difficult to conceptualize how it can be accomplished without some meaningful participation by the national security establishment through reductions in the amount of resources available to fund the national security enterprise. Only those who are basically isolationist question the need for robust defense forces, especially those resources that must be employed in distant locations arguably not in defense of American interests. The overwhelming majority in both parties agree on the need for a vigorous commitment to common defense and to the generous allocation of resources to guarantee the ample security of the United States against its enemies.

This basic agreement is not all encompassing, and there is disagreement at the peripheries of the public consensus. Three are worth mentioning because they will recur in later discussions. The most basic form of dissent is over the underlying nature of the threat and thus what levels of resource commitment are necessary to keep Americans safe from foreign harm. As reflected in the discussion of threats and risks in Chapter 2, it centers on the psychological dimension of security (what makes people *feel* safe, a matter of disagreement). As a budgetary matter, more expansive views of the threat are obviously more expensive than narrower views.

A second form of dissent comes from what are viewed by many as inefficiencies in the way national security dollars are spent. In the 1980s, concerns arose around so-called waste, fraud, and abuse of budgetary resources, and there is a lingering belief that there is considerable "fat" in the budget that can be pared in ways similar to attempts to make other parts of the budget leaner. This argument is emphasized as budget cutters search for places to make reductions in expenditures. The third concern, which is relatively new, is the fear that the national security sector is accumulating dangerous levels of continuing costs that will be a drain on future resources and thus budget balances. The most frequent source of these concerns surrounds long-term health care, both medical and psychological, for returning veterans of the wars in Iraq and Afghanistan. Exactly how these expenses will be met is a matter of ongoing concern.

What is possibly most notable about the issues surrounding the commitment of national resources to security is that none of them question or attack, at least before Trump, core assumptions about the role and commitment of the country to national security. The expense of the wars of the twenty-first century has contributed to budgetary deficits, but no one is placing the primary blame for those deficits at the doorstep of the national security enterprise. National security becomes entwined in the entire budget cutting exercise basically for two reasons that have little to do with security per se. One reason is the argument that the budget deficit is so great that it is impossible to achieve the goal of budgetary balance without reducing resources currently committed to national security: a balanced budget is impossible without cuts to the defense budget as part of the eventual deal.

The second reason is one of budgetary equity. Reductions in government spending must clearly be a large part of any scheme to balance the budget, and the question of where those reductions must come from amounts to a competition between the constitutional mandates of the common defense and the general welfare. Virtually everyone agrees that some portion of this burden must come from expenditures on the largest category of general welfare, entitlements. Clearly, cuts in either defense or entitlements will reduce the resources available to constituents of either category.

National security is not a primary cause of the budgetary crisis, but the resolution of the crisis may have major consequences on national security efforts depending on the extent to which resources devoted to national security become included in budget cuts to reduce deficits. Most experts believe that defense appropriations will be a real part of any scheme to reconcile government expenditures and revenues. The impact of reductions on national security will be one of the considerations in structuring those outcomes, but it may or may not be a controlling factor in how that outcome is shaped. In all likelihood, the national security effort will have to cope with consequences for its mission based on decisions that have budgetary savings rather than national security as their primary driving element.

The result is likely to be intermestic politics at its most basic and pure level. The budgetary debate has some international concerns, such as the vibrancy of the United States in the world economy and indebtedness to China, but it is at heart a domestic policy consideration both substantively and politically. Substantively, it is about how the American government collects and spends public monies; politically, it is about how the impacts of various substantive outcomes resonate with the voting public. National security, on the other hand, is primarily concerned with the international environment and external threats to the United States. Since it is a primary recipient of government revenues, however, it is and always has been a part of the domestic political calculation as well.

The Trump Factor

The advent of the Trump administration's approach to national security has been, to put it mildly, unorthodox. Trump has been broadly supportive of the defense establishment, advocating increases in the defense budget (the 2018 increase was largely at his insistence), the call for a massive military parade in Washington, DC, and even his proposal for a new American armed force, the Space Command. At the same time, his views on more conventional policy areas like those dealing with NATO and Russia have been extraordinarily controversial and would have created a spirited bipartisan debate in less confrontational times. The firestorm over Trump's Helsinki summit with Russia's Vladimir Putin, and his embrace of Putin's position on meddling in the 2016 election in contravention to established policy and the unanimous recommendations of the professional national security, are examples.

NATIONAL SECURITY AND DOMESTIC POLITICS

National security has not always been a primary player in the American policy or budgetary scene. For most of American history, the country devoted scant resources to peacetime national defense and security, and it was not until the aftermath of World War II that it seemed necessary for the United States to devote considerable, sustained amounts of national treasure to defending the country from outside threats. The context, of course, was the Cold War. The fear that drove that change was the protracted military competition with communism.

The Cold War setting prejudiced the American political system in favor of large and constant allocations of national resources to a robust defense. Such a priority was easily justified in the face of a menacing, strong, and implacable opponent, and over the forty-plus years of the Cold War, the United States developed the precedent for generally blanket support for military priorities as necessary adjuncts to national safety. That general attitude has survived the Cold War and the very different environment of a post–Cold War world. In a post–Cold War environment, national security is now subject to more of the rough-and-tumble of government than it previously was.

A balanced budget was once a talisman of the American political system. The country's first major deficit spending occurred during World War II, and the Cold War priority created deficits highlighted by spending on the Vietnam War while simultaneously implementing major entitlement programs. When combined with major tax cuts during the Reagan years, deficit continued through the end of the Cold War. The last president to balance the budget was Clinton in 1998. Regular deficits returned with George W. Bush's war on terrorism (notably wars in Iraq and Afghanistan) and his tax cuts. These were followed by Obama deficits created by the need to recover from the 2008 recession. Since the government has operated by continuing resolution since 2009, deficits have become institutionalized and have not been challenged by the Trump administration.

At the heart of the politics by which these alternatives are worked out is the budgetary process. It is a special case because of the intricacies, size, and complications that are associated with defense funding, and the discussion in this section begins with a brief review of the budgetary process and the problems associated with it. At the heart of the debate is the historic sanctimony of national security spending, and the discussion will thus move to the nature of the special position national security spending has had in that process and how it has eroded.

Defense Budgeting

The defense budget has been among the most invulnerable, even sacrosanct, elements within the federal budget. There are two basic reasons for this: the perceived necessity of adequately funding such an important mission of government and the complexity and incomprehensibility of the defense budget. The nature of the threat has made attacks on the defense budget seem unwise, even unpatriotic; the complexity of the budget had made it difficult to find ways to assault it. At the same time, the very large size of the national security budget makes it an inviting target for the budgeter's axe when questions of economy loom.

The critical nature of the mission of providing for the common defense in a hostile environment has insulated the national security sector from criticism on budgetary grounds. During the Cold War, the specter of the "Russian bear" offered such a frightening, physically menacing image that even the suggestion of limiting funds for defense was met with dire warnings that doing so would leave the country in perilous danger. The same arguments based in the communist threat that were quite successful during the forty-year confrontation with that system continue to dominate the core appeal for defense spending in the contemporary context where the problems and the financial aspects of their solution are not so obvious. The environment remains perilous, but the exact nature and budgetary means to deal with it have changed in ways that have not entirely been understood in the policy community. Policy is simply not as simple as it was during the Cold War: there is no Russian bear today.

The other source of resistance to reductions in defense spending arises from the complexity of the defense budget. Both the process and outcomes are complex to the point of being incomprehensible for most Americans, so much so that most feel inadequate or incompetent to assess or assail it. Although most will not admit it, this level of incomprehension extends to members of Congress and other actors in the political process who lack either mastery of the process or its outputs adequate to offer meaningful, real criticisms. Many defense actors like it this way because it shields them from levels of scrutiny policymakers in other areas must endure. Like the physical conduct of war, there is a strong tendency to leave the budget "to the generals."

Budget process procedures are extremely arcane and difficult to describe or to master. That process includes a long and convoluted process within the Department of Defense (DOD) that ultimately produces requests for budgetary allocations from the political system. This process includes executive branch requests within the overall federal budget, a legislative process that consists both of congressional response and reaction to executive budgets, and attempts to reconcile differences between the two houses of Congress and between Congress and the executive branch.

These processes can be presented in the form of a thumbnail sketch. It greatly simplifies the extremely complicated and detailed process, but nonetheless the budget process can be thought of in terms of four historically sequential steps: the formulation of the defense budget as part of the executive branch request for funding each year; the reaction to and enactment of a budget by Congress; the reconciliation of differences between the executive request and congressional predilections; and expenditures of funds appropriated by the process. Each step contains multiple sub-steps. Since a full federal budget has not been approved since 2009, the process is partially hypothetical since it is devoted almost exclusively to reallocating the basic amounts contained in the previous year's budget.

Formulating the Budget   For simplicity's sake, budget requests can be thought of as consisting of two separate actions. The first consists of the formulation of a budget request within the defense establishment for presentation to the president for modification and incorporation into the overall federal budget request. Because the Defense Department is a large organization with multiple forms of organization (by military department, for instance), this internal DOD process consists of formulating budgetary requests by the various services, which must be reconciled and aggregated into a coherent and reasonable request. Typically, this process begins two and a half years before the year in which the budget will be spent. Thus, planning for the fiscal year (FY) 2020 budget, funds from which begin to be spent in October 2020, began in early 2016. This process produces a budget request that is presented to Congress the following year for enactment and implementation beginning at the end of the following year. This long lead time means the DOD is concurrently dealing with three budgets at any point in time: the budget being initially prepared, the budget being enacted by Congress, and the current approved budget from which expenditures are being made. Once this request is formalized, it is sent to the White House for reconciliation and inclusion in the overall budget request of the executive branch, typically at the beginning of the calendar year after work began on it in the DOD.

Enacting the Budget   Once a budget request has been assembled, it is submitted to Congress for enactment. Technically, the budget request is merely a suggestion since the Constitution specifies that all bills to expend public funds must originate in the House of Representatives. That said, the president's recommendations represent the basic document on which congressional deliberations normally proceed.

The formal budget process begins with consideration of the requests by two sets of committees in each house. The Senate and House Armed Services Committees serve as *authorizing* committees that review the budget from a programmatic viewpoint and recommend what programs deserve support, whereas the *appropriating* subcommittees of the Appropriations Committees in each house recommend how much should be spent on each priority. These deliberations occur independently of one another in each chamber, and since they rarely coincide, the two committees in each house must meet and reach a common set of recommendations. When this has occurred (*if* it occurs), the Senate and House pass bills authorizing budget allocations. Since these rarely coincide either, the two houses must meet and try to negotiate a common bill acceptable to both.

Reconciling Executive Recommendations and Congressional Actions   Once Congress agrees on a defense budget as part of the overall federal budget, that document is sent back to the president for assent. The president's recommendations and congressional responses rarely coincide, and so attempts are made to reconcile the two documents in a way that is acceptable to both branches of government, which must then be scrutinized through the same procedures as before within the houses of Congress. If agreement can be reached, the result is a budget. Most of this labor is, of course, avoided when neither the Congress nor the Executive propose a budget (generally on the grounds the other branch would reject any proposal). In that case, most of this process is bypassed and the budgetary question is how the funds authorized by the continuing resolution (CR) will be spent.

Expenditures from the Budget   Once the executive branch receives authorization in the form of an acceptable bill for a given FY, it can spend the authorized amounts when that FY begins on October 1. The budget is a very thick document, and it is one of three somewhere within the budget process at any point in time. Each budgetary document contains literally millions of lines and accounts. Keeping track of all of them is a task only a few very dedicated specialists with particular expertise and interest can master and monitor. To most inside and outside the budgetary process, it remains a virtual "black box."

The extreme complexity of items within the budget adds to the difficulty of intelligent criticism. There are deep suspicions in the critical public that significant economies could be extracted from national security budgets without affecting the country's safety, and this suspicion is probably warranted. Many isolated examples of apparent misuse surface from time to time. In the 1980s, for instance, one particularly egregious example was the revelation that the DOD was spending $6,000 apiece for toilet seats on some of its aircraft. The very complexity of the budget instead focuses attention on so-called big-ticket programs, normally large and expensive weapons systems, that the military argues are necessary for security but the elimination of which could extract real savings in the budget. Sequestration has added to the tension in the process. Neither those who appropriate nor those who spend appropriated dollars like the process or its outcomes, but no one seems able or willing to undo it either, a source of deep frustration in the defense community.

The size and organization of defense spending makes it a formidable edifice to assault, but that same size makes it a tempting target. More than one in five dollars expended by the US government goes directly to defense, and if all the defense-related spending was added to the "official" total, that ratio would be more than one dollar in every four. Beyond entitlements, defense spending is the largest category of governmental programming for positive purposes (in other words, spending on other than debt service). It thus joins entitlement programs as tempting objects for those who seek to reduce federal spending.

The fact that the bulk of the federal budget is nondiscretionary leaves most of the budget immune from easy cutting. Entitlements and service on the national debt currently make up more than six out of every ten dollars the government spends, and that proportion is rising. Debt service payments can be altered only by defaulting on debts and are thus immune from legislation rescinding them; attempts to "reform" (a code word for reduce) entitlements have uniformly failed. Although a relatively small part of the federal budget (less than one dollar in five) is discretionary, well over half that total is in the national security budget, and most of the easily removable parts of non-defense discretionary budgets have already been attacked. The bulk of the more easily removed elements of funding lie within the realm of national security.

The Erosion of National Security Sanctity

Historically, even the discretionary budget elements within the national security budget have been effectively shielded from the budgeter's axe. That sanctity has been eroded by an arguably less intense threat environment and amidst general calls for governmental austerity. No two periods are perfectly isomorphic, but the comparison of the post-Vietnam period with the present helps complete the background in which the current domestic political battle is being fought. A milder version of the same phenomenon occurred in the early 1990s with the end of the Cold War and the expectation among some that this historic change meant the United States could reduce the size and expense of its commitments to national security.

The 1970s reaction to Vietnam offers some imperfect analogies. The United States had just ended a very expensive and ultimately unsuccessful military mission in Vietnam, and the American economy was saddled with crippling levels of inflation and the beginnings of a period of introversion born of a growing perception of American economic decline. Both mirror phenomena that surround the current milieu. In the 1970s, the response was to alter the national security footprint on society: the most visible symbol of the unpopularity of the war—conscription—was suspended, and the replacement all-volunteer force (AVF) limped through the decade with limited resources and, arguably, reduced readiness. When the Soviet Union collapsed, the external threat shrank dramatically. Many primarily liberal Americans argued for a so-called peace dividend of reduced defense spending in the face of a dramatic decrease in the threat facing the country. Those expectations were largely unfulfilled, however, as defense funds "freed" from the Soviet threat were reallocated to other unfilled defense priorities.

Such analogies are never precise. The wars in Iraq and Afghanistan have become unpopular, for instance, but opposition to them has never been as deep or encompassing as over Vietnam, largely because there has been no involuntary service as there was in Southeast Asia. The major public opposition to the military after Vietnam could be reasonably well assuaged by suspending the draft. There is no obvious analogy in the current environment beyond a general feeling that similar entanglements should be avoided. Whether that sentiment is transitory or permanent remains to be seen.

Two factors have contributed to the loss of sanctity surrounding the appeals for resources devoted to national security. The first is that, in the last decade, a lot of money has been squandered on national security. The chief examples are the wars in Iraq and Afghanistan, which have absorbed trillions of taxpayer dollars (exactly how many will probably never be agreed upon) on arguably unworthy actions. The belief is widespread that these wars, financed through supplemental appropriations rather than the regular budget process, represented money wasted that has contributed measurably to the current budgetary crisis. The other source of lost sanctity is the belief that the national security environment is less hostile than it was before and that the claim on resources is not so compelling. The first argument is reflective of the post-Vietnam domestic environment and the second of the immediate post–Cold War period.

The result is that those who defend the application of major resources for national security priorities enter the current debate in a more vulnerable position than they had previously occupied. As the debate has emerged, this vulnerability is notable in arguments that have surrounded the question of how to repair the federal financial ship. Advocacies of national security budgets have begun to intensify as the impacts of reductions on specific defense priorities become more evident.

Policy and Strategic Consequences

One of the very few matters on which there is an underlying agreement within the contemporary American political environment is that federal deficits are undesirable and that it must be a priority of the political system to find ways to reduce this overspending. Beyond that general level of agreement, consensus breaks down, largely on partisan lines. Although the depth of support for deficit reduction is more deeply held on some sides than on others, no one is willing to argue publicly that deficit reduction is not a high priority. Finding ways to accomplish this goal that are acceptable across the political spectrum has proven elusive, largely along ideologically based partisan political lines.

The principal political trauma this situation creates is that all solutions require imposing penalties on someone or everyone. Penalties come in the form of either increased taxes that must be paid or benefits that are cut from recipients as a result of budget reductions. The bottom line, however, is that some Americans will be punished through higher taxes or reduced benefits regardless of what actions are taken to improve the budget situation.

This definition of the problem, in turn, confronts political actors with two conditions they dislike and are historically unskilled at dealing with. Government is far better at giving things to people (entitlements and tax breaks, for instance) than it is at taking things away from people (reducing entitlements or increasing taxes, for example). At the same time, almost all proposals to deal with the problem allocate costs differentially: some people will face more losses than others. It is simple human nature that everyone wants to minimize their personal sacrifices even if they support the overall goal. As a result, people will defend, often quite vigorously, those who advocate solutions that minimize their own sacrifices while being less sensitive to the sacrifices of others who do not share in the benefit of the spending. Political actors are in the middle of this process of *loss allocation*, and because it means doing things *to* rather than *for* individuals, it is a position with which they are uncomfortable and thus have a difficult time coping.

In principle, the parameters of the debate over the deficit are straightforward: if the government is spending more than it is taking in, it can solve the problem by spending less, collecting more, or doing some of both. All solutions require sacrifices from some or all Americans, and the solutions that different groups advocate reflect comparative sacrifices. They also tend to cleave the major political parties in the United States: Republicans favor an emphasis on reduced spending rather than increased revenues, whereas Democrats favor an emphasis on increased revenues and lesser reductions in benefits/spending. Political centrists tend to favor a balance between the two. Each approach deserves some discussion.

Increased Revenues When government spends more than it collects, one solution is to collect more revenues to pay for the costs it incurs through spending. In the present context, the basis for "revenue enhancements" (i.e., new taxes) is the historic low rates on income and other taxes mandated by the Bush tax cuts of 2001 that expired at the end of 2012 but were largely reinstated by the 2017 Trump-advocated tax cuts across the board. Both bills provided more relief for the highest income brackets but less for most Americans below the top. Estimates suggest that the cuts in marginal tax rates that were the core of these reductions cost the government over $1 trillion in revenues. When combined with the unfunded wars in Iraq and Afghanistan (at least through regular budget allocations, as already noted), these factors formed the core of a trebling of the national debt during Bush's two terms in office. Expiration of the Bush tax cuts to pre-2001 levels (a rise of about four percentage points for the highest tax brackets) resulted in some increase in governmental revenues. Even champions of increased taxes do not, however, maintain that the amounts captured (or recaptured, depending on one's perspective) would negate the deficit; instead, such additional revenues would make the necessary cuts in existing expenditures, including those for national security, smaller than they would be in the absence of revenue enhancements.

The Republican Party led opposition to allowing the Bush tax cuts to expire and championed Trump cuts. The issue is rarely phrased in this manner but is instead described as opposition to any new taxes. In effect, this meant reinstating the pre–Bush era levels of taxation. The Bush cuts particularly favored individuals with the highest incomes, so opposition to revenue enhancement, by whatever rationale, is supported by the wealthy (who also happen overwhelmingly to be Republican). The heart of the GOP counterargument is that all reductions in the deficit must come from reductions in expenditures because, it was argued, reinstatement of higher tax rates will harm economic growth and that the proper course was to make tax cuts permanent. Democrats who favored allowing the Bush cuts to lapse argued that they enable the very wealthy to evade their fair share of the tax burden and that reductions in expenditures necessitated by the absence of new revenues would pose an onerous, unfair burden on less wealthy Americans. These basic arguments were largely replicated in 2017.

Decreased Spending   The alternative to higher taxes is decreases in federal spending, and virtually everyone agrees that reductions in what the government spends must be included in any effective solution to deficits. There are significant differences, however, on two central questions about the contribution of reduced spending to problem solution. The first is how much of deficit reduction should be borne by cuts in existing programs or from not funding new programs, which is in effect a question about future priorities. The second, and for current purposes more relevant, question is from where in the budget cuts should come. The prime categories for reduction are entitlement programs and national security since these constitute over three-fifths of the national budget.

Reductions in entitlement programs are politically poisonous since the benefits derived from them are disproportionately used by older citizens who also vote at higher rates than non-users. Opposing Medicare or Medicaid is politically perilous for those seeking election, and so they tend to avoid it. There is little disagreement that entitlement programs will or should take a "hit" in deficit reduction; the question is how much?

There are, of course, two alternatives to reductions in entitlement budgets. One of these is revenue enhancement so the government has more resources with which to pay for what it does. The other alternative is to reduce other federal budget elements, thereby lightening the relative load of entitlements in the process. Because it is the next largest category of vulnerable expenditures, resources expended on national security are a prime target.

Different Solutions and National Security Spending   The budget deficit debate, such as it is, thus moves to the area of national security. What is probably most notable about that inclusion is how the debate arrived at the participation of national security in the process. The debate did not begin from the proposition that defense expenditures are excessive and in need of cutting (although that case can be and sometimes is made). Rather, it begins from the implied assertion that every recipient of federal funding must sacrifice before the grail of deficit reduction and that national security is no exception.

The physical extent to which national security expenditures are affected by the deficit/debt process depends, of course, on how seriously budget cutting becomes in public policy. In recent years, deficits and debt have scarcely been raised because the short-term consequences have appeared minimal. The long war in Afghanistan, for instance, has been financed almost entirely by borrowing from foreign (mostly Chinese) sources, the repayment of which seems sufficiently distant not to be problematic (longer term consequences are another matter). Moreover, the two parties are so far apart on deficit/debt issues that a reconciliatory compromise seems impossible.

Particularly within the GOP there is an element that wants both to take tax increases off the table *and* to exempt national security spending from reductions. This alternative has some limited appeal within the generally conservative defense community. It concentrates all deficit reduction on entitlements, which would be an onerous burden on those programs and those who support and depend on those programs. As advocates of entitlements, such as the American Association of Retired Persons (AARP), constantly remind budget cutters, over fifty million Americans receive benefits under these programs and are part of the demographic group with the highest voting records. Thus, placing all the budget balancing burden on the backs of entitlement recipients reserves all the loss allocation on a segment of the electorate most likely to retaliate at the ballot box, as noted.

Deficit reduction will inevitably return to the political debate, and when it does, it is highly unlikely that defense spending will remain aloof from the budget-cutting exercise altogether. Advocates of a vigorous national security effort believe the problem becomes how to minimize the losses they will incur. Many are fiscal conservatives who oppose new taxes in principle, but they are on the horns of a dilemma in which following their ideological predisposition threatens the national security effort that is their central value. For some, reducing part of the deficit through new or reinstated taxes becomes the lesser of evils, but it is a bitter pill more easily swallowed when washed down with entitlement cuts.

Economic growth is the other means by which deficit reduction can occur in a politically painless manner. To the extent the economy is growing, it increases taxable income that can be collected under existing tax laws, thereby increasing revenues without changing tax codes. If growth is vigorous enough, these added revenues could largely remove the deficit altogether, and that they will do so remains the fervent hope of loss allocation–aversive politicians across the spectrum. Predicting large increases in growth rates is a standard political device by which politicians argue that they can reduce deficits without engaging in loss allocation by "growing the economy" at higher rates than previously. The idea is that increased growth will create new wealth that can be taxed without adding to the burden on current taxpayers. This device has occasionally worked in the past, but the predictions are routinely inflated to unrealistic levels, and thus the projections based on them tend to be excessive. As a result, they regularly fail to meet the expectations ascribed to them.

The New "Guns versus Butter" Debate These considerations recast the traditional debate between defense (guns) and non-defense (butter) spending in two different ways. First, they inject changes in how much money there is to allocate for either priority by altering the prospects of revenue enhancement or reduction through taxation policy, a politically divisive and explosive issue. Increasing the pot of funds available for increases in either priority through new taxes is essentially removed from the table, and the result is more of a zero-sum game where the advantage of one priority can only be achieved at the expense of the other. If tax cuts are added to the calculation, that competition becomes more pronounced, as it is over a smaller pot of government revenues.

Second, the new competition becomes more class and age based. Because so much of non-defense spending is devoted to entitlements disproportionately earmarked for the elderly and the poor, they add a very emotional social and ideological dimension to the basic argument. In effect, those who favor defense spending are effectively forced to oppose social spending, and defenders of entitlement programs must effectively oppose national security spending. The alternative is to ignore deficits and burgeoning debt as if they do not exist.

Many on both sides of guns and butter are uncomfortable with this dilemma. People in the military, for instance, tend to come from lower middle class backgrounds and thus are part of the group that needs entitlement programs. The military has its own benefit program for retirees, but many recognize that if the general public's entitlements come into question, so could theirs. At the same time, many who receive benefits are conservative on national security issues and favor strong support for defense. Both sides find themselves in something of a quandary as the guns versus butter arguments change and intensify.

THE IMPACT ON NATIONAL SECURITY

Due to sequestration, national security has been part of budget reduction since 2013, and it has already had enough negative impact that military leaders warn of adverse impacts in areas such as readiness and are among the strongest champions of suspending or rescinding the sequestration legislation.

The broader question is how the national security effort will be affected by the cuts it has been and will be forced to endure. The answer, of course, is that it depends on how much of a sacrifice must be made over how long a period of time, and estimates of what that means are thus difficult to determine in any reliable way, especially since the 2018 relaxation of the sequester. The answer depends, for instance, on the finally agreed upon balance between revenue enhancements and cuts in existing budgets and, within those cuts, the apportionment of losses among various budget categories and programs, including national security and specific defense programs. How long cuts will endure and at what levels in turn depend on the pace of economic recovery and growth and thus alleviation of the underlying deficit difficulties. All these variables are subject to enough sources of fluctuation to make estimation a highly inexact science, the predictive quality of which fades the farther into the future one projects it.

If it is impossible to predict with any confidence *how much* reductions in defense spending will occur, it is relatively safe to project that cuts will be incurred that will have some visible impact on the national security effort. Chapter 2 argued that the heart of national security is risk reduction, and the loss of national security resources reduces the available funds for capabilities in the formula (risk = threat − capability). The result is inevitably some increased risk at some level and in some areas. Budget reductions, in other words, have consequences, raising two questions. The first concerns where cuts in defense will occur, and the second is how these cuts affect the way the country conceptualizes and implements its national security policy.

Likely Areas of Reductions

Just as the overall federal budget has areas that are more or less vulnerable to being reduced, so too the national security budget contains budget categories that can and cannot easily be subjected to reductions. For the overall budget of the United States, the vulnerable areas are, of course, entitlements and national security; within the defense budget, the areas of greatest vulnerability are manpower, procurement, and research and development. Each presents different attractions and potential consequences.

The three areas are easy to identify in general terms. Manpower refers to the number of individuals employed within the defense effort. The general subcategories of personnel include uniformed personnel (both active duty and reserves) and civilians (part of both the defense bureaucracy and contracted personnel). Each of these subcategories can be broken down into subcategories—uniformed personnel by service and between active and reserve components of each service, for instance—further complicating the consideration of costs but enriching the roster or possible elements for cutting. Procurement refers to the things the defense establishment buys to carry out its business. Major subcategories include regular operations and maintenance costs and investment in weapons systems. Of the latter, major (what are called "big ticket") programs for major weapons systems have historically been most vulnerable. Third is research and development (R&D), which consists of investment the defense establishment makes in basic and applied scientific research with potential applicability to national security concerns.

Within this "menu" of budget items, the areas of spending most vulnerable to cuts are personnel, R&D, and, to a lesser extent, some areas of procurement, and there are definable consequences of cutting each that are most easily exemplified in the personnel and R&D areas. Cuts in personnel, especially when applied to active-duty personnel, affect so-called *end strength*, the size and thus the combat strength of forces the United States can put in the field. While cuts are possible in other areas, reductions in active personnel are almost always featured, both because of the impact on fighting ability and as an application of the so-called "Washington Monument ploy" described in Amplification 7.2.

Personnel cuts are attractive because one of the most prominent drawbacks of the current all-volunteer force system is that personnel costs are high in the AVF. To attract and retain qualified members of the professional force, the military must pay wages and benefits that are competitive with the private sector, and the result is a very high manpower cost per military member. This means that even modest reductions in the size of the force can bring about sizable effects. The cost is in end strength, a matter of concern as the AVF is fairly small anyway. The popularity of the AVF among elected officials largely insulates the military from the probability this option will be invoked, but it remains a possibility.

Research and development is a particularly tempting target for two reasons. One is that its activities are future oriented, geared toward enhancing capabilities at some future time, and thus the impact of the loss of funds is not so evident in the immediate, short-term environment in the way that reducing the number of soldiers and the equipment with which they work are. Second, about 11 percent of the defense budget is allocated to R&D, making it a tempting "pot" for potential raiding. The arguments against cutting R&D are that doing so is short-sighted since it means future forces will be deprived of technological fruits funded by R&D efforts that could make them more effective and safer and that adversaries may pursue to American disadvantage. In addition, defense funding through sources like the Defense Advanced Research Projects Agency (DARPA) has also funded efforts with enormous impacts on American society and prosperity. A partial list of DARPA-funded accomplishments include the Internet (originally developed to allow government defense scientists to communicate with one another); the Global Positioning System, or GPS (originally developed to increase battlefield awareness and to direct nuclear missiles to target); and high-definition television, or HDTV (originally funded to allow more precise visualization of battlefields from space-based satellite photography).

AMPLIFICATION 7.2

The Washington Monument Ploy

Although this term is infrequently used in contemporary discussions, the phenomenon it represents persists. The idea is that, when threatened with budget cuts, any agency will respond by reducing the services it provides that will most inconvenience the public and that are thus guaranteed to produce the most popular outcry in opposition. For the US Parks Service, the most frequently visited site in its jurisdiction is the Washington Monument, and thus, whenever cuts in its budget are proposed or imposed, it responds by restricting or denying access to the monument, thereby bringing howls of protest from visitors to Washington to reinstate its budget. The fact that the monument is an easy walk down the Mall from the Capitol building adds to the impact of protestations when Congress moves to deprive voters of access. For the DOD, reducing the number of soldiers in uniform has a similar effect. ■

National Security Benefits and Costs

For better or worse, budgetary considerations often drive debates about national security policy and strategy. In "good times" of abundant resources for national security, it is possible to think expansively about current or future commitments and about the purposes to which national security forces may be put. In a hostile national security environment like the Cold War, high levels of commitment may be dictated regardless of the costs and their impact on the availability of resources for other purposes.

Neither of these conditions obviously applies in the current environment. Resources available for any priorities are likely to be constrained by the absence of compelling threats or anti-spending sentiment, and noticeable expansions that could translate into new capabilities to expand missions and interests are likely to follow the arrival of such changes. Probably the only thing that could change the availability of public resources for national security would be some national emergency on the order of the September 11, 2001, catastrophe. Such an event is largely unpredictable, and even if its prospect justified maintaining robust capabilities as a hedge, the international environment seems unlikely to produce a major national security challenge to which the United States might have to respond through the application of major national security resources.

The basic conundrum with which policymakers and strategists must grapple in a resource-constrained environment is the relationship between threats and capabilities. Do capabilities allow the country to define threats in a constricted or expansive manner (in effect, narrowing or widening the range of threats in the psychological sense of security), or do threats determine the extent of capabilities that must be available? When gaps appear in capability to confront threats in the environment, after all, there are multiple ways in which to respond. As discussed in Chapter 2, these include both sizing capabilities to threat levels and restructuring perceptions of threat more closely to meet the capabilities available.

The present environment suggests that rethinking what is threatening in a narrower way may be the prudent planning model in the current climate of governmental gridlock. On the surface, this may seem an unattractive, even pusillanimous, approach for a country accustomed to a swaggering assertion of its power, but it has an upside as well. It is, for instance, almost certain that if the administration were to propose a military action today on the level of the wars in Iraq and Afghanistan, such a suggestion would be subjected to a far more critical appraisal than at the more economically flush beginning of the millennium and might well be rejected as unaffordable or inadvisable. Given the experience of the last decade or more, would that be such an unfortunate outcome?

Rethinking the nature of American national security, the structure of threats facing the United States, and various alternative ways to confront the challenges of the environment may be one of the signal characteristics of the debate over futures that has engulfed the national security sector. The situation has not been the result of national security decisions—although the costs of Iraq and Afghanistan have contributed to the problem—but it has certainly affected the environment in which national security problems are viewed and the solutions that are proposed. The question that remains is whether that contribution produces a healthy, constructive debate over national security or not. President Trump's proposal for a Space Force exemplifies this dynamic tension.

CHALLENGE!

Do We Need a Space Force?

On March 18, 2018, President Trump announced his intent to create a US Space Force (USSF) to become the sixth independent military force, joining the Army, Navy, Marines, Air Force, and Coast Guard. His announcement specified the creation of an effort that would be "separate but equal" from existing US

(continued)

military thrusts, including those associated with the United States Air Force's Space Command, which has been the country's primary leader on national security issues in space.

The proposal came as an apparently unanticipated shock to the DOD, although it was not an entirely new initiative. George W. Bush's secretary of defense, Donald Rumsfeld, announced a similar initiative in 2001, but it was lost in the national security response to 9/11. It has lain fallow ever since.

Reaction to the USSF was muted (largely because it was not a fully developed proposal) but largely negative, on two grounds, The first objection was redundancy, a cry predictably coming from supporters of the USAF Space Command, which has historically exercised the mandate in this area and personnel from which would almost certainly form the core cadre of the new force. The second, and more germane in terms of the arguments in this chapter, was budgetary: would the USSF be a wise and prudent use of scarce national security resources?

This raised at least two concerns. One was where the money to fund the Space Force would come from. The most likely source was the USAF Space Command, a prospect that was less than enthusiastically embraced by the USAF and the DOD. This was the model on which the DHS and DOE (discussed in Chapter 6) were funded, which has been less than totally successful. If the proposal moves forward (which is by no means a certainty), one can expect a great deal of infighting reminiscent of the DHS experience. A second concern was that the Space Force would be the smallest command within the DOD, and as such, it would be disadvantaged in the competition for the DOD budget: would the creation of the USSF decrease rather than increase the national fiscal commitment to space?

The stated purpose of creating the force was to ensure continued American preeminence in space, a goal that all Americans can agree to in the abstract. The question is whether this is the best way to go about maintaining that goal. What do you think about this proposal? ■

CONCLUSION: AN ONGOING DEBATE

The debate about the effects of the economy on the national security effort continues to be the eight-hundred-pound gorilla in the room that forms an important part of the backdrop and context of national security discussions. An assessment of threats and the efforts needed to counter those threats will remain the basic, underlying concern and point of debate and disagreement. It will be framed in terms of what responses to what threats are realistic and affordable given the structure of national security challenges and fiscal restraints under which the country will labor. As a result, national security planning will be more than ever an exercise in risk management, particularly given that reduced resources will mean that all threats cannot entirely be covered and some residual of risk will thus be left after efforts are assembled. A certain amount of uncertainty will inevitably be part of this calculation.

Despite this uncertainty, it is fair to assume that there will be constraints on resources available for national security until the current state of political dysfunction and economic disagreement has been replaced by a more congenial, consensual atmosphere that values solutions over ideological purity and fealty. There are two ways in which this situation can change. One is a return to a less confrontational tone in national politics, where the parties and branches of government become less institutionally divided and compromise becomes a valued purpose again. The other is a national security crisis that raises the prospect of a compelling national need to unite behind and use force—a war of necessity, not of choice. How likely are either of these contingencies?

In the remaining chapters, some of the historical and contemporary influences on these calculations will be introduced and analyzed in terms already presented. The opportunities and risks that may be attached to different problems and their potential solutions will be affected by how much treasure and sacrifice the United States is willing—or unwilling—to expend on the problems it faces and the attitudes it has toward those situations. The current malaise in which policy operates makes these processes more difficult than they might otherwise be.

STUDY/DISCUSSION QUESTIONS

1. What is the basic nature of the budget deficit problem? What are the possible sources of funding to alleviate the crisis? How is national security a "derivative" part of the process?
2. How is the deficit crisis a part of the hyper-partisan domestic political debate? How did the failure of the Super Committee in November 2011 help create the parameters of the problem and its solution? Include some discussion of the dynamics of sequestration (its origins, provisions, and effects) in your answer.
3. Discuss the budget process as it relates to national security. Why has national security historically been "invulnerable" to budgetary politics, and how and why has it lost some of that invulnerability? How and why has national security lost its "sanctity" within the political arena? How have devices like supplemental appropriations and continuing resolutions been used to deal with the national security budgetary problem and governmental dysfunction?
4. What is loss allocation? Why is it an important concept in the battle over deficits? Apply the concept to the deficit crisis in terms of the categories of potential sources of funds to reduce deficits. How do different loss-allocation patterns affect national security?
5. How will thinking about and preparing for national security be affected by different outcomes of the budget deficit reduction process? What are the likely areas from which national security reduction will come, and what are the benefits and costs associated with each possible outcome? Discuss.
6. What do you think are the best and worst outcomes to the current deficit crisis from a national security viewpoint?

SELECTED BIBLIOGRAPHY

Adams, Gordon. *The Politics of National Security Budgets*. Muscatine, IA: Stanley Foundation, February 2007.

——— and Cindy Williams. *Buying National Security: How America Plans and Pays for Its Global Role and Safety at Home*. New York: Routledge, 2010.

Bacevich, Andrew. *Washington Rules: America's Path to Permanent War*. New York: Metropolitan Books, 2010.

Blechman, Barry. *The Politics of National Security: Congress and U.S. Defense Policy*. New York: Oxford University Press, 1990.

Candreva, Philip J. *National Defense Budgeting and Financial Management*. Charlotte, NC: Information Age Publishing, 2017.

Chen, Greg G., Lynn A. Weikart, and Daniels W. Williams (eds.). *Budget Tools: Financial Methods in the Public Sector*. Washington: CQ Press, 2014.

Cheney, Richard, and Liz Cheney. *Exceptional: Why the World Needs a Powerful America*. Threshold ed. New York: Simon and Schuster, 2015.

Demarest, Heidi Bracken. *U.S Defense Budget Outcomes: Volatility and Predictability in Army Weapons Funding*. New York: Palgrave Macmillan, 2017.

Enthoven, Alain, and K. Wayne Smith. *How Much Is Enough? Shaping the Defense Program, 1961–1969*. Santa Monica, CA: RAND Corporation, 1966.

Jalal, Malik Ahmad. "The Number One National Security Threat?" *Harvard National Security Journal* (online), (March 28, 2011).

Korb, Lawrence J., Sam Klug, and Alex Rothman. "Defense Cuts after the Debt Deal: Bipartisan Recommendations from Four Budget Reduction Plans." *Center for American Progress* (online), (August 2011).

Krepinovich, Andrew F., and Barry D. Watts. *The Last Warrior: Andrew Marshall and the Shaping of Modern American Defense Strategy*. New York: Basic Books, 2015.

Linden, Michael. "Deficits and Debt 101." *Center for American Progress* (online), (September 2009).

National Defense Authorization Act for Fiscal Year 2012 (S 1867). Washington, DC: Congressional Budget Office, November 28, 2011.

Office of the Under Secretary of Defense (Comptroller). *United States Department of Defense Fiscal Year 2018 Budget Request*. Washington, DC: U.S. Department of Defense, 2017.

O'Hanlon, Michael. *The $650 Billion Bargain: The Case for Modest Growth in America's Defense Budget*. Washington, DC: Brookings Institution Press, 2016.

Packer, George. "The Broken Contract: Inequality and American Decline." *Foreign Affairs* 90, 6 (November/December 2011), 20–31.

Parent, Joseph M., and Paul K. MacDonald. "The Wisdom of Retrenchment: America Must Cut Back to Move Forward." *Foreign Affairs* 90, 6 (November/December 2011), 32–47.

Rubin, Irene S. *The Politics of Public Budgeting: Getting and Spending, Borrowing and Balancing*. 7th ed. Washington, DC: CQ Press, 2013.

Sapolsky, Harvey M., Eugene Gholz, and Caitlin Talmadge. *U.S. Defense Politics: The Origins of Security Policy*. 2nd ed. New York: Routledge, 2014.

Schultz, Tammy S. *U.S. Defense Budget and Strategic Overmatch*. New York: World Policy Review, November 6, 2011.

Snow, Donald M. *Thinking About National Security: Strategy, Policy, and Issues*. Routledge, 2016.

United States Department of Defense. *Defense Transformation: To What? For What?* Washington, DC, 2015.

———. *2014 Quadrennial Defense Review—Department of Defense Budget Priorities under Sequestration Cuts, Defense Strategy*. Washington, DC: United States Government Printing Office, 2014.

―――. *Defense Budget Priorities and Choices, Fiscal Year 2014*. Washington, DC, 2014.

Wheeler, Winslow, and Lawrence J. Korb. *Military Reform: An Uneven History and an Uncertain Future*. Palo Alto, CA: Stanford Security Studies, 2009.

Williams, Lynn M., and Susan B. Epstein. *Overseas Contingency Operations Funding: Background and Status*. Washington, DC: Congressional Research Service, 2017.

Zeliger, Julian. *Arsenal of Democracy: The Politics of National Security, from World War II to the War on Terrorism*. New York: Basic Books, 2009.

"Legacy" Military Problems

Thinking about and planning for large-scale war between conventional, World War II–style armed forces for symmetrical warfare and strategic nuclear war predate and postdate the contemporary period. The traditional roles of these forces were developed with the end of the Cold War, and only the United States retains a robust traditional capability, which it proposes to augment through force modernization. Critics say these large European-style forces are anachronisms in a world of shadowy, asymmetrical threats. Before assessing these criticisms, it is necessary to describe "legacy" forces and missions from the Cold War, first nuclear forces and then conventional forces, and the residual problems associated with each. Special operations forces and missions have their origins in the Cold War and before and have become a more prominent factor in the contemporary environment. These changing conditions also affect the nature of forces, notably in military manpower.

The past, it is sometimes said, is the prologue of the future, and nowhere is that observation more applicable than in describing military forces. War is an ancient institution that has evolved over time, but it retains significant continuities in how and why it is conducted. Doctrine—beliefs about the best ways to accomplish military ends—is persistent, and much of the doctrine employed today is rooted in the cumulative worldview that existed during the Cold War. The past is thus relevant to the future.

In the current environment, historical experience has been called into question as the United States seeks to grapple with the legacies of 9/11, especially in the Middle East, where the military problems tend to be unconventional and traditional ways and means of thinking about the use of military force are questionable. The result has been a drive to rethink and reorient the American military toward contemporary realities. This reorientation, of course, begins with traditional thinking and forces as its base.

What does it mean to refer to legacy problems, forces, and solutions? Within military circles, the term is used most often to describe forces that were designed for the specific circumstances of the Cold War, and these forces remain the backbone of American capabilities. The most obvious use of these forces is to deal with Cold War–like situations, thus the extension of the term *legacy* to describe the purposes of these forces.

This chapter examines the inheritance of three major kinds of armed forces during the Cold War competition: (1) thermonuclear forces and their potential use, (2) so-called conventional armed forces, and (3) not-so-conventional (or special operations) forces. All three capabilities were developed explicitly for a Cold War confrontation and environment that no longer exists, but the capabilities and plans for their use remain essentially intact today and still influence the current national security debate. Moreover, these forces frame what the United States can and cannot do militarily in the world and especially in the most militarily stressful situations it may face. Their continued relevance when hardly anyone else has a counterpart force is a major question.

In structure and configuration, strategic nuclear and conventional forces have formed the traditional backbone of US military capability. Although large-scale nuclear war and massive World War II–type war are no longer major operational probabilities, there are residual issues arising for each type. For nuclear forces, these include the problems of nuclear proliferation and missile defenses. For conventional forces, their relevance for contemporary warfare is a major concern since hardly anyone else retains large numbers of equivalent forces. For special operations forces, their prominence and the extent to which they can be effective in contemporary asymmetrical warfare is a major concern. These determinations are directly relevant to the question of who will fight: manpower policy.

NUCLEAR FORCES AND DETERRENCE

The nuclear age was formally born in the predawn hours of July 16, 1945, when the first atomic explosion lit the skies around ground zero at the Trinity Site at White Sands, New Mexico. The light from the explosion was visible as far away as Albuquerque, a hundred miles or so away. Robert Oppenheimer, the physicist considered the "father" of the atomic bomb, was so overwhelmed by the event that he said later, "There floated through my mind a line from Bhagavad-Gita, 'I am become death, the shatterer of worlds.'" General Lesley Grove, the military commander of the Manhattan Project that produced the bomb, intoned, "This is the end of traditional warfare," as he viewed the explosion.

The Manhattan Project began the nuclear age that continues today. It has proceeded through a series of steps, each of which has changed the nature and deadliness of nuclear weapons, from the explosion of the first nuclear bomb to the prospect of ballistic missile delivery and ballistic missile defense. Each is relevant to contemporary dynamics in dealing with ongoing proliferation problems like those posed by North Korea and Iran.

Seminal Events of the Nuclear Age

The nuclear age predated White Sands by nearly a century through more-or-less independent nuclear physics investigations in Europe and North America. The impending clouds of World War II and intelligence reports that Nazi Germany was attempting to harness and weaponize nuclear physics alarmed Albert Einstein to the extent that he wrote a letter at the behest of more politically active colleagues like Enrico Fermi to President Franklin D. Roosevelt, warning of the potential problem such weapons could pose in the hands of the Nazis. Roosevelt's response was to commission the Manhattan Project, which began the crash program that produced nuclear bombs shortly before the end of the war. The first operational atomic bombs were used against Hiroshima and Nagasaki, Japan, on August 6 and 9, 1945, to shorten the war in the Pacific by forcing Japanese capitulation short of an anticipated bloody invasion of the Japanese home islands. When the second bomb exploded, the American arsenal was temporarily exhausted; for the last time, the world had no nuclear weapons.

The Atomic (Fission) Bomb　The successful conclusion of the Manhattan Project was *the* seminal event of the nuclear age since it was the first step in the process. The original atomic bomb was what is known as a fission device—the basic physical reaction that makes the bomb explode and produce its deadly effects by the breaking apart (or fission) of atoms of unstable isotopes of uranium. The atomic bomb represented a quantitative change in the deadliness of war. The delivery of an atomic bomb could produce deadly effects that otherwise could be produced only by literally hundreds or thousands of attacks by conventional bombardment. Atomic bombs made bombardment incredibly more "efficient" than it was in the prenuclear weapons age.

The Hydrogen (Fission-Fusion) Bomb　The second major event was the successful development of a qualitatively larger form of nuclear explosive, the fission-fusion, or hydrogen, bomb. Known as the "Super" at the time because of the order of magnitude by which its deadly effect had increased, a prototype was successfully tested by the United States in 1952. The Soviet Union followed suit a year later. As the name implies, the physical reaction behind this new form of nuclear explosion involves two steps—the explosion of a small fission "trigger" to induce the second step, which is fusion.

This reaction involves the fusing together of atoms of heavy hydrogen (deuterium or tritium), which releases an enormous amount of energy—more than possible with a fission reaction.

The effects are awesome. Fission bombs produced yields that were the equivalent of thousands of tons (*kilotons*) of TNT; fission-fusion devices can produce explosions with destructive effects measured in *megatons (MT)*, or the equivalents of *millions* of tons, of TNT. Thermonuclear bombs altered the calculus of nuclear weapons and their use in two ways. First, they undermined the calculation of surviving a nuclear war. A society might endure grievous damage from an attack with atomic bombs, but it could reasonably anticipate surviving it. The same attack with thermonuclear bombs made survivability questionable. Second, during the early 1950s, scientists achieved considerable success in designing bombs that were more compact and much lighter than the Hiroshima and Nagasaki prototypes, making possible the delivery of these deadly weapons by missiles.

The Intercontinental Ballistic Missile (ICBM) The effort to weaponize rocketry began in the period between the World Wars, when the first rockets were developed and tested in Germany and the United States, among other places. In World War II, the first prototypes, the V-1 "buzz bombs" and the V-2 rockets, were used against Great Britain in a desperate act by the Germans to break British will. These were so grossly inaccurate that they had little impact on the war, and rockets were considered little more than terrorist weapons. By the 1950s, advances in rocketry allowed nuclear weapons to be transported over intercontinental ranges and land close enough to their targets to destroy them.

These advances fundamentally altered the impact of nuclear weapons on war more than either of the other seminal events. The reasons are profound and cumulative. The thermonuclear bomb removed the ability to calculate surviving a nuclear war if many of these devices were used. The ICBM produced the perfect delivery device for such weapons since there was (and arguably still is) *no proven defense against a nuclear rocket attack*. In the 1970s, a process known as fractionation allowed multiple nuclear bombs to be placed in the tip of a single rocket. MIRV (the multiple independently targetable reentry vehicle) further enhanced nuclear deadliness. In this situation, the only way to avoid being killed in a nuclear war was to avoid having such a war at all. Nuclear war avoidance (nuclear deterrence) became and remains the prime value and concern.

Ballistic Missile Defense (BMD) A possible means to lessen potential nuclear horror—defenses against missile attacks—has not yet definitively been achieved. The pursuit of BMD is not new, and its appeal is obvious. The current round of concern with BMD implications centers on the recurring threat from a nuclear-armed Democratic People's Republic of Korea

(DPRK, or North Korea). A truly effective missile defense could largely relieve that concern. Investigation of how to try to destroy incoming ballistic missiles proceeded parallel to the development of offensive applications of rocketry, and all the theoretical problems of missile defense had been solved before the first ICBM was launched in 1957. The problem has not been the concept, but rather the execution, of the proposed mission, a formidable technological task that would, if achieved, change nuclear calculations fundamentally. Imagine how little attention would be focused on North Korean leader Kin Jung Un's threats to use nuclear weapons against the United States if this country could shoot down all DPRK missiles before they reached American soil.

A truly effective, reliable defense would thus remove dependence on deterrence as the only basis on which to prevent the ravages of a missile-launched nuclear war. Rather than relying on the threat of robust retaliation after absorbing an attack (the basic threat under theories of deterrence developed during the Cold War), an airtight defensive system would make nuclear weapons "impotent and obsolete," in President Ronald Reagan's depiction in the early 1980s. A truly effective defense would rank with the ICBM in importance in nuclear evolution and change basic thinking about nuclear weapons.

Nuclear Proliferation   The alternative method to deterring nuclear war is to avoid or lessen the likelihood of war by controlling the number of states that have access to them. The premise is that the fewer that had a "finger on the nuclear button," the less countries could start a nuclear war. The logic implies opposing new members of the nuclear "club" and reducing the number of current "members." Both are relevant to the DPRK situation.

In simplest terms, proliferation refers to the attainment of or threat to attain nuclear weapons by a country that has not previously had them; avoiding that (non-proliferation) is the objective of policy concerns. Proliferation is always referred to as a problem because it is assumed that the addition of new members to the nuclear weapons "club" makes the use of nuclear weapons by them or someone else more likely. Based on actual nuclear weapons employment over the more than sixty years of the nuclear age, of course, there is no evidence of the truth of this assumption or assertion.

In form and substance, proliferation is as old as the nuclear age. When the United States was rushing to weaponize nuclear physics, the effort was largely motivated by the perceived danger that Nazi Germany would "crack" the atomic equation first. The purpose of the US program was partially to head off the German program and to end the war before Germany became a nuclear state. Immediately after World War II, the problem was keeping the Soviet Union from getting these weapons—a pure proliferation concern. Anti-proliferation efforts have recurred every time some state has expressed a nuclear weapons interest or moved toward the capability. The DPRK and Iran are the most recent examples of the proliferation problem dynamic.

Much of the criticism surrounding proliferation comes from analysts in the one country that has used these weapons in anger against other humans. Partly, this has occurred because many of the states that are potential proliferators are either not overtly friendly with or subject to much influence by the United States. India and Pakistan are good examples. At the same time, countries hostile to the United States either have exercised the nuclear option (e.g., North Korea) or might (e.g., Iran), and the prospect of attainment by such states that could threaten the United States with them is a legitimate national security concern. The dynamics of proliferation are the same when an American friend or ally has exercised the option (e.g., Great Britain, France, or Israel) but have been of lesser concern. This dichotomous treatment puzzles some states. The United States never publicly comments on (and certainly does not condemn) Israeli possession of nuclear weapons (which Israel does not admit it possesses), but this arsenal greatly concerns Israel's Islamic neighboring states (see Amplification 8.1).

The traditional nuclear proliferation concern has been augmented by contemporary complications. The first is that the proliferation concern has broadened beyond nuclear weapons, which are difficult to acquire, to other forms of weapons of mass destruction (WMD), such as biological and chemical weapons, that are less deadly but more accessible. Syria is an example. The second concern is that WMD, especially nuclear weapons, might fall into the hands of non-state actors and, more specifically, terrorist organizations. Because of their much greater destructive capabilities, nuclear weapons are the bigger concern. The fear that Saddam Hussein's Iraq was developing WMD and possibly planning to provide them to terrorists—allegations that were never convincingly demonstrated—was crucial in the 2003 decision to invade Iraq and overthrow its government.

Forms of Proliferation: N + 1   Nuclear proliferation can take on two guises. The first is *horizontal proliferation*, which refers to the spread of nuclear weapons to states that do not currently possess them. This is the most common cotemporary proliferation problem. There is a second form, however, called *vertical proliferation*, which refers to growth in the arsenals of current nuclear weapons states. As the superpower nuclear arsenals mushroomed after the advent of MIRV during the 1970s, this phenomenon became entangled with horizontal proliferation as potential new nuclear club members (notably India) argued that their continuing abstention from joining that club was tied (as specified in the Non-Proliferation Treaty) to a reduction in the arsenals of the superpowers.

The dynamics of horizontal proliferation are captured in a construct called the $N + 1$ problem. In this formulation, N stands for the number of states that currently possess nuclear weapons, and +1 refers to the additional problems created if additional states gain these weapons. The heart of the $N + 1$ problem is the different perceptions of the two categories of states and the controversy it creates. The N states implicitly (sometimes explicitly) argue that the possession of the weapons by states that already have them is acceptable, and their evidence is that the current possessors have avoided nuclear war. Additional states, however, pose unpredictable new dangers and dynamics that are better to avoid, thus forming the basis for opposition. Implicit in this assessment is the premise that new possessing states would act more irresponsibly with the weapons than current possessors do. Since the same charges were made against current members before they joined N (China in particular), it is difficult to defend this position publicly without being openly condescending to the potential proliferators. The enigma is that states that were formerly considered proliferation "sinners" for proposing to get the weapons become "saints" by opposing new proliferators after they attain nuclear status themselves.

Potential new members (the + 1 states) discount that *their* possession would make things more unstable and argue that, if anything, their membership in the club would increase their own security. This seems to be a prime argument made by North Korea, which claims to need nuclear weapons to deter the *United States* from attacking them. Once + 1 states get the weapons, however, they tend to accept the argument that N (of which they are now a part) produces an acceptable balance but that additional members of the club would be unacceptable. The hypocrisy of this changed reasoning is obvious.

The divide over *whether* an $N + 1$ problem exists cannot be overstated. Put bluntly, the supposition that it is all right for currently possessing states to perpetuate their nuclear arsenals and destabilizing for other states to join them is discriminatory at a minimum and condescendingly racist at worst. The loudest detractors of nuclear weapons spread have been the United States, Russia, Great Britain, and France, all of which are European by tradition. Obviously, some possessors (China, India, and Pakistan, for instance) are not European, but they are also the most worrisome members of N. The possession of these weapons by Israel rarely evokes this concern in the West.

Many of the contemporary + 1 states come from the developing world. Partly this reflects the fact that essentially all the developed states have decided—one way or the other—whether they want to pursue the nuclear option. Claiming that some countries are more responsible than others in possessing these weapons in effect accuses the pretenders of being more reckless and irresponsible, which, at a minimum, is condescending. Iran and the DPRK are the states against which these accusations are most often made in the contemporary period. The reasoning is that such spread would be destabilizing, which effectively means those countries would likely be less responsible possessors. Operationally, this means they would be more likely to use nuclear weapons against their enemies (including the United States) or might provide access to terrorists. Why? Because the Kim Jong Un regime of the DPRK and the religious regime of Iran are alleged to be less responsible than the current possessors, a position reinforced by periodic, inflammatory rhetoric from Pyongyang and Tehran. That logic may make sense to Americans; it cannot possibly be viewed by North Koreans or Iranians as anything other than insulting. There is no way to sugarcoat this quandary.

Non-Proliferation Efforts: The NPT   This logical dilemma infects the major international effort to discourage nuclear weapons acquisition, the Non-Proliferation Treaty (NPT). It was negotiated in 1968, entered into force in 1970, and creates a nuclear caste system. On the one hand are the states that already possess nuclear weapons, who are required not to encourage or help non-possessors gain these weapons and who are committed to reducing their own possession to zero. These states have proven to be better at meeting the former requirement than the latter. Non-possessing states are required to renounce their intention ever to build these weapons. Those states unwilling to make that pledge (Israel, Pakistan, and India have been the most prominent examples) have simply refused to become members of the treaty. (North Korea and Iran *are* or have been members; the DPRK has dropped out.)

The intent of the NPT is clearly to arrest horizontal proliferation, preventing the spread of nuclear weapons to non-possessing states and encouraging possessors to reduce their arsenals and disarm. It also has a vertical proliferation intent in its entreaties to possessors to reduce the size of their arsenals as they move toward disarmament. This latter emphasis has proven to be stillborn; major powers like the United States have reduced arsenal size since the end of the Cold War, but the NPT admonition has not been the reason.

How does one deter horizontal proliferation? There are two basic approaches. One is *acquisition deterrence*, which consists of attempts to dissuade countries from acquiring the weapons. The techniques for accomplishing this form of deterrence include positive incentives not to engage in provocative actions, such as providing safeguarded nuclear fuels (fuel sources that cannot be transformed into weapons-grade materials) and monetary incentives for demurring from weapons development, and negative actions, such as sanctions. Both techniques are currently being used against the DPRK (sanctions when the North Koreans engage in nuclear developments and promises of assistance such as nonnuclear fuels and foodstuffs when they comply) and are part of the non-proliferation agreement with Iran from which the United States withdrew in 2018. If countries like North Korea, for instance, cannot be dissuaded from developing these weapons, then one must revert to *employment deterrence*, which consists of efforts to avoid the use of nuclear weapons by states who gain them. The techniques for doing so tend to be those associated with traditional bilateral US–Union of Soviet Socialist Republics (USSR) deterrence during the Cold War.

A major contemporary concern is the addition of non-state actors (most prominently terrorist groups) to the list of nuclear pretenders. Arguments about the irresponsibility of this category of potential nuclear club members are much more convincing than the same arguments made against states. Notably, the allegation is made that a terrorist group like Al Qaeda (AQ) would be more likely to use such weapons if it had them because its members lack the fear of the consequences—retaliation—that impedes state possessors. There are two reasons for this. On the one hand, the principle of martyrdom is built into the ethos of many of these groups, who would thus not fear retaliation the way most states would. On the other hand, non-state actors lack identified, claimed territorial bases against which to retaliate. Should AQ launch a nuclear attack somewhere (blow up a bomb in an American city, for instance), what would the United States annihilate in retaliation?

There are currently eight admitted members of the nuclear club (in order of "admission": the United States, the Soviet Union/Russia, Great Britain, France, China, India, Pakistan, and the DPRK), one state that neither confirms nor denies its possession but is universally considered a member (Israel), and one state that developed these weapons but subsequently dismantled them and renounced their possession (South Africa). DPRK nuclear saber-rattling toward the United States arguably elevates its status to that of most troublesome possessor. Predictions made several decades ago suggested that twenty to thirty states might by now have gained the capability, but they have not. Moreover, proliferation has not been accompanied by its most dire possible consequence, nuclear war. The potential that other states and, more ominously, non-state actors might join the club keeps the concern over the proliferation problem lively because the potential consequences of a rogue + 1 entity gaining possession of the capability are so dire.

The proliferation question remains controversial. No one—except countries attempting to obtain the weapons—thinks proliferation is a good idea or the world would be a better place with more states possessing nuclear weapons. At the same time, there is disagreement about *how much* of a problem it is, as already suggested. In recent years, there has been an additional and dynamic concern among potential proliferators that they may need the weapons to protect themselves from current possessors like the United States. The DPRK publicly identifies the United States as its nuclear enemy, for instance, justifying their need to develop and maintain their arsenal.

The irony about proliferation in the current context is that countries seek nuclear weapons in order to guard against being attacked by their enemies—a deterrence argument. The possession of nuclear weapons, it is argued, provides status and respect from potential predators. The irony is that this argument is currently voiced most prominently as a reason for gaining nuclear weapons in Iran and North Korea, and the country they publicly seek to deter with those weapons is the United States. To support this concern, some argue that Saddam Hussein's greatest mistake was *not* pursuing nuclear weapons because, if he had possessed them, the United States might not have attacked him for fear of a nuclear retaliation by Iraq.

This latter argument has powerful resonance in Iran. Many Iranians fear being attacked by two nuclear states, the United States and Israel. Both states have identified a nuclear-armed Iran as unacceptable, and the Israelis have frequently threatened military actions to prevent the Iranians from obtaining nuclear weapons. Such threats were made and carried out by Israel against Iraq and Syria, adding credence to them. One way for Iran to negate that threat would be to obtain the weapons and their deterrent properties. This prospect contributes to the additional concerns suggested in Amplification 8.1.

AMPLIFICATION 8.1

Iranian Proliferation, Israel, and the United States

The agreement between Iran and a coalition of six prominent powers (Great Britain, France, Germany, China, Russia, and the United States) under American leadership by which Iran agreed not to pursue nuclear weapons status for at least a decade was finalized and went into effect in 2015 over the loud objection of the majority of the American Congress. From the perspective of the states negotiating with Iran (all of whom are nuclear weapons states except Germany), the purpose was to prevent or deter Iranian proliferation. For Iran, the principal benefits were economic: having crippling sanctions lifted and regaining funds frozen in the West.

The agreement has been intensely controversial, with major opponents in both the United States and Israel. In the harsh, largely partisan debate in the Congress and the Trump White House, questions of effectiveness have been raised, largely in proliferation terms: Will the agreement actually muzzle the Iranians, or does it have loopholes they will exploit to evade compliance?

(*continued*)

Will the results be destabilizing and dangerous for Israel because the Iranians cannot be trusted? Are there sufficient safeguards in place against noncompliance? Critics believe American negotiators gave away too much to get what these critics see as a "bad" deal. The Trump administration accepted the negative argument when it withdrew from the agreement. They are also deeply affected by their support for Israel, which has expressed strong, vocal opposition to the accord.

The Israelis view the situation more desperately, fearing a nuclear-armed Iran might attack them or provide the weapons to terrorists who would use them against Israel. Additionally, Iranian acquisition would void Israel's nuclear monopoly in the region, a major pillar of their effective military domination of the Middle East. To the Israelis, the alternative is to place their country in an assured-destruction embrace with the Iranians (where either could destroy the other preemptively or in retaliation and where many Israelis believe the Iranians will not be deterred by the assured-destruction prospect). The Israelis and their American champions do not publicly admit this dynamic, but it is fundamental to an aggressive Israeli stance on issues like the West Bank. Despite their silence, it nonetheless exists as a pillar of Israeli defense policy. ■

CONVENTIONAL FORCES AND THE FUTURE

The future nature and uses of US conventional forces have also come into question. The bulk of American military forces and the expenses associated with them have been devoted to maintaining, adapting, and modernizing a force that was largely designed and configured to fight World War III in Europe. The end of the Cold War made a conflict of this nature and scale extremely unlikely. No realistic potential adversary has emerged to confront the United States in traditional European style (symmetrical warfare where both sides fight a stand-up, Western-style war), and none is likely to emerge anytime soon. Saddam Hussein challenged the United States on American military terms in the Persian Gulf War in 1990–91, and he failed miserably. His experience was instructive for anyone else who might conventionally challenge the West, and especially the United States, in the future. The end of the Cold War started the process by which the United States' traditional power has grown in comparison to the rest of the world to the point that it has made itself virtually obsolete. The result has been a kind of self-fulfilling prophecy in which American prowess has eliminated the problem for which it was devised and is a behemoth with no opponent.

American continued military predominance in these traditional forces thus has helped create a debate on the continuing relevance of their size and capabilities. The last time the traditional force structure and model were applied in toto was in the Persian Gulf War of 1990–91. In modified form, it was also the model for the invasion and conquest of Iraq in 2003. As one looks at future possible scenarios where the United States might contemplate involvement, traditional conventional-style scenarios and wars are hard to imagine. Because they do reflect American superiority and are strongly advocated by the armed forces themselves, they do retain considerable political support.

The Vietnam War highlighted a variant of another model of warfare, unconventional or asymmetrical war, a form of armed conflict where the structure and mission of forces do not conform to the traditional model. This generic style of war has been encountered in the post-invasion (occupation) phase of the Iraq War and in Afghanistan and is the kind of conflict that seems most likely elsewhere. Preparing for and conducting this form of warfare is very different than conventional force and warfare.

These opposing views, and the roles, missions, and forces that implement them, form the basis for ongoing debate in the United States. One model, the extension of traditional uses of force, can be called conventional and the forces it emphasizes "heavy." The other model is unconventional and the forces it emphasizes "light." This model includes a distinctive sub-category, special operations, that is different enough to warrant separate discussion.

The Heavy Forces (Conventional) Model

World War II was the major formative period for the contemporary configuration of American military forces. The purpose of that conflict was the defeat of Nazi aggression by large, heavily armed, mechanized forces organized and fighting the same way as their opponents. That war still served as the model for the Korean conflict, with some peripheral modifications to reflect technological innovations (such as jet aircraft and helicopters). This force remained largely intact after Korea. Rather than following the American tradition of mobilization for war and then rapid demobilization at war's conclusion, the conventional force for the Cold War was one with which veterans of World War II were comfortable and familiar. Only the adversary changed, and since the Soviets were similarly organized and were likely to fight the same way in a future conflict, the model seemed vindicated and of continuing relevance. This force structure has largely survived reductions in size since the end of the Cold War.

The bulk of the American nonnuclear armed forces can be reasonably accurately described using two adjectives, *heavy* and *conventional*, and these together define most *legacy* forces. The term *heavy* refers to the way the force is configured and how it is equipped to perform its mission. More specifically, it describes a force designed to fight in large-unit, concentrated-firepower combat, using mobile mechanized units against a similarly configured opponent in brutal, positional land, air, and naval warfare. The symbols of heavy warfare are tanks and mobile artillery on land, bombers with large payloads in the air, and large capital ships (battleships, aircraft carriers) on the sea. By contrast, *light* forces feature more lightly armed and mobile forces capable of engaging in a variety of forms of warfare and generally not preferring the kinds of direct confrontations between armies, navies, and air forces typical of heavy forces.

Heavy forces are designed to fight *conventional*, traditional warfare, which is the style that was perfected during World War II and is also called European. Sometimes referred to as the "Western way of war," its military purpose is to overcome adversary "hostile ability" (the capacity to resist the other side's armed forces physically) through the direct confrontation of armed forces. The military purpose is to destroy "in detail," or to break the cohesion of enemy armies, sink enemy navies, and shoot down enemy air assets. Collectively, the objective is to gain military superiority over an adversary in order to impose political objectives on that enemy by overcoming its physical ability to resist that imposition. Warfare employing heavy forces is most closely attached to wars of total political purpose (in which the objective is the overthrow of the enemy government), such as World War II, although in some circumstances these forces are effective in lesser contingencies. Heavy forces are designed and best suited for confronting similar forces possessed by an opponent.

A heavy force was appropriate for the Cold War confrontation with the Soviet Union and its allies. US and Soviet armed forces were virtual mirror images of one another physically, and both shared similar plans in the event of war. The doctrines of both sides emphasized mass (having a heavier, more firepower-intensive force at the point of engagement than the enemy). A war between them, it was assumed, would resemble World War II, except that it would be much bloodier and more violent, and one side or the other would exhaust its weaponry and its ability to continue first. Moreover, such a war would likely be total in purpose, with one side or the other having its government overthrown (unless, of course, the war escalated to system-destroying nuclear war, in which case both sides would lose). The heavy model proved durable for fighting and winning World War II and confronting the Soviet Union short of war during the Cold War.

Much of the debate over the continued ascendancy of heavy forces is concentrated on how forces are equipped and modernized. Heavy forces are inherently expensive because they rely on large quantities of costly weapons systems that define their "heaviness." Moreover, the advantages of these forces over adversary counterparts can be transitory, as technological breakthroughs and applications make old weapons obsolete and vulnerable and thus in need of constant upgrading and replacement.

These "large ticket" systems are expensive and the backbone elements of service budget requests. Updating and replacing these kinds of systems is a major Department of Defense (DOD) priority under the sequester suspension of 2018.

The Light Forces (Unconventional) Model

The alternative approach is the light forces model. *Light forces* is a term that generally refers to military structures that deemphasize large military equipment and that, at the extreme, are largely limited to equipment that can be carried physically by soldiers on foot or transported by helicopter or similar conveyance (e.g., rifles, small-caliber mortars). The emphasis of light forces is on speed, flexibility, and surprise. They are not designed to confront and "slug it out" with heavy forces, against which they stand little chance in conventional European-style warfare. Rather, they are best adapted to rapid movement, to special assignments for which speed and deception are critical, and to missions that heavy forces cannot accomplish because of their relative lack of speed and flexibility—capturing fugitives or rescuing hostages, for instance. They are also arguably the best kinds of forces with which to confront other light, unconventional opponents.

In the developing world, light forces have often been associated with countering guerrilla warfare, particularly in the jungles of the mountainous "green belt" surrounding the equator and similar inhospitable physical environments, where it is easier for such forces to maneuver and to engage in hit-and-run tactics in the face of more firepower-intensive heavy forces. The Viet Cong were classic practitioners of this style of warfare during the Vietnam War, and it consistently frustrated the efforts of much more heavily armed American regular forces until they adopted similar approaches.

The light forces model has always been a part of the Western tradition, although its relative importance has varied. Some might suggest that the mounted cavalry is the prototype for light forces in the American system, comparing the cavalry on horseback with helicopter-borne "air cavalry." Special Forces and Rangers are a variation of the light forces model, but they are distinct enough to warrant separate consideration.

A major criticism of light forces is their inability to match up with heavy forces in direct combat; a soldier with a rifle stands little chance against a tank. This criticism is valid and carries considerable weight when the opponent is heavy, in which case heavy forces are the necessary counterweight. A light force facing a heavy force can deal with it successfully only by avoiding the kind of direct confrontations in which the superior firepower of the heavy force can be brought to bear to "frame" and destroy the lighter force. Heavy forces, however, have not always prevailed over light forces in unconventional asymmetrical warfare, especially in places where heavy forces have difficulty operating (e.g., tanks operating in rugged terrain where there are no good roads or bridges). Vietnam provides ample evidence of these situations. If the future is likely to hold more asymmetrical than conventional warfare, then the primacy of heavy forces should not be taken for granted.

This dichotomy is not between two fundamental alternatives. There are military missions that heavy or light forces can perform that the other cannot. Light forces are generally superior for fighting similar enemy forces, and heavy forces are better at combatting other heavy opponents. Heavy forces are necessary for some priorities for which light forces cannot substitute, an argument frequently and forcefully made by their proponents. At the same time, the number of military situations in which this is true have shrunk while the situations where light forces are more useful have expanded.

Light forces have always been held in less than total respect by an American military establishment that has been dominated by proponents of heavy forces, and this has been especially true of uniformed leaders in the armed forces themselves, most of whose basic military specialties have been in heavy systems (e.g., tanks, strategic bombers). The tasks these light military services traditionally performed—dealing with insurgents in Central America early in the twentieth century or leading amphibious assaults on Japanese-held Pacific islands during World War II—represented missions at which conventional heavy forces are not adept; hence, uniformed leaders tended to downplay them and their military significance. This disregard has also represented the treatment endured by a distinctive category of light forces, special operations forces.

Special Operations Forces

Unconventional military forces—or special operations forces (SOFs)—have become the "darlings" of nonnuclear forces among the aware public and many political figures. The sources of this infatuation are diverse. Special forces have been the centerpiece of some of the most visible, spectacular military operations in recent years: the Navy Sea, Air, and Land Team (SEAL)–led raid that captured and killed Osama bin Laden in Pakistan is the most obvious example. They have been attached to methods that more conventional or other light forces have not proven well suited to accomplish: counterinsurgency (COIN) operations in developing world internal conflicts (DWICs) and foreign force training are exemplary.

Historically, special forces have been unpopular, and subject to disdain, especially within the traditional hierarchy of the American military itself.

This dislike has been especially pronounced within the Army hierarchy, although in the current atmosphere of enthusiasm about special operations, this disdain is muted. There are several reasons for the popularity and the controversy that surrounds SOFs. Both are extensions of the "special" military roles that SOFs provide.

What principally distinguishes SOFs from other forms of force is that they perform tasks that conventional forces either cannot or will not perform. SOFs are basically "light" forces as the term was used in the last section, and their activities are both examples and extensions of what conventional light forces do. Typically, SOFs operate in small, specialized units (often called "teams") independent of conventional units. It is their hallmark and their badge of honor that they can do things that more conventional, and especially heavy, forces cannot do. An exemplary list of SOF missions includes reconnaissance and surveillance, training of the military forces of other states, counterinsurgency support, counterterrorism, sabotage and other "fifth column" actions, and hostage rescue. No list is definitive because the SOF mission expands as it is given (and usually enthusiastically embraces) new kinds of tasks that others cannot do successfully. Adaptability is what makes SOFs special.

In the contemporary context, much SOF popularity arises from the perception that they are more adept at combatting asymmetrical warfare efforts than are conventional forces. As will be argued later, much of the utility of asymmetrical approaches is that they reduce the advantages of conventional heavy forces like mass and firepower. A prominent method is through small-unit organization and operations that deny conventional forces the kind and size of opponents that heavy forces are adept at defeating. This same basic approach is shared by SOFs. They both understand and resemble asymmetrical forces, which can make them more relevant and effective against such opponents.

This symbiosis has historical roots. The use of large, massed (conventional) armed forces is largely associated with the military traditions of Europe, whereas SOF-style missions are more akin to the Eastern, Asian tradition that dates back at least to Sun Tzu and is more typically practiced in East Asia and the Middle East (see Chapter 9). The American tradition in what is now called special operations has roots in subduing indigenous Native Americans as the United States spread westward across North America, but it is especially associated with American military contacts with Asia at the turn of the twentieth century, including the Boxer Rebellion in China and the Filipino insurgency following the Spanish-American War. The first formal American foray into special operations was conducted by the Marine Raiders in the Pacific theater in World War II, which employed counterinsurgency, intelligence gathering, and unconventional operations against the Japanese, as did the newly formed (1942) Army Rangers, an airborne light force roughly modelled on the British Special Air Service

(SAS). The other unconventional warfare arm of the US government during this time was the Office of Strategic Studies (OSS), the lineal predecessor of the Central Intelligence Agency (CIA).

The need for a formal special operations capability became obvious as American military imperatives turned toward Asia after World War II. The Army Special Forces were commissioned first in 1952, and the Navy SEALs, which the Navy considers an outgrowth of the Marine Raiders and Underwater Demolition Teams (UDTs), were formally commissioned in 1962. The US Air Force followed suit with its own Special Force as part of its formation of the Air Force Special Operations Command (AFSOC) in 1983. The Marines have continued their tradition of unconventional missions that dates to their founding—they have always, in a sense, been special operators.

Conventional military practitioners have opposed special operations forces on essentially four grounds. First, SOFs are different. Conventional armed forces rely heavily on doctrine—beliefs in the best ways to conduct military operations. Conventional warfare is conducted within a structure of rules of engagement (ROEs) that lend a certain predictability to situations, and a prime measure of the virtue of a conventional warrior is the ability to recognize situations and to apply the proper doctrinal solutions to them. Orderliness and conformance to doctrinal principles are prime values. Special operations tend to be unique and not amenable to applications of doctrinal solutions. Learning doctrine is not a prime value since all SOF situations are different; thinking creatively how to solve a totally new problem is the important characteristic of the special warrior. The result is a very different mindset within each group. In caricature, conventional warriors see special operators as undisciplined "snake eaters" crawling through jungles; special operators see their conventional counterparts as plodding, unimaginative conformists.

Second, conventional warriors see special operators as competitors—especially for scarce budget resources. The traditional military commands very strongly opposed the formation of the Special Operations Command (USSOCOM) as part of the Goldwater-Nichols Act of 1986. Provisions of that act unified the various service efforts into one command and thus strongly enhanced the ability of the special operators in their requests for funding. The recent advocacies of increased usage of special forces against terrorists have been especially troubling to the traditional heavy force elements for this reason.

Third, the heavy warriors oppose the special operators on the grounds of ineffectiveness in the ultimate military role of confronting and destroying enemy armed forces. This argument is an extension of objections to light forces generally. In the contemporary context, the conventional heavy warriors argue the special operators can help weaken an asymmetrical enemy but that it requires conventional "boots on the ground" to destroy them.

Finally, special operations forces are opposed because they *are* special and thus arguably elite. The Army has a very long tradition of opposition to any imputation of elitism in its ranks, and a segment of its forces that disdains the grail of doctrinal obeisance and replaces it with independent, original thinking is suspicious at the least. The tension between the "regular" Army and the SOFs reached a pinnacle in 1962 when President Kennedy singled out the special operators for recognition by giving them the "Green Berets." The Army virtually fell all over itself providing different colored berets for the soldiers of units with other specialties to demonstrate the SOFs were really nothing special.

Unconventional military forces have become a major part of the military array available to the United States. Their rise in prominence—and the simultaneous decline of traditional forces—has been the result of a changing military environment in which conventional forces have lost some of the salience they had when confronting a symmetrical Soviet opponent. For as long as asymmetrical warriors pose the major military threat to the United States, the unconventional special operators will be a prominent part of the military equation the armed forces employ. Not even the most vocal proponent of SOFs argues they will replace conventional forces. There are things small, clandestine SOFs can do that conventional forces cannot, such as secretly infiltrating enemy-held territory to locate targets for aerial bombardment. At the same time, SOFs cannot stand toe-to-toe with and defeat an organized army on a conventional battlefield.

Light Forces, Heavy Forces, or Both?

The comparison of heavy and light (including special) forces is not an either/or proposition but rather a question of comparative emphasis. If the heavy forces model served the United States well in the twentieth century, is it equally durable, serviceable, and adequate for confronting the environment of the twenty-first century? Clearly, the contemporary environment has changed. The prospect of fighting a conventional war against heavy forces using conventional means has all but disappeared. In the words of the original 1997 Quadrennial Defense Review (QDR), a review of American strategy and forces mandated by Congress once every four years, the United States lacks a "peer competitor" or even a foreseeable adversary that poses the kind of military threat for which those forces have been historically appropriate. The question becomes whether this type of force and this style of warfare are appropriate for the challenges ahead. In the meantime, the use of SOFs expands quietly, as illustrated in Amplification 8.2. The further question is whether the United States can afford the continuation of its current light/heavy mix of forces and whether that mix is appropriate to the contemporary threat environment.

Special Forces and the War on Terrorism in Africa

The experience of combatting terrorism by inserting traditional American forces into Middle Eastern countries where they have been active during the 2000s has not been especially positive, and there is virtually no support for the idea of sending regular military units into other places that might end up like Afghanistan or Iraq—long, protracted, and costly engagements with questionably successful outcomes. Yet the problem of foreign terrorism has not gone away. Rather, it has moved into Africa, which is not well prepared to deal with terrorist intrusions but does not want the presence of American military forces to deal directly with the threat foreign-based terrorists pose. Moreover, suggesting the insertion of sizable numbers of American forces into any African country would be unacceptable politically in the United States. The United States wants to help Africa deal with its terrorist problem, but how can it do so without creating domestic and foreign opposition to any effort?

The answer has been the use of special forces. The Congress has been willing to provide material assistance to African militaries conducting terrorist suppression missions, but the problem is that many of these countries lack the expertise to employ this assistance optimally. The solution is to take advantage of one of the functions at which SOFs are adept, which is the training of indigenous military personnel on how to use military assistance to carry out their missions. Thus, for instance, the US government can provide helicopters to an African country, and the SOFs can train pilots to fly them and use them tactically to their best advantage.

An added feature is that the SOF teams sent into these countries can be quite small, so they can enter and operate within a country without being noticed. This has the dual advantages of not alarming Americans about the danger of "mission creep" (a slow expansion of commitment) and not alarming the indigenous population about being "occupied" by the Americans.

Until recently, SOF teams had quietly aided indigenous militaries combatting terrorist organizations like Al Qaeda and Boko Haram in several African states (the US Africa Command, which has jurisdiction over these operations, does not publicize where and for how long missions have been underway) under the public radar. In October 2017, however, four American SOFs were killed in a terrorist ambush in Niger, where the SOF team was leading a training mission of native forces. Political figures in the United States were enraged that they did not know the missions existed (a testimony of sorts to their effectiveness), but after a brief controversy, the issue faded and the SOFs presumably went back to their jobs. That, of course, is how the special operators like it best. ∎

CONVENTIONAL RESIDUES: MANPOWER

Questions about the proper types and amounts of traditional military forces and their applications in today's environment are further complicated by a question that is not often raised in public discussions but arguably should be—and will be in the future: who will do America's fighting? The question is influenced by American military efforts in Iraq and Afghanistan, where the quantitative limits of the current manpower system were tested. In fact, the experience of the 2000s has called into strong relief two related residual questions about these forces that must be answered for the future application of traditional forces. The first is quantitative: how many forces will be needed for what purposes? The second question is: how will the United States acquire the forces it needs? The two questions are related: how many forces the country needs depends on how they will be used.

Adequate military manpower has not been a major issue since the country moved to the all-volunteer force (AVF) system in 1972. Before that year, American forces consisted of a mixture of volunteers augmented by draftees. Typically, relatively few Americans were conscripted during peacetime, but the numbers of involuntary recruits grew when the country was at war and voluntary accession could not fill manpower needs. As the Vietnam War dragged on, a proportionately growing part of the force consisted of conscripts, a situation that became politically impossible to sustain. The result was the creation of the AVF. Because the United States had no major military actions for the rest of the last century, the AVF provided adequate numbers of military personnel.

The Iraq and Afghanistan commitments greatly stressed American manpower resources in ways that reveal both the nature and the limits of the AVF concept. Because all AVF members are volunteers who want to be in the military, the result is a highly motivated, competent, professional force. It is, however, a relatively expensive force because professionals must be paid well, and it is relatively small, since only a limited number of Americans will volunteer under most circumstances. To deal with limitations on size, the armed forces resorted to multiple tours of duty in Iraq and Afghanistan for active-duty members and extensive use of the Reserves, each of which has created its own problems, particularly in the field of post-deployment mental and physical disabilities and reenlistments.

The result was a manpower problem, which had three major components and one major implication for the United States at the time. The first component was recruiting shortfalls—all the services have, at one time or another, failed to meet their recruitment goals, and at times, the deficits were substantial. The problem was most acute for ground forces—the so-called combat arms—as is normally the case. The combat arms problem is especially acute in the Guard and Reserves. The second component was lower-than-normal reenlistment rates for current military members. Once again, the greatest part of the problem was in the Guard and Reserves, where non-reenlistment rates approached 50 percent in some cases and might have been higher except for "stop loss" orders, which kept soldiers involuntarily in uniform and deployed for set periods of time beyond the periods of their enlistment.

The effective withdrawal of American forces from Iraq in 2011 relieved these problems, but circumstances like a major deployment in the event of a crisis somewhere like the Korean Peninsula could cause them to return. However, this did not directly address the third problem, which is combat stress disorders suffered by American forces, especially those subject to multiple deployments. The result has been highly elevated rates of mental illness and suicide among Iraq and Afghanistan War veterans. As a shocking example, more American military personnel continue to die as the result of committing suicide than from other causes. Dealing with the lingering effects is expensive, and it is not clear that the US government has yet fully solved this problem. It will be a long-term obligation and drain on the resources available for defense under any circumstances, and it is certainly a problem for which there is scant evidence the government made adequate provision in advance.

What can the United States do about this problem? The answer is parallel to the discussion of risk. One way to reduce risk is to increase capability to deflect risk; the parallel for the military is to increase the size of the armed forces. The question is how. One way is to increase recruitment, either by creating greater incentives to join (e.g., more money for college tuition, signing bonuses) or by offering better terms of service (e.g., shorter enlistment periods, fewer overseas deployments). The other way to increase force size, of course, is through involuntary service—conscription or the draft—a prospect that is politically suicidal.

Another way to reduce risk is to reduce the threat. In military manpower terms, the parallel is to decrease op tempo for the force. With fewer overseas deployments, for instance, major objections to enlistment would be eased, and more current members would likely reenlist (especially Guard and Reserve elements). Clearly, the way to decrease op tempo most dramatically will be to end American involvement in overseas conflicts.

The components of the current strain over manpower policy reflect deeper questions about military service in the United States, with philosophical, political, and practical implications for national security. Five will be raised and discussed here.

The first factor is "who serves?" It is primarily a philosophical question. An artifact of the AVF has been that only a small proportion of the American public ever serves or faces the realistic prospect of having to serve in the armed forces. As a practical matter, this has meant that a large and influential demographic segment of the population effectively is shielded from the prospect that they or members of their families will be subjected to the deprivations and dangers of military service, including most prominently combat. These exclusions mean that in addition to the well-publicized very rich part of the American population, there is a second group of "one percenters" who perform the country's military chores. At the same time, the more politically active, affluent, and well-educated segments of the population, who are also the most politically influential, never have to concern themselves with the personal consequences of military decisions. War is somebody else's business.

The second factor is that this situation is extremely politically popular. Elected politicians love the AVF because it allows them to avoid an especially explosive potential area of loss allocation—compelling their constituents to serve in the military against their wills. Those political figures who champion the AVF in Congress and the executive branch, of course, support the fact that the military's reliance on voluntarism protects it from the need even to consider forcing anyone to serve in uniform. The public at large would solidly oppose any movement away from the AVF, a further reason why already timid politicians and officials who oppose government intrusion on citizens' lives would not support a transition away from the AVF.

This leads to a third philosophical and practical concern surrounding the AVF. That is whether such a force is easier to employ than a conscript force in which citizens are all equally vulnerable to service and thus participation. The AVF is a professional rather than a strictly citizen force; it is composed of willing citizens and some foreigners who hope to use their service to gain permanent residence or citizenship. It is not widely demographically representative, socially or economically, and one can only speculate whether those who make the decisions to commit forces to combat would be as willing to do so if those forces were drawn involuntarily from people more demographically like themselves. A hypothetical question sometimes raised in this regard is whether members of Congress would have voted to authorize the use of force against Iraq in 2003 if their constituents' sons and daughters might have been drafted to do the fighting.

The fourth concern, to which allusion has previously been made, is the limitation on the size force a volunteer method of recruitment can produce, which limits the ability of the country to protect its national security interests with force. The simultaneous deployments in Iraq and Afghanistan tested the practical limits of the AVF and required actions the military would rather not have exercised and would prefer to avoid in the future. One action was multiple deployments, which hurt retention and probably contributed to the number and severity of postwar traumas within the force. The other response was to hire contractors, private individuals and organizations, to perform military-related services for which AVF resources were inadequate. These contractors are generally much more expensive than even AVF personnel, adding to overall costs. Some perform innocuous services (food providers, for instance), but others provide quasi-military functions. In some cases, the military has not been able to exercise complete command control over these contractors (many of whom are former soldiers), and they have engaged in actions embarrassing to the US government.

The fifth concern is with the alternative to an entirely volunteer force structure. It is not widely advertised, but the United States maintains the structure to reinstitute conscription if it receives positive approval to do so. Some advocates argue at least a partial return to the draft would be beneficial on grounds of democratizing the social structure of the force and making it more difficult to deploy forces in harm's way without a compelling basis for doing so (see Snow, *The Middle East, Oil, and the U.S. National Security Policy* for a discussion). As long as the country's military needs can plausibly be met under the existing AVF structure, however, the possibility of a return to conscription is essentially nonexistent.

Military manpower recruitment under the all-voluntary concept is not immutable or irreversible. The national experience has been that most of the time when the country was at peace, its forces were composed basically of volunteers. The exception was the Cold War, when the selective service system (the draft) augmented voluntary accession because the confrontation with Soviet communism dictated larger forces than voluntary appeals produce. The lesson from this is that when there is a sufficient threat that the public agrees must be met, it will permit its citizens to be conscripted to meet the challenge. The chances of this are not great, but there still are "legacy problems" for which legacy forces might still be needed, a dynamic explored in the *Challenge!*.

CHALLENGE!

North Korean Nuclear Forces: A Legacy Problem

The confrontation between the United States and the Democratic People's Republic of Korea is the purest active legacy situation in the contemporary world. Its roots are in the Cold War competition: the communist DPRK invaded and attempted to conquer the non-communist Republic of Korea (ROK) in 1950 as the first full clash of that competition, and the United States (under United Nations auspices) moved to prevent that from happening. In 1953, an armistice halted the fighting with the two sides approximately where they had been before the war. An armistice was established, but it has never been supplanted by a peace treaty (which is a DPRK goal). The United States and ROK and North Korea have glared at one another across the thirty-eighth parallel ever since, with occasional flareups such as the crisis over the DPRK nuclear program in 2017. Unlike other parts of the world, the end of the Cold War has not visibly altered the geopolitical situation. The fact that the most dangerous aspect of the confrontation involves the signature form of potential warfare, nuclear weaponry, makes the analogy more complete.

The confrontation gained momentum during 2018 as the North Koreans tested newer and more powerful thermonuclear warheads and conducted ballistic missile tests with rockets capable of reaching North American targets once operational. The final physical in completing the North's arsenal would be the wedding of its fission-fusion weapons with true ICBM delivery capability. This possibility is the basic outcome the United States most seeks to avoid. The Trump administration's efforts culminating in the Singapore summit have been aimed officially at full denuclearization of the DPRK, but the likelihood they will completely dismantle these weapons seems remote.

The entire confrontation has a decidedly Cold War aura surrounding it, and it continues to occupy major American energy. The Unites States maintains around twenty-eight thousand conventional troops along the DMZ between the two Koreas, and warfare on the peninsula is one of the few scenarios that might involve large numbers of American conventional legacy forces. Confrontations flare periodically, and except for escalated rhetoric from Trump, the 2018 crisis seems likely to peter out the same way previous crises between the two countries have. They do, however, remind us why we had the legacy forces we did and why there is at least some residual reason not to dismantle them. ■

CONCLUSION: THE CONTINUING RELEVANCE OF LEGACY FORCES

By and large, the traditional military problems and solutions discussed in this chapter are artifacts of the Cold War and thinking about that period, conditioned by the experience of the first half of the twentieth century (notably the World Wars). The end of the Cold War provided a reprieve from the worst possible consequences of the Cold War going "hot" and produced a decade of relative relaxation of military concerns, effectively reversed by September 11. The first decade of the 2000s was dominated by 9/11-generated defense efforts, but it has been followed by a more force-aversive attitude in the early 2010s. What is next?

The military requirements of the post–September 11 defense environment are considerably different than those of the Cold War. The large end of the scale of threat, with huge arsenals of nuclear weapons and massive conventional forces facing one another in what could have been mankind's most destructive, and possibly last, war, has largely disappeared from operational consideration. Russia, the successor to the menacing Soviet Union, is no longer the significant opponent it once was, and even if it is often less than a friend, not even saber rattling and provocations like those in Syria are likely to devolve to war that would draw in the United States. The titanic clash that once seemed inevitable now seems a mere fanciful possibility. The military artifacts of that confrontation like massive nuclear arsenals seem oddly archaic as well.

The small end of the scale is now the most likely source of scenarios. The threats to American security come from more remote places where American interests are less engaged and where the scale and nature of American involvement are less well defined but generally more limited. The terrorism of bin Laden against the American homeland was the apparent exception to that rule, but it is not yet entirely clear whether this, or some other, form of terrorism will fill the center stage of concern that may engage SOF-style and SOF-sized responses but not larger entanglements.

How relevant are the military concerns and forces of the Cold War for the present and the future? Certainly the conventional forces and structures inherited from that era proved to be highly useful during the Persian Gulf War of 1990–91, which helps explain why a more thorough critique of future roles was delayed as long as it was. The defenders of tradition received a reprieve in the Kuwaiti desert. That critique was further delayed by the more immediate need to react to 9/11 and its spin-offs in Afghanistan and Iraq. American combat operations in Iraq are now completed, and the apparent inadequacy of the effort in Afghanistan has caused questioning of the operations there. The United States has been less than spectacularly successful in either country. Heavy forces have been especially suspect, and the SOFs and other light forces have seemed more useful.

The huge nuclear arsenals and the elaborate constructs for their deterrent roles seem particularly anachronistic, which has led to initiatives to reduce them. Nuclear weapons are not completely irrelevant, of course, because several states possess them, and others, including terrorists, may attempt to get them. Both the United States and Russia will clearly maintain arsenals adequately large to promise that an aggressor contemplating attacking either one with WMD would have to consider the suicidal consequences of such actions. In the meantime, the emphasis will be on arsenal reductions, non-proliferation, and securing forces from undesirable hands. Nuclear worries remain part of the equation but now focus on the peripheries in places like Iran and the DPRK, not on questions of central nuclear war.

The structure of conventional forces is also in limbo. As noted, the heavy composition of American (and most other Western) forces was designed for a massive, Western-style World War III clash with like forces from the Soviet world. Now, the only countries that possess those kinds of forces are American allies or friends, and it is not clear how adaptable those forces are for other contingencies, especially the kinds of asymmetrical wars that may seem to be the future.

Conventional forces are buffeted from both ends of the spectrum. On one hand, their relevance in the face of unconventional forces bent on devising ways to negate their advantages has not been proven. If technological proficiency and mass always prevail, the United States would have won in Vietnam. Newer and more sophisticated means of conducting traditional warfare have been developed and proposed for deployment, but their fate seems dubious. Despite these concerns, there has, until recently, been little criticism of a force structure arguably inappropriate for and anachronistic in a threat environment where that structure may not address all the problems encountered. The heavy legacy forces, which are very expensive to develop and maintain, look increasingly like a questionable investment to some budget-minded analysts, at least in the numbers and configurations in which they have traditionally existed.

STUDY/DISCUSSION QUESTIONS

1. How are current American conceptions of traditional military problems tied to the Cold War? What are legacy forces? Why have these conceptions become matters of debate in the contemporary environment?
2. Discuss the evolution of strategic nuclear forces and plans for their use in terms of the seminal events of the nuclear age, the concept of deterrence, and US nuclear strategies of deterrence.
3. What is nuclear proliferation? Discuss its aspects and evolution, its dynamics (the $N + 1$ problem), and the current state of the concern, including the problems associated with attempts to limit proliferation. Apply the discussion to Iran and North Korea.
4. Discuss the traditional role of conventional forces, including the debate over heavy and light forces. Place this discussion in the context of the current threat environment and budgetary constraints on defense spending.
5. What are the "not-so-conventional" special operations forces? Discuss their historic and evolving roles in the configuration and uses of American forces. What are their advantages and limitations?
6. What is the contemporary debate over military manpower? How has this debate been made livelier by the Iraq and Afghanistan Wars? What are the major concerns affecting manpower? Discuss.
7. How do changes in the international security environment have an impact on the future evolution of legacy forces?

SELECTED BIBLIOGRAPHY

Bailey, Beth. *America's Army: Making the All-Volunteer Force*. Cambridge, MA: Harvard University Press, 2009.

Besel, Jennifer M. *The Navy SEALs*. Mankato, MN: Capstone Press, 2011.

Borden, William Liscum. *There Will Be No Time: The Revolution in Strategy*. New York: Palgrave Macmillan, 1946.

Brodie, Bernard. *Strategy in the Missile Age*. Princeton, NJ: Princeton University Press, 1959.

———. *The Absolute Weapon: Atomic Power and World Order*. New York: Harcourt Brace, 1946.

Cha, Victor. *The Impossible State: North Korea, Past and Present*. New York: ECCO, 2013.

Clark, Ronald W. *The Greatest Power on Earth: The International Race for Nuclear Supremacy from Earliest Theory to Three-Mile Island*. New York: Harper and Row, 1980.

Clausewitz, Carl von. *On War*. Princeton, NJ: Princeton University Press, 1976.

Cohen, Eliot. *Citizens and Soldiers: The Dilemma of Military Service*. Ithaca, NY: Cornell University Press, 1985.

Dockery, Keven. *Navy Seals: A History*. Parts I—III. New York: Berkley Books, 2001–2003.

Drew, Dennis M., and Donald M. Snow. *Making Strategy for the Twenty-First Century: An Introduction to National Security Processes and Problems*. Montgomery, AL: Air University Press, 2006.

Engbrecht, Shawn. *America's Covert Warriors: Inside the World of Private Military Contractors*. Washington, DC: Potomac Books, 2010.

Gates, Robert M. "A Balanced Strategy." *Foreign Affairs* 88, 1 (January/February 2009), 28–40.

Guertner, Gary L., and Donald M. Snow. *The Last Frontier: An Analysis of the Strategic Defense Initiative*. Lexington, MA: Lexington Books, 1986.

Harrison, Selig. "Did North Korea Cheat?" *Foreign Affairs* 84, 1 (January/February 2005), 99–110.

Kaplan, Fred. *The Insurgents: David Petraeus and the Revolt to Change the American Way of War*. Reprint ed. New York: Simon and Schuster, 2014.

Kilcullen, David. *Counterinsurgency*. New York: Oxford University Press, 2010.

Kim, Sung Chull, and Michael D. Cohen (eds.). *North Korea and Nuclear Weapons: Entering the New Age of Deterrence*. Washington, DC: Georgetown University Press, 2017.

Kramer, Andrew E. "Russia Steps Back from Key Arms Treaty." *New York Times* (online), (July 14, 2007).

Lieber, Kier A., and Daryl G. Press. "The Rise of U.S. Nuclear Superiority." *Foreign Affairs* 85, 2 (March/April 2006), 42–54.

McCaffrey, Barry R. "Looking Beyond Iraqi Freedom: Future Enemies Won't Roll Over So Easily." *Armed Forces Journal* 140 (July 2003), 8–9.

McNamara, Robert S. "Apocalypse Soon." *Foreign Policy* (May/June 2005), 28–35.

Naylor, Sean. *Relentless Strike: The Secret History of the Joint Special Operations Command*. New York: St. Martin's Press, 2015.

Nuechterlein, Donald E. *A Cold War Odyssey*. Lexington, KY: University of Kentucky Press, 1997.

Payne, Keith B. "The Nuclear Posture Review: Setting the Record Straight." *Washington Quarterly* 28, 3 (Summer 2005), 135–152.

Perkowich, George. "How to Be a Nuclear Watchdog." *Foreign Policy* (January/February 2005), 28–35.

Pilat, Joseph F. "Reassessing Assurances in a Unipolar World." *Washington Quarterly* 28, 2 (Spring 2005), 59–70.

Porch, Douglas. *Counterinsurgency: Exposing the Myths of the New Way of War*. Cambridge, MA: Cambridge University Press, 2013.

Quadrennial Defense Review. Washington, DC: U.S. Department of Defense, 1997, 2001, 2006, 2010, and 2014.

Rhodes, Richard. *The Making of the Atomic Bomb*. New York: Touchstone Books, 1998.

Robinson, Linda. *The Future of Special Operations Forces*. New York: Council on Foreign Relations, 2013.

Sawyer, Ralph D. *The Seven Military Classics of Ancient China*. Boulder, CO: Westview Press, 1993.

Snow, Donald M. *Cases in U.S. National Security: Concepts and Processes*. Lanham, MD: Rowman & Littlefield, 2019 (see especially Chapter 6).

———. *The Middle East, Oil, and the U.S. National Security Policy*. Lanham, MD: Rowman & Littlefield, 2016.

———. *The Necessary Peace: Nuclear Weapons and Superpower Relations*. Lexington, MA: Lexington Books, 1987.

———. *Nuclear Strategy in a Dynamic World: Policy for the 1980s*. Tuscaloosa: University of Alabama Press, 1981.

Specter, Arlen, and Christopher Bradish. "Dialogue with Adversaries." *Washington Quarterly* 30, 1 (Winter 2006–2007), 9–26.

Stanley, Bruce E. *Outsourcing Security: Private Military Contractors and U.S. Foreign Policy*. Washington, DC: Potomac Books, 2010.

Stoessinger, John G. *Why Nations Go to War*. 11th ed. Belmont, CA: Wadsworth Publishing, 2010.

United States Department of the Army. *Field Manual (FM) 3–05: Army Special Operations Forces*. Washington, DC: Department of the Army, 2006.

Wiegley, Russell F. *The American Way of War*. New York: Palgrave Macmillan, 1973.

Wright, James. *Those Who Have Borne the Battle: A History of America's Wars and Those Who Fought Them*. New York: Public Affairs Press, 2012.

The Contemporary Environment and Challenges

This part examines the major national security challenges, particularly those for which the employment of US force has been or may be dictated. The four chapters look progressively at the structure of violence in the system, how the United States has dealt with those kinds of situations in recent years, the places and settings where instability and conflict are most prevalent, and applications of force short of major violence.

Chapter 9 introduces and explains the novel form of challenge arising from the fact that traditional, conventional warfare between large national armed forces has all but disappeared and has been replaced by asymmetrical warriors whose purposes and methods seek to frustrate conventional military forces like those of the United States. Chapter 10 sets the table for projecting into the future, looking at the three major outcomes of national security response to 9/11 in the forms of a concerted campaign against Al Qaeda (AQ)–prototype terrorism and the wars in Afghanistan and Iraq. Each situation has changed since 2001, and their individual legacies (or "lessons learned") help define the forward-looking environment. The most prominent of the challenges arising from those legacies is the phenomenon of so-called asymmetrical warfare.

Chapter 11 looks at those places and situations where violence and instability are most prevalent—the lethal landscapes of the world—and where the United States has been most likely to insert or to consider the use of American force in the contemporary period. This pattern has been most vivid in the Middle East and other parts of Asia, but American efforts have not been uniformly successful in achieving the goals for which they have been employed, raising questions about the propriety of continued pursuit of interests there by lethal means.

Chapter 12 systematizes the asymmetrical trend into the prospects and activities—the menu of responses—the United States may contemplate in the future. Modern wars occur in developing-world countries, where traditional measures of military success are either irrelevant or inadequate to describe their dynamics or outcomes. Nation building and development are responses to these new problems but have often failed to produce the desired outcomes, and their mixed success raises some questions about the advisability of American future involvement in these kinds of situations.

The Structure and Consequences of Modern Violence: Asymmetrical Warfare

What is now commonly called asymmetrical warfare is by no means a new phenomenon in military history or in the American experience. The situation where opposing military forces adopt sometimes radically different approaches to warfare dates to the first military encounters between armed groups. It has become more prominent in the last half century, particularly since the end of the Cold War. Asymmetrical warfare at heart is a methodology for conducting hostilities by a weaker party confronting an insurmountably superior military opponent if fighting occurs on the stronger party's terms. Since the United States is militarily the most powerful state in the world, with both the broadest interests and the most potent conventional military forces, choosing asymmetrical means is the most obvious manner by which a potential opponent can confront American military power. Fighting asymmetrical opponents is a very different military proposition than opposing enemies who fight in a similar fashion for like reasons. The prospect of meeting asymmetrical foes, such as those against whom the United States has competed in diverse places and situations from Vietnam to Afghanistan.

How the United States will use force in the future is one of the central national security questions the country faces. During the 2000s, the country engaged in two wars against foes in places where conventional legacy forces were not clearly appropriate. Iraq and Afghanistan reintroduced this country to asymmetrical warfare, and it was not a style at which the United States has proven wildly successful. Is this the wave of the future?

These experiences from the last decade offer some glimmers of what that future may hold. The Iraqi and Afghan opponents of the United States refused (or were unable) to confront the United States in a conventional Western military manner and thus employed different ways of fighting to try to avoid defeat by the United States and its Western military allies. These alternative methods did not produce unambiguous success for those opponents, but neither did they result in the abject defeat such forces would have expected had they tried to compete with the United States in the conventional warfare the United States has traditionally preferred and in which its greatest advantages lie. The lesson for those who observed these conflicts is that unconventional methods provide at least the chance of being able to compete successfully against the American military colossus. Knowing this, it is the kind of national security future for which the United States must prepare as well.

There is certainly nothing new about asymmetrical warfare. The purpose of the methodology is to reverse the military disadvantage combatants faced when confronted by insurmountable force and thus increase the odds of success by creating a more "level playing field." The objective is to change the military situation so the weaker side's weakness is nullified or reduced. As such, it is the strategic approach of the weak when faced with a superior force. This adaptation is as old as the first armed conflicts between groups of men and has been an enduring legacy of mankind. The Romans, whose legions represented the consummate conventional (or symmetrical) force of their time, certainly viewed the Huns who eventually defeated them as asymmetrical warriors, even if they did not use the term. For Americans, the campaigns against the various Native American tribes they encountered, and particularly those on the Plains and in the Southwest, represented an early exposure to the phenomenon.

The contemporary American experience with a form of asymmetrical war was in Vietnam in the 1960s and early 1970s. The variant of asymmetrical war American forces encountered there was something known as *mobile-guerrilla warfare*, a style adapted from the Eastern tradition by Mao Zedong during the Chinese Civil War in the 1920s through the 1940s and further refined by the Vietnamese strategist Vo Nguyen Giap (this form of war is discussed in more detail later in the chapter). Its military aspects are very much part of the tradition employed against Americans by the Taliban in Afghanistan and by the insurgents who arose to oppose the United States during the mid-2000s in Iraq. Apologists often argue that the Vietnam analogy is spurious because politically the war was part of a Cold War/proxy confrontation between communism and anti-communism, with significant conventional qualities. This criticism is both valid and misguided: the form asymmetrical warfare takes is a matter of military circumstance, not of the political goal it is employed to serve.

Asymmetrical warfare appears in various guises depending on the time and place one encounters the phenomenon. The heart of understanding this tradition is to think of it as a *methodology* rather than a *method*. Asymmetrical warfare is a mindset, an approach to the problem of the inferior when faced with a superior opponent rather than a set of guidelines or rules by which such an endeavor should be conducted (a method). Part of the methodology suggests that the asymmetrical warrior should observe what others have done in similar situations, adopt what has succeeded, reject what has failed, and then tailor those lessons to the physical and political setting where the conflict occurs. As a result, the implication is that no two asymmetrical efforts are exactly alike, and this adds to the frustration and difficulty of a country trying to prepare itself for opponents who may adopt this methodology. As a result, there is little reliable doctrine for opposing asymmetrical opponents.

The US military has traditionally not been enthusiastic or particularly adept at fighting asymmetrical opponents, and its historical record is not exemplary in dealing with asymmetrical foes. In one sense, this situation is ironic because this tradition of warfare played an important role in the formative stages of the American republic. Most of the Continentals with any military experience had what would likely now be called counterinsurgency backgrounds, having engaged in activities against unconventional Native American opponents on the frontier (particularly in the French and Indian War). During the revolution itself, the Continental Army generally failed when it met the British Army in the symmetrical warfare of the time—linear battles between clashing armies on open fields—where the superior training and discipline of British forces usually prevailed. Rather, the Continentals succeeded when they adopted unconventional ways of fighting, as they did at Saratoga and at Cowpens. American Revolutionary War military heroes like Francis ("the Swamp Fox") Marion in South Carolina and Nathaniel Greene in New England were among the great asymmetrical warriors of their time.

That early experience was not embraced by an American military establishment more comfortable with conventional European-style warfare. The modern American military tradition dates to the American Civil War, which was fought as a thoroughly symmetrical, conventional conflict when the Southern side probably would have been much better served by an unconventional, guerrilla-style approach that was more sensitive to Southern terrain and the weakness of Northern support for the war. The experience in Vietnam could have provided a wake-up call, and the inability to prevail in Afghanistan suggests that Americans have learned about the *methods* our asymmetrical opponents adopt more than we have learned about combating the *methodology* of asymmetrical warfare.

The American frustration in Afghanistan and, to a lesser degree, Iraq has to be encouraging to any hostile group that faces the possibility of being drawn into conflict with the United States. Potential future American opponents may conclude that the American military machine can be effectively countered by adopting an asymmetrical approach. If that is true (and it may not be), understanding asymmetrical warfare and what can and cannot reasonably and effectively be done to oppose it successfully is a major part of the assessment of the American future.

The rest of this chapter attempts to provide the basis for some of these judgments. It begins by putting into context how and why this form of warfare has been elevated to the place that it now occupies—or arguably should occupy—in American national security policy. The discussion then moves to the dynamics of asymmetrical warfare, including defining the approach and the dynamics of its practice, its appeal to some groups, and two of the most articulate examples of its practice in the recent American military past. The chapter concludes with an extensive examination of the implications of asymmetrical futures for American national security policy, including the effects of such an emphasis on asymmetrical warfare for overall national security policy.

THE CONTEXT OF ASYMMETRICAL WARFARE

The generic style of fighting that forms the heart of asymmetrical warfare represents the coalescence of two different but overlapping military traditions. The first is the problem of how a weaker opponent gains an equal or superior military footing to a seemingly stronger opponent. It is a response to a problem dating to antiquity. The superior forces of the time sought to exert their will and overcome the opposition of those on whom they sought to impose that will. The weak attempt to avoid that imposition in the face of forbidding odds. As such, asymmetrical warfare is the methodology of the weak against the strong.

The second tradition is that of indirect, rather than direct, warfare. In a sense, it is a clash between the Western, European tradition, featuring the direct confrontation of armed forces built on the principle of massive application of force attempting to destroy or break the cohesion of the opponent, and the more indirect Eastern approach to warfare that seeks to achieve military victory through maneuver and superior strategies that break the opponent's will to resist or continue the competition. The direct, Western approach is best exemplified in the campaigns of Napoleon or the bloody landscape of Western Europe during the World Wars of the twentieth century. The Eastern tradition dates back at least to the writings of the great Chinese military writer Sun Tzu (discussed in Amplification 9.1) as refined and brought forward by subsequent practitioners such as Mao

Zedong in China to the present. The two traditions coalesce in modern warfare as it is practiced today in Asia, including the Middle East.

Unconventional warfare has been a historical constant, although its relative importance in any particular period has varied greatly. In this sense, it is not entirely dissimilar to the phenomenon of terrorism, which from one perspective is just an asymmetrical method for the weak to bring their causes to the strong. Wherever there are disadvantaged groups who seek somehow to create political or other conditions more congenial to their particular interests and who have concluded that only violence has any chance of producing favorable change, the methodology of asymmetrical warfare will be considered and, in one form or another, may be adopted.

AMPLIFICATION 9.1

Sun Tzu on Asymmetrical Warfare

Little is known about the life of Sun Tzu, a Chinese military thinker who advised several warlords in China approximately three thousand years ago. Some historians argue that he did not exist at all and that the work attributed to him was the collection of the work and experience of others. Regardless of these arguments, his classic military manual, *The Art of War*, was a guide to action similar in intent to Machiavelli's political manual *The Prince* in the sixteenth century. It was little studied in the West until the twentieth century when it became known as one of the sources of inspiration and guidance to Mao Zedong in his campaign to seize control of China over a twenty-year period ending in 1949.

The heart of Sun Tzu's advice centered on knowing when and how to fight, and it would have been familiar to many practitioners of what is now called asymmetrical warfare. His philosophy is rooted in the ideas of indirection and asymmetry, and it is captured in the military advice he offered to leaders of his time. The most basic statement of this advice comes in the following admonition: "When the enemy advances, we retreat; when the enemy halts, we harass; when the enemy seeks to avoid battle, we attack; when the enemy retreats, we pursue." In other words, only fight on your own terms. In addition, he adds that the victor on the battlefield is the combatant who has a superior understanding of his opponent that allows him to deceive and thus alter the battle to his own advantage. "All warfare," he writes, "is based on deception. . . . To subdue the enemy without fighting is the acme of skill." The outcome of warfare, in other words, goes to the more intelligent, not necessarily the most physically powerful, combatant. The heart of asymmetrical warfare, of course, is turning disadvantage into advantage, which is at the core of Sun Tzu's advice. ∎

The current period is one in which asymmetrical warfare has become a highly visible, prominent part of the national security environment worldwide. One can even argue that confronting and neutralizing those who practice asymmetrical warfare is *the* dominant military problem confronting those in power or those who support people in power, and the United States stands at the forefront of countries for which this challenge is particularly poignant.

Why is the emergence of asymmetrical warfare so important in the contemporary world? Several factors have contributed to elevating this problem to the forefront. They include the end of the Cold War, the US emergence from the Cold War as by far the most powerful symmetrical military force in the world, and the shifting emphasis toward concern with violence in the developing world. These factors coalesced around a United States that was at the center of the globalizing system and increasingly saw its important interests in global terms and the pursuit of those interests in activist terms. These factors are interrelated to one another. The terrorist attacks of September 11 served as the catalyst to ignite the current set of concerns.

The Cold War Effect

As is true in so many areas of American national security, the American posture on asymmetrical warfare has its roots in the Cold War experience. The Cold War was the quintessence of heavy (including nuclear), symmetrical, European-style military preparation, and that structure absolutely dominated the military effort and mindset of the US military. The Cold War confrontation was the ultimate worst case, and if it was not managed successfully, nothing else mattered. Asymmetrical warfare was not part of the worst case.

The Vietnam War was the first chink in the traditional armor. The United States entered that conflict assuming the symmetrical forces and strategies they employed would quickly defeat the primitive indigenous opposition they faced, an expectation that seemed justified at the first major encounter with the North Vietnamese Army (NVA) in the Ia Drang (river) valley, an encounter captured by Moore and Galloway's book and motion picture, *We Were Soldiers Once . . . and Young*. American firepower won that battle and seemed to vindicate orthodoxy. The enemy concluded they could only win by adopting an asymmetrical strategy that would nullify American firepower superiority. Their strategy worked and served as a model for other future developing world opponents to the United States. The United States has been trying ever since to figure out how to deal with asymmetrical war.

The United States as Hyperpower

When the Cold War ended, the dominance of traditional symmetrical warfare came into question as well in several ways to which the military is still adapting. As the Cold War receded as a major organizing national security problem worldwide, many of the world's countries responded by reducing forces, the size and expense of which had been necessitated by Cold War obligations and perceptions of threat. This phenomenon occurred to a lesser degree in the United States, where the size of American forces was cut by about a third during the 1990s. Because of these shallower cuts, the American military power position in the world increased in relative terms. It became common to talk about American military hegemony—the United States not only as the sole remaining superpower but as a *hyperpower*.

The basic expression of this military superiority was and remains in the qualitative and quantitative advantage of the United States in *conventional, symmetrical* war capabilities. When combined with a growing confidence and resiliency in the United States about its reasserted world leadership, the result was an assertive American stance based, to some large degree, on the ability and willingness to implement American preferences with military force that no one else could match.

The reaction was what has become an enigma for the United States. As its great advantage in conventional armed force widened to a chasm (in the 2000s, for instance, the United States spent as much, or nearly as much, as the rest of the world combined on defense), no country stood a chance against the American military machine, and the global response was to abandon the competition. The American walkover against Iraq in the Persian Gulf War of 1990–91 was a wake-up call for potential opponents elsewhere: it is futile and suicidal to contest the United States on the terms on which the Americans prefer to fight. If American interests and your own come into conflict, you must find other ways to wage the contest or lose.

The net result of American overwhelming advantage at conventional, European-style warfare was that it has effectively made that form of war obsolete. The only other countries organized in the same way as the Americans were friends, allies, or others (like Russia) who had concluded that the competition was unbearable, current Russian resurgence notwithstanding. Countries in the developing world had no chance of resisting the Americans on their own terms and abandoned trying (Saddam Hussein's token resistance against the American invasion in 2003 is the clearest evidence of this). Instead, the only way to resist the Americans was to find a way to negate American sources of superiority. Through the adoption of asymmetrical approaches designed to negate the American advantage. By perfecting the historical "American way of war," the United States also made that style obsolete and inapplicable in the national security environment in which it found itself.

September 11 and the Shift in Dominant Forms of Violent Activity

The trend toward asymmetrical forms of violence has increased since 9/11. The terrorist attacks were acts of asymmetrical warfare from the vantage point of the perpetrators (who considered them acts of war): they used unconventional weapons (airliners full of jet fuel) in an unconventional manner (effectively as cruise missiles) against targets that were unprepared for them. Swooping from the sky unsuspected and undefended, they attacked their targets in a surprise operation with all the elements of a scene straight from *Lawrence of Arabia*. American planners realized they had to learn how to fight against a very different kind of opponent.

The emergence of asymmetrical warfare in the Middle East context represented the convergence of related phenomena at that place and point in time. The terrorist assaults of 9/11 came from a Middle Eastern–based organization that was headquartered in Afghanistan and drew its members from nationals from multiple Middle Eastern countries, thus making the area a natural ground for American reaction. Similar qualities of fear motivated the United States in Iraq. At the same time, the reactions in Afghanistan and Iraq were also the first major occasions when the enormous predominance of American symmetrical superiority first demonstrated in Kuwait was brought to bear, and it was unclear exactly how opponents would respond to the apparent inevitability of the American hyperpower flexing of its muscles.

THE DYNAMICS OF ASYMMETRICAL WARFARE

The academic use of the term "asymmetrical warfare" first appeared in an article by Andrew Mack that contrasted the experiences of the Americans and the French in their respective unsuccessful military conflicts in Vietnam and Algeria. Titled "Why Big Nations Lose Small Wars," it appeared in a 1975 issue of the academic journal *World Politics*. It received some attention at the time, but it receded into academic obscurity until the post–Cold War period, when the name and phenomenon were revived in policy circles to describe the difficulties the United States and others were encountering in the developing-world military encounters.

The term is more novel than the phenomenon it represents. This style of warfare is and has been described in many ways, such as unconventional warfare and insurgency, among other designations. Asymmetrical warfare is a novel way to depict the battle between unequal and dissimilar opponents, however, because of the geometric analogy it conjures. The heart of the notion of symmetry is balance between the constituent parts of whatever is being described using the term. In geometry, saying something is symmetrical means it has two similar halves, each of which is in balance with the other. A bisected circle is a good example of perfect symmetry. Asymmetry, by contrast, describes the opposite condition of symmetry, where there is imbalance between the two sides of the object. Extrapolated to warfare, this basic distinction helps one start unravelling the problem of asymmetrical warfare that confronts American national security policy and that has confounded some recent US military efforts.

Defining the Differences between Symmetrical and Asymmetrical Warfare

The basic definition and distinction of symmetry can be extended to the various basic concepts underlying warfare. At the risk of some oversimplification, these include the reasons for which groups (countries, groups within countries) go to war (the objectives of war), the organization of the forces they bring to bear to accomplish their goals (military structures), and the methods (strategies) and rules (laws of warfare in a normative sense) they employ in the conduct of war. Some of the other ways in which styles of war are contrasted include insurgency and counterinsurgency, for instance, to describe a method by which asymmetrical warfare can be carried on. The dichotomy between conventional and unconventional warfare provides as good a synonym for symmetrical and asymmetrical warfare as is available.

The two terms need to be defined and contrasted. *Symmetrical* (or conventional) warfare refers to the situation where both sides have the same general goals, organize and equip their forces in similar ways, and operate through similar strategies and according to similar rules of engagement and standards of acceptable conduct. In such wars, both sides adopt, in other words, roughly the same conventions of war, such that both sides mirror one another and are thus in some form of balance or symmetry.

A symmetrical war can be fought between any two forces that have the same general orientation and is not dependent on any single source or manifestation of symmetry. The American "way of war" reflects the European tradition of warfare as politically driven military actions (goals) fought between similarly equipped and organized forces (for instance, troops wearing distinguishable uniforms and organized along similar rank structures and chains of command) under similar accepted methods of conduct (rules of war). For the most part, the large European wars of the twentieth century were symmetrical, conventional wars in these terms, even if there were some unconventional activities at their peripheries (e.g., partisan guerrilla warfare in the Balkans or in parts of the Pacific). Because these very large conflicts were so important to the history of the twentieth century and were, in a real sense, the apex of the European military tradition, most Americans think of warfare fought in this manner as "normal." By contrast, wars fought in different ways are "abnormal," a notion that almost certainly prejudices the objective consideration of asymmetrical alternatives.

The idea of symmetry does not connote devotion to any specific way to fight wars, merely to the notion that both sides fight in similar ways. Thus, for instance, one can imagine two sides fighting insurgent-style each with nontraditional (at least in Western terms) forces in a guerrilla war. Such a war would be unconventional but symmetrical. The wars between Native Americans on the American plains before the introduction of European influences were of this nature. This same style became unconventional or asymmetrical only when it confronted an opponent driven by other methods—in this case the European-inspired Spanish and then the Americans. The adjective *symmetrical*, in other words, only describes the balance between sides within a specific context, not some universal standard.

The problem is that adherents to one particular military tradition have a cultural tendency to equate their set of conventions with right or proper behavior and to denigrate variations from it. In order to indoctrinate members to undertake actions deriving from a particular set of conventions that will put those members at physical risk, it is helpful to convince them that what they are being asked to do is the "correct" and even the "honorable" way to conduct themselves. By implicit or explicit contrast, those who act in different ways are somehow less honorable and their choice of methods less morally acceptable than one's own. When the colonials in the American Revolution flinched at confronting the British Army in the linear battles at which the British were considerably more adept and instead adopted tactics they had learned from the Native Americans, such as ambush from behind trees and rocks, the British viewed their actions as cowardly and dishonorable, part of what one British commander referred to as the "dirty little war of terror and murder." For the inferior force, symmetry may mean suicide, however, and that can be a powerful incentive to adopt other means—to act asymmetrically.

If symmetrical approaches to war suggest balance or similarity in how and why war is waged, asymmetrical approaches suggest the opposite. *Asymmetrical* warfare refers to the situation where two combating parties differ in the purpose for which they are fighting, the ways in which they are organized to conduct their military operations, and the rules or conventions of warfare under which they operate. The two sides, in other words, are dissimilar and do not mirror one another. The contrasts between them can be on any of the three basic levels of comparison (objectives, organization, methods), and the degree of asymmetry of their resulting clash varies to the extent they do not reflect one another on one or more of these levels and the extent of the differences within each level.

Asymmetrical warfare occurs whenever two sides fight differently. The most common and familiar example for Americans is, of course, the situation where one side fights conventionally and the other unconventionally. In contemporary terms, this form of asymmetrical warfare involves an American force fighting in the conventional European manner—with clear politically defined goals for forces organized along familiar lines of authority wearing standardized military uniforms and discernibly marked conveyances—by rules of engagement specified in the Geneva Conventions on Warfare. The opponent, on the other hand, eschews some or all of these characteristics. The opponent's goals may be nontraditional (not aimed at the traditional Western objective of political control in the post-conflict peace). It may be organized informally, utilizing part-time "soldiers" who blend in with the civilian population and do not wear uniforms distinguishing themselves from the surrounding population or answer to any discernible hierarchy of command. Most importantly, they may not accept the conventions for conduct in war that represent the norm for "acceptable" as defined by the opponent or by international standards.

The most visible and controversial aspect of asymmetrical warfare is the rejection of conventional means of conduct by one side. Refusing to be bound by the accepted "rules of the game" is an important and often necessary aspect of the attempt to level the playing field and thus to provide an opportunity for a disadvantaged force to gain a chance not possible otherwise. One example is for an asymmetrical warrior force to imbed itself in a civilian population, hiding from detection by, among other things, not wearing identifying uniforms that would allow them to be detected. Such behavior is prohibited by the Geneva Conventions, but it is a prohibition that works to the advantage of the powerful at the expense of the weak and is thus a form of rule breaking that may reduce the weaker side's disadvantage. For the traditional European-style warrior, finding the enemy, fixing him in place, and applying superior firepower to destroy that enemy is a major purpose of conducting military operations. To that end, the rules of war specify that combatants must wear distinguishable uniforms and not commingle with noncombatants. From the vantage point of the asymmetrical warrior, adhering to such rules makes them little more than easily identifiable "sitting ducks."

The example also illustrates why those adhering to the prevailing conventions are likely to hold the asymmetrical opponent in disdain. Hiding in urban areas among women, children, and the elderly is cowardly behavior under normal rules of European-style warfare. An opponent engaging in such behavior is likely to be viewed as cowardly because of such acts of self-survival. The party who adopts the tactic of blending into civilian populations also compounds the military problems for conventional forces, which are not routinely trained for such combat and must learn new ways to deal with them effectively.

Overcoming cultural biases is a major part of the difficulty of dealing with an opponent who chooses to fight asymmetrically because that opponent rejects mores, conventions, and rules that are an integral part of the symmetrical warrior's value system. Overcoming the prejudices that may be implicit in the clash of values and cultures is clearly part of the process of unravelling the problem of dealing with asymmetrical war.

The Lure of Asymmetrical Warfare

The problem facing the potential asymmetrical warrior is difficult. That warrior seeks to create (or re-create) some political condition he or she favors but is faced by an overwhelming preponderance of opposing power that must be surmounted before those goals can be attained.

The question facing the potential asymmetrical warrior is how his or her goals can be realized. For some aspirants, the answer is the terrorism variant of asymmetrical means, but terrorism has the undesirable characteristic that it rarely succeeds in achieving the broad objectives for which it is adopted. Terrorism certainly meets the criteria of asymmetry: the forms of organization that are associated with terrorists are clearly not those of traditional military entities, and terrorists egregiously violate and even flaunt their rejection of traditional values of warfare and civil law.

The problem is that terrorism, in fact, rarely works in the ultimate sense, and the potential asymmetrical warrior is likely to reject terrorism as a primary operating method for this reason. There are, however, two exceptions. One is that terrorism is often the method of the extremely weak, which is to say that usually terrorists commit the acts they do because they are incapable of much else: necessity dictates options. The other exception is that some acts of terrorism may be a part, if not the central feature, of asymmetrical means to achieve goals, and those confronting the asymmetrical warrior may find themselves tempted to invoke terrorist means against an asymmetrical opponent, such as the use of torture to extract information from terrorists.

The obvious allure of asymmetrical warfare resides in its underlying methodology: the search for means to confront and neutralize the advantages presented by a physically superior foe. The need for such a calculation begins from the perception that fighting by the acceptable orthodoxy is futile and that only changing the rules will make possible an outcome other than total disaster and loss. Asymmetrical solutions may or may not be capable of producing "victory" in the traditional, European sense. Usually the preexisting power imbalance means the asymmetrical warrior cannot realistically hope to achieve the traditional, European military goal of decisively defeating the other side's armed forces and causing them to surrender or quit the field in defeat. That may be the dream of the asymmetrical warrior, but it is little more than that.

Within warfare, it is conventional to talk about victory in terms of three outcomes (see Snow and Drew for a more complete discussion). One of these is the overcoming of *hostile ability*, the physical ability of an opponent to resist the assertion of one's power. Because the balance of traditional power disfavors the asymmetrical warrior, this is not generally a viable goal. In most cases, it is the goal of the symmetrical opponent. The second is to overcome *hostile will defined as conversion to support for the objectives of the other side*. Deciding that the objectives of the opponent may be superior to those one has held may be the ultimate goal of both sides, but it rarely occurs until the physical war has ended and is a condition for stable and enduring post-conflict peace. Asymmetrical wars rarely conclude in such a neat and decisive way.

This leaves the third goal, which is overcoming *enemy will defined as cost tolerance*. This term refers to the willingness of one side or another to continue to endure the suffering associated with war and to continue resistance as opposed to giving in to the demands of the other side. Cost tolerance is in effect a measure of the endurance and degree of commitment that one party or the other has to the pursuit of their conflicting goals. If a particular country or movement has a very high level of cost tolerance, this translates into a very high threshold to be surpassed before that party concludes that continuing to persevere is no longer worth the effort or the sacrifice. Conversely, a party with a low cost tolerance is less committed to the outcome and has a lower threshold for concluding that the worth of the endeavor does not justify the sacrifices its pursuit entails.

There are clearly two major elements that go into determining cost tolerance: the importance of the objective and the degree of sacrifice one is willing to expend pursuing that objective. The two elements are clearly related: the more importance one attaches to a particular outcome, the more pain and sacrifice one is likely to be willing to endure to realize it; the less important the outcome is, the less perseverant one is likely to be.

The calculation of cost tolerance as an objective is a core part of the methodology of modern asymmetrical warfare. Most potential asymmetrical warfare situations, and particularly the developing world internal conflicts (DWICs) in which the United States is likely to become involved, are situations where the United States has overwhelming power but the level and intensity of its interests are at least open to debate. By contrast, the potential adversary lacks the physical power to impose its will against an opponent that includes the United States, but it is likely to have a much higher level of interest and thus resistance to the imposition of a hostile will. In other words, the cost tolerance of the potential American opponent is likely to be higher than is its American counterpart's. If the contest can somehow be redirected so that it becomes a test of wills, the playing field is considerably leveled and the weaker side has a chance of prevailing in a situation where it could not do so otherwise. If the contest can be framed successfully in these terms, the question becomes what kinds of methods and what rules the weaker side can adopt to maximize cost tolerance—sapping effects on an opponent whose will to resist is probably already lower. The methodology of asymmetrical warfare thinking does not prescribe a "guidebook" of actions that should be taken toward this end, but instead provides a menu of sorts of possible activities adaptable to an idiosyncratic situation and opponent.

The concept of cost tolerance reframes the nature of war between asymmetrical and symmetrical foes. The traditional warrior seeks to impose conditions where the bulk of arms (firepower and mass) define the battlefield and outcome. The asymmetrical warrior wants to frame the war as a test of wills. The side to which the outcome is more important will persevere the hardest to accomplish its goal. It is a matter of muscle versus determination.

The discussion to this point may seem confusingly abstract, but the kind of reasoning that has been introduced can be and has been applied within different contexts, producing somewhat varying patterns since World War II. A historically prominent form—mobile-guerrilla warfare (MGW)—illustrates the underlying dynamics, their concrete application, and some future problems that may be associated with asymmetrical warfare and efforts to resist it.

The Asymmetrical Base Model: Mobile-Guerrilla Warfare

This form of unconventional warfare dominated much of the twentieth century, providing the inspiration and guidance for variations practiced during the second half of the 2000s. The Vietnam War from 1965 to 1973 is the most intimate encounter the United States had with the application of a variant of the basic strategy by the North Vietnamese strategist Vo Nguyen Giap and was one of the inspirations for Mack's designation of asymmetrical warfare. The strategy derived in large measure from Mao Zedong's application of Sun Tzu's principles in his successful civil war against the Nationalist Chinese. Its dynamics provide a fundamental insight into how the weak can defeat the strong.

Like other forms of asymmetrical warfare, MGW requires a perception of the need for violent change within enough of the target population to create adequate support. When support is inadequate or cannot be created, movements usually do not endure or succeed. MGW explicitly highlights and emphasizes gaining and nurturing popular support, which is a major reason it is used here as an example of asymmetrical warfare. The necessity for support provides one of the major lessons and cautions for intervention in these kind of wars.

Stages of Mobile-Guerrilla Warfare   MGW can be depicted as a three-stage operation. These stages are adapted from an earlier presentation in the author's *Distant Thunder* and are depicted in Table 9.1. The categories summarize, but do not precisely reflect, the designations of individual theorists or practitioners.

Four general points can be made about the overall model. The first is that it assumes the insurgents will enter the contest at an overwhelming initial disadvantage because the opposition's (normally a regime they are attempting to overthrow) conventional military force will be superior. The insurgency has no chance of success in a contest based on the regime's preferred means of fighting. The problem is thus the classic difficulty for which asymmetrical approaches are attractive. Second, the strategy mixes asymmetrical and symmetrical elements. The early stages of the contest, organization and guerrilla warfare, are asymmetrical, particularly during the guerrilla stage where the insurgents adopt unconventional methods to blunt their opponent's advantages in firepower and mass. A unique part of the Mao/Giap strategy, however, is that it includes the development and employment of conventional forces to confront and defeat the opposition's symmetrical forces to complete the revolutionary process conventionally. Third, the strategy works best, and may only work at all, in developing, primitive physical settings where the government lacks both the information/intelligence to learn about the insurgency when it is first forming (and very vulnerable) and the infrastructure to deny the insurgency a safe haven

TABLE 9.1

Stages of Mobile-Guerrilla Warfare

Stage	Forces Employed: Guerrilla (G) or Conventional (C)	Major Activity	Objective
Organizational	Avoid use, G as required	Recruitment, protection	Establishment, survival
Guerrilla	Emphasis on G, preparation of C	Attrition to weaken opposition	Shift in balance of power
Conventional	Integrate G and C, emphasize C	Enemy destruction	Power capture

where the government's forces cannot penetrate and destroy it. Fourth, the strategy is particularly flexible and adaptable to circumstances. Typically, movements using the basic mobile-guerrilla approach have been very patient—prepared for long, protracted campaigns—and the stages are also flexible in application, allowing practitioners to move back and forth through the stages as circumstances dictate.

The organizational stage is the period in which the insurgent movement is weakest, most vulnerable, and most susceptible to destruction. Indeed, if an insurgent movement is not destroyed before it completes this stage, it becomes extremely difficult to eradicate. The stage is critical to the insurgents because it forms the basis for all that follows. During this stage, the insurgency has three primary, sequential goals aimed at allowing it to form, survive, and prosper.

The first task of the insurgents is to find, establish, and fortify a safe place in which they can operate without danger of destruction. Such a sanctuary should be physically remote enough that the government cannot successfully attack it and in an area where the population is unsympathetic to the government and can be converted to the insurgent cause.

The second task is to form a support base in this "liberated" area, where the insurgents provide the population with protection and a better existence than before so they in turn provide physical support for the insurgents in the forms of recruits, food, shelter, and the like. The third task is to obtain armaments during this organizational phase from whatever sources it can.

The purpose of this organizational phase is to strengthen and to make the insurgency gradually stronger so it can begin the contest for power. The insurgents avoid direct clashes with the enemy because they are too weak and untrained to prevail. Rather, the purpose is to create the infrastructure with which to confront the opponent. This phase aims at leveling the playing field by increasing the relative strength of the insurgency.

The second stage of MGW is the guerrilla phase. During the first phase, Mao dictated the necessity of both a military capability emphasizing asymmetrical, guerrilla war tactics and methods and the beginnings of a conventional army symmetrical with that of the government. The purposes of the guerrillas in the second stage are to engage the government's forces using asymmetrical tactics and methods such as ambushes while avoiding contacts where the guerrillas are not superior at the point of engagement. The purpose is to win victories that slowly, gradually, and inexorably shift the balance of power away from the government and toward the insurgents. This pattern is designed to have both military and political impacts on the balance of power between the two sides.

Militarily, a major effect is to undercut the morale of government forces, who come to believe they lose whenever they engage the guerrillas. In the process, as failures increase, some government forces defect to the guerrillas, others flee, and the government finds it increasingly difficult to replace the forces it loses. The result is a gradual strengthening of the insurgency and deterioration of government power. Politically, the military success of the insurgents and failure of the government translates into an increased perception of the insurgents as winners, aiding the process of erosion of government political support and increasing the popularity of the insurgency.

This shift in the balance of power is often very slow, and it requires considerable patience to implement. Moreover, its progress can be impeded or interrupted, most dramatically when someone (like the United States in Vietnam) interferes by siding with the government. The strategy thus requires the ability to be both patient and flexible because reversals may not only delay but require the insurgents to back away from one stage and revert to an earlier stage.

If the second stage is successful, the Maoist model calls for a movement to the third, conventional phase. In classic Maoist terms, at this stage, the conventional army that has been in training but withheld from engagement is mobilized to confront the government in conventional, symmetrical warfare designed to create a decisive defeat for the government. This phase is necessary to break the opponent because light guerrilla forces are often incapable of delivering the *force de main* to destroy the opponent's ability to resist the insurgents.

MGW in the Contemporary Context   Maoism has essentially disappeared from the world political scene, and the MGW military model has fallen into some level of disuse as well. This is not entirely surprising: the MGW model is one method that is compatible with the methodology of asymmetrical warfare rather than a definitive guiding blueprint for conducting asymmetrical warfare. Maoist MGW is rarely practiced anymore except in a few isolated places in the world because the conditions for its success no longer exist in most places, notably the nurturing conditions for the critical organizational stage. The underlying dynamics—discontent and minority status—still exist and are as relevant as they were before.

There are still isolated places, primarily in Asia where the strategy was born, where movements fight or have fought for various causes employing some of its prescriptions. Most of these actions have been in remote places largely inaccessible to government forces. The Tamil revolt against the government of Sri Lanka that was formally ended in 2002 but springs back occasionally is one example, as are the Islamist separatists on the Philippine island of Mindanao. A small but persistent movement that is explicitly Maoist in orientation continues in the Indian countryside, the so-called Naxalites (named after the village in which the rebellion began). Attacks are waged in remote areas, difficult to penetrate and pacify by conventional forces.

Formal applications of the Maoist-based MGW strategy have largely disappeared. It is difficult, for instance, to imagine many places in the world where a revolutionary group could get through the classic organization stage of an MGW campaign without successfully being identified and subjected to probable decimation by the government it was organized to assault. It is still possible for a movement to arise and elude a particularly inept or corrupt government in a few places in the world, as the Yemen civil war exemplifies. The Islamic State (IS) was able to replicate the MGW sanctuary for a time in the remote, lightly populated areas of northern Syria and Iraq. Similarly, it is hard to imagine how a movement could clandestinely assemble and train an armed force for the climactic third stage of the strategy.

The underlying principles remain even if the tactics do not. It is, after all, a core characteristic of asymmetrical methodology to study the past and adopt those elements of prior experiences that remain applicable to individual situations. The guerrilla stage of MGW remains a viable model in some situations, tactically as both a way to negate the advantages of a heavier, conventionally superior opponent and to undermine the enemy's will to continue resistance (cost tolerance).

This process of adaptation continues to be well practiced by the Taliban in Afghanistan and Pakistan. Before the introduction of Western forces in 2001, the Taliban and the Northern Coalition were fighting what amounted to a symmetrical civil war for control of Afghanistan in which neither side had shown the ability to dispatch the other decisively. Both sides were fighting in ways that would seem unconventional by Western standards (essentially guerrilla style with lightly armed forces), but since they were both using essentially the same methods, the war was symmetrical under the definition of symmetry in warfare.

The introduction of Western-style forces upset this situation and impelled the Taliban toward asymmetrical warfare that included elements of MGW. Western forces changed both the nature of the war and Taliban calculations of prevailing in it. The introduction of Western forces, especially American troops, altered the prospects of success for the Taliban. While it was possible to calculate circumstances under which the Northern Coalition might be defeated militarily (overcoming hostile ability), it was not possible to imagine physically vanquishing NATO (North Atlantic Treaty Organization). In this situation, the Taliban were also forced to shift to overcoming American cost tolerance and causing them to quit the endeavor as a goal, before turning on the Afghan government and its Western-trained forces. This methodology, adapted from the second stage of MGW, was also highly congruent with the historical Afghan tradition of dealing with invaders who also represented far superior forces militarily, and these kinds of efforts have historically been successful.

The point of this comparison is not to show the continuity of MGW or the extent to which the Taliban or others may or may not be adhering to it. In a literal sense, the Taliban are not following the MGW "game plan" as a method of conducting their asymmetrical insurgency. Rather, the example suggests that, as a methodology, the Taliban operate partially from principles espoused and successful techniques developed by past practitioners as they need to be adapted and modified for the circumstances of asymmetrical warriors today and in the future. It is the lesson of flexibility and adaptation that is the legacy of studying past examples of asymmetrical warfare.

ASYMMETRICAL FUTURES?

Whether and how much understanding asymmetrical warfare are important to the United States depend to a large degree on how prevalent these kinds of wars will be in the future, especially in situations where the United States may feel impelled to involve itself. Any assessment is, of course, to some degree speculative. The dynamics of recent years suggest that Iraq and Afghanistan are not the last places the United States will confront a potential adversary who, if challenged, will respond asymmetrically to any American involvement. Asymmetrical responses are, after all, designed to negate the enormous advantage the United States enjoys in conventional arms, and potential opponents are almost bound to look at how American opponents, from the North Vietnamese to the Taliban, have used asymmetrical approaches to rebalance the playing field against the United States in situations that would be clearly suicidal for them. If the United States cannot develop effective ways to deal with this problem, it will be a source of frustration when it does become involved with and will provide further encouragement for other potential asymmetrical opponents.

With these rejoinders in mind, it is possible to suggest some lessons for the United States that may apply to the future. These include an assessment of the political situations where American involvement may be contemplated; some judgments about the military characteristics, and thus requirements, for combatting future asymmetrical foes; and the implications of both for planning in a resource-constrained political environment.

Both raise political and military questions. Asymmetrical conflicts occur in developing countries with histories, politics, and societal conditions with which the United States may be less than fully conversant and where prospects and solutions that make sense in an American context may not in local terms. Militarily, these conflicts are contested in unfamiliar settings and against forces the Americans do not understand or even recognize. Current American effective opposition against the Houthis in the Yemen civil war illustrates these vagaries, as depicted in Amplification 9.2.

AMPLIFICATION 9.2

The United States–Houthi "War"?

Most Americans have never heard of the Houthis and are only vaguely aware that there is a very bloody civil conflict going on in their home country, Yemen, that Brookings Institution analyst Bruce Riedel described in December 2017 as "the worst humanitarian catastrophe in the world," featuring a relentless bombing campaign by Saudi Arabia against the Houthi, who are the primary rebel force in the country, that has caused widespread hunger and starvation in the bleak Yemeni countryside. It is all part of a geopolitical struggle between Iranian-backed Shiites (of which the Houthi are a sect) and the Saudi-backed Sunni government.

The conflict has been ongoing for years in one of the world's poorest countries and most abject failed states. The United States has no direct interest in the politics of the country beyond the suppression of Al Qaeda (AQ) and other terrorist organizations there: the major manifestation of that interest was the assassination of American-born AQ leader Anwar al-Awlaki in a 2011 bombing raid. Beyond that imperative, it is difficult to discern any direct interest in the politics of Yemen. Yet recent reports have indicated that American special forces have been operating near the Yemeni border in Saudi Arabia in support of Saudi efforts to defeat the Houthi insurgency. Why?

The Houthis have considered the United States one of their opponents since the American invasion of Iraq in 2003, at which time they issued an inflammatory response: "God is great, death to the US, death to Israel, curse the Jews, and victory for Islam." At least regarding the United States, there is no publicly available evidence the Houthis have ever implemented this threat. The "war" between the Americans and the Houthis consists of this declaration and a handful of American special forces attempting to foil Houthi missile attacks into Saudi Arabia: there is a real war between Saudi Arabia and the Houthis over who will rule Yemen.

Why is the United States involved in this asymmetrical contest? The United States has no inherent interests in Yemeni politics and governance beyond the terrorist problem, and terrorism is not a major part of the civil war, which is basically an Iranian/Shiite/Houthi and Saudi/Sunni proxy conflict. The only discernible US interest is its long relationship with the Saudi monarchy, to which it is supplying massive amounts of arms to use against the Houthi.

Who will win this contest? Who knows? What difference will any outcome have on US national security interests? The latter is the key question for American national security, and no coherent explanation has been forthcoming. Can US interests (whatever they are) prevail? Or has the United States simply stumbled into yet another asymmetrical war it does not understand? ■

The Political Legacy: Be Careful Where You Intervene

The United States became involved in Afghanistan and Iraq when it was in the thrall of two relevant but different political forces that distorted its vision of these two quite distinct situations. The first force, created by the reaction to 9/11, was a quite understandable and irresistible obsession with revenge against the perpetrators (AQ in Afghanistan) and to avoid a possible recurrence (Iraq). The emotional heat of that motivation made an American violent reaction ineluctable. It also facilitated the United States' ability to distort the situations into which it was entering, including a clear vision of the end state of the missions. The second force, a product of the 1990s, championed by the neoconservatives in the Bush White House, was an overly optimistic evangelical belief in the ability to spread the "gospel" of American ideals in the world. This force ignored or overestimated its ability to transform the world in its image.

Any analysis of the political dynamics of situations where the United States might involve itself must begin with two fundamental recognitions. One is an objective view of the places in which one proposes to involve itself, and the other is recognition of the limits of the realistic levels of change the United States can induce or impress upon subject countries. The two concerns are related: the degree of instability that precedes American involvement makes the possible extent of change more problematic. Both dimensions counsel caution in decision making. (They are discussed in more detail in Donald M. Snow, *The Case against Military Intervention*.)

The "need" for American action presupposes that something is wrong in places where involvement is contemplated, and where that involvement seems warranted indicates how much must be wrong there. Simply put, there is a problem that has resulted in a level of instability or other pathology that tempts American action, and this problem must be of sufficient scope that it cannot be solved domestically.

The situation in Afghanistan, for instance, was a civil war between ethnic groups, and more specifically a power struggle between two branches of a single ethnic group, the Durrani and Ghilzai Pashtuns. That conflict is centuries old, has endured American efforts, and will still be there when the United States leaves. There is no indication that those who made the decision to go to Afghanistan knew of this central dynamic (although American experts on Afghanistan did). Once the AQ problem was settled one way or the other, that dynamic would continue and would be the central factor in a war in which the United States had become a central player. It was not then and is not now clear that Afghanistan can be made over into the kind of country the United States initially wanted it to be (a stable democracy) or even the more modest Afghanistan outcome it later espoused as a goal (a stable, strong central government). Two other things are not clear: whether the Afghans really want either outcome, both of which would be novelties in their history, and whether either outcome has been important enough to the United States to justify an open-ended American military involvement. In Iraq, deposing a despotic Saddam Hussein regime seemed a laudable goal, especially if there was a viable outcome that represented a real improvement (a stable democracy). It is not clear that this will be, or ever could have been, the actual outcome. Exchanging one sectarian autocracy for another was a more likely outcome. What is increasingly clear, however, is that American intervention has not been the critical element in whatever outcome will eventually occur in either country.

The failure to appraise the preexisting situation realistically, the depth of the situation's intractability, and the inability of the United States to change the situation can lead to adopting political objectives that are unrealistic or unrealizable under conditions politically sustainable in the United States. The question is not whether Americans have the will to pursue difficult goals, because there is little reason to believe they do not. The real question is whether the actions proposed are *worthy* of pursuit and are *attainable* within acceptable boundaries of sacrifice and energy. Americans, unsurprisingly as citizens of a democracy, like clear, praiseworthy, and measurable commitments; they do not like open-ended, protracted commitments with dubious or ambiguous outcomes. Afghanistan and Iraq more closely resemble the latter rather than the former, as do many of the other places where the United States might contemplate future involvement.

The delineation of clear political objectives is thus cautionary as one looks at the future. The kinds of places where the United States might invest itself with military force are not places with few, easily remediable problems; if they were, force would probably not be necessary to address them. Rather, they are likely to be in deeply troubled locales where it is not at all clear that outsiders, including Americans, can have a satisfactory impact within the parameters of political acceptability in the United States. This reality should be blindingly self-evident, but it clearly has not always been. The result is to leave the United States faced with one or more of three dilemmas if it becomes entangled in asymmetrical warfare situations.

The first dilemma is the *interest-threat mismatch*, first raised in Chapter 2. The heart of this mismatch is whether important interests and threats coexist in the same place or not, which is another way of raising the case of worthiness of US involvement. Many of the places in which the United States might become involved are, or historically have been, places American interests are nonexistent, minimal, or certainly not rising to the level of vitality. An application of the realist paradigm would leave less-than-vital places outside eligibility for US intervention. The second dilemma, raised throughout the book but not in these terms, can be called the *resources-threat mismatch*. Roughly, this mismatch involves the availability of resources, in this case monetary resources and manpower (treasure and blood), for adventures of varying importance to the United States. The current atmosphere of austerity within the American domestic political scene would suggest husbanding available resources to meet only the most important threats, a standard that most of the developing-world conflicts that might tempt American commitment arguably do not achieve.

The third dilemma is the *force-threat mismatch*, reflecting a problem raised in Chapter 8 in the context of American "legacy" forces. The underlying question is whether the physical forces and plans for their usage by the United States are effective in dealing with the kinds of threats with which they are now faced. The structure of American forces was designed to confront similar, and thus symmetrical, European-style forces on the northern European plain with its accompanying developed infrastructure of roads and the like. The armed forces and locales of essentially none of the places in which asymmetrical wars occur match these characteristics; indeed, in many cases the problems one encounters in them are direct results of actions taken to negate and neutralize the effectiveness of such forces. It is whether forces as configured can be employed in acceptable ways to asymmetrical challenges that forms the military legacy of asymmetrical futures.

The Military Legacy: Future Asymmetrical Foes

The American historical experience in asymmetrical military situations is ironic. When the United States has been the asymmetrical warrior, as it was in part of the American Revolution, or has been placed in situations where it essentially had no choice but to emulate its opponents to subdue them (e.g., mounted cavalry against mounted Native Americans in the American Southwest), the track record is exemplary; when the United States has sought to bring its overwhelming might to bear in faraway asymmetrical conflicts, from the Philippines to Afghanistan, the results have been much more problematic.

In some ways, this should be no surprise. The US military tradition does not embrace the ways of fighting that are generally associated with asymmetrical warfare, and much of the American military hierarchy has resisted institutional adaptation. This is particularly true of those services that have peripheral roles in asymmetrical encounters (the Navy and Air Force) and those parts of the Army (armor, artillery) that are not clearly central to asymmetrical, as opposed to symmetrical, warfare. Indeed, the only elements of the US military structure that embrace or at least do not shy away from thinking and planning in asymmetrical terms are the US Marines and the special operations forces in the various services. It is not coincidental that the Marine tradition is that of light infantry and that special forces' "specialness" derives from the unconventional nature of the tasks they undertake and the methods they employ to achieve those tasks.

Asymmetrical methods add to the problem because they are designed specifically to frustrate the conventional characteristics of heavy, European-style forces. This adaptation is necessitated by circumstance: it is hard to imagine how a place like Afghanistan could nurture a military tradition other than a basic light infantry, guerrilla style. At the same time, adopting methods to negate the inherent advantages of traditional forces is the heart of the methodology of asymmetrical warfare: making life more militarily difficult for the opponent is the objective for the asymmetrical warrior.

Two other elements contribute to the frustration facing the opponents of asymmetrical warfare and thus the calculus of becoming involved in such contests. One is a *clash of cultures* that defines the contrast in acceptable ways of fighting between symmetrical and asymmetrical opponents. Essentially all the situations where intervention may be considered are in places where the population is culturally distinct from the West. Topography and climate are also factors: the employment of massed armies cannot be sustained in tropical jungle-covered mountains and barren deserts without roads amenable to the movement of large-tank armies. Forms of warfare that evolved in Europe are simply inapplicable in other areas. In the American experience, for instance, the settlement of the West required the adoption of a number of Native American–like tactics and practices by the US Army to subdue relatively small numbers of nomadic tribesmen moving across vast, and in some places virtually featureless, landscapes, where European-style military maneuvers simply would not work.

The cultural clash is intensified when conventional forms of warfare are incompatible with those of the indigenous people. The use of drone aircraft by the United States in Afghanistan and Pakistan against suspected Taliban and AQ personnel is an example. Even when such attacks are highly successful, they almost always produce unintended civilian casualties. This so-called collateral damage is not proscribed by the Geneva Conventions on War, but it terribly violates the culture of the Pashtuns who are its victims. Their culture includes the "set of individual and social norms collectively known as *Pashtunwali*," according to the US Marine Corps manual *Afghanistan: Operational Culture for Deploying Personnel*. The code includes both the notions of *nang* (roughly honor) and *badal* (revenge). In the event of the killing of a relative, the code of honor demands revenge from surviving family members, meaning collateral damage creates people who seek revenge and thus become additional enemies. The Marine manual summarizes the consequence: "dishonor—particularly involving the spilling of blood—must be avenged by all male relatives." Following acceptable Western tenets of war can be potentially self-defeating since it may create more opponents than it dispatches and violates the *indigenous set of rules of honorable conflict*. In this case, who is the asymmetrical warrior? More to the point, who is the rule breaker?

The other element is the inherent difficulty of preparing for asymmetrical opponents since no two asymmetrical wars are ever exactly the same. It is a basic premise of military training to prepare soldiers to anticipate and act uniformly according to doctrine (belief in the most effective ways to handle situations), and these are based on past experiences one anticipates will be repeated in the future. The methodology of asymmetrical war, however, challenges this logic. What is constant about asymmetrical wars is their uniqueness. The more preparations to fight asymmetrical foes are based in previous encounters, the more they are likely to overlook whatever innovations and changes the current opponent has adopted. The element of surprise is a constant in asymmetrical warfare, and doing the unexpected is one of the ways the asymmetrical warrior tries to level the playing field.

All these factors complicate the contemplation of and preparation for future national security actions. How does one prepare and equip American forces to fight in unanticipated places against unpredictable opponents, assuming one cannot reasonably afford to prepare for everything? Moreover, the kinds of asymmetrical situations into which the United States might be drawn also contain significant, expensive nonmilitary requirements that go beyond the clash of arms. These are emphasized in Chapter 12. The basic dilemma, however, is discussed in the accompanying *Challenge!* box.

CHALLENGE!

Planning for Symmetrical or Asymmetrical Foes

Because asymmetrical warfare is physically and conceptually different than more traditional warfare, preparing to fight in asymmetrical environments is substantially different than it is for traditional military venues. It requires resource priorities that may result in a substantially different kind of force and different uses for that force than does preparing for traditional war. A particularly configured force may be very good at one kind of war but not the other. In its simplest depiction, it suggests an approach to the heavy forces/light forces distinction raised in Chapter 8 weighted more toward light and special, rather than heavy, forces if asymmetrical warfare is to be emphasized. That solution flies in the face of the American military tradition and is likely to be resisted by traditional military thinkers.

The choices are not mutually exclusive. The United States cannot abandon "heaviness" without leaving itself potentially vulnerable to a resurgent heavy power like Russia—the worst case. At the same time, too much emphasis on countering asymmetrical opponents may produce capabilities tempting the country to engage itself in places it might otherwise avoid in the absence of that capability.

The case for one alternative or the other is thus not ironclad, and arguments can be made in favor of either emphasis. Based on what you know at this point, which emphasis do you think makes the most sense? Why? What imponderables make a choice easier or more difficult? How do you come out on the issue? ■

CONCLUSION: ASYMMETRY AS THE PRESENT AND FUTURE?

Asymmetrical warfare is far older than the name used to describe it. The idea of a militarily inferior force attempting to change the situation more to its favor—or less to its disfavor—is venerable, and it is an idea and dynamic that has been part of American military history. It is not, however, a part of that tradition that those charged with contemporary American national security have clearly embraced or with which the United States has had notable success.

A central part of the concern with asymmetrical warfare is that it is concentrated in the developing world. This emphasis is also not a twenty-first century phenomenon; in fact, since World War II the United States may have placed its major intellectual efforts and resources on thinking about and planning for major symmetrical warfare, but the United States has employed armed forces into combat exclusively within the developing world. There simply are no meaningful exceptions to this generalization.

An emphasis on conflict situations in the developing world opens a number of avenues of controversy. The question of the importance of such situations to the United States (worthiness or vitality of interest) arises, and the evolving dynamics of asymmetrical methodologies applied in places like Afghanistan and Iraq raise additional questions about the ability of the United States to prevail and impose what it considers acceptable outcomes in asymmetrical situations—questions of attainability. Both factors have a direct, eroding influence on American cost tolerance when faced with asymmetrical situations, a dynamic captured in the mismatches raised in the last section and coming into focus when discussing places like Iraq and Afghanistan.

Asymmetrical prospects continue to present themselves to the United States because possible future opponents have seen the asymmetrical methodology applied to the United States with apparent success and are likely to be encouraged by what clearly inferior forces can accomplish against the American giant. The likelihood of a decisive US intervention in many

DWICs has been diminished by the American record confronting asymmetrical opponents. Whether the United States will rise to the bait of involvements where it may face an asymmetrical opponent is a major policy question for the future. That assessment goes beyond the purely military problem of defeating asymmetrical opponents, however, and the additional requirements are raised and discussed in the next chapter.

STUDY/DISCUSSION QUESTIONS

1. What is asymmetrical warfare? Is it a new phenomenon? What does it mean to describe it as a methodology rather than as a method?
2. Place the asymmetrical tradition into its historical and geographical context and how those phenomena interact to affect it as an approach. What factors have contributed to its contemporary prominence? How?
3. How are the terms *symmetrical* and *asymmetrical* descriptive of contemporary warfare? Why is this form of warfare attractive to some groups in some circumstances? Elaborate.
4. What is mobile-guerrilla warfare? Describe the stages of the strategy and how it exemplifies the principles of asymmetrical warfare more generally. What is its importance in understanding contemporary warfare, especially the wars in Afghanistan and Iraq?
5. What are the past political and military legacies of the asymmetrical experience for the United States? Elaborate on each. Apply them to the Houthi situation depicted in Amplification 9.2.
6. Based on your understanding, how do you think the United States should adapt its national security policy to the prospects of involvement in future wars that are or could become asymmetrical in nature? Include in your answer some discussion of the "mismatches" described in the text. Defend your position.

SELECTED BIBLIOGRAPHY

Barnett, Roger W. *Asymmetrical Warfare: Today's Challenge to U.S. Military Power.* Washington, DC: Potomac Books, 2013.

Boot, Max. "The Struggle to Transform the Military." *Foreign Affairs* 84, 2 (March/April 2005), 103–118.

Brandt, Marieke. *Tribes and Politics in Yemen: A History of the Houthi Conflict.* Oxford, UK: Oxford University Press, 2017.

Brodie, Bernard, and Fawn M. Brodie. *From Crossbow to H-Bomb: The Evolution of Weapons and Tactics of Warfare.* Bloomington, IN: Indiana University Press, 1973.

Cooper, Helene, Thomas Gibbons-Neff, and Eric Schmitt. "Army Special Forces Help Saudis Combat Threat from Yemen Rebels." *New York Times* (online), (May 3, 2018).

Gallagher, James J. *Low-Intensity Conflict: A Guide to Tactics, Techniques, and Procedures.* Mechanicsburg, PA: Stackpole Books, 1992.

Giap, Vo Nguyen. *People's War, People's Army.* New York: Praeger Publishers, 1962.

Goulding, Vincent J., Jr. "Back to the Future with Asymmetrical Warfare." *Parameters* 30, 4 (Winter 2000–2001), 21–30.

Hill, Ginny. *Yemen Endures: Saudi Adventurism and the Future of Arabia.* Oxford, UK: Oxford University Press, 2017.

Kaurin, Pauline M. *The Warrior, Military Ethics, and Contemporary Warfare: Achilles Goes Asymmetrical.* New York and London: Routledge, 2016.

Keegan, John. *A History of Warfare*. London: Hutchison, 1991.

Lacquement, Richard A. *Shaping American Military Capabilities After the Cold War*. Westport, CT: Praeger Publishers, 2003.

Mack, Andre J. "Why Big Nations Lose Small Wars." *World Politics* 27, 2 (April 1975), 175–200.

Mao, Zedong. *The Collected Works of Mao Zedong*. Vols. 1–4. Beijing, China: Foreign Languages Press, 1967.

———. *Mao tse-Tung on Guerrilla Warfare*. Translated by Samuel B. Griffith. New York: Praeger Publishers, 1961.

Moore, Lt. General Harold G., and Joseph L. Galloway. *We Were Soldiers Once . . . and Young: Ia Drang: The Battle That changed the War in Vietnam*. New York: Harper and Row, 1993.

Riedel, Bruce. *Who Are the Houthis. And Why Are We at War with Them*. Washington, DC: Brookings Institution, December 18, 2017.

Romaniuk, Scott N. *The Future of U.S. Warfare*. New York and London: Routledge, 2017.

Snow, Donald M. *Cases in US National Security: Concepts and Processes*. Lanham, MD: Rowman & Littlefield, 2019.

———. *The Case against Military Intervention*. New York and London: Routledge, 2016.

———. *Thinking About National Security: Strategy, Policy, and Issues*. New York and London: Routledge, 2016.

———. *Distant Thunder: Patterns of Conflict in the Developing World*. 2nd ed. Armonk, NY: M. E. Sharpe, 1997.

——— and Dennis M. Drew. *From Lexington to Baghdad and Beyond: Wars and Politics in the American Experience*. 3rd ed. Armonk, NY: M. E. Sharpe, 2009.

Sun Tzu. *The Art of War*. Translated by Samuel B. Griffith. Oxford, UK: Oxford University Press, 1963.

United States Army and United States Marine Corps. *Counterinsurgency Field Manual: Army Field Manual 3–24, Marine Corps Warfighting Publication No. 3–33.5*. Chicago, IL: University of Chicago Press, 2006.

United States Marine Corps. *Afghanistan: Operational Culture for Deploying Personnel*. Quantico, VA: Center for Advanced Operational Cultural Learning, 2009.

Van Creveld, Martin. *The Transformation of War*. New York: Free Press, 1991.

Residues of 9/11: Terrorism, Iraq, and Afghanistan

Three national security events have dominated American efforts in the new century. The terrorist attacks of September 11, 2001, spawned efforts that remain the major elements of the present and immediate future in Afghanistan and Iraq. The strongest and most enduring response was the campaign to eradicate the international terrorist threat represented by Al Qaeda (AQ) and highlighted by the assassination of its founder, Osama bin Laden. In addition, 9/11 prompted an American military intervention in Afghanistan and the invasion and occupation of Iraq. Each mission was different, each has had different outcomes, and each offers important lessons for the future.

The terrorist attacks of September 11, 2001, defined twenty-first-century national security policy for the United States and for many other areas of the world. They shattered the relative tranquility of the national security environment of the 1990s. The event was seismic and shaped the national agenda in ways similar to the impact of Pearl Harbor and the assassination of President John F. Kennedy for earlier generations.

There had been warnings during the 1990s that terrorism was emerging from the shadows in which terrorists have habitually dwelled. The Manhattan World Trade towers were the victim of an unsuccessful assault by AQ in 1993, and there were isolated precursor attacks against American targets overseas in the eight previous years, such as the American embassies in Nairobi, Kenya, and Dar es Salaam, Tanzania, and the USS *Cole* in Yemen.

The aftermath of 9/11 created three distinct national security responses. The first was the direct response to the attacks itself. It was initially conceptualized as a "war" on terrorism represented by AQ, and its objective was to eradicate that organization. The term *war* is put in quotation marks because the effort has not been a war in the traditional sense. The campaign has evolved as a broad intergovernmental effort that is domestic and international, is conducted by multiple governmental agencies, has resulted in the formation of a specialized terrorism suppression bureaucracy centered on the Department of Homeland Security, has an open-ended agenda, and is unconventional and asymmetrical.

The direct response to 9/11 also spawned two other national security efforts. Within a little over a month of the attacks on American soil, the United States became engaged in Afghanistan, a commitment that represents the longest war in American history, the duration and extent of which was unintended and seems open-ended, as noted earlier. The initial reason for intervention was that the Taliban government was providing a haven for the AQ terrorists who conducted the 9/11 attacks. The US government demanded that the Taliban hand over bin Laden and his cohorts. The Taliban refused, and the United States began a campaign directly against AQ in Afghanistan that almost inadvertently entwined the United States in an Afghanistan civil war that remains the central operational feature of American military involvement.

The attacks of 9/11 also provided the rationale for the American military war effort in Iraq. The presence began with an American invasion, conquest, and occupation of Iraq in March 2003, was justified on the basis of the "war on terrorism," and was framed in arguments that the government of Saddam Hussein was both building weapons of mass destruction (WMDs) and consorting with terrorist organizations that might provide AQ with WMDs that could be employed against the United States. None of these allegations have ever been demonstrated, and in some cases, they have been largely discredited.

Each of these responses is distinct, and they will be examined separately. The analysis will begin with terrorism, briefly defining terrorism and its evolution as a problem, how the campaign against it has been framed, and the general success of those efforts. It will then move to the American effort in Afghanistan and will then examine the formally concluded war in Iraq. Both Afghanistan and Iraq will be examined in terms of whether they should have been undertaken in the first place, what they accomplished, and the influence they could have on the situation and thus on the propriety of engaging in similar kinds of efforts in the future.

THE DIRECT TERRORISM RESPONSE

Terrorism, like asymmetrical warfare, is nothing new. It has been a part of the relations among peoples and countries for at least two thousand years:

historians of terrorism generally identify elements of the Jewish resistance to the Romans in Palestine (e.g., groups like the Zealots) as the earliest practitioners of the kinds of violence now called terrorism. It has flared occasionally in places around the globe. The contemporary environment is witnessing the most recent "spike" in the frequency and threat posed by terrorists.

The modern practice of terror, from which the term *terrorism* is derived, is generally considered an artifact of the French Revolution, associated most closely with the French extremist revolutionary Robespierre and the infamous "Reign of Terror" that was one phase of the French Revolution. The reign married the unique forms and purposes of terrorist violence with explicit political goals and objectives, a union that continues to the present forms of international terrorism.

Terrorism has evolved since then. Anarchism was a popular banner for terrorists of the nineteenth and early twentieth century, and variants of terrorist practices became the chosen methods of anticolonial movements in parts of the developing world during the early and mid-twentieth century; of a small number of anti–Vietnam War activists in the 1960s and 1970s; and, most recently, of religious fringe groups. The methods employed by terrorists have evolved from the knifing assassinations of the *sicarii* of biblical times to the use of improvised explosive devices (IEDs) by contemporary terrorists.

Terrorism is a persistent problem. Individual terrorists and groups come and go. Terrorism, however, continues because it is a methodology for achieving certain ends that are unattainable by other means. It has been an enduring part of the landscape that will continue to exist periodically until all the grievances for which it is invoked disappear. It is difficult to be sanguine about realizing this condition.

Terrorism has been the centerpiece of American national security policy since 2001, and it will remain a prominent part of the national security landscape. The discussion will proceed sequentially through three steps: a discussion of what terrorism is and why it is invoked, methods of combating terror and the current state of application of those methods against international terrorism, and the status of the campaign against the international terrorist opponent.

Why and How Terror?

Terrorism is a difficult phenomenon for most people to grasp. The public image of terrorism is the aftermath of the horrific things terrorists do: killing people (often in hideous fashion) or destroying often iconic places and things. In the most extreme cases terrorists engage in self-immolating acts incomprehensible to most people. More personally, a major terrorist objective is to convince people they could be the next victims unless compliance with what the terrorist wants occurs. Revulsion mixes with potential fright.

The difficulty of understanding begins with a definition of exactly what terrorism *is*. A review of the extensive literature on terrorism shows there is a general agreement on the core of definitions, but there are also major disagreements, at least at the margins. An acceptable definition of terrorism, however, allows the observer to distinguish terrorist from other phenomena and is a precondition for understanding why there is terrorism. For present purposes, the definition that will be adopted is that terrorism is *the commission of violent acts against a target group to gain compliance with some set of conditions the terrorist demands*. This definition contains three basic elements that are common to most definitions of terrorism: terrorist acts, terrorist targets, and terrorist objectives. Some definitions (for instance, the one employed by the US government) add other criteria, such as the kind of group that commits terrorism.

Terrorist Acts   As the name implies, terrorist acts are the violent actions terrorists commit. They are the most public "face" of terrorism and the part of terrorism with which most people are most familiar. Terrorism would be something else—and almost certainly less concerning—were it not for the mayhem in which terrorists engage. Several points are relevant to understanding this part of terrorism.

The first is that terrorist actions are uniformly illegal wherever they occur. The principal behaviors in which terrorists engage are acts of violence—murder and the destruction of property—universally condemned by all societies. Most of these crimes purposely target human victims, generally people who are part of a class of people the terrorists seek to influence. The fact of personally directed criminality prejudices people against terrorists.

Terrorists dispute this depiction since considering terrorism as a crime demeans what they view as the higher reasons for their actions. If terrorism is merely crime, then terrorists are mere criminals, and terrorists believe they operate for higher purposes that glorify and justify what they do in ways that are sullied by the criminality depiction.

The second point is that terrorism seeks to create fright in the target audience. Some acts of terror are more direct, seeking to eliminate opponents by assassination, for instance. Often the terrorist's motive is to influence the future behavior of the target group, and terrorist acts are aimed at frightening the audience into compliance. The dynamic is conceptually simple: terrorist acts succeed when they exceed the target's cost tolerance by convincing the target that it is more efficacious to give in to the terrorist demands than to continue to resist and live in fear. Additional purposes of terrorist acts can include gaining special concession for the group (e.g., ransom to finance other activities, freeing of members from incarceration), getting publicity for the terrorist group or cause, demoralizing the target society by revealing its vulnerability, provoking government overreaction that discredits the government and adds legitimacy to the terrorists, enforcing obedience or cooperation by the target population, and punishing those who have disobeyed the terrorists. Jessica Stern adds the use of successful terrorist attacks to maintain or increase the morale of members of the group.

Terrorist groups are generally small, and this limits their ambitions to random efforts to terrorize people. When they adopt larger designs, as the Islamic State (IS) did in 2014, they tend to fail because they have overcommitted themselves, as suggested in Amplification 10.1.

AMPLIFICATION 10.1

The Rise and Demise of the Islamic State

The Islamic State burst onto the world stage in 2014 as one of the most effective groups fighting the Syrian regime in the Syrian civil war. The group was based on the remnants of Al Qaeda in Iraq (AQI), which was largely decimated in 2007 and went underground. It reemerged as part of the Sunni opposition to Bashar al-Assad's rule, and it was the best organized and most effective part of the resistance. Its success led to an expansion of its role from terrorist to the leader of Islamic extremism as it announced its intention to form a religious state: the caliphate in Syria and Iraq. It was a conceptual expansion beyond its means: a bridge too far.

At first it appeared very successful as it spread across remote parts of the two states. The reality, however, was that most of its expansion was into virtually unpopulated regions that could not resist. The experience was euphoric, however, and IS continued to expand. That was its undoing: it tried to move from being a terrorist organization to an insurgency without the resources for the task.

It got caught in the "sovereignty trap." As a state, it had territory it had to administer and defend, and it lacked the resources to do so. As it expanded, it alarmed people in the way, who resisted, as did their governments. The momentum slowed, stopped, and was reversed. The caliphate no longer exists except in the minds of its most ardent supporters, and it has reverted to being just another Middle East religious terrorist group. ∎

Terrorist Targets If the major purpose of terrorists is to frighten people into complying with their demands, what maximizes the fear and dread they seek to create? Put another way, what can terrorists attack that will maximize the prospect that their opponents' cost tolerance will be exceeded? A critical calculation in target selection is what form of suffering will undermine the will to resist most effectively. The basic alternatives are people or physical objects: killing as many people as possible or demoralizing the population by destroying iconic places like the Golden Gate Bridge. Ideal targets are places where people believe they are invulnerable or places that maximize disruption and create associated dangers.

The nature of potential targets provides some inherent difficulties for those opposing terrorists. For one thing, there are a virtually infinite number and variety of targets from which terrorists may choose. As a practical matter, it is physically impossible to protect them all, meaning some targets are always going to be at risk, and antiterrorism efforts are always an exercise in risk management, not elimination. Moreover, terrorists can (and do) engage in *target substitution*. As the name implies, if one category of target or specific target has been made resistant to attack, the terrorists can always substitute a different, less protected target.

These limitations on protecting targets lead to a particularly vexing problem for those seeking to suppress terrorism: *cost-effectiveness at the margins*. This term was initially developed to describe the relationship between strategic nuclear offensive and defensive systems. The idea was that in any attempt to defend against a strategic nuclear missile attack, it is always cheaper to build additional offensive systems to overwhelm defenses than it is to build additional defensive systems. Thus, in any competition between offense and defense, the advantage always resides with the offense since it can compete more cheaply than the defense.

This dynamic also applies to terrorist targeting. In terms of expense, all terrorists must expend resources on are preparations to attack discrete targets, and part of their intent is to be sure those who oppose them do not know in advance which targets. Terrorism suppressors, on the other hand, must cover the entire category of potential targets, a much more expensive proposition than defending only discrete ones. The advantage in terms of marginal expenditures thus lies with the terrorists, not those trying to defend against them.

Terrorist Objectives Because terrorism is a political act, its objectives are normally measurable in terms of the political conditions they seek to attain. To amend the Clausewitzian dictum slightly, "Terrorism is politics by other means." In the emotion that surrounds the commission of and reaction to terrorism, the underlying objectives are sometimes lost or obscured, yet it is against their goals that their success or failure must ultimately be measured.

At least three factors complicate identifying terrorist objectives and assessing their attainment. The first is what is sometimes referred to as "noise." In many cases, it is difficult to know exactly what terrorists ultimately seek to accomplish. They may not articulate their goals publicly, or their expression may be in such harsh, hysterical rhetoric that outsiders, including their targets, have difficulty understanding what end states the terrorists seek.

Noise is compounded by a kind of "levels of analysis" problem that can be expressed as a strategic versus tactical definition of objectives. The strategic level refers to the broadest political objective the terrorist organization may seek to attain. The tactical level refers to the success of actions taken to move toward attaining the strategic objective. In the case of terrorists, this is probably the successful commission of a terrorist attack. The attacks of September 11 were a major tactical victory for AQ, probably intended to demoralize the United States and to weaken its resolve to continue to resist broader AQ political objectives. Since they increased, rather than weakened, American cost tolerance, however, they were hardly a strategic success.

The third factor is the differential success of terrorists and those who oppose them. For terrorists, the bottom line is their continued survival, without which they cannot possibly pursue their broader, strategic goals. Terrorists succeed ("win," in some sense) by not losing (avoiding annihilation). If the terrorist organization exists, it poses a threat.

The success of those who oppose terrorism is more exacting. Those opposing terrorism can only truly succeed by removing the source of that threat, the terrorists themselves, altogether. Thus, the only way the opponents of terrorists succeed is by destroying the terrorists. In conventional terms, those opposing terrorism only "win by winning."

Dealing with Terror

Suppressing international terrorism is a major US national security focus. That effort has evolved since President Bush stood on the wreckage of the Twin Towers in lower Manhattan and declared the national determination to bring those who had committed the dastardly attacks to justice. Those efforts can be summarized around four loosely sequential areas of concern: definition of the appropriate objects of the terrorism-suppression effort; the goal of suppression efforts; the most efficacious means for accomplishing the goal; and designating jurisdictions among appropriate enforcement bodies.

Objects of Effort The first question for terrorism suppressors is what is being confronted by the effort. There are three possibilities: terrorism as a phenomenon, the terrorists conducting the terror, or the underlying ideas that inspire the terrorism. Each is different and poses distinct problems, but determining an appropriate emphasis helps shape both the methods employed and the prospects of success.

The most ambitious and comprehensive opponent is terrorism itself. A campaign with this emphasis seeks to demonstrate that terrorism is always an inappropriate, self-defeating method to achieve the political goals for which it is contemplated. This is a particularly ambitious approach because terrorism has persisted for over two thousand years. Its accomplishment would require a suppression of all terrorist organizations so absolute that nobody could make an effective argument for trying it again.

The second, slightly less ambitious, possibility is a campaign aimed at the terrorist threat one confronts—the concrete terrorists rather than their method. Such an approach has the advantage of being directed at a concrete object the elimination of which is clearly desirable and measurable. It is not a total solution like destroying terrorism, since the eradication of one terrorist group does not preclude the emergence of successors.

The third possibility is to attack the underlying reasons that motivate terrorists—terrorist ideas. The goals of terrorist groups are normally articulated around a set of political conditions they seek to create (the restoration or promotion of some set of religious values, for example). Generally, these ideas are not widely shared by the target society, and this rejection drives terrorists to a strategy that promises the possibility of success against long odds. A strategy aimed at terrorist ideas seeks to discredit those ideas and turn potential and actual recruits away from the terrorist goal.

Goals of Effort   Which of these objects is pursued depends at least partially on the goals at which they are directed. The two major goals that can be adopted are the total eradication of the object or its reduction or control. Terrorism is such a physical and moral evil that eradication may seem the only obviously morally defensible goal. However, it may be an unattainable goal.

This distinction was vividly demonstrated in a 2004 exchange between President George W. Bush and his Democratic opponent, then Massachusetts senator and later Barack Obama's secretary of state John Kerry, during their second televised debate. When asked what he would do about the terrorist threat, Kerry replied that he would seek to control it within acceptable boundaries since efforts to remove terrorism altogether were likely futile. Kerry drew an analogy between terrorism and social evils like gambling and prostitution, neither of which could be erased altogether but which could be held within acceptable bounds. Bush retorted indignantly that the terrorist threat was such an outrage that only its total eradication was morally acceptable.

Who was right? The answer is that it depends on what each man was identifying as the object of the terrorism effort. If eliminating the phenomenon of terrorism is the aim, Kerry's response was probably the more defensible since a goal of totally eradicating terrorism defies experience—a utopian pie in the sky that may have rhetorical appeal but not make practical sense. Eradication is clearly the moral high ground in this debate, and if terrorist groups are the objective, it is at least in principle attainable. In the current context, the United States is clearly devoted to the goal of eradicating the terrorist threat represented by AQ and similar groups, but it has never articulated ending all terrorism everywhere or the total discrediting of the concept of terrorism as its goal.

Means of Conduct   The third question remains how to eradicate the threat. In traditional terrorism circles, the possibilities are grouped around two strategies and approaches, *antiterrorism* and *counterterrorism*.

Antiterrorism is defined in terms of primarily defensive efforts to reduce the vulnerability of targets and to lessen the impact of terrorist attacks when they do occur. Antiterrorist efforts start from the premise that some terrorist attacks either will be carried out or attempted and thus that efforts must be undertaken to thwart those attempts or to lessen the results of those that do happen.

These intentions lead to two different strands of antiterrorism emphasis. The first is trying to create conditions that make it make difficult to carry out attacks in the first place. The most prominent and symbolic form is the attempt to deny terrorists access to vulnerable targets like airplanes. Since September 11, the most controversial symbol of that effort has been the Transportation Safety Agency (TSA) and its ubiquitous security checks at airports. The second strand is to mitigate the impacts of terrorist attacks that do occur. One effort includes making targets more difficult to assault successfully. Locating new public buildings away from the street is a way to prevent their being blown up by car bombers (the method used in the 1995 bombing of the Murrah Federal Building in Oklahoma City); shutting off Pennsylvania Avenue in front of the White House to vehicular traffic is another example.

Antiterrorism alone is insufficient to deal with terrorists. It is very expensive. The target set against which the antiterrorist must prepare is very large and subject to expansion due to the ability of terrorists to engage in target substitution—the problem of cost-effectiveness at the margins. This problem is compounded by the inherently defensive character of antiterrorism: by emphasizing *responses* to terrorist problems, it forfeits much of the initiative to the terrorist, who can effectively set the agenda within the bounds of his or her resources.

The second approach is counterterrorism, defined as offensive and military measures against terrorists or sponsoring agencies to prevent, deter, or respond to terrorist acts. The heart of counterterrorism consists of both preventive measures (offensive actions that prevent terrorists from mounting or attempting to mount attacks) and defensive actions (retaliations after a successful attack to prevent or deter a reprise). Preventive actions can take on a variety of guises, from penetrating terrorist cells and arresting or debilitating its members to overt violent acts like assassinations against key terrorist personnel. These actions may be carried out by law enforcement personnel or military or paramilitary forces. Retribution is generally carried out by military or quasi-military means.

Counterterrorism is intuitively appealing. Preventive measures are proactive, and punishment includes the inherent satisfaction of bringing direct retribution for wrongs committed. Preventive action also reverses the terrorist advantage of possessing the initiative and places the terrorist on the defensive. Such efforts are also politically popular. They are macho and virile, always a valuable characteristic in testosterone-driven American politics. Evidence of this was the enormous surge in the popularity of President Obama after the successful completion of the ultimate counterterrorist operation, assassinating Osama bin Laden on Pakistani soil in May 2011.

The problem with counterterrorism, like antiterrorism, is that it is insufficient alone to quell all terrorism. Preventive actions against foreign-based terrorist organizations require a level of intelligence about the structures and plans of terrorist operations that is difficult or impossible to attain in actionable detail, and terrorists, acute to electronic and other efforts at penetration, constantly seek to magnify those difficulties. The absence of a state base for terrorists makes it difficult to carry out either preventive or retaliatory strikes because limited intelligence can lead to imperfect knowledge of the location of desirable human targets and can lead to deadly attacks against civilian targets that create opposition to the United States.

Jurisdictions and Responsibilities   Efforts against terrorists can occur in three different physical environments: within the foreign countries where virtually all terrorist leaders and organizations are located; at the US border, across which terrorists must pass to carry out attacks on American soil; and within the physical territory of the United States. Each location is the physical jurisdiction of a different agency of the federal government and involves different kinds of personnel performing different missions. Each jurisdiction has a designated lead agency of the government with primary responsibility for operations within its venue. Ideally, the various functions of this triangular relationship are well coordinated such that each makes the job of the other less difficult; in practice, this ideal is not always met.

Foreign operations are aimed at identifying foreign terrorist organizations, monitoring their activities (especially of budding attacks on the United States or its allies), taking appropriate actions to undercut whatever plans are hatched, and coordinating and engaging in preventive or retaliatory actions against foreign-based terrorist organizations. The primary emphasis of foreign operations is counterterrorism, and because the bedrock of success is the gathering of information about terrorists, the agency assigned primary responsibility for foreign intelligence operations—the Central Intelligence Agency (CIA)—is the designated lead agency.

At the operational level, many of the actions carried out on foreign soil are military (e.g., air strikes against terrorist camps) or semimilitary (e.g., the use of special operations forces, or SOFs, to capture terrorists in foreign locations). As a result, the CIA shares some responsibility for foreign operations with the military. Both the CIA and the military have access to Predator drone aircraft, for instance, and they share access to Defense Department–controlled satellites for tracking and guidance of these assets. The most famous instance of this cooperation was the 2011 raid that ended with the death of bin Laden: the intelligence that located him and the plan that was devised against him were largely fashioned by the CIA and executed by SOFs.

Border operations have as their primary functions monitoring the people who enter or leave the United States, including the interception and apprehension of terrorists attempting to enter (or leave) and the identification of people who might pose terrorist threats but are not subject to apprehension. Identifying and detaining possible terrorists is an extension of the normal border-monitoring function of the government, and the federal agency with lead responsibility is Immigration and Customs Enforcement (ICE), the successor agency to the Immigration and Naturalization Service (INS) after the reorganization of the terrorism effort with the Homeland Security Act of 2002. These efforts are primarily antiterrorist in nature.

Domestic operations involve both counterterrorism and antiterrorism elements. The primary function is to capture terrorists who have penetrated American territory. This function involves both elements of activity: counterterrorism aimed at intercepting and destroying terrorist groups planning attacks and antiterrorism monitoring and apprehension efforts to make it more difficult for terrorists to execute their plans. These are primarily law enforcement problems, so the agency with primary responsibility for federal law enforcement is the Federal Bureau of Investigation (FBI). If a terrorist attack succeeds, the Federal Emergency Management Agency (FEMA) has the lead agent's task of dealing with the resulting devastation, an antiterrorist activity.

These are, of course, not the only agencies involved in the effort. Foreign operations involve close coordination between the CIA and the military, among various other intelligence agencies of the US government, and with intelligence agencies from other countries. Border security includes thwarting attempts to enter the United States at illegal crossing points and thus involves cooperative efforts with agencies with that primary responsibility. Domestic law enforcement efforts are shared with state and local law enforcement agencies, and local and state first responders are part of the disaster-relief exercise.

Status and Prospects   What exactly is the status and ultimate objective of the campaign against terrorism? If it is the eradication of terrorism as a phenomenon, it is unlikely ever to succeed, although that would clearly be a desirable outcome. If it is the elimination or control of a specific terrorist threat (e.g., IS), that is a measurable goal toward which apparent progress can be noted, and in cases like IS, it has clearly occurred.

It is difficult, even impossible, to demonstrate why something does not happen, and this limitation suggests one should use some caution in reaching conclusions, particularly about what has and has not "worked" in the effort to deal with the problem of terrorism. It is almost certainly true that the effort has substantially weakened the terrorist opponent, but the endpoint of an international environment in which the threat of terrorism has been expunged is not so clearly in sight.

The AQ threat has been diluted in recent years. Counterterrorism efforts have been successful in attacking and either killing or aiding in the apprehension and confinement of substantial numbers of AQ leaders and followers. Claims by the government and other observers suggest that the direct threat posed by the original is a shadow of its former self. Its leadership has been decimated and its active force of terrorists reduced to something in the low hundreds (or even fewer) worldwide. The killing of leaders like bin Laden and Anwar al-Awlaki points to the success of these very active counterterrorism efforts; if these continued efforts were to yield the same results for Ayman al-Zawahiri, the Egyptian-born physician who succeeded bin Laden in 2012, what terrorism analysts like Bruce Hoffman refer to as Al Qaeda Central (the original structure) would all but disappear.

The elimination of AQ is not, however, the same thing as the elimination of terrorism as a force in international politics or as a national security concern for the United States. AQ will almost certainly fail—as virtually all terrorist movements before failed—in achieving its strategic goals, but it has succeeded tactically in enough cases that it provides a "model" for some aspiring, desperate movements elsewhere in the world. Some of these are spinoffs of AQ (like IS). Others have roots in AQ but have grown beyond it. Still others, especially in Africa, will be spawned or inspired by the "successes" of AQ. Not all these movements pose current threats to the United States, of course, and thus American interests are not necessarily engaged enough to warrant an extensive American effort against them. As long as these groups exist, however, they will be potential American national security problems to which the US government will devote resources. The use of SOFs, as introduced in Amplification 8.2, may be a model for these efforts.

THE WAR IN AFGHANISTAN

The terrorist attacks provided the rationale for the two major military adventures of the United States during the 2000s, the wars in Afghanistan and Iraq. They are two separate and individually justified and conducted military adventures, tied together only by a shared rationale in the campaign against terrorism and geographic proximity to one another. One (Iraq) is basically concluded; the other (Afghanistan) is not.

The discussion of each war will be organized around three central emphases. The first is the justification for the war effort, including how it may have changed across time. The central question is, "Why did the United States go to war?" The second is the validity of the objective, including its importance and attainability and the success in achieving the goal. The central question here is, "Was it worth it?" This raises questions about the clarity of the objective, its importance and attainability, and whether it has (or could have) been reached. The third concern is the lessons of the war. "What should or has the experience taught the United States that can or should be valuable in the future?"

The discussion begins with Afghanistan. Chronologically, the American intervention in Afghanistan preceded the American invasion of Iraq by nearly a year and a half. It began with the insertion of some American SOFs and the introduction of American airpower into Afghanistan in October 2001, barely a month after the September 11 bombings (the American invasion of Iraq began in March 2003). There was a direct and tangible connection between the terrorist attacks and the initial American actions in Afghanistan, which was largely an attempted retaliation and punishment of the Afghanistan-based AQ terrorists the Taliban refused to turn over to the United States.

Justification of the War

When the United States initially decided to take military action in Afghanistan immediately after the 9/11 events, the reasons for doing so were clear-cut, unambiguous, limited, decisive, and highly supported by almost everyone in the country. The action arose from the realization that AQ operatives who had enjoyed sanctuary in Afghanistan since 1996 protected by the Taliban government had executed the atrocity. The United States demanded that the Afghan government turn over bin Laden and his followers to American authorities. The Taliban, who had granted a haven to AQ after it was expelled (partially at American insistence) from Sudan five years earlier, refused. In this situation, the United States decided to mount a campaign in Afghanistan to capture and bring AQ to justice. Hardly anybody worldwide questioned this American reaction.

The mission was, however, complicated by the situation in Afghanistan in ways that would foreshadow future developments. The Taliban, a fundamentalist Islamic movement dominated by young Afghans (*talib*, from which the name Taliban is extrapolated, means "student"), had seized power in 1996 after several years of chaotic and corrupt rule following the final expulsion of the Soviets from the country in 1989. The Taliban movement came almost exclusively from the Ghilzai Pashtun ethnic group of Afghanistan, the Pashtun being the largest tribe in the country. Although by no means all Pashtuns supported it, almost everyone who did was a Pashtun. The Taliban government was opposed by elements who disapproved of the highly ascetic program of the Taliban and by tribal groups that generally opposed Pashtun rule. Since the Taliban shielded AQ, the United States found itself in direct opposition with the government.

When the Americans decided to enter Afghanistan, the Taliban government was engaged in a civil war with a coalition of opposition elements collectively known as the Northern Alliance. The alliance was composed mostly of non-Pashtun ethnic groups (of which the Tajiks were the largest group) and even some Pashtuns, including Hamid Karzai, a warlord leader from the Kandahar area who was a member of the Durrani branch of the Pashtuns. As is often the case in Afghanistan, this civil war was proceeding with no apparent winner at hand.

The United States almost inadvertently became part of the civil war on the side of those opposing the Taliban. Before the American intervention, the United States had expressed reservations about some of the extremist practices of the Taliban government against its own people but had no compelling interest in the outcome of the civil war. US Afghan interests essentially began and ended with AQ.

The crystalline objective of the United States—the capture of AQ—failed, and the American objective changed in two distinct ways. The action that implicitly, and later explicitly, broadened the objective was the assistance the United States gave to the Northern Alliance. The critical element was the provision of American airpower and SOFs to attack and weaken the Taliban, helping push the military balance in the civil war toward the insurgents. Aided by the United States, the Northern Alliance drove the Taliban from power, an objective they had basically achieved by the end of 2001 as the defeated Taliban retreated to the tribal regions of Pakistan dominated by fellow Pashtun Pakistanis. This internal change brought Hamid Karzai to power, implicitly aligned with the United States and other Western countries. The promotion and retention of the Karzai regime evolved into the primary operational objective of the United States.

The United States failed to achieve its primary objective, which was the capture and destruction of AQ. The United States pursued AQ into the mountains of eastern Afghanistan along the Pakistan border, where Operation Anaconda, drawing upon the analogy with the snake after which it was named, was supposed to envelop, slowly strangle, and kill the terrorists. It failed because AQ managed to slip out of the noose prepared for it in the Tora Bora Mountains along the border and escape into tribal areas of Pakistan. Some disagreement continues about how and why this occurred but centers on the diversion of crucial military assets needed to complete the mission to preparations for the invasion of Iraq.

The net effect was to change the objective of the ongoing mission. In a sense, the mission succeeded in ridding Afghanistan of AQ in that it fled to Pakistan and has not returned. It failed to provide retribution for the 9/11 attacks since it neither captured nor killed bin Laden or his associates at the time. What did occur was a de facto commitment of the United States to defend and promote a non-Taliban government in Kabul, a task that at the operational level has provided the rationale and, implicitly, the basic US objective ever since.

These two objectives are separable and distinct, although they tend to be conflated in justifications by war apologists. A major defense of continuing the war effort is still voiced in terms of the original antiterrorist objective, but there has been no real AQ presence in or threat from Afghanistan for a long time. If there is a continuing AQ threat, it comes from places other than Afghanistan, like Pakistan, and the relationship between current efforts in that country and the original objectives are tenuous. They rely on the hypothesis that if the Taliban were to return to power, they would bring AQ with them and thus pose the same kind of threat present at the time of 9/11. This proposition is, at best, debatable.

The question that must be raised about the change of the objective is the comparative worth of the two objectives to the United States. There is no controversy surrounding the original objective of subduing and destroying AQ; there is, however, a question about whether the implicit adoption of the secondary objective of supporting and buttressing the government in Kabul was or is wise.

Validity of the Objective

The original objective of American military actions in Afghanistan was a textbook example of how to establish a political objective and the means to achieve it. It met all the major criteria for a "good" objective: it was clear and unambiguous; it was clearly an important response to the 9/11 attacks; it was apparently attainable by discrete, bounded operations; and its achievement was clearly measurable. Unfortunately, actions diverting from the objective contributed to expansion and distortion of the mission and the controversy that has surrounded the war effort ever since.

Those who have defended the continuing Afghanistan campaign and counsel a longer military presence generally ignore or downplay this transformation of objectives, but it is arguably *the* critical element in understanding the war and the crucial factor in assessing it. At the time the decisions were being made to become involved in Afghanistan in late 2001, there was never any public discussion, and thus support or opposition, for a political objective that included the development and stabilization of an anti-Taliban government there. Instead, the failure to capture bin Laden and his associates in the Tora Bora region created a felt need to manifest conditions in that country that would impede or block the return of an AQ that was supposed to have been destroyed in the original American military operations. Had Operation Anaconda been successful, there would have been no potential AQ return against which to act. The failure to destroy AQ, however, led to the expansion of purpose under the original objective, avoiding the need to engage in a separate decision process about Afghanistan. Had AQ been destroyed in 2001, most of what happened subsequently would not have occurred to the United States.

Why no separate process of formulating, justifying, and adopting a new objective occurred is a matter of speculation. At the time, military leaders and decision makers could easily have viewed the change as little more than a tactical adjustment to the failure to reach the original objective in a timely fashion, thereby not necessitating a separate decision and justification process. Initially, there were few operational alterations for the United States, so the change occurred "below the radar" of public and media attention, thereby avoiding any public clamor for a reassessment.

Assessing the objective in Afghanistan as it evolved rather than as it started leads to a very different set of conclusions that can be examined by applying the same four criteria that were used to examine the original objective. Unlike the original objective, the reason for supporting the Afghan government has never been entirely clear. What end state does the United States have in mind (possibly quite distinct from the preferences of the Afghans themselves)? Saying the objective is a stable government that can and will resist a Taliban return is not enough. Must it feature strong central governance (which contrasts with the Afghan tradition)? Must it take the form of some form of democracy (also not part of Afghan tradition)? Must the outcome represent some ethnic balance of power (most historic Afghan governments have been dominated by the Durrani Pashtuns)? What are acceptable levels of economic development that must be achieved to assure future political stability in one of the world's most impoverished countries? All these questions were pertinent but essentially unasked and unanswered in 2002, and they remain questions that surround present politico-military efforts. Most contemporary defenses of the continuing American presence simply maintain things would be worse if the United States left—hardly an inspiring rationale.

If the objective defies specificity, how important is it? No one seriously questions whether defeating AQ was a worthy goal, but what about any postwar political outcome or structure in Afghanistan itself? Historically, the United States has had no more than the most passing interests in Afghanistan and its politics, and these have certainly not translated into any vital interest in who governs Afghanistan. Does the connection of the Afghan political situation to the likelihood of an AQ return override the traditional lack of interests? In other words, is an unfavorable outcome in Afghanistan's internal struggle for power enough to justify war?

Then there is the question of attainability. Whether the original objective was attainable had the United States not diverted from it is interesting but academic. In some sense, the assassination of bin Laden, combined with the relentless campaign against the upper levels of AQ, have marked an achievement of the original objective. This achievement is not, however, directly attributable to the American campaign in Afghanistan and can only questionably be used to justify the sacrifice in blood and treasure the United States has made and continues to "spend" in Afghanistan.

Whether the goal of leaving behind a stable, anti-Taliban Afghanistan is achievable remains highly questionable. The standard defense for continued participation is "progress," but progress toward what is rarely specified. The achievement of the second objective in Afghanistan requires a massive application of nation building in that state, a concept and dynamic that has widely fallen into disfavor in the United States and has disappeared altogether in the Trump administration.

The question of attainability also relates to the methods employed and their appropriateness. The use of controlled, specialized force was, by virtually all accounts, the proper tool for realizing the first objective of taking down AQ; failure is normally ascribed to the inadequacy of the resources applied to the siege of Tora Bora and assistance from pro-Taliban tribesmen, not the basic nature of the method.

Whether US forces can contribute positively to achieving these goals is not clear. The Taliban returned in 2003 as insurgents rather than as the government, and they have established themselves as a formidable opponent. The application of American force has not subdued them or allowed the emergence of a united, stable Afghanistan. Part of the reason is that not all Afghans share the vision of their state contained in the objective, which raises questions about whether the goal itself is realistic. At the same time, the transformation of Afghanistan requires political and economic change, and it is not entirely clear that a primary reliance on force—and especially force applied by outsiders against whom Afghans have always shown resistance—is appropriate for the task. The political situation in Afghanistan is so complicated and the military criteria for success so unconventional and complex as to make measures of success treacherous. It is increasingly clear a small residual American force cannot be decisive in a final resolution—whatever that may be.

Lessons of Afghanistan

Since the war continues, its ultimate "lessons" are unknowable. Despite its length and lack of progress toward any discernible conclusion, it has not become unpopular enough that the public demands withdrawal. It drags on with limited American combat involvement—about ten thousand "military trainers" (see Coll, *Directorate S*), a few of whom become casualties—with no clear end in sight. The US government no longer predicts when an acceptable conclusion (whatever that may be) will be achieved.

Determining the lessons the war may eventually teach requires asking at least three questions that reflect previous discussions. The first is whether the United States should have gone to war in Afghanistan in the first place. The answer depends on which objective one is discussing. The second is how the outcome might have been different under other circumstances (including different American actions). Finally, there is the question of what can be gleaned from the experience to help inform the process of future engagements.

Was Afghanistan important enough to the United States to justify the use of American armed forces? In realist language, were American vital interests at risk that could only be defended through the application of that force? The answer, of course, depends on why that force was employed. If the objective was to combat or destroy an AQ threat that had brought thousands of deaths to Americans on American soil and that might have been repeated if the United States failed to respond, the answer is almost certainly positive, assuming the goal could be realized by American arms.

The answer is cloudier regarding the expanded objective of supporting and stabilizing the political situation in Afghanistan and keeping AQ and IS elements from stealing back across the border. Stabilization has never represented a high American national security interest and certainly not one that most would raise to the level of vitality. Unlike the original goal, the secondary objective has lacked specificity in terms of both its desired end state and the means that could produce that result. Both the importance and attainability of the ongoing goal—which is, de facto, why the United States remains in Afghanistan—are questionable at best.

What could—or should—have been done differently in Afghanistan to avoid the situation in which the United States has found itself? Virtually no American in 2001 would have supported American involvement in one of Afghanistan's perpetual, inconclusive civil wars. They were not, of course, asked that question. One can debate why and more specifically the importance and attainability of whatever outcome we supported. One possibility is that things turning out the way they have could not have been anticipated. That answer would be disingenuous because elements within the government (in the State Department and the CIA) did indeed predict what would happen and why, and there were other warnings, largely ignored outside government, and the outcome had copious historical bases.

This leads to the third question, which concerns the lessons of Afghanistan. The lessons depend on the reason for going into and staying in Afghanistan. If the goal was solely to eliminate AQ, the mission was well worth the effort, but the execution was flawed. Once the effort failed, the question of what to do next should have been addressed publicly on its own merits, and it was not. Such an assessment might well have concluded that a massive allied outside intervention in Afghanistan, a country that has been resisting and repelling the invasion of outsiders for its entire history, was not in American interests and was, if anything, an unnecessary diversion that would not serve the country well. Had there been such an open reassessment of Afghanistan at the end of 2001, it might well have concluded the inadvisability of what was subsequently done. The question that remains is what to do now. The broad possibilities are explored in Amplification 10.2.

AMPLIFICATION 10.2

Afghanistan Options

There are three conceptual options available to the United States to try to bring to conclusion what Coll calls in *Directorate S* "at best a grinding stalemate" that is approaching two decades of inconclusive conduct. None of them is compellingly more attractive than the others.

The first, and least discussed or advocated, is a major escalation of American participation in the war to cause the decisive defeat of the Taliban and to produce a pro-American regime in Kabul. This solution suffers from two drawbacks. The first is whether it would work, and negative assessments arise from the lack of broad support for any side in the war (including the government the US supports) and the long Afghan experience resisting the imposition of outside solutions to their problems. Second, and more importantly, this solution would have almost no public support in the United States and would be politically suicidal even to propose.

The second solution is simply to pack American bags and leave. This is essentially the solution to which the country turned in Iraq, and it did result in extrication. This solution is supported by the political left as admission Afghanistan is a mission impossible, but it is opposed on the right because it admits defeat and could lead to an AQ/IS return to the country.

The third solution is to continue what the United States has been doing, but somehow to do it "better" to produce a happier solution. This is the choice embraced by the Trump administration, which announced the appointment of

Lt. General Scott Miller, commander of the Joint Special Operations Command, to head the US military mission in 2018, accompanied by a modest increase in troops. The idea is that putting in a Special Ops leader will result in a more aggressive, innovative approach to the campaign against the Taliban. Whether it will break the "grinding stalemate" remains to be seen. ■

THE IRAQ WAR

The invasion, conquest, occupation, and eventual withdrawal from Iraq by the United States has become one of the most controversial military actions undertaken in American history. Originally publicly justified as part of the national response to international terrorism, the war was the second longest war in the American experience after Afghanistan at eight and a half years (by the same standard, the third longest war, Vietnam, lasted eight years). The war has been criticized so relentlessly that even its original apologists no longer offer more than a token defense for it. Iraq may well occupy the dubious distinction of being viewed as America's most unpopular and unnecessary war.

There is an irony in what transpired because at one time or another most of those who crafted policy at the highest levels recognized that invading Iraq was a bad idea. President George H. W. Bush did not send troops into Iraq in 1991 because he feared the result would be a civil war. In 1994, George W. Bush's future vice president, Richard Cheney, declared such an invasion would result in a quagmire. In 1997, then Texas governor George W. Bush told a San Antonio newspaper he agreed with his father's assessment. Those earlier assessments were prescient; they were also apparently forgotten.

The details of the specific criticism of what Ned Parker described as "the United States' disastrous misadventure" in a 2012 article have been chronicled extensively elsewhere. Those criticisms can be organized in terms of the categories used to dissect the war in Afghanistan. The justification has been questioned in terms of both its vitality and the honesty of its advocacy. Like Afghanistan, the objective changed over time, although in the case of Iraq, it became more modest rather than broader. Moreover, the ways in which various stages of the operation were conducted have been the subject of scrutiny in terms of both their vitality and attainability. Since the formal operation ended at the end of 2011, it is possible tentatively to look at the post-occupation phase.

The Iraq War can only properly be analyzed in terms of four distinctive phases. The first step was the *pre-invasion phase* that included the planning and rationalization of why the United States needed to go to war against Iraq. The second step was the *military invasion phase*, the period from the initial American incursion into Iraq to the collapse of the resistance and the fall of Baghdad. The third step was the *occupation*, the eight-year-plus period when American forces occupied and, with some growing power sharing, ruled Iraq. Finally, the Christmas holiday season of 2011 saw the end of the occupation and the full restoration of Iraqi sovereignty; this *post-occupation phase* continues to unfold.

These distinctions are important because different controversies have attended each phase. Two phases are most controversial. The pre-invasion phase is controversial because of questions about the honesty and prescience of the arguments that were made to justify the war. The other highly controversial phase was the occupation, with most of the critiques aimed at the planning (or lack thereof) for the occupation, its generally inept administration, and how mistakes made during the occupation prejudiced the outcome. The brief period of less than two months between March and May 2003 when the invasion was successfully carried out receives the least criticism. Defenses of the war tend to concentrate on this brief period. The extent to which the post-occupation phase will or will not become controversial depends both on how far domestic circumstances in Iraq move from the intended American objectives and on how the United States responds to any divergences that do occur (a concern raised in the *Challenge!* box later in the section).

Justification of the War

The official rationale for invading Iraq was based in the "war" on terrorism and rested on two major allegations. The first was that the Iraqi regime of Saddam Hussein was engaged in clandestine efforts to develop WMDs. The second was that he had developed links to AQ terrorists, and that, most darkly and implicitly, should he attain WMDs, he might share them with terrorists who would use those weapons against the United States. Formulated in this manner, it made a compelling case that the situation posed a threat to vital American interests.

The problem was that the truth of these accusations was never demonstrated, was shown to be false, or was proved illogical after actions to address them had occurred. The George W. Bush administration never managed to produce any positive evidence of an active Iraqi WMD program (which had apparently been abandoned in the 1990s) or ties with the AQ terrorists. Shortly before the war began, President Bush declared that "you can't distinguish between Saddam Hussein and Al Qaeda," but provided no explanation. Such ties also failed logical tests since the comparatively secular Sunni regime of Hussein and the radical fundamentalism of AQ made them enemies, not potential collaborators. The justifications were factually challenged.

These incongruities were hotly debated at the time of the invasion, but much of the public and the Congress accepted them. If taken at face value, they certainly appeared to make the case for using American force, especially given the extreme concern Americans felt about the threat emanating from 9/11 and the possibility it might be repeated. In that atmosphere, both houses of Congress passed resolutions authorizing the president to take whatever measures he deemed necessary to deal with the Iraqi threat. His response was to invade Iraq, beginning on March 19, 2003, and then declare the mission to have been successfully completed on May 1, a mere six weeks later. This phase of the operation was a clear and unambiguous success and achieved the objective of overthrowing the regime of Saddam Hussein, an interim necessity to end his alleged production of WMDs and his relations with the terrorists.

The stated objectives of the Iraq War rang slightly off-key, even at the time. A minority of Americans felt the alleged behavior justifying the action was either bogus or insufficiently demonstrated, a suspicion later largely validated. At the same time, there was always an important subtext to the stated objective. This semi-hidden agenda came from a group of close advisors to President Bush known as the neoconservatives, a group of defense intellectuals, many with close ties to Israel, who had advocated the overthrow of Hussein since the 1990–91 Gulf War and even before that. Their argument in 1991 was that the victory in the Kuwaiti desert had been incomplete because it did not include a march to Baghdad and the overthrow of the Iraqi dictator. To the neoconservatives (often abbreviated to "neo-cons"), the overthrow of Hussein would serve two important and sequential purposes. First, it would end the Hussein tyranny and replace it with a democratic regime in Baghdad. This regime would be the first Arab democracy in the region and would act as a shining example others in the region would emulate. A democratic Iraq and a democratizing Arab world would contribute to their second (and many suspect primary underlying) goal, promoting the security of Israel: a democratic Israel and like-minded Arab regimes would have less to fight about under these circumstances (democratic peace). There is also a lingering suspicion, most often associated with neo-con supporter Vice President Richard Cheney, that many coveted access to Iraqi oil as well.

The neoconservative vision became the de facto objective of the Iraq War. Once the fighting ended, it became clear that the original goal either had been achieved or had never needed achieving, yet American forces were still on the ground in Iraq as occupiers, and their removal would have resulted in chaos since the United States had destroyed the old regime but had not replaced it. The Bush administration had apparently not adequately considered the possibility of an extended stay in Iraq (Secretary of Defense Donald Rumsfeld had declared during spring 2003 that he expected there to be the need for no more than six thousand American forces by Labor

Day, 129 days after the invasion). Since there were no WMDs to dismantle (despite a furtive search for them) and no links to terrorists to be severed, the war needed a new objective. The neo-con vision became the de facto substitute.

With the original justification in tatters, the rationale of the long occupation that ended in 2011 was to prepare Iraq for the restoration of its full status as a sovereign, and hopefully stable and democratic, state. Just as the objective implicitly changed in Afghanistan after the original objective failed, so too the objective in Iraq needed to be changed after the original purpose was demonstrated to have been false.

This implicit change in direction occurred as the war effort was becoming more controversial anyway. The occupation was the subject of increasing scrutiny and criticism, with escalating claims of amateurism and incompetence in its administration (Chandrasekaran and Packer, among others cited in the suggested readings, particularly make these points). The decision to dismantle the Iraqi army and much of the civilian bureaucracy because they were dominated by Sunni supporters of the toppled regime when there were no ready personnel or structures to replace them is often cited as particular evidence of this incompetence. Largely sectarian resistance began to emerge by 2004, emphasizing questions that had earlier been raised by critics of the original war decision.

Defenders of the Iraq War generally do not like to phrase its assessment in these terms. They prefer to downplay the controversy about the original objective, an explicit adoption of the neo-con dream of Iraq as a democratic regional beacon suggests a kind of starry-eyed idealism most of them explicitly reject. Instead, their defense of the long occupation and in some cases their rejection of its sudden and total termination are phrased in other terms, such as needing a stable, vibrant Iraq to be a regional counterweight to Iran.

Validity of the Objective

Was the war in Iraq worth it? Critics deny vehemently that it was. Iraqi WMDs and ties to terrorism certainly rose to the level of affecting vital American interests. Critics argue that once these threats were discredited, the other rationales for the war—including democracy promotion and a stable alternative to the Sunni dictatorship of Saddam Hussein—were less worthy, leaving the war one of choice—a war that did not have to be fought to protect vital American interests.

The basic argument against the war is found in applying the realist paradigm to the situation. If the original charges were true, the realist case could be made on vital interest grounds. With that rationale debunked, however, many concluded that the justification fell short of the realist threshold. Many supporters of the war, including leading neoconservatives, counter that the realist paradigm was too restrictive as a criterion for force employment.

This debate about the validity of the Iraq War can be examined in terms of the same four criteria used to structure the discussion of Afghanistan. The first criterion is the clarity of the objective, and once again, the assessment is mixed. Eliminating WMDs and severing Iraqi ties to terrorists were clear, measurable objectives; they just turned out not to exist. The secondary, implicit promotion of a stable, democratic Iraq was less tangible, and it is not clear what exactly would have demonstrated its attainment. For instance, is a Shiite-dominated regime, the selection of which is based on the principle of "one man, one vote" but that suppressed minority Sunnis and Kurds, acceptable? What about a democratic but indecisive regime that cannot make decisions that will result in economic prosperity? What if stability can only be achieved by the de facto or total de jure partition of Iraq into three autonomous regions or sovereign states? Which, if any, of these outcomes is acceptable?

The second criterion is the importance of the objective. The original objective met that standard, but the secondary objective of regime change arguably did not. Was an alternative regime to Saddam Hussein's in Baghdad important enough to justify an eight-and-a-half-year effort that cost over 4,500 American lives (and hundreds of thousands of Iraqi casualties) and well over a trillion American dollars? For all his other considerable faults, Saddam Hussein was an implacable opponent of the Iranians and their expanded influence regionally. By removing him and sanctioning his replacement by Iranian coreligionists (Shiites), the United States effectively, in the view of many, handed influence in postwar Iraq to Iran on a platter.

There is also serious debate about whether the secondary objective is, or ever was, attainable. Criticism of the war on attainability criteria stems from a negative assessment of whether Iraq was ever a realistic candidate for the democratizing makeover the neoconservatives proposed. Iraq is a classic artificial country with a relatively short history and tradition of statehood (Iraq has existed as a state since 1932) and has deep and well-documented cleavages along sectarian (Sunni versus Shia) and ethnic lines (Arabs versus Kurds) that are also geographically defined (the Shiite south, Sunni center, and Kurdish north of the country). None of these divisions has been resolved and remain deep, arguably unsolvable sources of division and disunity. These divisions existed and were known at the time of the attack.

Whatever the goal in Iraq, it is hard to argue it has been attained. There are no WMDs, and the only ties to terrorism were the result of Sunni resistance to the American occupation (AQ in Iraq) and IS, the reincarnation of AQI that arrived in 2014. Hussein is dead, but stability has remained elusive. How much credit goes to the American invasion? The outcome remains largely in the hands of the Iraqis themselves.

Lessons of Iraq

In *What After Iraq?* this author (writing in 2008) titled the chapter on the lessons of Iraq "No More Iraqs," strongly suggesting a parallel with the post-Vietnam experience of the United States and reflecting a negative assessment of the experience. The question, then and now, is what the content of "no more Iraqs" means, another way of asking what the United States should learn from the experience.

What is not clear is whether Americans care much one way or the other about post-occupation Iraq. Harkening back to the Vietnam experience that provided the model of "No More Iraqs," the United States turned its back on the final outcome of the Vietnamese civil war in which it had chosen sides for eight years of combat. When Saigon fell to the North Vietnamese two years after the last American combat troops evacuated from the country, there was hardly a murmur of concern.

CHALLENGE!

Is Syria the Lesson of Iraq?

If the 2000s were a decade of considerable American military activism flowing from the reaction to 9/11, the 2010s have, to this point, been a decade of considerable military retrenchment, where the country has avoided the kinds of involvements Iraq and Afghanistan represented. The reluctance to become involved even in tragic, hideous situations has not been part of the recent landscape for American security policy. Partly, this has almost certainly been because no trauma of 9/11 proportions has demanded a forceful American response (some might argue the rise of IS came close). But is part of the reason that Iraq has taught the United States a useful lesson about military involvement in the Middle East?

Syria is the obvious example of change. When the civil war broke out and reports mounted of atrocities by the Assad government of those opposing him, there were virtually no calls for a forceful American response. There was some sentiment to assist the opposition with weapons, training, and the like (which came to nothing because the US government could not find a faction it trusted to whom it could funnel aid). The Syrian situation is, of course, different than what the Americans faced in Iraq and Afghanistan, but is that the reason the United States acted in the 2000s but not in the 2010s? Or did the United States learn a valuable lesson about the consequences of forceful action in a part of the world it really does not understand? ■

The ill will surrounding Iraq is different than it was in Vietnam. The military operation in Vietnam bore much of the tarnish from that war, and that is not true in Iraq. Negative reactions to the Iraqi experience tend to center on the objectives of the war: the honesty and prescience of the original objective and the attainability and reality of the revised objective. Whether those who advocated war on Iraq did or did not know their charges against the Saddam Hussein regime were disingenuous, many of them (notably the neo-cons) saw such reasons for war as a pretext for doing something they more firmly advocated: getting rid of the hated dictator and conducting the democratizing experiment. They succeeded in the first of these goals and failed in the second.

There is also the question of the attainability of the secondary objective. Iraq was and is not the poster child for a country ripe for democratic reform in a Western sense, and there is little indication that those who advocated trying to do so fully understood the political and cultural barriers that made their goal quixotic. Toppling Hussein was the easy part, and it was carried out successfully. Rebuilding from the ruins after the invasion turned out to be not so easy. The reason was partly the inept way the occupation was conceived and implemented, but partly it was the result of pursuing an unattainable vision.

CONCLUSION: CONDITIONING THE FUTURE

The terrorist attacks of September 11, 2001, triggered the series of national security–based commitments that dominated American efforts for the balance of the decade and extended into the early 2010s. The nearly three thousand Americans and other nationals who died in the Twin Towers in New York and at the Pentagon were a major wake-up call for Americans and set in motion policies and actions that are still evolving.

In any objective sense, the direct terrorist threat to American soil has probably passed its peak and is on the wane. It has not disappeared altogether, as new international terrorist groups have come into being, some of which are spinoffs from AQ and others in other parts of the developing world. The need for vigilance in the terrorism effort remains a major continuing element in the national security equation for this country.

The "spin-offs" of American military efforts in Afghanistan and Iraq remain parts of the landscape as well. They are different, of course, in status and dynamics. The war in Iraq was entirely an event of American doing since it began with the American invasion of Iraq and continued for as long as American forces remained on and in control of Iraqi soil. There was already war in Afghanistan when American forces arrived, and although the introduction and continued presence of those forces altered that war's conduct and duration, it was not a conflict the United States started. American combat participation has ended in Iraq but continues in Afghanistan. No one in the decision process admitted the possibility that the American involvement in either would be as long and costly as it has turned out to be; knowing that possibility undoubtedly affects current decision processes.

The legacies of these events of the 2000s are important for two other reasons. The first is that neither Iraq nor Afghanistan has been a conspicuous success in either a military or a political sense. The United States did not lose on the battlefield in either case, but neither conflict has produced the political outcome for which it was undertaken. These facts are cautionary as the United States views the landscape of future military adventures in the contemporary environment. The second reason is that these adventures were terribly expensive. Much of the cost of the campaign against terrorism may have been unavoidable, but whether the American recovery from the Great Recession would have been hastened if the United States had not expended resources measured in the trillions of dollars in Iraq and Afghanistan remains a debatable proposition in an era of at least rhetorical fiscal frugality.

STUDY/DISCUSSION QUESTIONS

1. What national security responses were triggered by the September 11, 2001, attacks? Relate each response to those attacks.
2. Discuss the major problems associated with terrorism and its study, including the definition of terrorism and the various elements of terrorism deriving from that definition and its context as part of war and politics.
3. How can terrorism be combated? Against what objects can one aim efforts? What are the goals, conceptual means, and institutions by which to conduct terrorism suppression? What is the status of American efforts to combat the phenomenon?
4. What have the two objectives of the United States in Afghanistan been? Describe each. How did they evolve? Assess them in terms of their worth and attainability (validity).
5. What are the principal lessons of Afghanistan described in the text? Critically assess this list. What options does the United States have in Afghanistan?
6. The text suggests that the Iraq War was conducted in four phases in pursuit of two different objectives. Describe each phase and objective, relate them to one another, and show how one led to the other.
7. How was the Iraq War justified? Were these justifications valid (important and attainable)? Were they achieved, and what can the United States do if they were not? Critically assess.
8. Compare the lessons of Afghanistan and Iraq. What do they suggest for the future of American national security policy in the current political environment?

SELECTED BIBLIOGRAPHY

Atwan, Abdul Beri. *The Secret History of Al Qaeda*. Berkeley, CA: University of California Press, 2006.
Barfield, Thomas. *Afghanistan: A Cultural and Political History*. Princeton, NJ: Princeton University Press, 2010.

Biddle, Stephen, Fotini Christia, and Alexander Thier. "Defining Success in Afghanistan: What Can the United States Accept?" *Foreign Affairs* 89, 4 (July/August 2010), 58–60.

Chandrasekaran, Rajiv. *Imperial Life in the Emerald City: Inside Iraq's Green Zone*. New York: Alfred A. Knopf, 2007.

Coll, Steve. *Directorate S: The CIA and America's Secret Wars in Afghanistan and Pakistan*. New York: Penguin Books, 2018.

———. *Ghost Wars: The Secret History of the CIA, Afghanistan, and Bin Laden from the Soviet Invasion to September 10, 2001*. New York: Penguin Books, 2004.

Dershowitz, Alan M. *Why Terrorism Works: Responding to the Challenge*. New Haven, CT: Yale University Press, 2002.

Ewans, Martin. *Afghanistan: A Short History of Its People and Politics*. New York: Harper Perennial, 2002.

Goldberg, Jeffrey. "After Iraq." *The Atlantic* 301, 1 (January/February 2008), 68–79.

Hoffman, Bruce. *Inside Terrorism*. 2nd ed. New York: Columbia University Press, 2006.

Jalili, Ali Ahmed. *A Military History of Afghanistan: From the Great Game to the Global War on Terror*. Lawrence, KS: University of Kansas Press, 2017.

Johnson, Robert. *The Afghan Way of War: How and Why They Fight*. Oxford, UK: Oxford University Press, 2011.

Jones, Seth G. *In the Graveyard of Empires: America's War in Afghanistan*. New York: W. W. Norton, 2009.

Law, Randal D. *Terrorism: A History*. 2nd ed. Boston: Polity Press, 2016.

Miller, Paul D. "Finish the Job: How the War in Afghanistan Can Be Won." *Foreign Affairs* 90, 1 (January/February 2011), 51–65.

Nacos, Brigette I. *Terrorism and Counterterrorism: Understanding Threats and Responses in the Post-9/11 World*. New York: Penguin Books, 2006.

O'Connell, Aaron B. (ed.). *Our Latest Longest War: Losing Hearts and Minds in Afghanistan*. Chicago, IL: University of Chicago Press, 2017.

Packer, George. *The Assassin's Gate: America in Iraq*. New York: Farrar, Straus and Giroux, 2005.

Parker, Ned. "The Iraq We Left Behind: Welcome to the World's Next Failed State." *Foreign Affairs* 91, 2 (March/April 2012), 94–110.

Polk, William R. *Understanding Iraq*. New York: Harper Perennial, 2006.

Rapaport, David C. "The Four Waves of Terrorism." In *Attacking Terrorism: Elements of a Grand Strategy*, Audrey Kurth Cronin and James M. Ludes (eds.). Washington, DC: Georgetown University Press, 2006, 46–73.

Rashid, Ahmed. *Taliban: Militant Islam, Oil, and Fundamentalism in Central Asia*. 2nd ed. New Haven, CT: Yale University Press, 2010.

———. *Descent into Chaos: The United States and the Disaster in Pakistan, Afghanistan, and Central Asia*. New York: Penguin Books, 2009.

Ricks, Thomas E. *Fiasco: The American Military Adventure in Iraq*. New York: Penguin Books, 2006.

Sadat, Kosh, and Stanley McChrystal. "Staying the Course in Afghanistan: How to Fight the Longest War." *Foreign Affairs* 96, 6 (November/December 2017), 2–8.

Serwer, Daniel. "Iraq Struggles to Govern Itself." *Current History* 109, 731 (December 2010), 390–394.

Shahrani, M. Nafiz (ed.). *Modern Afghanistan: The Impact of 40 Years of War*. Bloomington, IN: Indiana University Press, 2018.

Sky, Emma. "Iraq, From Surge to Sovereignty." *Foreign Affairs* 90, 2 (March/April 2011), 117–127.

Snow, Donald M. *Cases in International Relations: Principles and Applications*. 7th ed. Lanham, MD: Rowman & Littlefield, 2018.

———. *The Middle East, Oil, and the United States National Security*. Lanham, MD: Rowman & Littlefield, 2016.

———. *What After Iraq?* New York: Pearson Longman, 2009.

———. *September 11, 2001: The New Face of War?* New York: Pearson Longman, 2002.

——— and Dennis M. Drew. *From Lexington to Baghdad and Beyond.* 3rd ed. Armonk, NY: M. E. Sharpe, 2010.

Stern, Jessica. *Terrorism in the Name of God: Why Religious Militants Kill.* New York: ECCO, 2003.

US Department of State. *Patterns of Global Terrorism.* Washington, DC: US Department of State (annual publication).

US Marine Corps. *Afghanistan: Operational Culture for Deploying Personnel.* Quantico, VA: Center for Advanced Operational Cultural Learning, 2009.

Lethal Landscapes: The Future Menu

Most national security planning tries to anticipate the nature of future threats and how they can be countered. When the future appears to be very similar to the past, this task is simple and straightforward. The future today is not so comforting. There is no predictable, concrete opponent on the short-term horizon that greatly taxes American resources or substantially threatens the United States. The Islamic State (IS) appeared to provide a strategic threat in the middles of the current decade, but that threat has largely dissipated itself. The result is less focused "lethal landscapes" that center on developing world internal conflicts (DWICs) and continuing interest in the turbulent Middle East that dominate the "menu" of violence.

Military threats are changing in terms of severity and importance, location, and conduct. The American "way of war," concentrated on the European tradition and reaching its epitome in World War II, is essentially archaic today. There has not been a major cross-border war fought between sovereign states employing conventional means for well over nearly three decades, unless one counts Russian "hybrid" incursions in Ukraine, and there is little likelihood that such a conflict will occur anytime soon. The opponents and the rules by which people fight have simply changed.

This does not mean that the international system (the landscape) has become any less dangerous (lethal). Warfare continues inside many countries, mostly in parts of the developing world, and occasionally these conflicts spill across boundaries. They can be quite deadly in terms of local casualties, and the ubiquitous presence of electronic recording of the bloodiest aspects of these conflicts makes them harder to avoid than in earlier times. Modern technology means that individuals with cell phones now chronicle man's abundant inhumanity toward his fellow men. The ubiquity of violence has become more difficult to ignore.

Contemporary lethal landscapes arise from this context. The dominant form of violence in the system today is internal to states—groups of people, sometimes overlapping sovereign jurisdictions—fighting one another for control of political space and power, and the discussion begins by looking at these developing world internal conflicts. Among other things, the DWICs tend to be fought asymmetrically, using some variation of the methodology that weaker forces employ against conventionally superior opponents. These dual characteristics make it difficult, and often impossible, for outsiders (including the United States) to affect these situations positively: internal political differences can only be truly resolved by the internal factions that hold different positions, and conventional force has not been particularly effective in defeating unconventional warriors in developing world venues. In somewhat different ways, Iraq and Afghanistan both display this dynamic and provide some caution about the kinds of international violence of which the United States should become a part.

For the last quarter century or more, the bulk of the mayhem has been concentrated in two areas of the world: Africa (particularly the northern half) and the Middle East. The two areas overlap geographically (much of Saharan Africa is also part of the Middle East) and religiously. Islam is a common denominator because it is zealously present in both areas. In its most extreme instantiations, that zealotry employs terrorism as a primary or sole tool. The United States has become most involved in Middle Eastern conflicts: Andrew Bacevich points out that the United States has employed force in fourteen Middle Eastern countries since 1981, far more than in any other part of the world. The Middle East has provided the showcase for American arms, although it is not entirely clear in all instances where American interests lie and whether the country can effectively defend its interests with the use of American military power.

PROBLEM OF DEVELOPING WORLD INTERNAL CONFLICTS

The concentration of violence in the developing world presents the United States with two distinct conceptual problems, both discussed earlier. The first is an *interest-threat mismatch*, where America's most important (vital) interests are hardly threatened and where the threats that do exist are to less-than-vital (LTV) interests that, under the realist paradigm, do not warrant the use of American force. The irony of the mismatch is complete because where American interests are most important—Western Europe and Japan, for instance—there are hardly any threats.

The second conceptual problem is the *threat-force mismatch*, where American forces are robust and effective in places where interests are greatest but where threats are minimal—the European land mass. In situations where American force might be employed because of instability and violence, the forces have not proven to be especially adept. This difficulty is most apparent in developing-world situations where asymmetrical opponents negate the enormous firepower advantage. The United States possesses unparalleled capability to fight wars that no longer occur, but this capability is not so appropriate for conducting wars that do occur.

A concentration of systemic violence in the form of DWICs is not new. Internal conflict within many developing-world states was an outcome of decolonization. Many European colonies were politically imperfect, even grotesque, in terms of the peoples they aggregated. Independence was generally given to the old colonial units, meaning the new states inherited all the animosities and imperfections that had been perpetuated by the colonial experience. Generally deficient in resources that could ameliorate their problems and lessen their differences, the situations bred the development of warring factions along ethnic, tribal, religious, or other bases. These sources of international instability were present in all the areas of the world that underwent decolonization (Africa and Asia, including parts of the Middle East), and they often erupted in occasionally extreme violence.

Cold War–era DWICs were overshadowed by the central East-West confrontation. To the extent developing-world countries were considered Cold War concerns, it was as pawns and surrogates in the broader contest. They were pawns if they could somehow be persuaded to side with one side or the other, and they could be surrogates where the superpowers could compete without any great danger it might devolve into direct conflict between them. In the process, the actual problems of the developing parts of the world, including violence, were either ignored or left to former colonizers to deal with. The very real and deep divisions in many of these countries were hidden behind the veil of the Cold War.

THE NEW NORM: DWICS IN AFRICA AND THE MIDDLE EAST

The changed emphasis of global violence has been startling for traditional powers like the United States accustomed to a Euro-centered world where European political problems (largely interstate in nature) and violent means of resolving them (conventional, European-style military forces) were the norm. Europe and most of the world heavily influenced by the European model (e.g., most of South America) are remarkably tranquil, with outbreaks of violence confined to peripheries like the Crimea and Ukraine and the Balkans.

The disappearance of traditional wars has created a national security ambiguity to which countries like the United States are still adjusting. The old model was both familiar and compatible with the realist paradigm:

traditionally organized military force to protect the vital interests of states. In the new world of DWICs, neither of these characteristics always holds: traditional forms of force are not clearly decisive against asymmetrical opponents, and American vital interests are no longer unarguably engaged in the conflicts that tempt American (and other) outside participation.

The developing world is an incredibly complex pastiche of unique situations and circumstances so that talking about *a* developing world distorts the analysis. Most developing countries share a European colonial background, but that experience differed significantly depending on location (Asia, Africa, or Latin America), historical experience (length of colonial rule and time and nature of its termination, for example), the level of pre-colonial development, resource abundance or absence, and the nature of the culture and peoples who were colonized, to name five. Because of these and other, often idiosyncratic, factors, the experiences of no two post-colonial societies have been identical. Not all developing countries have been prone to violence. Those that have experienced violence, however, tend to share some characteristics that should provide cautions for outsiders contemplating involvement in the problems faced by these countries.

Developing World Sources of Conflict

The problems of the developing world are enormous, intractable, and enduring. The difficulties that existed at the time of independence—which began in the early 1950s and extended until the late 1970s—have often not been reduced significantly. Where they have not, the result has sometimes been a volatile instability that can become violent, sometimes in very bloody, even atrocious, ways. The factors that create this situation can be categorized as political, economic, and geographic.

Political Factors   The political factors are the most striking and often difficult. In the violence-prone countries, the major political problem is generally associated with nationalism or, more precisely, its absence. Nationalism is defined by Wikipedia as "a shared group feeling in the significance of a geographical and sometimes demographic region." Nationalism is supposed to be directed to the political entity of the particular state in which one resides, and it is supposed to be manifested in a primary political loyalty to that state and not to some political entity within or transcending state boundaries. Nationalism is characterized by primary identity with and political loyalty to the state. Characteristics of nationalism include a common language, common history, cultural and/or religious experience, and at the bottom line, simply feeling one's primary political loyalty is to the state. Americans, for instance, lack many of these characteristics but generally feel themselves so overwhelmingly to be Americans that American nationalism is very strong.

The problem in violence-prone developing countries almost always derives from the absence of a strong sense of national identification by some or all parts of the population. As a result, many of the countries are classic *artificial states*, arbitrary political designations for which there is no compelling loyalty rationale based in historical experience, popular loyalty, or anything else other than that they were areas on a map that European colonialists designated. This deficiency was the direct result of the colonial experience and the process of decolonization in two significant ways. One was the physical and demographic nature of the colonies to which independence was granted—sometimes peacefully and occasionally after a violent struggle. Most were assembled without any reliable prior knowledge of who lived in the colonial units and thus their loyalties and intergroup relations. The result was that colonies tended to aggregate various "nationalities" within their bounds. When independence occurred, it was usually granted to the physical colonial unit, meaning diverse and often antagonistic peoples with loyalties to varying political units were thrown together and told they were Nigerians or Iraqis or Pakistanis, regardless of how they felt themselves.

Second, it was a conscious concern of colonial administration to avoid integrating the peoples within their colonies into some coherent nationalism. The motivation was simple: colonies were established for profit and were considered as perpetual as they could be made to be. Bringing together members of diverse and antagonistic groups to form a unified sense of nationalism could only incite the population to decide that part of their common purpose should be to expel the outsiders, an outcome that hardly promoted long-term profitability. On the other hand, keeping native groups antagonistic facilitated a strategy of divide-and-rule, using some groups to keep others in line. The British were particularly adept at this approach.

When independence occurred, many developing-world countries started out with a severe handicap in nationalist terms. Mostly the problem was that the new state contained multiple subgroups to whom the members placed primary loyalty rather than to the new state of which they were a part.

These divisions tended to be manifested in one or both of two forms. One is *multinationalism*, the situation where there are multiple groups within a country to which the members proclaim greater loyalty than they do to the state. When these more parochial units come into conflict with one another—including over the issue of which one will rule—the result can be violence. Multinationalism is virtually universal in both Africa and the Middle East. Iraq, divided among Sunni Arabs, Shiites, and Kurds, is a familiar example. Christian Ibo, Muslim Hausa-Fulani, and animist Yoruba regions in Nigeria are another, as are the parts of former Sudan.

The other form of division is *irredentism*. Although the term was originally devised to describe divisions in Italy, the phenomenon refers to the situation in which state boundaries divide nationalist groups and where the members of those groups seek to be united into a single state. The problems that irredentism creates can be quite complex and can contribute to considerable internal and regional violence and instability. The most assertive contemporary irredentist group is the Kurds, who live in parts of Iran, Iraq, Syria, and Turkey and want to form a state of Kurdistan carved out from those states, all of which oppose this act of national self-determination. One cannot understand the politics of the region—especially Turkish attitudes toward IS, for instance—without including the Kurdish "card." Many Pashtuns of Afghanistan and Pakistan also yearn to create Pashtunistan.

An additional political problem surrounds post-independence governance in the developing countries. In the euphoria that accompanied the European departure, newly independent national leaderships tended to overestimate their abilities to overcome old animosities that had lain fallow during the colonial interlude and assumed they could create a comity and level of cooperation that was unattainable. Part of this problem was that the colonialists generally did little to promote post-independence governance—not training people to lead government departments, for instance. As a result, leaders have lacked the negotiating and interpersonal skills to facilitate formation of nationalist sentiment and were either so corrupt or inept that they were ineffective leaders. After the honeymoon of the post-independence period faded, subnational groups often moved to seize power and to try to suppress one another.

Economic Factors Developing countries are, by definition, not as economically advanced as their counterparts in the developed world. The countries of Africa, Asia, and Latin America that constituted the colonial empires of mostly European states were generally premodern in economic terms at the time of their conquest. Both their societies and economies were traditional—generally village-based structures that engaged in cottage industry at most and relied on subsistence agriculture. Their attraction to the Europeans was that they often possessed exploitable resources of one sort or another—minerals, spices, gold, and jewels were particularly desirable—and could serve as captive markets for goods produced in the "mother" countries.

Developing colonial economies did not serve European interests and was usually actively avoided. Development could spawn indigenous wealth and skilled labor and management that could produce anticolonial activity. Infrastructure developmental activities like building schools or energy grids for citizen usage could be expensive and did not contribute directly to colonial profit, the purpose of the enterprise. Economic activity was normally confined to actions directly benefiting the colonist, such as building a road or railroad from mines to the coast or widening and deepening ports to allow more efficient transport of raw materials from the colony to the mother country.

At independence, most developing countries lacked the economic structural development to provide general prosperity in the population and thus reinforce their satisfaction with the new political arrangement. The "lucky" new countries had some exploitable commodity—oil in Persian Gulf countries and elsewhere, for instance—but this wealth was often controlled by the elite and withheld from most of the population. In conditions of extremely scarce and inequitably distributed resources, there was little basis for creating the modern, prosperous economies that might aid the development of nationalist support for regimes or for the country.

Geography A great deal of the developing world is part of the equatorial "green belt" that circles the globe, a geographic swath generously intermixed with formidable deserts, mountains, and jungles. Numerous studies have sought to explain that geography, including its physical effects on people, is an important part of why the developing world did not develop in the same way as the European-dominated region of the Northern Hemisphere. Geography is important to contemporary national security concerns for two reasons.

First, most of the developing world is physically hostile to the operation of European-style military forces that are most effective in relative flat terrain with abundant infrastructure development like roads, bridges, and rail lines. A notable exception is the relatively flat and open desert area of much of the Middle East. In the Persian Gulf War of 1990–91, for instance, American forces were able to maneuver freely in this terrain, aided measurably by global positioning systems (GPS) that allowed them to know where they were in the featureless landscape (an advantage the Iraqi opposition lacked). In much of the developing world, mountainous jungle terrains with virtually no roads mean that modern military force can most readily only be delivered by air, which inherently lacks the mass associated with traditional ground force. Much of the developing world is a very tough neighborhood for Western military force to operate effectively.

Second, the geographic location of much of the developing world also places it beyond the effective vital interest orbit of countries like the United States. A major exception has been in the Middle East, where historic dependence on petroleum resources has created a vital interest in preserving secure access to this resource. The discovery and exploitation of petroleum and natural gas in shale formations has, however, greatly reduced that dependency and arguably the vitality of the region in American national security, as discussed in the next section.

Geography thus helps define the American relationship toward the developing world and its conflicts. Most of the conflicts—and thus potential sites for American activism—are in Africa and the western part of Asia (the Middle East). From an historical national security perspective, Africa has been of lesser interest and involvement. There is some concern with Muslim North Africa because of its petroleum reserves on which European allies depend (e.g., Libya), because of its instabilities and proximity to Europe (e.g., Tunisia), or because it is a large and historically important place (e.g., Egypt), but that interest is episodic. The Horn of Africa contains some terrorist activity that is of some interest, such as Al Shabab in Somalia and adjacent countries and Boko Haram in Nigeria, both of which have caused the United States to dispatch American special operations forces (SOFs) trainers to help the indigenous regimes deal with these problems.

The concentration of American national security concerns in the developing world has been and continues to be in the Middle East, where the bulk of American military deployments and force engagements have occurred. There are a variety of reasons for this concentration that include the petroleum dependence on the region by the United States and others; the special protective relationship between the United States and Israel; and, more recently, the concentration of international religious terrorism, some of which is directed at the United States.

The Internal Nature of DWICs: The Unique Problem of Interference

Almost all the difficulties of dealing with DWICs are present in the Middle East. Almost all the region's countries are multinational, artificial states (Egypt and Israel are arguable exceptions) that have long been politically contentious. Divisions within and between members of the populations are ethnic, linguistic, and religious, to name the most obvious sources, and they have been intractably enduring. Almost the entire region other than Israel is Islamic, but religion has been the most recurring and emotional aspect of this contention. Religious terrorism toward the United States that emanates from factions in both major Islamic sects has formed much of the contemporary basis for advocacies of American interference in the region on national security grounds. The United States embraced these rationales in the early 2000s in Afghanistan and Iraq.

The fact that the roots of these conflicts are internal should provide caution about such entreaties. I have argued since the 1990s (see *Distant Thunder*) and more recently (see *The Case against Military Intervention*) that direct outside military interventions in these conflicts is almost always a losing proposition for the intervening power. This is true for the three reasons introduced in Amplification 11.1 and elaborated upon in the next section.

The Folly of Outside Intervention

Intervention in civil conflicts does not produce the desired outcome for interveners because it is premised on three fallacies. The first is that internal conflicts normally arise from local issues that outsiders normally do not understand as well as the indigenous peoples contesting them. Outsider solutions may well prove both untenable and irrelevant to the underlying problems. If any resolution is possible, it generally must be achieved by the native population itself. Outside intervention is almost never decisive in reaching a desirable outcome. Additionally, outsiders often become part of the problem when their intervention becomes an occupation. Their presence is eventually resented and resisted by those the action is supposed to help. This resistance eventually causes frustration on the part of the intervener because it appears their actions are unappreciated.

The second reason involvements are ill advised is the comparative levels of interest outsiders and the internal population have in the situation. DWICs and their outcomes are *always* more important to the indigenous population than they are to the outsiders. DWICs occur in places not obviously vital to interveners, but they are life-and-death affairs to the indigenous factions. If those being opposed by the interveners can drag out the conflict by asymmetrical means, the interveners will eventually become frustrated, tire of the enterprise, and leave. The American experiences in Vietnam, Iraq, and potentially Afghanistan are testimony to this dynamic.

The third reason arises from the military nature of DWICs. Because of their locations and the relative balance of comparative force, they will invariably be asymmetrical campaigns that will likely involve some elements of terrorism as a tactic. For indigenous factions, there is really no choice. They lack the conventional firepower and organization to fight on the intervener's terms, and the absence of infrastructure development in geographically challenging settings further complicates employing conventional methods and militates toward unconventional methods. Fighting on familiar ground that is unfamiliar and hostile to the outsiders is a considerable physical advantage to the indigenous population; protecting loved ones from invaders adds a significant psychological, motivating advantage as well. Outside intervention in these situations usually results in a quixotic, self-defeating experience and outcome. ■

This discussion suggests that the most frequent contemporary opportunities and temptations for the United States to employ armed force are in hornets' nests where the chances of success are not great based on the historical experiences of this country and the nature of the situations where DWICs occur. Since 9/11, these employments of American force have been in the Middle East, with decidedly mixed results. For the immediate future, this concentration is unlikely to change greatly, making an examination of the region, its problems, and its prospects necessary. Recent history suggests that many of these temptations will continue to be in the Middle East.

THE MIDDLE EAST CRUCIBLE: *THE MIDDLE EAST, OIL, AND THE US NATIONAL SECURITY POLICY*

The Middle East has become the epicenter of American national security policy. This is partly by default: the absence of compelling violence and instability elsewhere in the world since the collapse of Soviet communism. Combined with relative tranquility in other places generally considered in the vital interests of the United States (Europe and East Asia), attention and activism have been devolved to this part of the world. The need for oil and the threat of terrorism have been the fundamental drivers of American policy, which has had more than a few unfortunate consequences.

Three initial, and admittedly controversial, comments about the Middle East (extracted from *The Middle East, Oil, and the U.S. National Security Policy)* frame the discussion. The first is that Middle Eastern politics is a mess, a hodge-podge of religious, ethnic, and national cleavages that ravages almost all countries in the region and often defines the highly imperfect nature of relations among them. The sources of these differences do not conform much to the political borders on regional maps. They often reflect cleavages within and among states that make it difficult, if not impossible, to fashion a common policy toward any of these countries and toward the conflicts in which they enmesh themselves. Efforts to rationalize and create order in policy are almost uniformly doomed to failure or, at best, incoherence and contradictions. US policy toward IS and Syria illustrates these problems vividly; attitudes toward the Kurds and the formation of Kurdistan are another prime instance.

Second, these differences are deep and longstanding and come from historical processes the United States played little, if any, role in creating or perpetuating. Many of them go back to antiquity. A major source of animosity is religious, born in the aftermath of the death of Mohammed in the seventh century and the struggle over who would succeed him as caliph. It has been an ongoing struggle ever since, and some observers believe an important part of the current instability is that Islam is entering what Ayaan Hirsi Ali calls a religious reform movement that resembles the same process that took place in sixteenth-century Europe. That process took more than a century of bloody conflict to resolve, and outside intervention (which, ironically, included attempts by Muslims) was indecisive in moving the process to completion. As John Owen puts it, "Just as the Ottoman Empire, the Muslim superpower at the time of the wars of religion, could not solve the strife among Christians in the sixteenth century, no outside actor can pacify the Middle East today. Only Muslims themselves can settle their ideological war."

Another source is ethnic and tribal; loyalties that go back to biblical times remain primary and have not changed much since, despite multiple political forms being grafted upon them. These tribes have been feuding for centuries, and many have added religious fraction to their divisions. The most recent pattern was created as the Ottoman Empire was dismembered at the end of World War I. The primary architects of what became essentially the contemporary political map of the region were the British and French, and their vehicle was the Sykes-Picot agreement (named after two functionaries of the two European powers who drafted it). As Scott Anderson in *Lawrence in Arabia* describes the agreement, it was "one of the strangest . . . accords ever penned." That document, drafted in January 1916, resulted in "much of the future map of the Middle East" that little reflected realities on the ground.

These are, of course, sources of conflict in which the United States played no role. No Americans influenced the seventh-century schism between Sunnism and Shiism within Islam, and the Old Testament–era animosities among tribal elements were not of American making, even if American armament policies may inadvertently contribute to keeping some of them lively. The United States was a very minor player in the dismemberment of the Ottoman Empire, with primary American presence limited to representatives of American oil companies. If the Middle East is a mess, its roots are hardly America's fault.

Third, since the United States had no real role in creating the basic problems of the Middle East and, for the most part, has little real understanding of them, it is unlikely the United States can do anything fundamentally to resolve them. It can meddle in some of the manifestations of these underlying problems, but only the people of the region can resolve them. The necessary, but not necessarily sufficient, conditions for some tranquility in the region are sectarian reconciliation and ethnic/tribal accord, and these are problems that only the Muslims of the region can resolve. Interference will likely not produce lasting benefits for either the United States or the people of the region themselves. Interference, especially physical intervention, simply adds to the problems of the region and to the frustration of Americans.

Despite these unpromising dynamics, the Middle East has been, for nearly three decades, America's primary fighting ground. As noted earlier, the United States has dispatched troops to fourteen Middle Eastern countries since 1980, and in some cases, American troops have intervened in

DWICs in the region on multiple occasions (Iraq, for instance). The results have not been obviously positive for either the host or the United States, at least partially for the reasons just stated: internal conflicts are only truly solvable by those directly involved, especially when the underlying conflicts are particularly longstanding and intractable. Yet factions in the United States continue to advocate the continued, even accelerated employment of American force in the region to the point that one is tempted to conjure Albert Einstein's definition of insanity: doing the same thing and expecting different results.

Changing American Interests and Prospects

If the Middle East has become America's primary fighting ground and seems destined to remain so in the absence of some major change in basic policy, the question is why? The answer reflects an assessment of American interests that emerged from the protracted competition with communism. This estimation of interests continues, at least implicitly, to guide American actions. There are, however, reasons to believe that those interests are changing both in intensity and in the threats to them. There may be an opportunity to reassess national security policy in the region as a result.

Current American interests in the Middle East arose from the rubble of World War II and reflected three components that result from the nature of the postwar environment. These factors evolved as the Cold War unfolded and ended. Each retains cogency but is different than it was at the time. The three elements are secure access to Middle Eastern petroleum reserves for the United States and its allies, the guarantee of a secure Israel, and the exclusion of the Soviet Union and its influence from as much of the region as possible. Different people place different degrees of importance on each of these, and one, the Soviet threat, has not existed for a quarter century. Each deserves some consideration.

These three factors are not always compatible with one another, and they enter another variable into the calculation of US interests in the area: conflict *between* interests in the region. American interests, as the following listing illustrates, are not always compatible with one another. As a result, discussing one interest (such as support for Israel) may make achievement of another interest (such as access to oil) more difficult. At the same time, pursuing one interest (such as support for Saudi Arabia) can result in de facto involvement in other situations (like the Yemen civil war) in which there are otherwise no interests.

From a classic realist vantage point, the most palpable and objective American interest in the Middle East has derived from the need for secure access to Persian Gulf petroleum reserves, the largest conventional sources of oil drilled from underground liquid deposits in the world. American interest in these reserves goes back to the turn of the twentieth century as petroleum was replacing wood as the principal energy source in the developed world. The geopolitical implications of control of Middle Eastern reserves developed during World War I and were a prominent part of the jockeying for influence and control after the Ottomans lost regional control at war's end.

Oil was also part of the competition in World War II, as the Allies undertook heroic efforts to ensure that the Axis powers like Germany were denied access to these reserves. After the war, the United States and the Soviet Union came to loggerheads over the Iranian province of Azerbaijan in 1946 since Soviet possession of that territory would have given them a leg up toward capture of Iranian and possibly Saudi reserves.

The situation has changed dramatically in the past few years for the United States and potentially for others. The reasons partly reflect conservation efforts by the United States that have reduced the demand for foreign oil and are partly the result of the successful exploitation of alternative sources of petroleum energy—shale oil and gas. Conservation has taken on numerous forms that include, most dramatically, better gasoline mileage in automobiles and alternate energy sources, and has reduced the overall American consumption of petroleum.

American allies do remain dependent on Persian Gulf oil, but actions by the United States can reduce that affliction by sharing shale technology with the Europeans. Europe, for instance, has considerable shale deposits, but most of the states with exploitable reserves are in the eastern parts of the continent, including Ukraine. An added benefit of shale exploitation could be to relieve Western Europe of its dependency on Russia for the gas necessary for heating Europe during the winter. The extension of the shale revolution into areas near Russia (which has very large reserves but lacks the wherewithal to exploit them) helps explain the tensions between NATO (North Atlantic Treaty Organization) and the Russians over Ukraine. The Middle East will not necessarily suffer inordinately if Western buyers abandon the region, since Eastern suiters (notably China and India) provide ready and potentially compensating markets.

The second American security interest in the region has been and continues to be the security of Israel. This interest is longstanding, emotional, and highly political. It dates to World War II and the Holocaust. When much of the remaining Jewish population of Europe, many of them displaced persons, fled to what became Israel, their migration was widely supported by a guilt-ridden world population seeking to atone for its failure to prevent or ameliorate the genocide. The United States co-sponsored (with the Soviet Union) the 1947 United Nations resolution to create the state of Israel; when the British decided to leave Israel in 1948 (the British had been the mandate power there since 1917), the United

States became the de facto protector and guarantor of Israeli security and even survival.

Holocaust-derived guilt provided the emotional basis for the American relationship with Israel, and reminders both of that horrible event and the genocidal pronouncements of some Arab groups and governments keep that emotion alive. This emotion translates into political terms. The United States is the largest Jewish diaspora outside Israel, and there are politically consequential Jewish voting blocs in several politically important American states, including New York, New Jersey, Florida, and California. Conservative Republicans have developed a strong affinity for both the State of Israel and its controversial leader, Benjamin Netanyahu, adding a further element to the political equation.

The American continuing interest in Israeli security combines the Israeli security situation, which it prefers to describe as a survival challenge, and the affinity between the two countries. The security equation has changed as Israel's nuclear arsenal has developed and diversified. Israel is currently (pending change in Iran's status) the only nuclear state in the Middle East if one discounts the "Pakistani bomb," which is mostly relevant to Indo-Pakistani relations. Israel's arsenal (which the Israelis neither confirm nor deny exists) is estimated at about eighty warheads, most of which are on invulnerable nuclear missile submarines that would survive even an attack that destroyed Israel and could then retaliate and destroy the attacker—the classic dynamic of Cold War nuclear deterrence. Except for terrorist incursions, Israel has not been the victim of a major attack since the Yom Kippur War of 1973. Although such an attack against the Israelis is still possible, it could only realistically be undertaken by a suicidal attacker. The other security basis is the close relationship between the two countries. Israel is the only political democracy in the region, and it is the most developed, Westernized Middle Eastern state. Israel has the most formidable armed forces in the region (another reason no Islamic state seems interested in more than a rhetorical battle with the Israelis). If drawn into a regional conflict, one would want the Israelis on one's side. Israeli settlements on the West Bank are internationally controversial and opposed by most countries other than the United States. American support for Israel thus creates conflicts of interest with those countries.

The final leg of US policy after World War II was excluding the Soviet Union from the region. The Soviets sought influence wherever they could find it in the region, both to foment difficulties for the Americans and potentially to become part of the energy equation. Their efforts achieved very mixed results. They were able to become the armorer of several states—notably Egypt—but atheistic communism was a very poor match for the religious beliefs of most Middle Easterners, thereby contributing to limits on their success. When Mikhail Gorbachev came to power and began to reduce expensive and unsuccessful worldwide commitments, the Middle East was one of the first places from which they withdrew. The Soviet challenge and the need for an aggressive opposition to that expansionism died with the end of the Cold War.

One of the very few countries with which the Soviets developed a true affinity and alliance was Syria. Even after the demise of the Soviet Union, that friendship continued, and Syria is the only country outside Russia where the Russians maintain a military base. This affinity helps explain why the Vladimir Putin government has taken such an aggressive stance in support of the government of Bashar al-Assad, including a limited military intervention.

Sources of Interest Conflict

Two major characteristics define the Middle East cauldron. One is the pervasiveness of conflict between its members and the actuality or potential for violence area-wide. Some part of the Middle East always seems to be on the verge of exploding. The other is the complexity and contradictory nature of these conflicts, both internally and in terms of American interests. Each conflict is not only unique, but each forces the United States to choose among conflicting interests that are affected differently depending on American interests. Moreover, whatever interests are engaged often overlap and contradict other American interests in the region. The United States often finds itself in a "damned if you do, damned if you don't" quandary when Middle East crises arise.

Conflict situations and differing, sometimes contradictory, American interests in and among them are recurring items on the "menu" American national security policy faces in the region. The result is often a confusing regional pattern that seems to (and sometimes does) demonstrate a level of incoherence and inconsistency in that policy. To illustrate the byzantine nature of the problem, this section will examine four instances of how Middle East problems ensnare and contort American policy. They are the rise and fall of the Islamic State, the ongoing Israeli-Palestinian conflict currently focusing on Jerusalem and the West Bank, the fate of the Kurds, and the sectarian showdown between Sunnism and Shiism featuring Iran and Saudi Arabia.

The IS Phoenix The legendary phoenix of Greek mythology is a fitting analogy by which to measure the ascent and descent of the Islamic State introduced in Amplification 10.1. According to legend, the phoenix was a mighty bird with a life span of up to five hundred years (a contrast with IS) that eventually self-immolated and died and was reborn from its own ashes to reign again in its domain. In modern usage, the term is associated with something "flaming out." The brief but spectacular history of IS has reflected the legend: it arose from a modest beginning, appeared to self-immolate in 2007, regenerated in 2012, and flew into the sun (one of the depictions of its demise) in 2017. It has arisen from its ashes to the extent of continuing to exist as a more "conventional" terrorist group since— possibly as a global competitor to AQ. In 2018, IS elements became active in Afghanistan and found themselves unwelcome, opposed by both the Taliban and the Afghan government when they appeared in territories controlled by either faction in the war.

The evolution of IS can be condensed for present purposes. The organization became active as part of the Sunni reaction to the American occupation of Iraq in 2003. It was formed under the leadership of Abu Musab al-Zarqawi in 1999 as Al Qaeda in Iraq (AQI) and continued to be active against the Americans until the founder was killed by an American air strike in 2006 and the American-inspired Anbar Awakening decimated the organization in 2007. The presumption at the time was that the organization had collapsed, but in its first phoenix-like act, it simply went underground, arising as the Islamic State of Iraq and Syria (ISIS) as part of the opposition to the Syrian government of Bashar al-Assad. It was reportedly the most militarily effective of the opposition groups, but it was refused outside assistance (notably by the United States) because of its terrorist roots.

The new leader was Abu Bakr al-Baghdadi, and in 2013, he declared that his intention was to create a new religious state, the caliphate. Initially, the territorial definition of the caliphate was mainly in eastern Syria and Iraq, but Baghdadi (who along the way declared himself as the caliph) expanded the desired realm to include most of the Levant and beyond to other territories with a Muslim majority. The leadership of IS was Sunni, and the realm over which the caliphate would rule would make subjects of Shiites as well as practitioners of other religions and anyone else who refused to declare fealty to the caliphate. As its ambitions expanded, IS became an actual or potential threat to almost everyone in the region.

IS was initially very successful, sweeping across apparently impressive swaths of territory in Syria and Iraq, reaching far enough east to conquer Mosul and establish it as their eastern "capital." In 2014 and 2015, IS seemed like an inexorable force that threatened regional and even global peace. Most Middle Eastern countries issued dire warnings about the seemingly unstoppable force—which proved to be a vast overstatement of the threat. Very few of them were willing to do much personally to stop the IS onslaught. The Kurds were the exception.

In retrospect, IS was less than it seemed. Its seemingly inexorable march across Syria and Iraq created the impression of a major military force, an impression reinforced by maps depicting IS-conquered territory in the movement's black flag that looked like an overturned ink bottle spreading across a sheet of paper. As 2014 and 2015 proceeded, it was not clear if *anything* other than a major counteroffensive by an advanced military power like the United States could stop the advance, and the Americans were not rising to the bait.

The threat was, of course, overblown. Although there were numerous reports of youth from Europe and North America rushing to the IS banner to join the IS army, in fact that force never numbered more than about thirty thousand, a small number to rule the large territory they initially subdued, and the territory they were conquering was either mostly uninhabited or peopled by sparse groups initially drawn to its ascetic Sunni values. The impressive amount of territory IS conquered and its evangelical profession of a new Islamic empire helped conflate the threat IS posed. IS looked more impressive than it was, but it was more of a Potemkin Village than anything else. It has not disappeared altogether. Reports aired on CNN in early August 2018 suggested there is still a sizable residual IS force, although its capabilities are unknown.

The most obviously concerned states did not respond uniformly to the IS onslaught. The most obviously affected state, Iraq, was still recovering from its long war and occupation by the Americans, and when IS first appeared on the scene, some Iraqi Sunnis thought they might be liberators to free them of remaining US influence and rule from Baghdad by Iraqi Shiites (numerous IS military leaders were former officers in Saddam Hussein's army, for instance). When the harshness of the IS sharia-based system of governance became obvious, they rejected Baghdadi and his appeals, but IS had occupied sizable parts of the country by the time Iraqi supporters rejected the intruders. The Gulf states and others like Turkey, which could have been threatened by the continued expansion of IS into their countries, generally stood passively by, limiting themselves to reinforcing their borders at most.

The Saudi role was, as usual, enigmatic and ambivalent. The highly ascetic, fundamentalist vision of Islam that Baghdadi preached was not very different from the Wahhabi gospel that is the state religion of the kingdom, and there were widespread reports that private Saudis were among the chief financial supporters of the caliphate. At the same time, the Saudi regime knew that if IS succeeded, the caliphate could pose a direct threat to their leadership of the Sunni world. As is so typically the case, the Saudis did not act overtly in the crisis beyond providing some financial assistance to governments rejecting the IS cause.

As the crisis continued, the Kurds emerged as the leading military obstacle to IS expansion. The reason was obvious but largely overlooked at the time. The initial territorial conquests by IS primarily occurred in parts of Syria and Iraq that are claimed by the Kurds as part of Kurdistan: much of eastern Syria is viewed by the Kurds as Rojava, a province of the Kurdish state, and IS advances in Iraq were in Kurdish-dominated territory that the Iraqi armed forces were not particularly interested in fighting for.

Kurdish militias, the *pesh merga*, jumped into the breach and proved to be the most effective force opposing the IS army. They were so successful that sentiment emerged in the United States and elsewhere somehow to transform the Kurdish forces into the lead military sword that would liberate the conquered ground and defeat IS. The sentiment, unfortunately, missed the point: the *pesh merga* was not an offensive army, it was a *territorial militia the sole purpose of which was to liberate their own Kurdish lands*, not an army out to defeat the IS force. The Kurds and IS were (and are) antagonists: the Kurds are not, for instance, Arabs, they do not speak Arabic, and they practice a far less fundamentalist version of Sunnism than does IS. The Kurds, in their campaign of territorial recapture, were instrumental in weakening IS, but they did so in the name of Kurdish nationalism, not Arab united opposition to IS.

The United States was in a quandary: feeling threatened by IS but faced with fractious regional actors. Given the circumstances in which AQI/IS burst onto the scene, the IS and Syrian problem became part of the same general concern for the United States. The American government and people opposed Syrian suppression and wanted to see Assad overthrown but were limited by their unwillingness to commit American forces to the effort out of fear of another Iraq/Afghanistan imbroglio, which the American people would not tolerate. The countries of the area were also divided. The Syrian government was controlled by Shiite Alawites, who in turn received help from Iran and groups like Hezbollah, but the major Sunni states like Turkey and the Gulf states preferred to sit out the conflict because no one could find a suitable Syrian rebel faction to support. IS was the most powerful of these, but their roots were known, and their ultimate goals were well established by 2014, when they began their attempt to carve out the caliphate.

The involvement of the Kurds made matters worse for coalition-building because, despite the successes of the Kurds kicking IS out of Kurdish-claimed lands, Kurdish proficiency was a double-edged sword: it reduced the strength of IS, which most favored, but it also increased the cogency of Kurdish independence claims, which countries like Turkey and Iraq opposed. The result was to further neutralize any united stance against IS. The United States, of course, viewed IS as part of the general war on terror, both as a potential source of terrorist acts against the United States and its allies and because some young Americans reportedly had joined IS, prompting the fear they would return home to commit IS-ordered attacks in America. At the same time, the IS problem even extended to US domestic politics, as Amplification 11.2 discusses.

AMPLIFICATION **11.2**

"Your Brother Created ISIS"

During the early stages of the 2016 presidential campaign in early 2015, an audience member confronted candidate Jeb Bush, the brother of former president George W. Bush, with the accusation, "Your brother created ISIS." At the time, it seemed an odd charge, and it did not survive long in the news cycle. It did, however, make an arguable point that illustrates the complexities, subtleties, and interconnectivity of Middle East politics and demonstrates how a Middle Eastern political concern could affect American domestic politics.

The logical flow of the assertion proceeds through two steps. The first is the 2003 invasion and occupation, which created the conditions that allowed for the formation and development of AQI. There was no need for such an organization before the invasion, and it would not have been tolerated by Hussein. Second, the American killing of Zarqawi in 2006 deprived AQI of its leadership and allowed the rise of Baghdadi and his more ambitious organization (IS) and agenda (the caliphate) to emerge. Without the first step, there would not have been a second step and thus the third step, which was the formation of IS. In that sense, George W. Bush indeed "created" ISIS by setting in motion the train of events from which it evolved. Richard Clarke, author of *Against All Enemies* and a leading terrorism expert, concurred in an interview reproduced by Fareed Zakaria: "ISIS," he said, "was a direct result of the American invasion." ■

The Kurds   Among its multiple political abnormalities, the overwhelmingly multinational nature of existing states manifests itself in the existence of the most prominent irredentist movements in the world. Many of the Pashtuns of Afghanistan and Pakistan would like to be reunited in an independent Pashtunistan, but the best publicized and most intractable cases of stateless nations are the Palestinians and the Kurds. The problem of creating an independent state of Kurdistan is among the most divisive and difficult issues in the region, and it presents the United States with difficult national security problems as well.

The Kurds have a long history in the region, although not as an independent entity. One of the notable events in their history came in 1514, when they negotiated a place in the Ottoman Empire, and when that empire collapsed after World War I, they petitioned the negotiators at Versailles to be accorded statehood. Unfortunately for them, the disposition of the region under the Sykes-Picot arrangement divided Kurdish areas among several other states under mandatory control, and the Kurds, divided among several jurisdictions, have been struggling for statehood ever since.

The territory the Kurds consider theirs is part of four Middle Eastern states, all of which oppose the establishment of a Kurdish state. They are most numerous in eastern and southeastern Turkey (also known as Northern Kurdistan), followed by northern Iraq (Southern or Iraqi Kurdistan), northern Syria (Western Kurdistan or Rojava), and western Iran (Eastern or Iranian Kurdistan). Although not all the census figures are terribly accurate, Kurdish nationalists claim that the population of a Kurdish state would be thirty to thirty-five million, one of the more populous states in the region. Moreover, the Iraqi-based *pesh merga* is one of the most formidable fighting forces in the region.

Kurdish statehood is opposed by the governments of the states in which they reside, and that opposition is one of the few things some of them have in common. That opposition is strongest in Turkey, which is home to eighteen to twenty million Kurds in an area roughly the size of Wisconsin (Turkey is about the size of Texas). Northern Kurdistan is critical to a Kurdish state, but it is also located in a part of Turkey (Anatolia) that is a key part of Turkish tourism and a source of needed water. The Kurdish Workers Party (PKK) has waged a sporadic insurrection (the Turks call it a terrorist campaign) against Ankara for decades, adding to animosities. Turkey has been the most vocal, adamant opponent of Kurdish self-determination. During the campaign against IS, the Turks stayed mostly on the side line, at least partly because they feared *pesh merga* success would worsen their Kurdish problem, a position at odds with that of the United States.

Iraq also has a significant problem with the Kurds, about five million of whom live in the Kurdish Autonomous Region of the oil-rich north. Particularly since the American occupation and withdrawal from that country, the Kurds have been the de facto government of the Kurdish region, and the desire for autonomy and the formation of Kurdistan is very strong, at least partially because the Kurds are ethnically unrelated to the Sunni and Shia Arabs of the rest of the country. There has been speculation that Iraq could split into three countries at some point, and the Kurds would be the first to leave, followed by the Sunni western part of the country and the Shiite south. In the campaign against IS, it is symptomatic that Iraqi armed forces were not especially zealous about coming to the aid of the Kurds and that the Kurds were much more interested in defending Kurdish lands than in evicting IS from other parts of Iraq.

Iran and Syria are the other states with sizable Kurdish populations who would join Kurdistan if it came into being. About eight million Kurds live in Iran in an area that would be the second largest part of the Kurdish state. The Iranians and Kurds have more in common than do the Kurds and the other states of which they are part. Like the Iranians, the Kurds are neither Sunni nor Arab, and their language is akin to Persian, but they have different religious traditions. The Kurds are least numerous in Rojava (about two million), where they live in the sparsely populated northern and eastern part of the country along the Turkish border. When the Kurds were leading the eviction of IS from its western "capital" in Raqqa, the Turks provided essentially no assistance to the Kurds, whom they consider enemies on par with the Syrians.

This dissonance creates headaches for American national security makers. The Kurds have long considered the American as champions of their cause, and an independent Kurdistan would likely have close ties with the Americans extending from ties between the Iraqi Kurds and American oil companies. The United States, however, has been a vocal opponent of IS, and although it has been politically unwilling to commit major personnel resources to the destruction of IS, it has provided considerable aid to the Kurds, and the idea of a Kurdish-based regional armed force was initially proposed by Americans. The opposition (Turkey) and reluctance of other regional states has complicated this effort and brought some level of strain in American relations with other regional powers.

Israel versus the Palestinians   The most famous irredentist situation in the world, and one that puts the United States more at odds with allies, friends, and foes alike, has been the Palestinian question. It began to emerge as an international issue with the declaration of the Jewish state of Israel in 1948 because the Palestinian Arabs who had shared what became Israel with the Jewish population fled the new country, fearful of violence against them. They migrated to various parts of the neighboring states, including Lebanon, Syria, the Gaza Strip (then part of Egypt), and the West Bank of the Jordan River, then a part of the Kingdom of Jordan. None of these countries could clearly accommodate this population influx, leaving the Palestinians a stateless nation.

The situation reached its present contours in 1967. In what is known as the Six Days War, Israel decisively defeated the assorted Arab states that had attacked it and in the process annexed territory from each of its major antagonists: the Gaza Strip and the Sinai Peninsula from Egypt, the Golan Heights from Syria, and the West Bank (including East Jerusalem) from Jordan. Israel and Egypt signed a treaty whereby the Sinai was returned to Egyptian sovereign control, and in 2006, Israel ceded jurisdiction of the Gaza Strip to the Palestinian Authority. Golan and the West Bank remain under Israeli control despite the objections of most of the international community, which considers the occupation of the West Bank and thus control of its Palestinian population to be illegal. The United States is the only major country that does not accede in that position, a point of dispute between Washington and the international community.

The result is an ongoing dispute about the rightful home of the Palestinians and, most importantly, their quest for statehood. Approximately a million Palestinians reside in pre-1967 Israel, and over two million live in Gaza, but the rest (about five million) reside on the West Bank, where they are under the effective control of the Israelis. The Palestinians have declared and continue to press their claim that the West Bank *is* the physical territory that would end their statelessness, a position the Israeli government refuses to accept. Instead, Israel has conducted a campaign of aggressive populating of the West Bank with Israeli settlers, mostly immigrants from the Jewish diaspora outside Israel. Attracting more of world Jewry to Israel has been a major policy emphasis of the current Netanyahu government since it has been in office, and there is virtually no habitable space in pre-1967 Israel where expansion can take place. If the Jewish state is to encompass a larger part of the world's Jewish population, there is little alternative to control of the West Bank, which helps explain Israeli intransigence on the issue.

The Israeli position also has a strong security component. When the Jordanian West Bank abutted Israeli territory, Israel was militarily vulnerable, with the distance between the Jordanian border and the Mediterranean Sea only about ten miles at the narrowest point. As a result, the Israelis were always vulnerable to being cut in half if Arab armed forces could breach that distance, thereby creating a near impossible situation for Israeli defense purposes. The long occupation, now over a half-century long, has eliminated that problem.

The status of Jerusalem also complicates the situation. Jerusalem has religious significance to the three modern religions that began in the Middle East (Judaism, Christianity, and Islam), and both Jews and Muslims consider the city both spiritually and politically crucial. The controversy centers on the old city of East Jerusalem, which was formerly part of Jordan, is occupied by Israel, and is claimed by the Palestinians. More to the point, both Israel and Palestine claim the city as their national capital. This mutual claim is a major point of disagreement, and the international community has sought to avoid involvement. When the United States moved its embassy to Jerusalem in 2018 (like all other countries, the United States had previously had its diplomatic personnel housed in an embassy in Tel Aviv), it represented a significant symbolic tilt toward the Israeli position.

The United States is in a difficult position regarding the Palestinian question. On one hand, the United States has since 1948 been the principal supporter and guarantor of Israel, with which it has felt a special relationship deriving from the Holocaust. This has historically put the United States at odds with Islamic states that have in the past opposed Israel, in some cases vowing to destroy the Israeli state and since 1967 concentrating more on the "injustice" of the West Bank occupation for the Palestinians. Anti-Israeli and pro-Palestinian rhetoric has become more muted in recent years, and now only Iran, ironically, champions the cause of Palestinian statehood with physical actions. The irony arises because the Iranians are

Shiites and the Palestinians are Sunni, and the most powerful Sunni states (e.g., Saudi Arabia) are largely mute on the plight of the Palestinians.

The American guarantee has been against aggression, but nukes
Solutions include 2 and 1 states: US and Israeli debates
Disagreement inside US, embarrassment, and long-term Israeli interests
Arabs have lost leverage with US due to oil situation
Result is to compromise US position in area and with allies

A major difficulty also involved how the United States could or should go about achieving either goal, especially the role of American force in that process. There are at least four possible avenues the United States can pursue, alone or in concert with others. The first two involve a sequential strategy of eliminating one opponent first (either the Syrian regime or IS) and then turning to the other. This strategy is at least implicit in rhetorical policy statements that suggest IS represents the greater evil and thus must be eliminated first. These options, of course, have the undesirable effect of indirectly promoting the cause of the second enemy. It is also a prioritization that will be opposed by those who would prefer the order or attention be reversed. It has the major advantage of allowing concentration of resources sequentially on one enemy at a time.

The third option is to oppose actively both at the same time. This strategic option has the virtue of being even-handed and clearly identifying that both opponents are equally worthy of defeat. It is also part of current strategy in the sense that the Obama administration in late 2015 declared that while destroying IS was the major physical priority, other forms of action, largely diplomatic in nature, should simultaneously be pursued, such as multilateral negotiations in Geneva, Switzerland, in November 2015. The question is whether this strategy can succeed: will different approaches to the two opponents yield satisfactory outcomes to either problem? The fourth approach is not to pursue either goal actively, especially with American armed forces. The rationale for such an approach would be that neither goal is truly in American vital interest and that these are problems that can only be solved by the parties themselves, not by outside interference.

The problem with any solution, but especially the fourth, is largely political within the United States. Within the poisonous partisan atmosphere of contemporary American politics, there is probably no level or direction of American action that would be acceptable across the political spectrum. A policy that suggested decisive action sequentially or simultaneously would be unacceptable to the majority of Americans who are war averse given the experience of the previous decade. A policy of sequential attention to the two opponents (in whichever order) would likely be long and protracted, whereas a policy of simultaneous engagement would require a large intervention that would test the operational limits of the all-volunteer force. Moreover, the

Iraq and Afghanistan experiences suggest that these efforts would not necessarily succeed, thereby causing additional political angst. A policy of inaction or limited action would (as it has) alienate more hawkish, activist elements, who would accuse the United States of pusillanimity in the face of adversity and of forfeiting its rightful leadership role in the world. Thus, political costs of doing or not doing something are all considerable.

What actions the United States should undertake are also affected by questions of the end result desired and whether that outcome can be attained. Removing Assad or dismantling IS are politico-military actions, but do they constitute ends in themselves? If Assad is forced to resign, what then? The invasion of Iraq in 2003 removed Saddam Hussein from power, but it did not visibly improve the situation in Iraq or elsewhere otherwise. Iraq traded a Sunni tyranny for Shiite rule, which pleased some Shiites but neither the Sunnis nor Kurds, and the situation is analogous in Syria. The ruling Alawite Shiites also represent a minority, and if they are deposed, will the majority (about 70 percent of the population) Sunnis simply turn the tables and suppress the Alawites and the Kurds? There is no indication that the United States knows of a viable alternative to Assad. How would replacing him improve the overall condition of Syria?

The problems associated with IS are not dissimilar. If IS was effectively destroyed, it would remove it as a disruptive force in Iraq and Syria and as a terrorist threat to the West, but would it do anything to alleviate the underlying sentiments that gave rise to IS or that sustain it? Iraqi Sunnis, who form much of the leadership backbone of IS, would not necessarily be any better off (and might be worse), and militant Muslims drawn to the caliphate would not likely be converted to moderation in the process. Would the destruction of IS simply create a power vacuum in the largely vacant areas of Iraq and Syria they now occupy?

Destroying IS and deposing Assad are regional problems, in the sense that the changes either action might bring about would have their greatest impact on the region itself. As already argued, the problem is that the fractious, feuding people of the region—those with the most at stake in any outcome—cannot agree either on what to do or why. Inflammatory rhetoric notwithstanding, the stakes are considerably lower for the United States. Beyond humanitarian indignity and embarrassment, the political situation in Syria does not greatly affect important American interests. IS, to the extent that it indeed provides a terrorist threat to American soil, has a higher salience, but one must ask why IS considers the United States to be its implacable enemy. The major connection is that the United States has declared itself to be the enemy of IS and has taken violent actions—primarily from the air—against the caliphate. Were the United States to remove itself from the violent elimination of IS, would the organization, which has plenty on its hands trying to establish a territorial state, not redirect its attention away from the Americans? If anyone has a vital interest in what happens to IS, it is regional groups adversely affected by the attainment of IS goals. Without the United States to provide the sword against IS, would some of them decide they had to do so themselves?

Finally, there is the question of the attainability of any policy option chosen. Political reality in the United States has dictated that an all-out invasion of IS-occupied territories on a scale akin to the previous effort in Iraq is unacceptable, and the precedent from the original event is hardly encouraging anyway. Much of any concerted effort against IS would have to occur in Sunni-dominated areas of Iraq. Such an action would probably be supported by the Iraqi government (assuming there were strict time limits on the intrusion) but would meet with at least some resistance among Iraqi Sunnis and might even provide a recruitment platform for IS, which has said they welcome an American intervention for that reason. Since it is also American policy to topple the Syrian government, Syria would not welcome an American intrusion.

There are two broad obstacles in the way of achieving the goal of destroying IS with a force led by the United States. First, IS would fight asymmetrically, employing methods at which the United States has not shown great proficiency in the past. All asymmetrical efforts are, of course, different, and the IS response to an American-led action would be distinctive. Because its aims are territorial (establishing and maintaining the caliphate), it cannot simply abandon territory the way terrorists do, and its "army" of twenty to thirty thousand is necessary for territorial defense and maintaining internal order. If it were faced with a concerted conventional armed intrusion, that army would probably be withdrawn from the central battle in much the same way the North Vietnamese Army was drawn back after the American intervention in 1965. In all likelihood, the conflict would then revert to the kind of resistance the United States faced in Southeast Asia in the late 1960s and in Iraq before the Anwar Awakening. Neither US effort was overwhelmingly successful. There is little reason to believe this time would be any different.

The major reason to question the attainability with American forces goes back to arguments that underpin *The Case against Military Intervention*. The IS onslaught is essentially an internal conflict within a part of the Middle East where political boundaries are artificial and the real point of contention is sectarian. Outside intervention is rarely decisive in these kinds of conflicts, which only the parties themselves can resolve. Outsiders may temporarily tip the balance one way or the other, but their continuing presence will eventually be resented, and their opponents will eventually move to a strategy of attrition aimed at waiting out the interveners until they tire of the effort and leave. It has happened before, and it would almost certainly recur in this instance.

The only military effort that might succeed would be one in which a coalition, preferably led by Middle Easterners and outside supporters that might include but would not be predominantly American, took on the task of destroying IS. The problem is assembling such a coalition: most of the Middle Eastern countries do not have large or potent ground forces (Iran may be an exception), and they have all been reluctant to place their military assets in harm's way. Their implicit battle cry has been, "Let the Americans do it!" Moreover, the divisions within the region make it virtually impossible to imagine them being able to come together to this end. The conundrum is that the kind of force that might be effective is probably unattainable, and the kind of force that could be fielded probably could not accomplish the mission.

This assessment of the threat may appear more pessimistic that it truly is. Many observers have suggested that the real long-term fate of IS will be self-implosion. The barbaric acts it commits and publicizes on social media have already alienated some in the region (e.g., the Jordanians after IS burned a captured Jordanian air force pilot), seem intent on alienating others outside the region (e.g., the Russians by bringing down a Russian commercial airliner over the Sinai peninsula), and show no indication of intention to moderate its actions to minimize the formation of a united front intent on bringing it down. That fate may not await IS, but it might.

CHALLENGE!

What Would *You* Do about the Islamic State?

What the United States should do about the Islamic State has been a major policy matter for more than two years, and as long as IS remains a force in the Middle East and poses some threat to the United States, it will remain so. That "something" needs to be done about the threat is one of the few things political Washington seems to agree on: everyone is in accord IS should be defeated, even destroyed. Where there is disagreement is how this can be accomplished or whether American action can be effective in the demise of IS.

What would *you* do about IS? In thinking about possible strategies, consider and try to answer the following concerns:

What should the policy goal be? Destroying IS, overthrowing the Syrian regime, or both? Can one strategy accomplish both?

How important is the objective? Does it represent a vital or LTV interest of the United States? Is the use of American force advisable or necessary? If so, what form should that force take?

If force seems necessary, can it succeed? What must armed forces do to accomplish the goal? Why would that use succeed when American regional adventures with not dissimilar purposes in Iraq and Afghanistan have not?

How will the American public react to your position? What if it either does not succeed or results in a lengthy involvement that, like in Iraq, ends with a long occupation? What about costs? Are the possible outcomes worth it?

None of these are easy questions, and no advocate on either side has successfully answered them all. Yet they must be answered. ■

CONCLUSION: TIME FOR A NEW APPROACH TO THE LETHAL LANDSCAPES?

The Middle East has been at the maelstrom's center of violence and instability in the world for at least a quarter century. It attained this status around 1979, the year in which the shah of Iran was driven from power by a militant Shiite religious movement, of which Ayatollah Ruhollah Khomeini was the symbolic driving force. This act resulted in what is generally described in the West as a radical Shiite theocracy in the region's most populous country. It also forced a heretofore unprecedented level of direct American involvement in the millenniums-old conflicts in the region.

Prior to 1979, the triad of American interests in the region—secure access to oil, support for Israel, and exclusion of Soviet influence—had been achievable with a minimum direct investment of American force. The Soviet influence was self-limiting because of the philosophical chasm between Islam and Marxism, and the Israelis had repeatedly demonstrated their ability to protect themselves with American material assistance. There was no compelling reason to invest large numbers of American "dusty" boots on the arid, desert terrain of the region.

Secure access to petroleum, the third pillar, was most upset by the shah's overthrow. During the period between the shah's return to power in 1953 (with the generous help of the CIA) and his departure from the Peacock Throne, an accommodation had been reached between the US and Iran under which the United States provided material and expert assistance to the shah's Westernization program, the so-called White Revolution, and a generous provision of arms to Iran (see my *Cases in American Foreign Policy* and Kinzer) that made the country the region's predominant power. In return, Iran provided secure safe passage of petroleum from the Persian Gulf to the West.

The transformation of Iran from close ally to implacable opponent destroyed that arrangement and forced the United States to personally take on that role itself. The principal military vehicle for doing so was the US Navy's patrol of the Gulf and accesses to it, but American air and ground forces increasingly became part of the mix as well. The symbolic act of transformation was American military leadership in evicting Saddam Hussein from Kuwait in 1991; events triggered by 9/11 expanded that role to places like Iraq, Afghanistan, and Yemen. The link between the expansion and the rise of anti-American terrorism may be related directly to a desire among some in the region to get the United States to leave.

Things have changed since the United States inserted itself so forthrightly into the Middle East cauldron. The Soviets are no more, and Russian involvement in Syria may be pulling them into the IS fray alongside, rather than in opposition to, the United States. The Israeli nuclear arsenal arguably now deters attacks against that country by anything other than the small strikes by terrorists, what David Galula called "the war of the fleas" a half-century ago. Most important, the shale oil and gas revolution has removed most, and potentially all, American dependence on Middle Eastern oil—this country is no longer a Persian Gulf oil "junkie"—and it can reduce the reliance of friends and allies it helped "hook" on that oil by extending shale technology to them.

All this means that the game has changed for the United States in this most violent part of the world. The United States maintains important geopolitical interests in the Middle East that are explored in this chapter, but these are not the same as the calculation of interests that has caused this country fairly automatically to consider and implement military responses to what it considers national security challenges. The potential insertion of American force into this lethal landscape is by no means automatically excluded by these changes, but neither is it the automatic response it has been. It may be time to begin rethinking the applicability of past policies to current and projectable environments and challenges.

STUDY/DISCUSSION QUESTIONS

1. How has the pattern of international violence changed in the past quarter century? How are today's "lethal landscapes" different, and what effects do changes have on American national security policy?
2. What is a DWIC? What characteristics do DWICs have that differ from traditional conflict? Are they anything new? Why are attempts to intervene in them so difficult?
3. What are the three major sources of developing-world conflicts and violence? Include political, economic, and geographic factors, as well as the legacy of colonialism.
4. What internal factors make developing-world violence so difficult? What are the unique problems of outside intervention in these conflicts?
5. Describe how the Middle East has become the "crucible" of violence in the world and the place where the United States uses force. What factors about the region help frame the debate?

6. What have basic American interests in the Middle East been? How is each changing, and what are the implications for American national security policy in the region?
7. Discuss the Islamic State. What is it? What is its history? What are its characteristics and objectives? How does it differ from "traditional" Middle East terrorist organizations?
8. What can be done to reduce or destroy IS? How is the calculation complicated by Syria and other regional actors with conflicting interests?
9. What goals can the United States realistically pursue (have a reasonable chance of attaining) against IS? Will force work? Why or why not?
10. Is it time for a "new approach" to the Middle East? Discuss.

SELECTED BIBLIOGRAPHY

Ajami, Fouad. *The Syrian Rebellion*. Palo Alto, CA: Hoover Institution Press, 2013.

Ali, Ayaan Hirsi. "Why the United States Should Back Islam's Reform." *Foreign Affairs* 94, 4 (July/August 2015), 36–45.

Anderson, Scott. *Lawrence in Arabia: War, Deceit, Imperial Folly and the Making of the Modern Middle East*. New York: Anchor Books, 2014.

Bacevich, Andrew C. "Even If We Defeat the Islamic State, We Still Lose the Bigger War." *Washington Post* (online), (October 3, 2014).

Boot, Max. "Should the US Send Ground Troops to Fight ISIS? Yes, Uproot the Enemy." *Time* 195, 8 (March 9, 2015), 32.

Brisard, Jean-Charles. *Zarqawi: The New Face of Al-Qaeda*. New York: Other Press, 2005.

Calabrisi, Massimo. "Caught in the Cross Fire." *Time* 185, 13 (April 12, 2015), 24–27.

Clarke, Richard. *Against All Enemies: Inside America's War on Terror*. New York: Free Press, 2004.

Cronin, Audrey Kurth. "ISIS Is Not a Terrorist Group: Why Counterterrorism Won't Stop the Latest Jihadi Group." *Foreign Affairs* 94, 2 (March/April 2015), 87–98.

Feaver, Peter. "The Just War Tradition and the Paradox of Policy Failure in Syria." *Foreign Policy* (online), (August 22, 2013).

Galula, David. *Counterinsurgency Warfare: Theory and Practice*. Westport, CT: Praeger Publishers (PSI Classics of the Counterinsurgency Age), 2006.

Kinzer, Stephen. *The Brothers: John Foster Dulles, Allen Dulles, and Their Secret World War*. New York: Times Books (Henry Holt and Company), 2013.

Latham, Michael E. *The Right Kind of Revolution: Modernization, Development, and U.S. Policy from the Cold War to the Present*. Ithaca, NY: Cornell University Press, 2011.

McCants, William. "Islamic Scripture Is Not the Problem." *Foreign Affairs* 94, 4 (July/August 2015), 46–52.

Owen, John M., IV. "From Calvin to the Caliphate: What Europe's Wars of Religion Tell Us about the Modern Middle East." *Foreign Affairs* 94, 3 (May/June 2015), 77–89.

Simon, Steven N. *After the Surge: The Case for U.S. Military Disengagement from Iraq*. New York: CFR 23, Council on Foreign Relations, 2007.

Snow, Donald M. *The Case against Military Intervention: Why We Do It and Why It Fails*. New York: Routledge, 2016.

———. *The Middle East, Oil, and the American National Security Policy: Intractable Conflicts, Impossible Solutions*. Lanham, MD: Rowman & Littlefield, 2016.

———. *Thinking About National Security: Strategy, Policy, and Issues*. New York: Routledge, 2016.

———. *Cases in American Foreign Policy*. New York: Pearson Longman, 2013 (especially Chapter 3).

———. *Distant Thunder: Patterns of Violent Conflict in the Developing World*. 2nd ed. Armonk, NY: M. E. Sharpe, 1997.

Stern, Jessica, and M. Berger. *ISIS: The State of Terror*. New York: ECCO, 2015.

Vick, Karl. "Should the U.S. Send Ground Forces to Fight ISIS? No Don't Take the Bait." *Time* 185, 8 (March 9, 2015), 33.

Von Drehle, David. "The War on ISIS." *Time* 185, 8 (March 9, 2015), 24–31.

Wood, Graeme. "What ISIS Really Wants." *The Atlantic* 321, 2 (March 2015), 79–80.

Zakaria, Fareed. "The Long Road to Hell: America in Iraq." CNN *Special Report* (broadcast) (October 26, 2015).

The Menu of Activism: Peacekeeping, State Building, Development, and Humanitarian Intervention

Modern violence goes beyond the battlefield when a country uses armed forces to achieve its national security objectives in the contemporary environment. Fighting and prevailing may be necessary preconditions to realizing a "better state of the peace," but there is more if peace and stability are to be achieved. The language and dynamics of peacekeeping (PK) are useful for moving from a state of war to one where all formerly warring parties embrace peace as a better alternative. Part of moving toward peace includes improving the physical condition in which people live, which is an exercise in development and state building. In contemporary times, states are also called upon to use armed forces to relieve the great suffering of others, a phenomenon known as humanitarian intervention. The wars in Afghanistan and Iraq offer examples of these factors and the consequences of failing to take them into account adequately in planning and executing the application of military force.

"We make war that we may live in peace," the Greek philosopher Aristotle wrote in *Nicomachean Ethics* nearly 2,500 years ago. Although that simple statement has been elaborated upon and expanded in the years since, it remains a central tenet that underlies using force in the contemporary world. In the period between the twentieth century's World Wars, the British strategist Sir Basil Liddell Hart put the same sentiment a slightly different way: the purpose of war, he said, was "a better state of the peace."

At one level, using violence to achieve peace seems anomalous, but it points to the inherent complexity of maintaining national security through the possession and occasional utilization of military force. The key element in reducing that apparent inconsistency is through the idea that military power is an instrumentality that facilitates creating a condition of peace that is superior to the peace that preceded the war. The need for war suggests that there may be barriers to an acceptable peace that must be removed by force before a "better state" of peace in which people "may live" is created.

In modern Western thinking about war, the prevailing (but by no means only) formulation of the role of force is captured in the Clausewitzian dictum ("War is politics by other means"), and war gains its meaning, purpose, and rationale as a way to create a postwar political condition that is more desirable than those conditions it seeks to replace. The notion that the recourse to war is intimately tied to the political reasons for which it is conducted remains a vital center of Western, and more specifically American, thinking on the subject.

War and the recourse to force are, however, more complex than simply the link between the successful application of force and a resulting better state of peace. In some cases, war may be a necessary condition to enable the creation of peace, but it is not in and of itself sufficient to ensure that such a peace ensues. The creation of a postwar peace may require the application of force to remove the preexisting barriers to an agreeable peace, but the removal of those barriers does not ensure that a satisfactory state of peace will be the result of successful military action on its behalf.

The removal of the barriers to a better peace is not, in and of itself, enough to guarantee the victor's goals will be realized in the peace that follows. For the postwar vision of the victor's peace to be enduring and stable requires that opposition to it must disappear as well. This can happen in one of two ways. One way is simply to impose the peace upon the losers and hence to force their acquiescence to the new reality. This is what is generally known as a *punitive peace*, in that its effect is to punish the losers by forcing them to abide by the conditions for which the victors fought. Extended, open-ended occupations are a good example of punitive peace. The other method is to convince the vanquished side to embrace the political outcomes for which the victors fought. This form of peace is known as *reconciliatory peace*. Its purpose is to convince the losers that their interests are better served by embracing the political goals of the victors as their own. If that can be accomplished, then a stable peace is a likely outcome to war.

This formulation of the objectives of war was devised in an earlier period when warfare was somewhat different than it is today. It is particularly applicable in decisive clashes between states where the military outcome is defined in traditional terms of overcoming hostile ability and is the goal of both sides. The two World Wars are clear examples of this formulation.

The World Wars also exemplify why military force alone will not necessarily create a better peace. At the end of World War I, the victors led by Great Britain, France, and the United States simply imposed harsh terms of peace on the defeated Central Powers (notably Germany). No real attempt was made to convince the Germans that their loss was for the best and that they should embrace the postwar conditions in Europe. Ultimately, the terms imposed proved so unacceptable that Germany rejected them, and the result was a second global conflagration twenty years later. The victorious allies in World War II consciously sought to convince the losers to embrace the outcome in 1945 by building a superior postwar condition the losers could adopt as their own. In this case, a reconciliatory peace settlement created a better state of peace that has endured for nearly three-quarters of a century.

War is about more than the simple clash of arms. War's dynamics are becoming more complicated in the contemporary environment of asymmetrical warfare. Contemporary warfare's asymmetry extends to why and how it is conducted. The asymmetrical warrior generally has no pretensions about overcoming the hostile ability of his militarily superior opponent but instead must attack and overcome that opponent's cost tolerance. The superior side usually has the destruction of the asymmetrical opponent as its goal, but accomplishing that objective normally requires the decisive clash of the two sides' armed forces, a climactic event the asymmetrical warrior avoids at all cost. The superior force can only prevail by a generally long, systematic sapping of the opponent's strength that has no dramatic, climactic point at which the opponent gives up and surrenders. Rather, the opponent's implicit action in "defeat" is more likely to be quitting the field or repairing to some safe place to refurbish capabilities in the hope of reactivating the contest at some later date (the Taliban after their defeat in 2001 is a primary example).

Contemporary wars are rarely cleanly decisive. The United States, for instance, has not participated in an armed conflict since 1945 in which the opponent surrendered in any formal, legal sense. The whole idea of surrender has become virtually archaic. At best, modern conflicts end with some form of negotiated agreement between the parties, and that dynamic results in a postwar peace that does not totally represent the prewar definition of a "better state" by either side. The absence of a decisive surrender rarely allows the imposition of the victor's peace, and the result is often the loser not embracing the victor's vision of peace.

For war to result in an enduring, stable condition of peace, Aristotle implies that its terms and conditions must be embraced by both (or all) contending sides. The employment of military force is often not, in and of itself, sufficient to create the conditions that allow that embrace. Partly, the reason is the inherently indecisive nature of modern warfare. Americans think of war as a discrete, temporary, and essentially pathological situation. War is thrust upon Americans, who fight, defeat, and subdue the enemy and then return home to the more normal and desirable condition of peace. Such a worldview segments the conduct of war from its aftermath and even sometimes the dynamics that created the pathology.

Unfortunately, the physical act of war does not always create all the conditions of a stable peace. That effect requires the embrace of the peace by all sides, and that embrace requires a process of political conversion away from the conditions that underlay the war toward the preferred policies of the victors. Indecisive military outcomes, which are a feature of modern warfare, make this process of conversion more difficult than when conditions—including benign, reconciliatory ones—can be in essence imposed and their benefits absorbed, as was done in postwar Germany and Japan. Instead, the conditions that can lead to reconciliation have to be the result of political persuasion, most of which can only occur in the aftermath of military hostilities. Doing so, however, is difficult for both foreign and domestic reasons.

Modern warfare is conceptually messier than traditional warfare. The motivation for entering hostilities may transcend traditional calculations of interests to embrace humanitarian motives that complicate both the reasons for war and its outcomes, a matter addressed at the end of the chapter. Once the decision to use armed forces is reached, fighting and winning (hard enough in and of themselves) must anticipate additional actions, all of which entail continuing, and sometimes expensive and effort-consuming, conditions that may surpass the will and attention span of the United States. They are likely to be the predictable consequences of an American involvement that does not have a decisive ending, so they must be addressed before the United States commits itself to any involvement. Failure to do so may result in an unacceptable outcome. The necessary conditions include physical assurances, such as presence, to guarantee that an established peace is not breached; assistance in building support for the new political realities; making people's lives better than they were before (development); and, partially as a result, movement to strengthen the structure of the government and system that exist in the country (state building). These actions are sequential, and each is the subject of individual examination.

PEACEKEEPING

In contemporary warfare, the cessation of organized violent conflict and the transition to peace in which continued acts of violence cease are not to be taken for granted. Parties neither surrender nor formally agree to end all fighting, so violence or its potential remains a prospect that can devolve into resumed hostilities. Thus, there remains a need to fill the vacuum between the end of formal hostilities and the desired state of peace. PK is a generic term that encompasses the various actions by different kinds of parties that may attempt to fill the gap.

The recent military experiences of the United States illustrate this condition between war and peace. In Iraq, the completion of the conquest of that country ended the formal state of hostilities between the two governments, but it did not end the fighting, which ignited periodically in one or both of two ways: actions taken by different Iraqi groups against one another to try to assert a new balance of power among them in Iraq and actions taken by the various Iraqi groups against the Americans to demonstrate their opposition to the American occupation. In this situation, American occupation forces acted as peacekeepers, trying to retard or extinguish the violence as a precondition to creating a durable peace. They did not entirely succeed, and violence has continued since the American departure.

The term *peacekeeping* is historically associated with efforts by parties not part of the original conflict to impose themselves between formerly warring parties, and such efforts have historically been associated with the United Nations (UN). During the Cold War, the principal physical contribution of the world body to international peace and security occurred in the role of creating and enforcing peaceful conditions on formerly warring parties. The first, and generally most successful, efforts were in interposing UN forces between countries that had been at war and had achieved some sort of military cessation the peacekeepers could enforce to assure the adversaries they would not be attacked while efforts toward a more enduring peace were negotiated or otherwise created. This process was particularly associated in the early Cold War years with missions such as the UN Emergency Force (UNEF) that separated Israel and Egypt between 1956 (the Suez War) and 1967 (the Six Days War), and it became the model for UN efforts elsewhere. Since it was one of the few truly positive areas of UN participation in the avoidance of war, the term *peacekeeping* was extended to essentially any UN intervention, including into situations that were dissimilar in content and requirements from those associated with the original concept of PK.

The United States has only infrequently been involved in formal UN PK missions. During the Cold War, the reason for American absence from such operations—other than to provide financial support for them through UN assessments—was purposeful. The most basic underlying principle of successful PK has always been the neutrality of the peacekeepers in their attitudes and actions toward the formerly warring parties whose peace they were supervising and reinforcing. Since almost any international or internal conflict during the Cold War had Soviet or American implications, the Americans and the Soviets generally had interests on the opposing sides that would compromise their neutrality and might even add Cold War considerations to an already difficult problem. By common agreement, both superpowers acquiesced in physically avoiding interference in PK operations.

The prohibition on American direct involvement in UN PK has been relaxed somewhat since the end of the Cold War, but it has not become an intimate part of American national security efforts. Because of superior logistics capabilities, for instance, American naval and air power are often used to help insert and support UN forces in remote locales, and in a few limited situations, some American forces have been assigned to UN duty, such as creating and maintaining the peace in parts of the Balkans (Bosnia and Herzegovina, Macedonia, and Kosovo) beginning in the 1990s. Ongoing violence in places like the Middle East rarely reaches a point where there is any peace to enforce. The peacekeeping force in Sinai, an artifact of the Israeli-Egyptian peace accord of 1982, is an exception in which American forces take part.

American formal participation in UN PK remains a peripheral part both of such operations and of American national security more generally. Unlike countries such as Canada and Sweden, for instance, the United States does not dedicate part of its forces to potential UN duty, and there is no direct allocation of defense budgetary resources to UN PK. On its own, US participation in UN PK operations would hardly warrant more than a passing mention in a text on American national security.

PK in its original usage to describe UN operations to influence and reinforce world peace is different from the kinds of dynamics that are discussed here under the generic term *peacekeeping*. The principles and dynamics associated with more traditional uses, however, are germane to the central questions surrounding American actions in the world designed to enhance national security. Aside from formal UN PK responses, the situations that PK solutions seek to address—the nether world between war and peace—are very useful in describing the kinds of involvements in which the United States has been a part in the twenty-first century, and they are likely to continue to be relevant in the future. UN PK may be a fairly minor part of the equation of American national security, but the problems and dynamics of PK are highly relevant to the achievement of better states of the peace everywhere.

The Dynamics of Peacekeeping

The term *peacekeeping* can be a misleading way to depict all the various phenomena typically implicitly or explicitly encompassed by the term. Taken literally, it means "keeping peace," and that clearly is its most important aim. Phrased in this manner, however, PK implies that there must be a peace to be kept before PK can be invoked, but often the situations for which peacekeepers are suggested are more complex—and dangerous. There is simply more to situations where PK is invoked than monitoring peace. The

TABLE 12.1

"Peacekeeping" Situations, Missions, and Forces

Situation	War	Unstable peace	Stable peace
Mission	Peace imposition (PI)	Peace enforcement (PE)	Peacekeeping (PK)
Forces Required	War fighters	War fighters/police	Police

full dynamics of PK require thinking about three related, sequential sets of conditions and actions captured in Table 12.1.

Before fully explicating the distinctions and their implications, it is first necessary to recognize what they seek to depict and describe. The table asserts that in a situation of war or its aftermath, there are three possible factual situations on the ground. These vary from a situation where fighting remains active or likely in the absence of some kind of restraint (war), to circumstances where the fighting has concluded but could easily resume without constraint (unstable peace), to conditions where there is a genuine desire for peace on the part of all concerned that requires nothing more than monitoring implementation of a durable peace (stable peace). The result is a continuum of levels of violence or peace, rather than the sharp break between war and peace that has been integral to the preferred American view of war. The table much better captures the situations in many particular developing-world conflicts. It further suggests that the term *peacekeeping* only truly applies to situations at one end of this war/peace spectrum, since in most cases a peace is not present to be kept or is only tenuous and may require a more active, assertive posture than is implied by the more passive mode associated with traditional UN PK.

The movement of violent situations is clearly a multi-step operation that involves more than simply keeping the peace, and it requires different kinds of forces and actions to conduct the mission. Conceptualizing missions as PK implies that the appropriate way to deal with them is to dispatch lightly armed, defensive forces whose job is essentially to keep the parties apart and to monitor their compliance to the order that has been established. These forces keep the peace by enforcing the arrangements or laws to which the parties themselves have agreed. This form of PK is a preferred UN approach for several reasons, two of which are exemplary. One is that the UN is in the peace "business": it was, after all, established to enforce the peace after World War II and to avoid a recurrence, as had happened after World War I under the League of Nations. This conviction is part of the basic worldview of most people who are part of the

UN, and thus it is more comfortable for them to think of their missions in peace-oriented rather than war-oriented terms. Second, peacekeepers are generally cheaper to raise and maintain than more active fighting forces. Since the UN exists in a perpetual state of underfunding, it is a much more affordable form of activity than more active military roles.

The distortion this creates is that many real-world problems are not, in fact, PK situations but rather circumstances in which peace has not clearly been established as the consensual preference of all parties. In these circumstances, the passive, monitoring activities associated with UN PK may prove inadequate to deal with the exigencies on the ground.

A final introductory note about the continuum is that the overall goal of what are called peacekeepers is to move situations along the continuum from states of war toward stable peace. In a pure sense, the two ends of the spectrum represent concrete, discrete points, whereas the large center (unstable peace) represents a gradually changing balance between war and peace. PK efforts seek to move the situation along that continuum from war to a state of stable peace. Depending on the place and circumstance with which one is dealing, this can be a particularly difficult process, with both military and nonmilitary implications.

The military part of the puzzle is how to end fighting among the parties: in other words, peace imposition (PI). This may be especially difficult when the peace imposers are part of the ongoing state of war, as the United States was in Iraq, and, indeed, one way this *may* be accomplished is by removing the outside (in this case American) forces that may have acted as an irritant contributing to the continuation of violence. Stopping the fighting is the goal, and it is a necessary precondition to moving toward peace. The political implications revolve around changing the attitudes of the parties toward the condition of war. In a situation of war, all (or most) of the parties prefer the continuation of war to any state of peace in which their goals are not fully realized. In this case, war is preferred to peace. The goal of PK is to change those perceptions to a consensus that peace under some kinds of terms is preferable for all. Such a change in perception is necessary for the situation to move across the continuum away from war to stable peace. The perception by all or nearly all that peace is preferable to war is a necessary condition for true PK, which aims to ensure against backsliding by the opponents.

In national security concerns for the United States, this model is applicable to developing-world situations where the United States has been or may become involved, which is at the heart of the relevance of the model. This interest flows across the kinds of national security actions the country may take and what it can reasonably be expected to accomplish.

Peace Imposition Although the idea of UN PK was born in response to situations where conditions of war (normally between sovereign states) had occurred and ended, most contemporary scenarios do not meet those conditions. Normally, the preexisting condition to American involvement features some form of internal situation, either of active or of potential civil conflict, or involves a regime whose policies the United States disapproves of and seeks to change. Afghanistan is an example of the former and Iraq the latter.

When there is no peace but instead a condition of war or its likelihood, the first action is to end the fighting. If the warring parties are fighting, the cessation of violence must be forced upon them; in other words, peace must be imposed, hence the name for this stage in the process. The difficulty of imposing peace varies depending on the preexisting situation and the level of commitment of one or all parties to pressing military action toward a successful ending. In some limited cases, the party that becomes the instigator and champion of the peace process may have been the party that broke the peace in the first place—the United States and the invasion of Iraq, for instance— and in other situations, the side suffering the most may call for peace.

PI can be more or less difficult and enduring. One clear variable is the level of commitment of both sides of the conflict to continue or to end fighting. In wars, there is sometimes a dynamic that favors continued fighting regardless of the situation on the ground: whoever is winning wants to continue until total victory is attained, and whoever is losing may prefer to "double down" rather than seek peace, fearing that war termination when it is losing will weaken its bargaining position in discussions of peace terms. The losing side may also believe it can reverse its fortunes and improve its negotiating position.

In either case, the intervention of peace imposers is likely to be greeted with less than enthusiasm by one or all sides to the conflict, and the peace imposer can thus expect opposition rather than cooperation from some or all. A second variable in the calculation of difficulty is whether the outside peace imposer has the overwhelming *and appropriate* kind of force to impose peace. In Iraq, the United States had such overwhelming conventional force that it quickly brushed aside the symmetrical forces of the Hussein regime and imposed peace on the situation, at least until Iraqi elements who did not desire the new status quo could organize and mount asymmetrical responses.

Since PI operations are at heart military campaigns designed to force the parties to cease fighting, they are the clear province of war fighters. The goal and mission of the intervening party or parties at this stage is to convince the parties to war that they will not be allowed to continue fighting and that if they resist that dictate, the intervening forces will suppress them and not permit them to continue or to resume fighting. The requisites of this phase are virtually entirely military and require the presence and employment of active combat forces.

The inclusion of a PI phase as part of PK differentiates the model described here from UN PK. The UN variant presumes that some form of peace predates its entrance into a situation or that its mere presence will create such a situation. The UN does not have pure combat forces at its disposal (at least partially because it cannot afford them), and the peacekeepers it deploys depend for their safety in large measure on the inability or unwillingness of warring parties to challenge them. In UN missions where this condition has not been met—notably the Congo in the 1960s and Bosnia in the 1990s—they have suffered as a result.

PI operations are only the first step in the movement from the chaos of war to an enduring, stable peace, and they are clearly not adequate in and of themselves to produce that peace. They may be a necessary first step on the road to peace, and retention of the ceasefire they impose is clearly a requisite to provide the "shield" behind which the process can move toward real peace. As Table 12.1 clearly indicates, as the process moves toward the peace end of the spectrum, different actors and different dynamics become part of the scene.

Peace Enforcement   Once fighting has been suppressed, the purpose of PK missions is to convince the formerly warring parties to embrace peace. As Table 12.1 suggests, this process is extensive as the situation moves from one of war to one of stable peace. At the outset, a PE operation is likely to experience resistance from some or all sides since the imposed peace may favor one group of combatants over others. As a partial result, not all sides may truly accept the virtues of peace over a return to war. The phase is described as one of "unstable peace" because it is likely that, in the absence of some forms of PE restraint that prevents a resumption of fighting, the situation might revert to the war end of the continuum.

The basic mission during the PE stage is gradually to increase opposition to continued (or renewed) warfare and to move toward broader, and eventually universal, support for peace. It is a gradual process wherein progressively more elements of the population come to prefer peace to war. As such, it is a phase where two goals are simultaneously pursued, where different kinds of forces and personnel are necessary to conduct them, and where the balance between activities and forces gradually shifts.

The two goals are the enforcement of peace achieved in the first phase and the gradual conversion of the target population toward a preference for and embrace of that peace. Since the early parts of this phase in particular are likely to include armed groups that are unconvinced they benefit more from peace than a reversion to war, it is necessary for peace enforcers to guarantee that war cannot and will not be tolerated and that efforts to restart violence will be met and suppressed. This requisite is primarily military, and it requires a combat, war-fighting presence. At the same time, the process of reconciliation and conversion to support of peace must begin.

This goal and its accompanying actions are essentially political and include concrete actions to convince the population they are better off at peace than they were at war. As this conversion progresses, those favoring war shrink in numbers and influence, and the primary emphasis of the peace enforcers moves from military combat to enforcing the new rules by policing forces that are more concerned with maintaining a more and more accepted set of rules than with suppressing opponents.

The PE phase is likely to be more or less lengthy depending on the environment in which it is implemented, but it will never be short, compact, or dramatically decisive. Since the conditions that lead to outside intervention generally occur in developing countries with underdeveloped economies and political traditions, the transition to some form of popular base support for a peace-promoting postwar environment means considerable beneficial changes must be made that are both difficult and problematic, but accumulating positive changes can move the process forward. One may, to invoke an old Vietnam analogy, build schools during the day to promote the welfare of the people but find that the structures are occupied by resisters to the effort at night, requiring those schools to be attacked and destroyed to enforce the peace. Peace is built by increments.

The PE phase is not only likely the longest stage in terms of physical duration, it is also the most stressful on the participants. During the PI, the situation is one of war, and combat is the appropriate and understood role of forces sent to create peace. The situation is adversarial, and the rules of war govern engagement. At the other end of the spectrum, PK assumes that conflict has been overcome, that the peacekeepers are welcome, and that the requirement is basically to keep abnormal violations from occurring. The combat soldier becomes the urban beat cop protecting a supportive population against the occasional lawbreaker.

PE falls between the two situations, containing elements of each. Unstable peace means not everyone supports the conditions that are being enforced. At the same time, most of the people with whom the peace enforcers interact probably support what they are doing and pose no threat. Much of the time, peace enforcers have little way to know who is who in these terms, which creates tensions and stress among the peace enforcers, as captured in Amplification 12.1.

Movement along the continuum included under the label PE is the essential description of American twenty-first-century involvements in places like Afghanistan and Iraq. During the 1990s, US interventions were in situations where peace could be more easily imposed (e.g., Haiti, Bosnia) and where PE was easier at least in terms of suppressing a return to violence.

One can argue that American efforts arising from 9/11 have failed to move across the PE spectrum toward approximation of stable peace. Most of the institutional effort in both cases has been directed toward the military aspects of PE, such as training indigenous armed forces and gendarmes to enforce the peace against potential violators but not including meaningful changes that make embrace of the peace a clearly superior alternative. The United States left Iraq, but support for the Islamic State (IS) demonstrates that not all groups have embraced the postwar situation as their own. In Afghanistan, the situation continues to hover on the brink between war and unstable peace, and Americans remain in more of a PI role.

AMPLIFICATION 12.1

The Talk/Shoot Dilemma in PE

A major part of PE involves patrolling former combat areas to ensure that the imposed peace is not breached. In this circumstance, the peace-enforcing individual, normally a soldier, inevitably encounters people whose orientation toward him and the peace he enforces is unknown. His dilemma is how he should treat such people, and his decisions have real consequences for himself and the peace he seeks to enforce. Should he act as a wary soldier facing a potential hostile enemy? Or should he act as the friendly "cop" on the corner interacting with the neighbors?

His difficult calculation is captured in the talk/shoot dilemma. A combat soldier knows when he encounters potential opponents that he must assume hostility and dispatch his opponent to avoid being killed: he shoots first and talks afterward. A policeman, on the other hand, does not assume lethal hostility and generally seeks to defuse situations without recourse to violence: he talks first and shoots only if that fails. The dilemma is that in individual cases, the peace enforcer may not know whether those he encounters are friend or foe and thus whether his proper role is that of soldier or policeman. If he encounters a foe and tries to talk to him first, he may end up dead. If he treats that same person as an enemy and shoots him when he in fact was not the enemy, he will be accused of being a foreigner slaughtering innocent natives, and his action may make matters worse for everyone. It is a difficult, often split-second decision. It is little surprise that it is stress-inducing or that returning veterans who have been placed in peace-enforcing roles have heightened instances of stress-related disability. ■

Peacekeeping   The opposite end of the spectrum from war is stable peace. This condition refers to the situation where all (or substantially all) formerly warring parties have accepted the peace as preferable to that which preceded it, and thus a reversion to war is unlikely even without some kind of military coercion. This is the state of affairs for which UN PK is most clearly designed since the requisites for such a force to succeed have been met. It is also a condition in which any outsider (like the United States) can envisage its withdrawal, reasonably confident that doing so will not result in a return to the preexisting conditions that caused it to become involved in the first place.

Achieving stable peace is not easy for several reasons. The first is that it requires a process of reconciliation and forgiving among the formerly warring parties that the state of war has almost certainly made difficult to achieve. There are always old wounds that only heal slowly. At the same time, the creation of a "better state of the peace" is much easier if the PE process has produced a better life for all concerned, thereby making embrace of the new condition obviously beneficial and supportable. The problem is that the resources to make improvements have historically not been available due to societal poverty or misapplication of resources. Creating internal resources to cause improvements may be difficult, and, as will be argued in the next sections, outside sources are problematic as well.

If an outside intervening party has been involved, reaching a peace that is stable enough to justify its withdrawal is often difficult, and this is particularly a dilemma the United States has faced and will likely continue to face. When outsiders are peace imposers and peace enforcers, their mere presence is likely to be an irritant to internal processes of reconciliation, and one of the few things disputants are likely to agree on is their common desire to see the outsiders leave. Even this desire will not be universal as some groups invariably benefit from foreign presence and are likely to suffer when it is removed. The outsider must justify its presence and provide an assessment that what it has done has been successful enough that a withdrawal is possible without undermining whatever goals caused it to intervene in the first place. The situation is rarely so clear that such a decision can be made with absolute confidence. At some point, the outside party must adopt some version of the "Aiken solution" (named after former Vermont senator Claude Aiken, who stated during the Vietnam War that the United States should simply declare victory, withdraw, and let others figure out what victory meant). Doing so implies the very real possibility that, once the outsider has left and can no longer influence events, the situation will simply revert to unstable peace, guaranteeing the outsider's solution is not realized. This outcome becomes particularly likely if the preferred outcomes of the people in the target country and those of the outsider were not identical in the first place.

The situations in Iraq and Afghanistan demonstrate this dynamic. In Iraq, the United States overthrew the Hussein government to end its ties to weapons of mass destruction (WMDs) and terrorists and to institute some form of political democracy that would represent a stable peace for

Iraq and meet US regional and antiterror goals. The problem is that the PE process did not clearly include a conversion of the whole Iraqi population to the American vision since internal divisions remain. The American occupation period failed to create the kinds of conditions in the country that would guarantee future support for the preferred American solution. When domestic pressure in the United States caused the American withdrawal (the desirability of which was one of the few things upon which most Iraqis agreed), the Americans were left hoping that stable peace had been achieved, which has not yet happened. They recognized, however, there was little that could be done if it was not. In Afghanistan, the pressures for American withdrawal began to mount well before the Afghan situation had moved beyond a state of open war (a clear PI problem), and it remains a PE problem at best.

Peacekeeping and the Future

Situations with dynamics like the continuum from PI to PK are likely parts of any future US potential military involvement in the developing world. The circumstances will not be identical to those the United States has encountered in places like Iraq and Afghanistan. A variety of differences will be apparent, from demographics to political structures to topography and geography to the kind of asymmetrical warfare tactics opponents employ. These differences will simultaneously give pause and encouragement to those either for or against inserting American forces into foreign situations. Knowing such involvements will likely be asymmetrical conflicts posing new and unforeseen challenges will cause skeptics to counsel restraint and to oppose military commitments. Enthusiasts will simultaneously find comfort in that same uniqueness, arguing that the problems may not be as insurmountable as past situations suggest.

Those who choose to downplay past experiences must confront and provide suitable answers to at least two observations that seem to emerge from past experiences within a PK perspective. The first is that these kinds of situations are difficult and complex, and generally more difficult, than traditional planners have recognized (or admitted). In Iraq, for instance, the Bush administration and its planners implicitly argued that success in PI would quickly lead to a stable peace. In reality, of course, the United States found itself in a lengthy PE process that lasted for over eight years, cost more than four thousand American lives and trillions of dollars, and arguably was not totally completed when the last American forces withdrew in 2011. In Afghanistan, there is equally little indication that planning proceeded beyond the limited goal of exterminating Al Qaeda (AQ) in 2001 and that the United States was, in partial consequence, unprepared for the nature of the situation to which it contributed: a state of war requiring PI that has not yet succeeded to the point that the situation has become a PE, much less a PK, problem. The critical lesson should be that the intrusion of American arms is likely to create a source of resistance in and of itself to the creation of a stable peace. Any projections that suggest American intrusion will somehow be "easy" should be viewed with considerable jaundice.

The second observation is that successful outcomes for these adventures are likely to be problematic. The United States can apply overwhelming conventional force to military situations. These efforts sometimes succeed in ending overt opposition (successfully impose peace), but that does not mean they will succeed in achieving the long-term PE and PK goals and objectives. Past experiences, of which Iraq and Afghanistan are examples in different ways, suggest that real success requires a viable, workable strategy for getting through the crucial PE stage, and it is not clear the United States has such a strategy. In Iraq, prewar planners implicitly denied the PI to PK progression existed and thus were totally unprepared for the process of resistance to American goals and the US occupation that followed: there were no PE provisions. In Afghanistan, there has been some recognition of the need to engage in positive processes of conversion to move the population toward embrace of a stable peace, but these have not been decisive successes, and Afghanistan remains a PE problem at best that occasionally looks like a PI challenge.

If the United States is to engage in successful attempts to influence developing-world violent situations in directions it prefers, it must generate ways to move those situations through the PK process. A viable strategy will have to contain both military and political components. The military aspect centers on developing an effective way to deal with the various permutations of asymmetrical warfare, a difficult task and one it is not clear the United States has mastered. The political aspect centers on winning "the hearts and minds of men." This aspect requires political conversion that includes demonstrating the superiority of the preferred American peace to other solutions. Since the targets of this conversion process are developing world populations, much of the traditional emphasis has been aimed at improving economic conditions simultaneous to or accompanying political development. Development and state building are both controversial and problematic processes, concerns to which the discussion now moves.

DEVELOPMENT AND STATE BUILDING

One way to think about the process of moving from war to peace is that it consists of both negative and positive actions and intentions. The first stage of the PK process (PI to PE) mostly emphasizes negative actions: military and semimilitary actions to keep former combatants from engaging in negative acts of war and gradually making reversion to violence both less possible and less desirable. Keeping bad things from happening is not necessarily enough to make the recourse to violence unthinkable in the future. As a result, positive actions with the intended result of providing a better condition of life for former fighters are often the necessary second element in strategies for stable peace. These processes fall under the general category of development and state building.

The broad context of this rationale begins with the enormous gulf in living standards and quality of life between the most developed countries and the rest of the world. Based largely in constructs that developed countries are more prosperous, more stable, and more democratic, the rationale is that if the poorer countries could be made more similar to the developed countries, the result would be a more peaceful and secure world. Academic constructs supporting this thesis began to emerge shortly after World War II and became rapidly entwined in the Cold War, when the less developed countries were emerging from colonial rule and became battlegrounds for influence and control between the Cold War antagonists. This conjunction tied together the inherent, humanitarian basis of making life better with the national dictates of the worldwide geopolitical struggle.

Development and modernization are controversial ideas. Two major questions arise about the disparities in standards of living between the most and lesser developed countries. The first is responsibility for the disparity: whose fault is it? In most cases, the poorer countries of the world have been former European (including American) colonies. Prior to colonization, most were "premodern" or "traditional" societies, meaning they did not resemble the countries of the developed world in organization and economic levels of achievement, among other things. During the colonial period, there were normally minimal developmental efforts by colonialists within their colonies, but these were generally aimed at making colonies more profitable rather than at removing economic disparities. When independence came to the developing world, gaps were wide, and the colonial period had created an awareness of comparative deprivation that the new countries wanted ameliorated. The question was who had caused this disparity.

The first question led to the second: whose responsibility was it to do something about developmental disparities? The question itself presupposes the situation was someone's fault and there was a resulting obligation to rectify it. Not everyone agrees there is such an obligation. Defenders of colonialism, for instance, argue that had colonialism not occurred, the traditional societies they colonized might never have been aware of differences and would have remained premodern, making their relative positions even worse than they are. Developmental advocates argue that the disparity is the "fault" of the Western world, which has a resulting obligation to alleviate the condition. This obligation can be argued on moral grounds of right and wrong or on more pragmatic grounds dealing with the relative security of developed and underdeveloped parts of the world. A further question, assuming a positive answer to the existence of an obligation, is who within developed countries should promote development—governments or private entities. This is an extension of the liberal/neoliberal argument that can be applied to both the international and domestic levels.

At various times, the debate over development has had both an academic and a policy emphasis, and for much of the period since World War II, the two emphases have coincided and intermingled. Academic constructs of development have largely been positive and expansive, suggesting the likelihood that development could, in one academic rendering, "speed up the course of history" by systematically reducing the disparities between the rich and the poor and thereby contributing to greater global tranquility. These arguments, underwritten by federal subsidies in the 1950s and 1960s, have faded both within academic circles and within policy circles where they always had less currency. The underlying idea that development must somehow be part of any process leading to a more peaceful world has, however, not disappeared.

The Rationale and Evolution of Development

Various terms are used to describe what development means. It is a Western construct that generally refers to more or less concerted efforts by governments and private entities to increase the economic wealth of communities and individuals and groups within those communities. The implicit model or goal in the present context is some general approximation of the form and levels of economic attainment of Western democratic societies. Terms that are used somewhat synonymously within the contemporary context include *modernization* and *Westernization.*

Arguments for and against governmental activity to create development can be found in the debates over both domestic and foreign policies. In the American debate, for instance, there is an ongoing disagreement over what the federal government should and should not do to improve the situations of the poorest Americans—in other words, what should be done to aid in their development. This debate, in turn, has both philosophical and practical roots that are reflected in the international realm. The domestic debate, for instance, becomes entangled in philosophical bases about liberal versus neoliberal (or conservative) notions regarding the appropriate level of governmental activism to induce change versus the degree to which market forces should impel change.

These issues are also present in the international debate over development, with the contribution to national security added to the equation. When political liberalism—with its generally positive, expansive views of the role of government in inducing change—was the prevailing philosophy between the end of World War II and the sour ending of the Vietnam War, the orientation was positive. Academic "theories" of development appeared to provide road maps about how to implement developmental strategies in the exploding developing world. These prescriptions were partly humanitarian, partly a matter of assuaging guilty feelings among colonial rulers, and partly based in national security concerns. The national security connection was established in the late 1940s and provided a "hard" geopolitical basis for engaging in efforts to uplift the conditions of the downtrodden.

The geopolitical argument is worth noting because it has endured as part of the stable peace equation. The underlying rationale for including developmental efforts within national security calculations arose from the assumption that the appeal of communism was greatest in conditions of squalor, deprivation, and unhappiness, all of which contributed to a "devil's workshop" of discontent in which communism thrived. Since the geopolitical battle between the West and the communist bloc was largely defined in terms of which system would gain global supremacy, efforts to remove disparities through development served a national security goal by making antidemocratic alternatives less attractive. This basic rationale has been revived in the context of those environments in which terrorism is spawned and grows. One popular construct among students of terrorism suggests, for instance, that terrorism "breeds" in a "swamp" of deprivation and hopelessness and that the antidote is to "drain the swamp" through developmental efforts.

Support for the developmental emphasis has never been universally held. Domestically, the debate is partially philosophical, as noted. There is sharp disagreement among Americans about whether government or the private sector, or either, should provide for the developmental disparities within US society. Some of the criticism of government efforts is founded in the ineffectiveness such efforts have often demonstrated. The 1960s War on Poverty, with its particular emphasis on conditions in Appalachia, is often cited as evidence of the failure of such efforts. Supporters of domestic developmental efforts often argue that no other entity but government can or will do these things and that most of the failures of the past have been the result not of flawed logic but of inadequate resources being available to implement them effectively. This latter criticism is particularly important in ongoing debates about development as a strategy for peace promotion in a resource-constrained environment.

The United States has always been the primary champion and symbol of developmental efforts worldwide. Historically, this leadership reflects the conditions of the immediate post–World War II environment in which the developmental initiative was born. The United States became the bulwark against expansionist communism and had the world's most vibrant economy, both contributing to conjoining the economic and national security rationales for development.

The neoliberal challenge represents a fundamental disagreement both on the philosophy underlying developmental efforts and on the efficacy of government versus private action in promoting development. If one rejects the notion that the developed world has any moral or other obligation to assist in development in the poorer countries, then what is the rationale for doing so? The neoliberal answer is that developmental efforts should arise from the perception of self-interest of the giving parties. It reframes the approach to development to acts that help private enterprises enhance their profits and as a side effect help improve the conditions in the countries in which they invest (the heart of so-called "trickle-down" economics). In the process, the major vehicle of developmental assistance shifts from public, governmental sources ("foreign aid") to private investment.

The neoliberal position has a restricted view of the role of government at its core, and this principle clearly extends to the international realm. For neoliberals, the market is supposed to correct for disparities in resources and wealth, and it does so through private investment in developing economies and in the dynamics of free trade, both mechanisms of globalization. The "hidden hand" of the market is responsible for making adjustments, and government is relieved of many of these responsibilities, which resultantly fall outside the parameters of its planning activities.

The neoliberal approach was clearly applied to the problem of moving the situation in Iraq from the realm of war to stable peace, bringing the discussion directly into line with the thrust of this chapter. One of the reasons little thought or effort was directed at the political and economic consequences of the invasion of Iraq was because outside governments are not supposed to play a prominent role in directing development decisions. Partially as a result, very little effort went into prewar planning for dislocations that would have to be remedied after the invasion on the assumptions that the expenses would be minimal, that Iraqi oil revenues would pay for them, and that foreign private investment after the fall of Hussein would provide the impetus for development and its consequent prosperity. All these assumptions proved false, of course, and the result was that major segments of the Iraqi economy remained chaotic even when the United States finally left in 2011, providing very little positive incentive for Iraqis to follow American suggestions about how the country should operate when they were gone.

The broader critique of the neoliberal performance in Afghanistan and Iraq goes beyond the adequacy of the physical planning and performance of the United States in addressing social and economic concerns as part of the political conversion process. Rather, the real heart of the criticism has to be whether the underlying disdain by neoliberalism for governmental activism predisposes it to ignore or downplay the importance of the political conversion process and to assume these kinds of problems are both so minor and unimportant that they will, in effect, "take care of themselves."

The final verdict on Iraq and Afghanistan is not, of course, complete, but any interim assessment must be somewhat skeptical of the idea of operating PE through private means.

The rationale underlying development as a part of national security policy is vulnerable on grounds beyond its philosophical conformance with the worldviews applied to different situations. It may be fairly clear that some form of economic and political change is a necessary part of the process of political inducement needed to proceed through PE toward a landing point in stable peace, but it is not so clear that development as it has historically been undertaken always produces desirable outcomes. As a result, an examination of the efficacy of development as an approach to these matters must include some review of critiques of the concept.

Impediments to Development

Two criticisms are generally made of development policies. One is philosophical and reflects the liberal/neoliberal disagreement. The important offshoot of this debate is the kind and quality of development that occurs based upon each philosophical predisposition: is government aid or private enterprise the best road map to development? The other criticism is that the record of developmental efforts has not been so uniformly positive in general or in particular situations as to provide clear evidence of the superiority of either one approach or the other: do developmental efforts work? Both concerns can be, and in the present political environment are being, applied to domestic as well as international problems. In turn, how one ultimately assesses the viability of developmental efforts affects both the wisdom of its continuation and the national security proposition about efforts in developing countries, including prominently how such efforts can contribute to movement from civil war (PI situations) to stable peace.

Disagreement begins with what developmental efforts should be undertaken and, by extension, whether governments or private actors should undertake them. One of the more obvious and pressing problems in developing countries is an infrastructure deficiency, manifested in primitive transportation, education, and public service capabilities. Such capabilities are necessary to improve the lot of citizens in countries and, importantly, to make countries attractive to outside private investors. The argument for a strong infrastructure is, of course, familiar in the contemporary domestic debate, although generally in terms of updating and improving rather than in creating a modern infrastructure.

The question is who should engage in infrastructure development in the developing world. There are three candidates for the role. One of these is the country itself. By definition, a developing country is poor and lacks sufficient resources to improve its condition and thus cannot develop these kinds of infrastructure components on its own. Even where some infrastructure development may have occurred, the impact of war may harm or destroy parts of it, requiring repair (Iraq is a prime example) and resources that are unavailable. In addition, one of the common characteristics of developing countries is governmental corruption, which may mean available resources are misappropriated. Thus, the developing countries generally cannot build their own infrastructures or they already would have.

The second possible source of funds for infrastructure development is foreign private sources, whose participation can be rationalized on the grounds that doing so creates the preconditions for successful investment in those countries. Thus, before a company can contemplate the profitable operation of a factory in a country, it must have a developed power-generation system to provide electricity to its plant, a workforce with sufficient education to perform factory tasks, and a transportation network that can move its products to market. The problem is that the investments necessary to create this vital infrastructure are generally not attractive investments to profit-driven enterprises. Most infrastructure items are, in the language of economic development, *non-self-liquidating:* these enterprises do not directly and accountably pay for themselves, which would allow private investors to recover their expenses, much less make a profit. A school, for instance, may be a legitimate investment that, by virtue of educating citizens to make them more productive, benefits the society that creates it. The "payoff" from education is not direct or measurable for accounting in profit-and-loss terms. Thus, private investors are likely to be attracted to places that *already have* developed infrastructures and are likely to be repelled from places that do not.

The third option is public foreign investment, or what is called developmental assistance or, more pejoratively, foreign aid. Such assistance does not have the same accountability standards in terms of profit-and-loss ledgers but can be justified by way of long-term, less directly measurable effects, such as increased standards of living, citizen support, and the like. Developmental assistance was a major part of the underlying rationale of international efforts that emerged in the 1950s as part of the academic, liberal approaches to development and modernization. Its eclipse in recent years is partly the result of the neoliberal assault that questions the desirability of governmental activism, but it has also been questioned on the grounds of its effectiveness in achieving its goal and, more recently, its affordability in a resource-constrained environment.

The second foundation of the critique of development is that it does not work, and more particularly, that government-sponsored programs of development in foreign countries have often had disappointing results. The early confidence of postwar developmental theorists regarding the dynamics and prospects for improving conditions in the developing world has proven either incorrect or overly optimistic. Part of the reason for this is that the problems of development are both more complicated and localized than was initially recognized so that one-size-fits-all solutions often proved inappropriate. Development is simply more complex than was originally envisaged. Moreover, the amount of resources available for developmental purposes has always been much less than enthusiasts argued was necessary. The criticism of an inadequate physical commitment has come with particular force from the developing countries themselves, who have consistently advocated greater wealth transfer from the rich to the poor countries and maintain that the workability of developmental strategies remains unknown until adequate resources are devoted to it.

These arguments, of course, come up in the contemporary domestic debate. The role of government in promoting the solution of problems versus a more constrained role for government is at the heart of much liberal/conservative disagreement and currently finds voice in, among other places, debates over who should take the lead role in developmental areas like infrastructure refurbishing and modernization. If government will not do these things, who will? At the same time, neoliberal critics question the efficacy of governmental, liberal activism in solving problems, particularly on the question of affordability. The dynamics also apply to the process of establishing stable political systems in developing countries, also known as state building.

State Building

The idea of state building draws together the PK and development strands of dealing with the developing countries. When the United States becomes involved in the violent affairs of developing-world states, its objective is normally a stable peace where fighting is ended, where it will not recur, and where its causes have been rectified. In Afghanistan, for instance, that means a stable, representative, strong central government that is resistant to the return of the Taliban. In Iraq, it originally meant a strong and stable democratic government, but the democratic requirement has been relaxed somewhat by ongoing conflict.

The purpose of state building is to move situations from the point where PI has more or less succeeded to the point of stable peace, where essentially all former combatants prefer and will support a peaceful order. Doing so makes it possible, but not inevitable, that support for the national political system will thrive as well.

Getting from a condition of war to one of peace requires a process of conversion and consensus building that contains both military and developmental aspects and in which each form of success is a necessary condition for the hoped-for outcome. Military success may remove barriers to putting in place an order that both those imposing the solution and those upon whom it is imposed can agree is preferable to the prewar situation, but the process of achieving that success comes with major caveats regarding the application of state-building solutions to local situations. Success at PK can lead to state-building success.

The Afghanistan War once again provides an example of the difficulty of appropriate state building. The United States' objective in its state-building efforts is to create a strong Afghan state that will be powerful enough to resist future radicalization, notably the return of AQ (or some other terrorist successor) to power. In the American view, this means a fairly strong central government, and American efforts have generally been directed toward that end. To move away from the PI end of the PK spectrum, it has attempted military pacification to transform the situation on the ground to an unstable peace so peace enforcers can provide a shield behind which state-building activities can proceed. These efforts have included programs to increase the indigenous ability of the Afghan government to provide for security against the Taliban by building the Afghan National Army (ANA) and gendarme as part of constructing the Afghan National Security Forces (ANSF). More modest developmental efforts have been directed at infrastructure development (e.g., building schools and hospitals, providing funding for farmers to grow crops other than opium poppies).

These programs have been no more than partially successful. Part of the reason may be flaws in the PK and developmental programs that have been instituted, but part of it may be that the state structure the United States wants to institute is not what Afghans want. Afghanistan has rarely had a strong central government through its history, at least partially because most of its people did not want one. One of the roots of Afghan tribalism is a desire for local autonomy for population groups, who have always resisted efforts from Kabul to impose strong central rule upon them.

What this discussion suggests is a third element in calculating success in intervening to affect foreign countries with armed force. State building requires an effort like that described in the PK model to provide a shield behind which a movement can be undertaken to build consensus for the better state of peace that is sought. One of the necessary tools in that process is to convince citizens of the superiority of the new order, which, in the developing world where such struggles occur, means some process of development. Both PK and development are necessary to create a stable peace, but for that peace to take hold, the state being built must be one that can be and is embraced by all parties. Accomplishing all three of these is difficult, as the thumbnail sketch of remaining problems in Afghanistan depicted in Amplification 12.2 suggests.

Peacekeeping, Development, and State Building in Afghanistan

The achievement of stable peace represents the ideal ending for an outside power that has intervened with armed force in the affairs of another country—the better state of the peace in which that outsider can claim success and terminate its involvement on a victorious note. How close is the United States to achieving this end state?

Clearly, the situation is not there, and the categories used in this chapter (and the last) are useful in helping us understand why not and even what the future prospects may be. The discussion of asymmetrical war suggests that dealing militarily with these situations is both alien to the American experience and difficult to master. After greater than a decade of more or less concerted action, the United States and its allies (including the Afghan government) have not vanquished the Taliban from the field, although they may have weakened Taliban capabilities. In the meantime, the situation hovers between the PI and PE phases of PK and cannot move toward the stable peace end of the spectrum as long as there is active Taliban resistance. The situation, in other words, is at best one of unstable peace where some (notably the Taliban) prefer the continuation of war to a peace in which they lose all power. In this situation, the Taliban actively oppose developmental efforts, which generally languish, thereby impeding the process of convincing the population of the superiority of the proposed peace. It also remains unclear that the state-building vision of the United States and its fractious allies in Kabul is universally shared within the country.

In these circumstances, is the American achievement of its goals reasonable or a chimera? Is it possible to move the situation to an outcome the United States can embrace as successful? If not, what is possible? What does the dilemma posed by this complex problem suggest for future American policy toward Afghanistan and in other places? ■

HUMANITARIAN INTERVENTION

On November 14, 2015, the *Washington Post* entreated the international community to take action to prevent a slaughter of civilians in the east African country of Burundi. Titled "The World Should Act to Prevent Atrocities in Burundi," the editorial reminded the world that when it was part of the country of Rwanda-Burundi, the citizens of Burundi had witnessed the slaughter of upward of a million members of the Hutu tribe by Tutsi in 1994. In that case, there was no international intervention, and a humanitarian disaster of epic proportions ensued. The editorial called for the international community to prevent a recurrence in Burundi.

The appeal was purely on humanitarian grounds: no major state has particular interests in Burundi, certainly none that rise to the level of vital interests. The parallel with 1994 was eerie, however. Of that catastrophe, then president Bill Clinton said that American inaction was the worst decision of his presidency. The world could have acted to prevent a violent humanitarian disaster and did not. From that crucible, international humanitarian interests were added to the reasons to intervene in developing-world problems.

Historically, the reasons countries involve themselves in violent outbreaks like typical developing world internal conflicts (DWICs) reflect geopolitical calculations: that it is in the presumably vital national interests of the United States (or other countries) to influence the outcome in a particular direction. American interest in most Middle Eastern conflicts arises, at least indirectly, from some calculations that the conflict will affect access to petroleum resources or, more recently, international terrorism directed against the United States or allied soil. The debate over what to do about IS usually is phrased in these terms.

The end of the Cold War allowed the introduction of a new rationale for using force in DWICs: humanitarian intervention. The basic argument comes from natural-law philosophy and the position that there are certain conditions of life that all people are entitled to and that, if they are dishonored by governments or others, the international community has an obligation to redress. Suppression and slaughter of civilian populations is the penultimate violation of natural rights.

This entire area is of relatively recent vintage. Many of the most obvious atrocities in the contemporary environment fall under the rubric of *genocide*, a term that was not invented until 1944. Prior to that time, positivist international law had held the position that outsiders had no standing or right to interfere in the internal affairs of other states and that those states could do essentially whatever they wanted to their citizens free from international repercussions. This position may seem archaic today, but it provided a "right" to suppress and, in some cases, even to extinguish parts of populations on the grounds that what governments did to their own citizens was strictly their own business.

The Holocaust discredited that notion. As Nazi Germany moved to murder its Jewish and Roma (Gypsy) citizens, the idea that this was acceptable came into disrepute (if not disuse). Those most responsible for humanitarian atrocities in the war were tried, convicted, and in many cases executed. After the war, the Convention on Genocide was passed by the United Nations and created an atmosphere in which "crimes against humanity" have become a prominent part of war crimes. The International Criminal Court (ICC) at the Hague regularly tries international transgressors on humanitarian grounds in which sovereign rights are overridden.

The contemporary demand for humanitarian activism comes in the form of something called the "Responsibility to Protect" (R2P). It begins from the premise that there is a fundamental obligation to protect those against whom atrocious violations of human rights have occurred and that this obligation meets the test of vitality to all countries and to humankind. The debate has centered on the UN as the leader of the movement to protect "vital humanitarian interests." Alex Bellamy explains the rationale and need for such a movement. "All too often the world's response to genocide and mass atrocities," he wrote in *Responsibility to Protect*, "has been slow, timid, and disjointed."

R2P has not been embraced operationally by major governments, but neither has it been denounced. There are two major objections raised to it. One comes from the realist paradigm and questions the vitality of humanitarian disasters in places that are not otherwise within the vital interests of the state for using force. The question is not whether these situations are tragic or should be ignored, it is whether there is an unavoidable moral or geopolitical mandate to deal with them. Moral arguments in this regard are ambivalent about the extent to which one is obligated to rescue others if doing so means putting oneself at risk. The other objection is more practical, based on the frequency of humanitarian violations in the contemporary world and thus the international ability to solve them all. This objection falls within the purview of a general reluctance to commit American forces into DWICs, a concern raised earlier.

Humanitarian and geopolitical factors often comingle in DWICs and thus in what to do in the international reaction to Syria and IS. When the issue was largely focused on Syria in 2013 and early 2014, much of the concern was humanitarian: the apparent slaughter of civilians by the Assad regime. This sentiment ran into negative attitudes toward intervention. In this case, humanitarian considerations gave way to geopolitical reluctance. When IS entered the picture, the balance of justifications changed. IS posed both a geopolitical threat to the region and beyond and committed atrocious acts against civilians in areas it occupied. In this case, geopolitics and humanitarian concerns overlapped and even reinforced one another. Even this combination did not create broad international support for decisive action until IS broadened its activities to terrorist attacks against the Russians and the French in late 2015.

The rationale for humanitarian intervention is much stronger in the abstract than it is in real cases. Truly gross humanitarian violations like genocide are relatively infrequent: Cambodia in the 1970s and Rwanda in the 1990s are exceptional cases, but gross violations continue to occur, as in the case of the Darfur and South Sudan regions of Sudan. It is relatively easy to bemoan these situations and to issue abstract pleas that something be done to alleviate them. Doing so, particularly if it involves personal sacrifice, is a much more difficult decision, as the *Challenge!* box suggests.

CHALLENGE!

How Important Is Responding to Vital Humanitarian Disasters?

Humanitarian disasters, and thus the question of whether the international community—including the United States—has any obligation to mitigate them, are simply a part of the environment of modern conflict and violence. Most of the contemporary instances occur within countries, usually involving competing nationalities within its borders, and they are often committed either by subnational groups (e.g., IS) or state governments (e.g., the Syrian regime of Assad). There is little reason to believe this regrettable practice will simply disappear.

This phenomenon cannot be avoided as a national security question. It occurs frequently enough that some kind of national stance toward it seems desirable, both to guide reactions and to let perpetrators know what consequences they should anticipate from the United States if they commit humanitarian atrocities. There is a general global agreement that humanitarian intervention is desirable, but it is not backed by any strong concrete plan of action: R2P, for instance, is more an exhortation than an action plan. The most recent instance in Burundi reminds us they will recur.

The debate about American reaction is clouded. At one level, we decry these events and argue that something should be done about them. At the same time, we are reluctant to become involved in messy internal situations based on unsuccessful past experiences (e.g., Iraq, Afghanistan) and the projection that involvement could be costly and inconclusive. What should we do?

It is not an easy question. The late 2015 case of allowing Syrian refugees into the United States illustrates the point. There is no question that almost all the refugees had been the victims of humanitarian atrocities and deserved respite—the positive side of humanitarian involvement. At the same time, there was a fear among many Americans that allowing them to enter the country would also provide a kind of Trojan Horse effect in which IS terrorists would also enter the country intent on wreaking havoc on Americans—the negative side of the ledger.

Where do you stand on this issue? Is there some kind of moral imperative to help fellow humans in disastrous situations? What is that obligation? ■

CONCLUSION: THE COMPLEXITY OF POSTWAR PEACE

War has never been as conceptually simple as many common depictions. In popular renderings, war is depicted as the clash of arms, where forces collide and one side prevails while the other loses. War has a clear beginning and a clear end; there are states of war and states of peace, and they are easily discernible. This is the basic image of the "American way of war," with referents to supposedly simpler times, such as World War II, a terribly stressful and difficult war fought for lofty principles that justified sacrifice and concluded with a just and lasting peace.

Warfare since 1945 has seldom been so conceptually tidy, and its conclusions have not been so neat and determinant. The last time the United States conclusively "won" a war in the sense that it faced and defeated a foe on distant battlefields and the other side formally capitulated was at the end of World War II. Warfare since has been more complex, with greater nuances surrounding why and how it is fought, what constitutes success or failure, and the terms on which it ends. The Korean War, which ended with an armistice that stopped the fighting but contained no surrender, and Vietnam were the signal posts for this change in the last century. It is a pattern that, in unique permutations based on the locales in which it occurs, continues to this day, and it is likely to be the basic pattern with which the future must contend.

Three conclusions about these processes are necessary takeaways from this examination. The first is that the motivation to fight is different: humanitarian intervention is an example. The second is the problematic nature of outcomes. The processes of PK and development are complex, and they are not clearly understood in general and especially in the often idiosyncratic circumstances in which they may be applied. The nature and thus "success" of adventures that inevitably engage these processes are very difficult to predict with any precision. Third, these additional processes and requirements add to the duration and expense of modern warfare. It should not be a surprise that the two longest wars in American history have occurred in the twenty-first century because war now contains significant elements of what used to be thought of as postwar activity that makes the action linger. It is one thing to occupy a country that has surrendered and place it under one's domain, for instance, but it is quite another when parts of the population remain in active, deadly opposition to that occupation. This duration contributes to the expense of warfare, and the requirements of development and state building are also expensive, adding measurably to the total "bill" for military activities.

The dynamics contained in this chapter should counsel caution in the contemplation of future warfare and should suggest questions that must be raised and answered before the call to arms is acknowledged, especially at a time when the expense of war for questionable purposes and with dubious, unpredictable outcomes may be increasingly difficult to justify and sustain. Would, for instance, the American population have accepted the challenge to arms in either Iraq or Afghanistan had they understood the situation into which the country was getting itself?

These kinds of dynamics are not the only matters that demand consideration on the national security agenda. In addition, there are other problems that are conceptualized in national security terms of making Americans feel safe that go beyond traditional military conceptualization and for which solutions framed in military terms are not clearly appropriate. A complete view of the national security agenda requires looking at these as well, which is the purpose of the next chapter.

STUDY/DISCUSSION QUESTIONS

1. What is the traditional Western conception of war? For what objectives is it fought? How does modern warfare vary from that conceptualization? What do these changes mean for traditional ideas about peace and war?
2. What are the three distinct phases of peacekeeping described in the text? Describe the dynamics of each phase, including the set of circumstances in which it occurs and the mission and forces needed in each phase. Emphasize particularly the dynamics of peace enforcement and why it is especially relevant now and in the future.
3. Describe the concepts of development and modernization. What is the basic rationale for each? How has this process worked over time from both a liberal and neoliberal perspective? What are the impediments to the realization of development, including the problem of who pays for it and why that is a problem in the contemporary environment?
4. What is state building? What are its goals? What are its dynamics, and what criteria must be met for it to succeed from the vantage points of both target countries and outsiders who may involve themselves in state-building exercises?
5. Relate peacekeeping and state-building processes to one another. How do they fit together on the peacekeeping spectrum? How do they relate to the overall process of involvement in contemporary war?
6. In your view, should considerations regarding peacekeeping and state building be included in the process of deciding to go to war? Would such considerations have affected decisions in places like Afghanistan and Iraq? How and why should they (if they should) factor into future decisions?
7. What is humanitarian intervention? What kind of events have given rise to it? Cite examples. How important a concern should it be in American national security policy?

SELECTED BIBLIOGRAPHY

Atwood, J. Brian. "The Development Imperative: Creating the Preconditions for Peace." *Journal of International Affairs* 55 (Spring 2002), 333–349.

Bellamy, Alex J. *Responsibility to Protect*. Cambridge, MA: Polity Press, 2009.

Boutros-Ghali, Boutros. *An Agenda for Peace: Preventive Diplomacy, Peacemaking, and Peace-Keeping*. New York: United Nations, 1992.

Clausewitz, Carl von. *On War*. Rev. ed. Translated and edited by Michael Howard and Peter Paret. Princeton, NJ: Princeton University Press, 1984.

Cordesman, Anthony H. *The Iraq War: Strategy, Tactics, and Military Lessons.* Washington, DC: Center for Strategic and International Studies, 2003.

Diamond, Larry. *Squandered Victory: The American Occupation and the Bungled Effort to Bring Democracy to Iraq.* New York: Times Books (Henry Holt and Company), 2005.

Durch, William (ed.). *The Evolution of UN Peacekeeping: Case Studies and Contemporary Analysis.* New York: St. Martin's Press, 1993.

Editorial Board. "The World Should Act to Prevent Atrocities in Burundi." *Washington Post* (online), (November 14, 2015).

Eisenstat, Stuart, John Edwin Porter, and Jerry Weinstein. "Rebuilding Weak States." *Foreign Affairs* 84, 1 (January/February 2005), 134–146.

Evans, Gareth. *The Responsibility to Protect: End Mass Atrocities Once and for All.* Washington, DC: Brookings Institution Press, 2008.

Goldstone, Jack A., and Jay Ulfelder. "How to Construct Stable Democracies." *Washington Quarterly* 28, 1 (Winter 2004–2005), 9–20.

Hanson, Victor Davis. *Between War and Peace: Lessons from Afghanistan and Iraq.* New York: Random House, 2004.

Jones, Seth G. *In the Graveyard of Empires: America's War in Afghanistan.* New York: W. W. Norton, 2009.

Kemp, Geoffrey. "Losing the Peace." *National Interest* 76 (Summer 2004), 46–48.

Kilcullen, David. *The Accidental Guerrilla: Fighting Small Wars in the Midst of a Big One.* Oxford, UK: Oxford University Press, 2009.

Latham, Michael E. *The Right Kind of Revolution: Modernization, Development, and U.S. Foreign Policy from the Cold War to the Present.* Ithaca, NY: Cornell University Press, 2011.

Liddell Hart, Sir Basil. *The Real War 1914–1918.* Boston: Little Brown, 1964.

Mueller, John. *Remnants of War.* Ithaca, NY: Cornell University Press, 2003.

Nardin, Terry. "The Moral Basis of Humanitarian Intervention." *Ethics and International Affairs* 16, 1 (March 2002), 57–70.

Natsios, Andrew S. *Sudan, South Sudan, and Darfur: What Everyone Needs to Know.* New York: Oxford University Press, 2012.

Rachman, Gideon. "Democracy: The Case for Opportunistic Idealism." *Washington Quarterly* 32, 1 (January 2009), 119–128.

Rashid, Ahmed. *Descent into Chaos: The U.S. and the Disaster in Pakistan, Afghanistan, and Central Asia.* New York: Penguin Books, 2009.

Ricks, Thomas E. *Fiasco: The American Military Adventure in Iraq.* New York: Penguin Books, 2006.

Sachs, Jeffrey D. "The Development Challenge." *Foreign Affairs* 84, 2 (March/April 2005), 78–90.

Snow, Donald M. *Thinking About National Security: Strategy, Policy, and Issues.* New York: Routledge, 2016.

Tripp, Charles. *A History of Iraq.* 2nd ed. Cambridge, MA: Cambridge University Press, 2001.

Weiss, Thomas G. *Humanitarian Intervention.* Cambridge, MA: Polity Press, 2012.

On the Horizon

The United States seems to be at one of its frequent crossroads regarding its national security posture toward the world. As always, the proper stance, including a new or revised national security paradigm, is clouded by dealing with the uncertainties of the future, some of which can be anticipated and some of which cannot. Part V's two chapters attempt to deal with some of these problems.

Chapter 13 looks at some of the new problems that are present in the contemporary environment but whose future impact are not entirely foreseeable and will be affected by American actions and policies. The four areas examined are border security, natural resource security, environmental security, and cyber security. All are examples of policy areas that have not historically been thought of as national security concerns but that are becoming more important today. Chapter 14 tries to extrapolate from the present to likely future national security environments in which the United States may find itself. It looks at possible policies and their effects and even suggests the parameters within which to consider a new national security paradigm to confront future challenges and threats.

New Dimensions and Approaches to National Security: Borders, Energy and the Environment, and Cyber Security

The language of national security is filled with highly emotionally charged words and concepts that can be appropriated by others. Strategy's clearest meaning is military strategy, but many people and entities have strategies for various objectives. War used to be reserved for armed clashes, but now we make war on poverty, ignorance, and a host of other nonmilitary objects. The same extension now applies to security. It has been extended to a series of nonmilitary subjects that can in some way endanger us. This chapter explores four of these policy areas that extend ideas of security in distinctly different ways: border security, natural resources security, environmental security, and cyber security. The latter area combines very old, traditional national security actions with very new, traditionally nonmilitary methods.

The traditional environment in which national security policy is honed and in which threats to that security are mounted has not changed markedly in the last decade, although relative emphases on different aspects of security have changed since 2016. Two major trends are likely to become prominent as the United States confronts the security environment of the next five to ten years. The first, resulting directly from the Iraq and Afghanistan War experiences, will be tension about military activism manifested in a reluctance to commit large-scale American military assets except under the most unambiguous conditions of need (a war of necessity). Arguments that some situations merit deployments of necessity rather than choice will be subject to great scrutiny because of this.

The second trend is likely to be a broadening of the matters on the national security agenda to include more concerns that either lack or do not prominently feature a traditional military component. Economic security is an obvious example that will be woven into the discussion. What all these nontraditional forms of security have in common is that they affect the well-being and prosperity of Americans and what makes Americans *feel* safe (the heart of the psychological dimension of security).

There is no universal agreement about what a list of these concerns should or should not contain, and there will be disagreement about the inclusion or exclusion of different concerns depending on individual interests and assessments: no list will please everyone. With no claims to inclusiveness, the author has chosen four areas for illustrative purposes. They all share the common characteristics of making Americans safe or feel safe and of having both some conventional and some unconventional security aspects. They are presented in rough descending order of conventional (i.e., military) content.

The four areas are border security, natural resource security, environmental security, and cyber security. Problems associated with each—borders breached by undesirables, interruptions in the flow of oil, environmental catastrophes, or interruptions in telecommunications—pose a threat to Americans (and everyone else), but each is unique in the threat it poses and how its risk can be reduced or eliminated. Border security, which has been a virtual obsession of President Trump, seems the most obviously security-related issue, but it is more complex than simply sanitizing or sealing the borders. Americans would clearly feel and be threatened by an interruption in the supply of natural resources to the country, but it is not clear whether or how, in different situations, the instrumentalities of national security apply to securing those resources. Environmental catastrophes of various kinds could represent the ultimate threats to security, even existence, but they lack obvious immediacy. Cyberattacks, with special reference to Russian interference with US elections, can be aimed at a variety of both public and private targets and represent a hybrid national security problem: cyberspace applications of traditional problems and intentions.

BORDER SECURITY

In some important ways, the security of national borders is the oldest and most fundamental of all national security issues. Protecting and defending national, sovereign territory is, arguably, the most important and vital priority and task of government. National (or homeland) security is, at heart, about protecting the citizenry from hostile others who might breach those borders and do harm to the population. Preparing to repel armed, hostile hordes has not been a prominent part of the American experience, but border security remains a fundamental part of the charge to government; it can be and often is argued that a government that cannot protect its borders from hostile invasion can serve no other useful function.

The contemporary border security issue facing the United States became a major emotional issue during the 2016 presidential campaign in two ways. One was what to do about the flow of undocumented people across the Mexican border into the United States, the Trump response to which has been a proposed physical barrier running the length of the border. The other was the supposed negative impact illegal entrants have on the country, an issue that has led to controversial efforts to deport undocumented immigrants and to stanch the flow of others into the country. Both issues are highly complex and contentious. Framing the border security problem and determining its security content require examining border security from two vantage points. These are the physical extent and dimensions of American borders and the nature and locales of threats to those borders.

The Physical Problem

The territorial boundaries of the United States are among the most extensive, complex, and difficult to secure of any country in the world. They can be divided into land and sea borders, each of which poses different security priorities and problems. The land borders of the United States are shared with Canada and Mexico. The land border between Canada and the United States is slightly more than 5,500 miles long (the boundary between Canada and the contiguous forty-eight states is 3,987 miles and that between Canada and Alaska is 1,538 miles). The border between Mexico and the United States is 1,933 miles long. Thus, the land borders of the United States total 7,458 miles. Even this total length pales in comparison to that of Russia, the world's largest country, which is twice as big as the United States and has land borders with fourteen countries that are approximately two-thirds longer than those of the United States.

Clearly, maintaining the absolute and inviolable sanctity of borders this long is physically impossible and would, for the most part, seem a low priority. Which parts of which borders will be secured (i.e., made inviolate) is a matter of risk assessment and risk reduction: what are the threats posed by permeable borders at different locations? The 2016 presidential campaign emphasized the principle of sovereignty that suggests all borders should be secure, but what priorities should be attached to making which borders more or less impermeable? Some of the answers are relatively simple: there is little reason, for instance, to expend major resources securing most of the border between remote areas of Canada and Alaska because little threat is posed by allowing transit back and forth (which could probably not be prevented under any circumstances). Large urban crossings and the long border between the United States and Mexico may be different matters.

The sea borders of the United States are an even more daunting physical problem. Two measures are used to describe these dimensions: coastline and shoreline. The coastline refers generally to a line drawn along the intersection of the coast and the ocean, not allowing for bays, inlets, and other coastal features, whereas the shoreline measures the total topography of the coast, including the shores of bodies of water emptying into the oceans and seas. Using figures provided by the National Oceanic and Atmospheric Administration (US Department of Commerce), the coastline of the United States is 12,383 miles and the shoreline is 88,633 miles.

As with land borders, sealing access to American territory along the seas is a daunting task, probably beyond physical possibility. Once again, the problem is differential. Almost 42 percent (5,580 of the 12,383 miles) of coastline is between Alaska and the various bodies of water that touch it (the Pacific and Arctic oceans, the Bering and Beaufort seas), and 35 percent (31,383 of the 88,633 miles) of shoreline is Alaskan. Parts of the Alaskan coast were important during the Cold War, and the 1,350 miles of Florida's coastline and 8,426 miles of its shoreline have long been a source of concern regarding both drug (and other) smuggling and illegal immigration.

The solution to the border security problem is thus a good bit more complicated and difficult than a simple call to "seal the borders." Physically, it is probably impossible and certainly impracticable in terms of the resources necessary to attempt it. Sealing great parts of the border would accomplish little toward achieving justifiable national priorities: most of the Alaska-Canada border and the Canada-US border traversing much of the Great Plains and West is, for instance, essentially unguarded because there is no national perception that they need to be protected.

These physical dimensions create enormous difficulties in trying to secure the country's borders. Clearly, continuously patrolling every inch of either the land or the sea borders goes beyond the capabilities of the various agencies assigned border protection tasks. The US Coast Guard, for instance, is the agency given the primary task of protecting the coastline and shoreline, but it clearly lacks the number or quality of sea craft to prevent all intrusions. Preventing all of these would require a vast expansion of its capabilities (both sea- and land-based) that would go beyond any reasonable political expectations. To announce that the entire coastline and shoreline will be sealed amounts to declaring a "paper blockade" of the coast. Similarly, the Border Patrol, which has comparable responsibilities for the land borders, cannot possibly seal every inch of the borders between the United States and Canada and the United States and Mexico. In both cases, it may be possible to provide a blanket protection of certain *parts* of the border or against unwanted intruders, but the attempt to seal it comprehensively is feckless.

A couple of real examples may help clarify the magnitude of the problem of comprehensive border protection. According to Stephen Flynn, one of the country's leading experts in border and port security issues, in 2000, "489 million people, 127 million passenger vehicles, 11 million trucks, 2.2 million railroad cars, 829,000 planes, and 211,000 vessels passed through American border inspection systems." Given the limited resources available to border guards, it is physically impossible to inspect in any detail all these entrants, and it is thus impossible to ensure all undesirable people or things are excluded. In addition, the border from the western extremity of Lake Superior to Boundary Bay, Washington, is monitored only at major crossing points; anyone who wants to walk across the border from Saskatchewan to Montana or North Dakota where there are no roads can do so with a high likelihood of success. To make matters more complicated, Flynn adds that one-third of all the trucks (almost four million) entering the United States annually cross over one of four bridges from Canada into Michigan or New York State. If a real attempt to monitor the movement of goods across these bridges were attempted (as was briefly tried on the Ambassador Bridge between Detroit and Windsor, Ontario), the result would be massive gridlock. In one actual attempt to do so, several Chrysler automobile assembly plants in the United States that depended on parts from Canada had to be shut down until the inspections were rescinded and normalcy returned. The problem is easily as great regarding the movement of vessels into the country's ports, where only a small percentage of incoming freight is or can be inspected. Advanced technology is improving both these situations, but significant barriers to an inviolable border remain.

Present political advocacies notwithstanding, it is by no means obvious that essentially sealing the border from outside intrusion is desirable. A truly effective system of screening people and goods and services entering the country would, among other things, impede the flow of people, ideas, and goods across the border into the United States, a direct challenge to the dictates of globalization and free trade. In summer 2007, for instance, the Bush administration found itself in the incongruous position (although it did not admit the incongruity) of simultaneously promoting additional trade within the NAFTA (North American Free Trade Agreement) trade area (which meant an increased flow of goods across the country's borders with Canada and Mexico) and arguing for increased border security that would have the effect of slowing and impeding, rather than facilitating, the very trade it was promoting.

Border Threats

The question of border security must thus be made more specific, basically stating who and what it is important to exclude from American soil and where that effort should be concentrated. An auxiliary question is to what agencies of the government different responsibilities should be assigned. This latter question is more complicated than it would seem on the surface, as the 2018 separation of illegal immigrant families at the border and the bumbling attempts to reunite separated children from their parents revealed.

Because the United States is historically a country that has sometimes opened its borders to immigrants from around the world, the idea of impermeable barriers to entry (or exit) from the country has not always dominated this item on the national security agenda. At the same time, it has also been true that the United States has always tried to keep what it viewed as undesirable people and unwanted things out of the country. The content of what or who is acceptable and unacceptable has changed across time: during Prohibition, for instance, it was a national priority to exclude alcoholic beverages from the country; at different times, the same exclusiveness has been aimed at different nationalities seeking to immigrate to this country (the Irish during the 1840s potato famine, for instance).

The current concern over border security must be placed in this context. Who and what does the United States seek to exclude from its sovereign territory? And how important is it that this exclusion be successful? In the current context, border security has come to be associated with the 1,933-mile US-Mexico land border, and the political cry has been to seal that border from undesired and presumably undesirable intruders. Even narrowing the problem to that level (thereby excluding the Canadian-American land borders and the protection of the coastline and shoreline), the problem is daunting.

The major question is against what threat border security is aimed. As Terry Payan points out, there are three aspects to the US-Mexico border issue, and each poses a different kind of problem, a different priority, and a threat of differing national security content. These three aspects are illegal immigration, drug trafficking, and terrorist penetration. Although they overlap some of the time (illegal immigrants may, for instance, carry drugs into the country, or they may also be terrorists), they are also distinct problems.

Immigration   The illegal immigration issue became a political hot-button topic because of the flood of Mexican citizens entering the country since the middle 1990s and the institution of NAFTA. Although the flow has changed in the last decade and statistics are notoriously unreliable, the number of Mexican and Central American citizens living in the United States who did not enter the country through prescribed means of immigration rose from about one and a half to two million before NAFTA to twelve to fourteen million today, although recent trends of Mexican immigrants suggests the trend has reversed modestly.

What kind of problem does illegal immigration pose? That it violates the sanctity of the border is true, but as a concern in and of itself, that raises the question, so what? Do illegal immigrants pose a security threat beyond the fact that they have violated the sanctity of the border by entering the United States? Most of the arguments to staunch and reverse the flow are not made on traditional national security grounds (they pose no military threat, for instance), but on grounds such as perceptions that these immigrants place additional demands on social services, do not pay other than use taxes (e.g., sales tax), and deprive American citizens of jobs. The truth of all these assertions is disputed. Placing these problems under the heading of "security" may have the implicit (or intentional) effect of elevating its perceived importance in the pantheon of national priorities, but it is not clearly a part of the national security agenda at all.

The illegal immigrant "problem" has been the core of the Trump administration advocacy of building a physical barrier—the fence or wall—the length of the border. The issue is more complex than the rhetoric. It may be impossible to contain the entire 1,933 miles (see Amplification 13.1). It is also not clear that the immigration is not beneficial: the United States has a surplus of unfilled jobs, some of which can be and are filled by immigrants who, among other things, will perform tasks Americans are reluctant to undertake, the so-called 3-D (dirty, difficult, and dangerous) tasks (see Snow, *Regional Cases in U.S. Foreign Policy*).

Drugs The second aspect of the border security problem is drug trafficking. Once again, precise determinations about the physical extent of the problem are probably unreliable, but Michael Shifter maintains, "Mexico is the transit route for roughly 70 to 90 percent of the illegal drugs entering the United States. . . . Along the US-Mexico border, the kidnapping trade, clearly tied to the drug trade, is flourishing." Illicit drugs entering the United States have an impact on the criminal justice system designed to interrupt that commerce and to punish those who engage in it, so it is also a domestic political problem rather than an obvious national security problem. It does, however, have strong indirect security implications: the deleterious effect of drug usage on Americans, and thus American society, and the political devastation to other countries (especially but not limited to Mexico) created by the actions of drug traffickers.

The damaging effects of illicit drug usage on the United States have been sufficiently alarming that the Reagan administration declared it a national emergency during the 1980s (Nancy Reagan's "Just say no to drugs"), and George H.W. Bush upgraded the national effort to the "War on Drugs" during his term in office. The "war" analogy was always more symbolic than real, but it did include significant use of, for instance, military resources from the US Southern Command (whose military mission covers Latin America) for identifying and destroying sources of drugs and processing facilities in South America and from the US Air Force and Coast Guard for preventing transshipment of processed drugs through and over Central America and the Caribbean. The interruption of drugs flowing into the United States, principally but not exclusively from Latin America, remains a high priority of the federal government.

If an argument can be made that drugs weaken the United States and thus are a legitimate national security concern, what solutions are there for the scourge they represent? Broadly speaking, there are two answers: demand side and supply side. Demand-side solutions are aimed at reducing demand for drugs so the drug trade becomes progressively less lucrative and thus less appealing. Education is a prime example: teaching and convincing people that drugs are bad for them and should be avoided (the analogy with antismoking campaigns is often made). Supply-side efforts aim at reducing the availability of drugs for people. Such have focused on the Mexican border.

The movement of drugs through Mexico and across the border creates tremendous difficulties and strains in US-Mexican relations. Drug smuggling is a big and very lucrative business, and it is difficult to interrupt successfully. Peter Andreas, for instance, contends that "the amount of cocaine necessary to satisfy US customers for one year can be transported in just nine of the thousands of large tractor-trailers that cross the border every day." At the same time, drug smuggling becomes intertwined with illegal immigration as those seeking to enter the country illegally are recruited as "mules" by drug smugglers to bring contraband across the border. Moreover, the dual goals of immigrant and drug interdiction bring both the Drug Enforcement Agency and the Border Patrol to the border with differing and occasionally conflicting priorities, hampering enforcement.

Drugs entering the United States must first transit across Mexico, and the result has been to corrode and corrupt the Mexican political process. Michael Shifter lays out some of these problems. Governmental corruption is an endemic problem in Mexico, and "the astronomical revenues generated by the drug trade fuel the rampant corruption that eats away at already fragile institutions." Drug money that bribes officials to ignore, at a minimum, drug trafficking has infected the system from top to bottom. At the local level, "the police are thoroughly corrupt, unreliable, and ill-equipped to handle increasingly violent traffickers," and the taint has extended to the top levels of the military and central government. The great danger is a general destabilization of the entire Mexican political system; Mexico in the throes of revolution would clearly pose a national security threat to the United States.

Much of the alleged criminal suppression element of border security is in fact drug-related. Most undocumented immigrants have economic motives: seeking a better, more prosperous life for themselves and their families. The crime rate among this group is lower than the rate for the US citizenry. Most border-related crime comes from smuggling drugs into the country, where they are consumed by Americans. It is not clear how much a border fence contributes to alleviating the American appetite for drugs.

Terrorism   The third aspect of the problem is the penetration of the border by terrorists. This problem affects both the Mexican and Canadian borders. One can argue that, since it is more difficult to enter Canada from elsewhere than it is Mexico, the problem is more severe along the Mexican border. Conversely, it is easier for a potential terrorist to cross the Canadian border than the Mexican border into the United States if that person can successfully get into Canada in the first place.

This terrorist problem has the clearest national security content of any border issue. The difficulty is that border solutions to the terrorist entry problem are the most difficult to implement comprehensively. Current efforts by agencies like the Border Patrol and Immigration and Customs Enforcement (ICE) are necessarily concentrated at the points of greatest transit of goods and services—major crossing points on the borders and international airports and ports, for instance—and are inadequate to control or seal the entire border. If someone coming from Canada into the United States wants to avoid detection, that person can likely succeed by steering clear of the busy and well-controlled urban border crossings and instead walking across the border into North Dakota. Moreover, the proposed fence along the Mexican-US border traverses so long a distance of remote areas that it is hard to imagine it can be made impenetrable.

The border security issue is thus much more complicated and complex than it is often depicted in the general political debate. In the abstract, one can talk about the sanctity of the border as a general political value, but in an applied sense, the matter is by no means so simple. One must start with an observation similar to framing the terrorism problem: what is the goal? In the terrorism case, the goal can be either elimination or control/reduction of the problem, with elimination as the ideal and reduction as the practical and attainable goal. The same is true of border security. It may, in an abstract sense, be desirable to make American borders impermeable to all undesirable outside intrusions, but the land and sea borders are simply too extensive for that to be practical. If one could construct an absolutely impenetrable boundary, it would greatly reduce or eliminate the movement of unauthorized immigrants, illegal drugs, and terrorists across the frontier, but it is not clear that building such a border would be desirable, a possibility explored in Amplification 13.1.

AMPLIFICATION 13.1

An Impenetrable Border?

If it were possible, would sealing the border be desirable for the United States? Certainly it would solve the problems of border penetration. But it might cause other problems that would be as bad or worse.

First, it would be enormously expensive both to construct and to maintain. Roughly 700 miles of fencing existed when Trump assumed office. Extending it for the other 1,200 miles would be physically difficult due to topography and would require amending treaties with some Native American tribes whose tribal lands include the border over which they exercise sovereignty and the US government has no jurisdiction. Electronic means of surveillance or flyovers by drone aircraft reduce human observation needs, but such a system would require a large and expensive manpower commitment, and ironically the less manpower intensive the system might be to operate, the more expensive it would be to build.

Second, such a system would, as already suggested, interrupt the flow of goods and services coming into the United States. In the most direct sense, the movement toward more secure borders runs directly counter to the greater globalization built into the full implementation of NAFTA and other trade agreements, although this is less a concern for Donald Trump than it has been for past presidents.

Third, there is the symbolism of greater border security. The United States has a long tradition of encouraging migration to this country, and relatively easy access is a part of that tradition. Fortifying the border—turning the Mexican-US border into something resembling the Great Wall of China, for instance—has symbolic importance. Does the United States still adhere to the Statue of Liberty's invitation to "give me your tired, your poor, your huddled masses yearning to breathe free," or does it prefer to build a wall to keep the barbarians out? ■

NATURAL RESOURCE SECURITY

All countries depend on natural resources that do not exist in adequate supply within their own territory for their well-being and their national existence. As pointed out in Chapter 3, resource dependency has not been a historic American problem because of the natural physical endowment of North America. At least up to the end of World War II, the United States was essentially resource independent, but that has changed. First, adequate supplies of some resources at economical costs for extraction have been depleted, making foreign sourcing either necessary or economically preferable. Until recently, petroleum has been the primary example, although the progressive exploitation of shale oil and gas is alleviating that problem. Second, modern technology requires some resources that are not present in adequate supply or at all on or under American soil. Titanium, which is necessary for jet engines, is an example. Third, Americans demand some commodities that are not indigenous to the United States and that must be imported. Spices and year-round access to some fresh fruits and vegetables are examples.

Not all the resources in inadequate supply are equally vital and thus the subject of security concerns. Americans, for instance, might not like being deprived of cinnamon from Southeast Asia, but the country would not collapse if cinnamon became unavailable. On the other hand, there are resources that are going to be clearly scarce and strategically important for the United States and much of the rest of the world. Some of these scarcities will (and do) have a direct impact on the United States: petroleum is the obvious example.

Petroleum Energy Security

For the United States, the continuing availability of acceptably priced foreign petroleum will continue to be a national security concern, but it is already easing somewhat as the transition to shale-based petroleum occurs. The problem is not exclusively American; it is part of a larger global concern with energy security of which petroleum is the biggest consideration. It is a dramatic and poignant American security concern both because of the heavy dependence of the American transportation system on petroleum and because of the obvious connection between petroleum and other, more volatile aspects of national security policy, notably policy toward the Middle East. It becomes an emotional issue because it gets wrapped up in the overall debate over energy policy and thus the heated disagreement between energy producers and conservationists.

The American petroleum problem is one facet of the global dilemma over this form of energy. The origins of the problem go back to the end of World War II, when those rebuilding the ravages of the war made the decision to reorient the rebuilding economies of Europe and elsewhere around petroleum from the Middle East—primarily the Persian Gulf littoral. When this decision was made, there was a geographically limited level of demand, and the supplies were controlled by Western interests.

The Petroleum Problem   The global oil situation is easy to describe, if not to manipulate. In its simplest terms, global production is tight, meaning demand and supply are so close that even marginal change in either supply or demand can upset the balance. As Leonardo Maugeri points out, this has been the result of a twenty-year trend: "Between 1986 and 2005, the world's spare oil production (the amount produced beyond current demand) dropped from about 15 percent to between 2 and 3 percent of global demand." The trend is not linear: some claimants like the United States have reduced their demands and others have either increased their demands or have become active oil users.

This problem could get considerably worse in the future. One reason is increases in global demand. The chief sources of increased demand are China and India. According to Infoplease data, China currently produces a little over half the oil it consumes, meaning it must import nearly half its requirements. According to David Zwieg and Bi Jianhai, China "accounted for 31 percent of global growth in oil demand" in 2004, and that demand is increasing. The Chinese government has adopted a policy of greatly expanded automobile production for Chinese citizens, meaning the demand for petroleum will continue to expand. The Indian example is slightly less dramatic but nonetheless significant: India currently imports about 1.5 million barrels per day, and even though Indian production had reached about 3 million barrels per day by 2010, it will continue to be an importer as the country undergoes growing economic development and enters the world automobile market.

What constitutes a satisfactory situation for the United States in these circumstances? There are two possible goals, with differing political appeal and feasibility. One is *petroleum substitutes and independence*, where the United States produces all the energy it requires and is thus independent of foreign sources of supply, a solution that may become possible due to the changeover to shale oil and gas. As long as energy prices remain high enough to make shale extraction economical, the switch to shale will continue, and one of its effects will be to move the United States toward overall energy self-sufficiency, even surplus. The United States will still import some oil, but the costs will be compensated for by the sale of American natural gas from shale sources. Such a solution would be highly politically desirable, and it could have a major effect on American policy in the Middle East, for instance. Shale production raises the prospects of independence from the Middle East oil producers like Saudi Arabia, thereby opening the prospect for less dependence on that country. A strategy of independence, however, is only possible if petroleum prices remain high enough that shale extraction is competitive with other sources. National security dictates and high oil prices are thus related, creating a dilemma discussed in the *Challenge!* box.

The alternative is *energy (petroleum) security*: the reasonable guarantee of access to adequate amounts of energy at reasonable, acceptable costs. The definition contains three variable elements: access, adequacy of supply, and cost. All three elements can change and be manipulated to affect the suitability of the supply availability. Most critical is the guarantee of access, which is, of course, not a problem in a situation of energy independence. Until circumstances of supply and demand change radically enough to make it possible to think about independence, the less satisfactory but more troublesome alternative of energy security appears the only realistic goal.

The Trump administration has added an additional strategy, *relaxation of environmentally dictated restrictions* on domestic oil reserves such as those in Alaska or off the Atlantic shoreline that have been closed to exploitation due to fears of environmental degradation. Actions taken to relax or rescind restrictions can increase domestic supplies but with an arguable environmental impact that could harm the ecosystem.

CHALLENGE!

National Security and the Price of Gas

One of the direct results of moving toward energy independence through a conscious shift to North American sources of petroleum would be to institutionalize and guarantee in the long run the perpetuation of reasonably high gasoline prices to American drivers because the cost of extraction and processing of those sources is rigidly high. The benefit of petroleum independence thus comes with a direct and unavoidable cost to American drivers. The benefit, of course, is to free the country of its dependence on petroleum from the geopolitically volatile Middle East, up to and including the possibility of substantial disengagement from the region's instability and violence. The dip in gas prices in 2015 may make this seem like a false dilemma, but the reason for cheap gas coming from foreign sources was to undercut shale production. Cheap gas is thus probably a temporary phenomenon.

Americans can respond in one or a combination of up to three ways to a return to expensive gas. One way is simply to accept the consequences and make the best of their personal economic choices. The other two reflect effectively enforced conservation: driving less to reduce fuel costs or driving smaller, more fuel-efficient vehicles. All have costs: absorbing costs reduces available resources for other priorities, driving less reduces mobility, and greater fuel efficiency means more cramped, arguably uncomfortable transportation.

Do the costs justify the benefits? The most obvious benefit would be to allow the United States to approach the Middle East in an arguably more objective, disinterested way than is possible under conditions of petroleum addiction, and this could mean, for instance, not becoming so involved in regional conflicts. The cost, of course, is in personal lifestyle. Is the price too high? What do you think? ■

Operationally, solutions to the petroleum energy security problem are changing. Historically, the question has been how the country guarantees the continuing flow of economical petroleum in adequate supply. This is a supply-side problem. This approach has been the easiest to couch in traditional security terms because it falls within the geopolitical paradigm of threats to security for which military solutions are applicable. Thus, one way to solve the problem of reasonable access to Middle East petroleum has been to have a military presence in the region that can assure physically that the oil continues to flow. That paradigm has arguably dominated since President Jimmy Carter issued the so-called Carter Doctrine as part of his 1980 State of the Union address, declaring continuing access to Persian Gulf oil a vital American interest. American leadership in the Persian Gulf War effort to expel Iraq from Kuwait, the continued presence of American military forces in the region after 1991, and the Iraq War can all be thought of as actions consistent with that approach.

The Shale Solution   There is a second possible solution to the problem: shale technology. As petroleum from shale increases and American dependence on Middle Eastern energy sources declines, the effect may be to make places like the Persian Gulf less important in a traditional national security way. Although exploitable shale formations are found widely around the world (especially in China), extraction technology is far more advanced in North America (the United States and Canada) than elsewhere.

The costs associated with petroleum energy, especially from the Middle East, have changed the traditional calculation of dependence. When the price of petroleum was much lower than it has become, remaining North American reserves were uncompetitive and uneconomical to exploit: foreign oil was cheaper. While there was (and is) a large pool of petroleum in the United States and Canada, it is expensive either to access (oil in the Oklahoma and Texas oil fields, for example) or to process (Canadian tar sand oil, for instance). The same is true of shale oil and gas. Eventually, the world's other shale-rich countries will learn how to exploit their holdings, and American advantage will be reduced. That change could take decades, during which the United States will be a world energy leader.

The second way to look at the shale issue is as part of a broader energy policy, an orientation that brings elements of both supply and demand into the equation. Framing the question in the broader context of energy policy widens the concern and moves it beyond the more conventional bounds of national security consideration because, unlike petroleum, alternative sources of energy are neither controlled overseas (solar or wind energy, for instance) nor subject to determination on national security grounds (whether the country invests in additional nuclear plants to produce electricity, for instance, is not at heart a national security issue). Much of the thrust of moving toward alternate energy sources reflects this position.

Subsuming the petroleum security question as part of energy policy opens additional strategic alternatives from both the supply and demand sides of the energy equation. From the supply side, overall energy policy can view alternatives to imported petroleum as solutions to needs currently serviced by imported oil. These can include alternate sources of petroleum, such as recovering hard-to-access petroleum in historical American oil fields, opening new domestic sources (the Alaskan wildlife reserves, for instance), tapping alternate sources of petroleum-based energy (Western oil shale or Canadian tar pits, for example), developing entirely different sources of fuel (corn-based ethanol), or moving to new energy sources (wind or geo-thermal). There are arguments, based largely in resource adequacy or cost, against each of these alternatives, but they are at least potential ways to reduce foreign petroleum dependency. A supply-side approach also looks at alternative sources of energy, from wind power to thermal energy to "clean" coal to nuclear power, as strategic options. All are aimed at reducing dependency on foreign oil and the baggage such dependency carries; all of them are also nontraditional approaches to a national security problem.

This whole area evokes strong emotions when the question is expanded beyond petroleum to encompass broader energy policy, especially when continued petroleum dependency is viewed as a *cause* of national security problems. Chapter 11 introduced the possibilities. What would American policy in the Middle East look like if the United States did not need *any* oil from the Persian Gulf? From that perspective, it can be argued that an obvious way to get the United States out of harm's way as a visible presence in that volatile region would be to reduce, and preferably eliminate, that dependence since it would remove the primary reason for a military role in regional politics.

ENVIRONMENTAL SECURITY

Determining what aspects of the physical environment contribute to security is more abstract than either border or natural resource security and is thus more difficult to conceptualize within the normal structure of national security thinking. The threat is more indirect: environmental catastrophes that could endanger people are either far into the future (projections about global warming, for instance) or the result of natural phenomena, such as hurricanes or tornadoes, over which there is little control or matters of disagreement. Environmental dangers lack immediacy, controllability, and consensus. Environmentalists argue many environmental threats are the result of human actions that create future hazards or make them worse, but these are not clearly purposive malevolent acts that can be identified and somehow stifled or reversed.

Yet the term *environmental security* has entered the lexicon of applications of the term *security*, and the question is whether the designation is legitimate or whether it is more akin to the overextension and overuse of the term *war* to describe efforts aimed at phenomena as diverse as poverty, drugs, and terrorism. Environmental security is simply not a subject covered in most traditional treatments of national security, so why add environmental security to the present endeavor?

Beyond the attempt to broaden horizons about what constitutes security, two reasons can be suggested. The first is that environmental factors, including those that may have consequences in the nebulous future, do indeed have direct implications for the safety and well-being of people. If the consequences of global warming are anything like those predicted by environmental scientists, they will have a major impact on the commodiousness and conditions of life for future generations. The second is that some of these impacts are already present, and although it has not been customary to think about them in national security terms, it might be helpful to do so. The prototypical example in this regard was the impact of Hurricane Katrina in 2005. Hurricanes Irma and Maria ravaging the Caribbean and Puerto Rico in 2017 are another.

Global Warming

Few issues in the contemporary political scene evoke as much emotion and disagreement as global warming. The emotions tend to center around the severe environmental consequences of unchecked carbon dioxide release (the source of most global warming along with several other gases like methane).

If the trends projected by most of the scientific community about global warming prove to be true, the results could be cataclysmic across a range of environmental concerns. Disagreement exists about the accuracy of these projected dynamics. Most scientists who have studied the problem of global warming concur generally in issuing strong, even dire, warnings about the failure to curb the practices leading to global warming, but a politically well-connected minority of scientists and others question the scientific basis of these dire projections and the policy implications that follow from those predictions. The disagreements are difficult to refute because almost all the phenomena in question and all the predictions are in the future and thus not subject to current scientific observation and validation.

To make matters more politically difficult, proposed remedies for global warming center on potentially vast reductions in carbon dioxide emissions. The vast majority of carbon dioxide excess (that amount above the ability of the environment to absorb and dissipate naturally) comes from the burning of fossil fuels that provide most of the energy used for transportation and industry in the world. Thus, conservation efforts intended to reduce carbon dioxide emissions target practices that are at the heart of the productivity, prosperity, and security of societies. Specifically, countries like the United States, China, and India, among the world's most populous states, have also been the greatest polluters.

Is global warming, as the leading emblem of worldwide environmental concerns, a legitimate national security issue that should be considered along with other, more conventional, national security matters? With no claim to inclusiveness or exhaustiveness, three perspectives can be examined to help formulate the answer.

The first way to think about the question is in terms of *threat*, the normal framework within which national security problems are considered. Does global warming threaten Americans (or citizens of the world in general)? That question is complicated because it is too simply put. Part of the answer is a matter of timing: global warming may pose some disquieting and inconveniencing short-term consequences (hotter summers, prolonged drought or rain-producing seasons, more violent weather generally), but it does not pose direct threats that people associate with national security. After unsettled weather that results in tornadoes ripping through the countryside, victims do not say, "If we had burned less gasoline in our cars, this tornado would not have happened." The longer-range consequence—the permanent flooding of low-lying coastal areas that will make them uninhabitable—certainly affects the security of people who either live or want to live in those areas, but this consequence has not been experienced and lies in the future. Thought of in threat terms, global warming is a *potential* rather than an immediate threat.

Second, the security *consequences* of global warming are more difficult to specify, making it harder to know who to punish or how to punish them. It is very hard to specify how individuals will suffer specifically from global warming and, more important, to *personalize* the causes and nature of that future suffering to motivate current actions by people. Consider an example: what if one could demonstrate that reducing the weight of automobiles by a certain number of hundreds of pounds would result in fuel savings (and lower carbon dioxide emissions) that would mean ocean levels would rise a concomitant number of feet less than they would without that reduction in automobile weight? If the result would predictably avoid inundating a specific amount of coastline within the lifetime of residents, the plea to act might be quite effective. That level of specificity cannot be demonstrated; thus the question of consequences is more abstract and less actionable.

Finally, at the level of identifying *solutions* to global warming, the issue becomes both more contentious and more directly security oriented. All solutions to global warming hinge on reduced carbon dioxide emissions. In general, such reductions require less burning of fossil fuels (principally petroleum) and the most carbon dioxide–emitting fuels, such as coal. Proposals for such reductions activate opposition on traditional national security grounds: reduced energy production and its impact on economic productivity and the enormous dependency of modern military forces on petroleum for operational purposes, for instance. The impact is to transform the argument into an either/or proposition: one can support traditional security *or* remedies to global warming, but since their consequences are incompatible (at least in the short run), one cannot support both.

The question remains: Is global warming a national security problem? Alternatively, is it a national problem that can usefully be considered within the framework of national security? The answer is unclear. On one hand, categorizing global warming in security terms elevates its visibility and the extent to which it is taken seriously within the political process: the designation of national security, for better or worse, endows an issue with greater gravity than it possesses without it. Since those who are most interested in the global warming issue tend not to be participants in the traditional national security process, categorizing global warming as a national security issue may broaden its audience. On the other hand, including global warming on the broader national security agenda can result in diluting its consideration (global warming as one of many problems) or in the presentation of contrary arguments not directly relevant to the issue (global warming is important, but other concerns like economic disadvantages are more important). All these problems and others have hampered international efforts to control pollution.

Hurricanes Katrina and Irma/Maria

Where does one place natural disasters within the priorities of national security? Clearly, natural disasters affect the safety and lives of people subject to them and are thus important national concerns, but they are rarely conceptualized in national security terms. Formal federal jurisdiction over such incidents resides with the Federal Emergency Management Agency (FEMA), a part of the Department of Homeland Security (DHS), thus implicitly according it national security status. The federal response to Hurricanes Katrina and Rita, and more recently Irma and Maria, raised serious concern about the actual priority assigned to this function.

The response (or lack thereof) to Hurricane Katrina by the federal government became something of a symbol for those critical of federal priorities. In terms of human devastation, for instance, official statistics indicate that as of August 2006, 1,464 people had lost their lives due to the impact of Katrina on New Orleans and the Gulf Coast (in parts of Louisiana and Mississippi and, to a lesser extent, Alabama), nearly half the number of people who lost their lives in the September 11 attacks. Much rhetoric surrounded federal efforts to respond to the human and physical suffering that centered on New Orleans, but even years later, parts of the city (notably the Ninth Ward) remained uninhabited and uninhabitable, and the same was true all along the affected Gulf Coast. The same criticisms have been made about federal responses in Puerto Rico since Maria in 2017, from which almost three thousand people died.

Should responses to natural disasters be part of the national security equation? If so, where should they be placed in the hierarchy of national security concerns? Is, for instance, planning for and funding programs against the possibility of a major earthquake in southern California as important as continuing funding for the military effort in Iraq or for a missile defense system in Europe or elsewhere? Or are these areas of concern so unrelated that they cannot and should not fall under the same umbrella of consideration?

Since the federal government elevated environmental disaster response to a national security concern by placing FEMA under the DHS, it is difficult for the government to argue disaster relief is *not* part of national security. The states concur in this judgment by placing National Guard contingents among the prominent first responders to national disasters within their jurisdictions.

Would the response to Hurricane Katrina have been different if it had been considered a threat to national security rather than a response to a horrific but naturally caused disaster? It is difficult to assign human blame for the occurrence of Katrina: no identifiable human enemy caused Katrina or made its effects worse or better for those forced to suffer them.

Where should priorities lie in the future? If the global warming theorists are substantially correct in their projections, one major impact of continued neglect will be an intensification of weather patterns, including the severity of storms and their impact: Hurricane Katrina and the 2017 storms may be the harbinger of things to come. At the same time, seismologists and other geologists maintain that a major shift in the earth's crust is inevitable in southern California in the upcoming years. Depending on exactly where the resulting earthquake is centered and directed (at the Los Angeles basin or southward toward Mexico), the resulting devastation could make Hurricane Katrina or September 11 pale in terms of human and property losses. Is that a matter of high national priority as important as threats in the Middle East or elsewhere? Should these possibilities be thought of separately or together? What national priorities should attach to each prospect, and should they compete for national security resources? The answers are not simple, straightforward, or necessarily obvious.

CYBER SECURITY

Cyber security has become the national security talisman of the computer age, and as such, it creates a gulf between traditional national security operators and the denizens of the electronic technology sector. Neither group truly understands the other: military analysts are often not computer experts, and electronically inclined people generally are not overly interested in national security problems. Cyber security, however, necessitates a bridge between the two groups: applying (or thwarting) electronic approaches to traditional national security problems. In 2010, the US Army established a command to bridge the gap in the form of USCYBERCOM, and the other military services (notably the Air Force) have also developed cyber capabilities. Cyber security has become an important, if eccentric, part of the national security universe.

The idea of cyber security, and especially cyber "war," relates to any assault on information technology. The figurative "battlefield" of this conflict concerns stealing secret information with traditional national security applications and using surreptitious access to operating systems that can destroy the effectiveness of traditional weapons. The activities often included under the cyber label are not new. Stealing secrets has been the purpose of spying since antiquity, disrupting enemy military capabilities is an age-old purpose of espionage, and destroying the capability to sustain traditional warfare is venerable. What *is* unique about cyber security is its intimate relationship to computers and electronic technology. Historical national security practices do not encompass and its operators do not understand the new environment. Cyber war is not war as traditional practitioners understand that term, and the practitioners of cyber security and those who assault that security—the cyber warriors—are a new breed who are not familiar with or interested in traditional military concerns.

What do people mean when they refer to cyber security? Basically, the subject encompasses information technology and focuses on protecting computers, networks, programs, and data from unauthorized access, change, or destruction. Those who create the cyber security problem include individual hackers, industrial cyber warriors, national governments, and subnational groups. The weapons they employ include breaking into databases, introducing viruses into computers, and interrupting the flow of information and the cyberspace through which it flows. Wikipedia condenses the definition of cyber activities to "actions by a government to penetrate another's computers or networks for the purpose of damage or disruption." Terrorism expert Richard A. Clarke adds a parallel definition: "hostile attempts by one nation to penetrate another's computers or networks."

These definitions share an emphasis on the international character of cyber security and cyber war. Attacks on or penetration of computers may be conducted by groups and individuals for a variety of purposes. Subnational groups include entities like terrorist groups or private groups attempting to steal corporate proprietary secrets to exploit in a militarily useful way, like IS using the Internet to recruit foreign fighters. Is the electronic manifestation not a form of cyber warfare? Likewise, governments such as China and individuals use the Internet to steal secrets or to break into others' networks for nefarious purposes.

Cyber security is, at heart, the current version of how very old problems are addressed. It is the direct consequence of new ways in which information is created, stored, and transmitted and in which information and operations of critical systems work. The innovations that cyber security seeks to protect are the direct result of computer-driven advances in each of these areas. Cyber "war" involves attempts by hostile forces to interrupt these processes to their advantage.

These objects of concern fall into two basic and thoroughly familiar categories. The ability to interfere with how others transmit and receive information and in effect to "steal" that information is, very simply, the heart of traditional espionage. Through most of human history, this information—intelligence to those who try to obtain it—has been the province of human intelligence (or HUMINT in the language of US intelligence). The collection of information has been carried by human agents, or spies. These spies now sit at computer consoles seeking ways to take advantage of weaknesses in the protection that their opponents devise to keep secret information inviolate. The cyber warrior seeks to breach the electronic walls intended to protect information in ways not dissimilar to how historical warriors scaled castle walls or breached enemy positions. The cyber warrior tries to protect against such breaches occurring, to repair the damage from past breaches, and to erect effective barriers to future electronic assaults.

These dynamics provide the battleground of cyber warfare, and protecting that information is the form of "combat" in which the cyber warrior mostly engages. The battlefields on which this warfare is conducted include intellectual locales such as information security, physical operations security, and telecommunications and network security.

Stealing information is not the only invidious aspect of cyber competition. In some ways, it is not even the most interesting part of cyber security in traditional national security terms. The other traditional activity where cyber elements have a primary role is subversion, the use of cyber attacks to disrupt or destroy the vital electronic or electronically controlled assets of an opponent. In common scenarios, cyber attacks could be used to disable communications networks (thereby rendering the opponent electronically "deaf") by disrupting power supplies to cities (in extreme form, disrupting the computer instructions to nuclear power plants) or scrambling communications capabilities in times of combat (taking out military satellites is an example).

The ongoing competition between cyber warriors is akin to a running battle between traditional armies moving across terrain to gain decisive battlefield advantage. One primary tool of the cyber warrior that illustrates this competition is through encryption of information—arranging messages in codes that can only be understood ("decrypted") by those for whom they are intended but not by opponents. There is also nothing new about this. During World War II, for instance, US forces in the Pacific used Navajo "code talkers" to communicate between military units, a method of encryption the Japanese could not break because they had nobody who spoke the Navajo language. The same principle is involved in breaking the encryption of opponents. During World War II, the Allies also developed a way to decrypt Axis communications that had been generated using the Enigma system, which the enemy never realized had been broken, to its great disadvantage. In the cyber world, encryption and decryption are generally done by dueling computers.

Interest in cyber security is keen in both the private and public sectors. A good bit of the competitive advantage nurtured by private enterprises is based in the development, application, and protection of information they solely possess in the form of proprietary right, which others seek to obtain by whatever means they can, including industrial espionage. Most of that effort is now a matter of cyber penetration of the electronic systems of competitors. Cyber protection is directed at other firms, and these same attempts to protect proprietary properties must also be directed at foreign governments or individuals in foreign countries also interested in systems penetration and theft or disruption of the information for espionage or even subversion. An entire branch of the cyber effort is devoted to solving this problem. Like counter-cyber efforts conducted by the national security apparatuses of government, the problem is an elusive, ever-changing problem as electronic capabilities are developed and evolve, complicating both the cyber and counter-cyber problems of all those involved in the process.

In perspective, cyber warfare and protection from it basically represent a new medium or forum in which to conduct very traditional national security (and other) functions. The goals of cyber attacks are traditional, and the underlying missions of the cyber warrior are nothing new: spies and encryption codes have been around for a very long time, and applying electronic means is today's way of carrying out these traditional functions. Amplification 13.2 looks at the most publicized cyber attack in the contemporary environment: Russian cyber activities to disrupt the 2016 American presidential election campaign.

AMPLIFICATION 13.2

The 2016 Russian Election Cyber Attacks

The use of cyberspace to manipulate international politics and national security affairs burst into the national spotlight when it was revealed that Russian "hackers" had penetrated the cyberspace in which the American electoral process

(*continued*)

took place. The details and proof of this activity remain largely classified and under both political and legal scrutiny that will occupy investigators for some time and will ensure that full public disclosure of what went on is somewhere in the future, but the American intelligence, including cyber, community is certain the Russians took cyber-based actions in the electoral campaign.

Two major forms of cyber intrusion have become public. One was the actions of Russian hackers, who broke into confidential records of the Democratic National Committee and presidential candidate Hillary Clinton and then selectively leaked that information. The other was apparent tinkering with electoral vote recording equipment, although there is no public record that whatever penetration occurred was used to affect voting outcomes. The exact reasons this activity was undertaken have not been revealed. It is generally agreed that Russian president Vladimir Putin, who allegedly authorized the campaign (which he denies), disliked Clinton and hoped the campaign would help ensure she lost. Whether the Russians acted specifically to promote her defeat is not known and is fiercely denied by the Trump administration.

The campaign is upsetting in national security terms. Countries, including the United States, have long interfered in one another's politics and nefariously intervened in electoral politics (see Kinzer), but the interruption of information and computing systems represents a new and difficult addition to the conduct of such activities. Efforts have been undertaken both diplomatically and through counter-cyber actions to prevent a repeat—and especially a sophistication—of these activities, which are presumably becoming more advanced and difficult both to detect and to counter. Russian attempts to engage in cyberwar in the 2018 off-year elections and the 2020 presidential election have been suspected virtually since the discovery of the 2016 actions.

This raises the additional national security dangers for the future and what to do about them. This problem exists at the individual level in terms of the security of electronic activity, but it also exists at the national security level. Most modern warfare capability has at least a cyber component, and often very important weapons systems like those that utilize electronic targeting and guidance to targets could easily be affected. There is a growing level of anxiety within the military community of a new arms race in the field, and even the possibility that a spiraling of cyber capability could underpin the basis for cyber warfare. Nobody knows exactly what such a trend could mean, and nobody really wants to find out. Russian intrusion in the 2016 election may only be the tip of the iceberg of the cyber future, and what lies beneath the surface holds some very concerning possibilities. ■

From a traditional national security perspective, cyber warfare, and protecting against it, represents a new medium within which to conduct very traditional national security functions in a new and potentially more difficult manner. Because it is wrapped in the encompassing and novel language and framework of electronic systems, it largely eschews the traditional language and concepts of national security formulations, even if its purposes and effects closely resemble more venerable ends and means. Espionage is about, among other things, stealing state (and other) secrets, regardless of whether the thieves are human spies or computers. What is unique about the cyber security framework is that it attempts to do things "warriors" have been doing for millennia in ways that are different in form and approach. The purpose of the traditional and the cyber warrior are the same: to provide advantage to the possessor and to deny advantage to an opponent. The weapon of choice of the two kinds of warriors may differ, but their intent does not. The generally unasked question is what will replace the cyber warrior some day in the future.

CONCLUSION: EXPANDED SECURITY HORIZONS

American national security policy has historically focused on the prevention and prosecution of major military threats to the United States. Seven decades ago, the country led the way in ending the largest war in human history, and that effort soon shifted to the prevention of a potential nuclear world war with the Soviet Union. National security policy was militarized and conducted on a grand, deadly stage.

The "lethal landscapes" introduced in Chapter 11 have changed. The danger of deadly encounters certainly remains in the confrontation with international terrorism, and occasionally the country will be drawn into developing world internal conflicts (DWICs) and other forms of violence and instability. The use of force remains a major part, but not the entirety, of what makes us safe or feel safe from harm.

The new agenda of national security is different. It does not replace traditional sources of national security concern, but it augments them. The new security "battlefields" are debates about how to "secure" the border between Mexico and the United States, whether to build the Keystone XL Pipeline to ship Canadian tar sand to southern American refineries for conversion into petroleum products, how to change the power grid to reduce carbon dioxide emissions into the atmosphere, or how to build better firewalls to keep hostile hackers from penetrating or disrupting electronic information systems.

All these are legitimate national concerns, and all contribute to the sense of safety (or lack thereof) that Americans experience in the contemporary world. Currently, there is a tension between the considerations of traditional and nontraditional elements of security. Part of the problem is that the two sources of security are very intellectually different. Great skill in dealing with military threats does not necessarily translate into concomitant expertise in dealing with environmental disasters like Katrina, where inadequate resources were devoted to disaster mitigation—a deficiency reprised in 2017 (Irma/Maria). At some points, traditional and nontraditional concerns do overlap: the problems of industrial and military espionage and subversion are not conceptually very different, and other problems like securing the country's borders combine military and nonmilitary approaches. The new and more traditional elements of security are different but not entirely discrete.

A second source of tension arises from the orientations and agendas of different groups and whether their supporters are more focused on traditional or nontraditional security. Traditional operators, policymakers, and experts inside and outside government have a deep and sometimes vested interest in maintaining the national security focus on "hard" concerns related to military force. Many of those who view "softer" concerns like the environment as legitimate decry the focus of the "hard men (and women)" in the traditional security realm. All too often, the two groups hold one another in some disregard, making the accommodation of security concerns with different content under one intellectual tent more difficult than it might otherwise be.

The third source arises from the competition for funding of the two different sets of concerns. There are points of coincidence: budgetary allocations for cyber security can be applied to both military and nonmilitary concerns. Areas like border, resource, environmental, and cyber security are additional items on the national security agenda that will require the devotion of additional energies and make demands on resources that might otherwise be allocated to more traditional national security areas. National security already has to compete for resources in a more budget-restrained environment where there is less funding for all public policy concerns, and thus a more furtive competition will ensue for those resources that do exist.

Will the nontraditional kinds of issues described here become a permanent part of the national security agenda? There is reason to believe both that they will and that they will not. Certainly, the kinds of problems discussed are likely to be enduring: global warming, natural disasters, petroleum dependency, control of the country's borders, and computer security are long-term problems that will not disappear in the short or middle term, and emphasizing them is a way to move the spotlight away from the military realm of national security. At the same time, there will be resistance to thinking about these issues in national security terms. To some, these nontraditional issues are indeed "soft" in a geopolitical sense, important in their own right but not on a par with the military threats to national existence. In their view, elevating environmental security, as an example, to national security status thus diverts attention from what is truly important.

A reorientation of national security emphases means adding concerns to the mix but not abandoning more traditional concerns, all within the bounds of fiscal austerity and hyper-partisan politics wherein any proposals for change will be subjected to very loud, wilting criticism that will be a damper on innovation. The inclusion of expanded horizons of what constitutes security is the final ingredient to the emerging casserole of concerns with which policymakers must cope in the upcoming years.

STUDY/DISCUSSION QUESTIONS

1. Why does the text maintain that nontraditional security concerns could become more prominent in the next five to ten years? Do you agree?
2. Define the border security problem in historical perspective. Why has maintaining a secure border been simultaneously so difficult and of such low priority historically for the United States?
3. Define the various aspects of the country's current border security problem. Briefly describe each aspect and the extent to which it is or is not a national security problem. Is an impenetrable border a feasible or desirable goal (or both, or neither)?
4. Why is resource dependency a national security problem? Using petroleum as an example, define what problem that dependency creates for the United States, what the consequences of that dependency are, and what can be done about the problem.
5. What are the major prospects for and consequences of an effort to achieve energy independence? Elaborate.
6. Define *environmental security*. Is it legitimate and/or helpful to think of environmental concerns like global warming and natural disasters like Hurricane Katrina in national security terms? Why or why not?
7. What is cyber security? What are its various aspects? Are its purposes novel or traditional? What about its means? How does it fit into national security concerns? How does Russian interference in the 2016 US election fit into this phenomenon?

SELECTED BIBLIOGRAPHY

Alden, Edward. *The Closing of the American Border*. New York: Harper Collins, 2009.

Andreas, Peter. *Border Games: Policing the U.S.–Mexico Divide*. Ithaca, NY: Cornell University Press, 2009.

Berjas, George J. *Heaven's Door: Immigration Policy and the American Economy*. Princeton, NJ: Princeton University Press, 2016.

Blau, Judith. *The Paris Agreement: Climate Change, Solidarity, and Human Rights*. London: Palgrave Macmillan, 2017.

Bonner, Robert C. "The New Cocaine Cowboys: How to Defeat Mexico's Drug Cartels." *Foreign Affairs* 89, 4 (July/August 2010), 35–47.

Browne, John. "Beyond Kyoto." *Foreign Affairs* 83, 4 (July/August 2004), 20–32.

Clarke, Richard A., and Robert Knake. *Cyber War: The Next Threat to National Security and What to Do About It*. New York: ECCO, 2011.

Deest, Brian. "Paris Isn't Burning: Why the Climate Agreement Will Survive Trump." *Foreign Affairs* 96, 4 (July/August 2017), 83–92.

Diehl, Paul R., and Niles Peter Gleditsch (eds.). *Environmental Conflict*. Boulder, CO: Westview Press, 2001.

Economy, Elizabeth C. "The Great Leap Backward." *Foreign Affairs* 86, 5 (September/October 2007), 38–59.

Flynn, Stephen E. *The Edge of Disaster: Rebuilding a Resilient Nation*. New York: Random House, 2007.

Futter, Andrew. *Hacking the Bomb: Cyber Threats and Nuclear Weapons*. Washington, DC: Georgetown University Press, 2018.

Gonzalez, Francisco. "Drug Violence Isn't Mexico's Only Problem." *Current History* 110, 733 (February 2011), 68–74.

Haas, Peter, Robert O. Keohane, and Marc A. Levy (eds.). *Institutions for the Earth: Sources of Effective International Environmental Protection*. Cambridge, MA: MIT Press, 2000.

Hennessey, Susan. "Deterring Cyberattacks: How to Reduce Vulnerability." *Foreign Affairs* 96, 6 (November/December 2017), 39–46.

Isikoff, Michael, and David Korn. *Russian Roulette: The Inside Story of Putin's War on America and the Election of Donald Trump*. New York: Twelve Books, 2018.

Jarmon, Jack A., and Pano Yannakogerorgos. *The Cyber Threat and Globalization: The Impact on U.S. National and International Security*. Lanham, MD: Rowman & Littlefield, 2018.

Kaplan, Fred. *Dark Territory: The Secret History of Cyber War*. New York: Simon and Schuster, 2016.

Kinzer, Stephen. *The Brothers: John Foster Dulles, Allan Dulles, and Their Secret World War*. New York: Times Books, 2013.

Klare, Michael. "Navigating the Energy Transition." *Current History* 108, 714 (January 2009), 26–32.

Klein, Daniel, and Maria Pia Carazo. *The Paris Agreement: Analysis and Commentary*. Oxford, UK: Oxford University Press, 2017.

Klimburg, Alexander. *The Darkening Web: The War for Cyberspace*. New York: Penguin Books, 2017.

Kramer, Franklin, Stuart H. Starr, and Larry Wentz (eds.). *Cyberpower and National Security*. Washington, DC: Potomac Books, 2009.

Krauze, Enrique. "Furthering Democracy in Mexico." *Foreign Affairs* 85, 1 (January/February 2006), 54–65.

Krupp, Fred. "Trump and the Environment: What His Plans Would Do." *Foreign Affairs* 96, 4 (July/August 2017), 73–82.

Lizza, Ryan. "As the World Burns: How the Senate and the White House Missed the Best Chance to Deal with Climate Change." *The New Yorker* (online), (October 11, 2010).

Nevin, Joseph. *Gatekeepers and Beyond: The War on "Illegals" and the U.S.–Mexico Boundary*. 2nd ed. New York: Routledge, 2010.

Nez, Chester, and Judith Schleiss Avila. *Code Talkers: The First and Only Memoir by One of the Original Navajo Code Talkers of WW II*. New York: Penguin Books, 2011.

O'Neil, Shannon. "The Real War in Mexico." *Foreign Affairs* 88, 4 (July/August 2009), 66–77.

Payan, Terry. *The Three U.S.–Mexico Border Wars: Drugs, Immigration, and Homeland Security*. Westport, CT: Greenwood, 2006.

Pirages, Dennis C., and Theresa Manley DeGeest. *Ecological Security: An Evolutionary Perspective on Globalization*. New York: Rowman & Littlefield, 2004.

Podesta, John, and Peter Ogden. "The Security Implications of Climate Change." *Washington Quarterly* 31, 1 (Winter 2007–2008), 115–138.

Roberts, Paul. "The Seven Myths of Energy Independence." *Mother Jones* 33, 3 (May/June 2008), 31–37.

Rockenbach, Leslie J. *The Mexican-American Border: NAFTA and Global Linkages*. New York and London: Routledge, 2001.

Rozenthal, Andres. "The Other Side of Immigration." *Current History* 106, 697 (February 2007), 89–90.

Segal, Adam. *The Hacked World Order: How Nations Fight, Trade, and Manipulate in the Digital Age*. New York: PublicAffairs, 2016.

Shifter, Michael. "Latin America's Drug Problem." *Current History* 106, 697 (February 2007), 58–63.

Singer, P. W., and Allan Friedman. *Cybersecurity and Cyberwar: What Everyone Needs to Know*. New York: Oxford University Press, 2014.

Snow, Donald M. *Cases in International Relations: Principles and Applications*. 7th ed. Lanham, MD: Rowman & Littlefield, 2018.

———. *Regional Cases in U.S. Foreign Policy*. 2nd ed. Lanham, MD: Rowman & Littlefield, 2018.

Springer, Paul. *Encyclopedia of Cyber Warfare*. New York: ABC-Clio, 2017.

Steinnon, Richard. *There Will Be Cyberwar: How the Move to Network-Centric War Fighting Has Set the Stage for Cyberwar*. London: IT-Harvest Press, 2015.

Stern, Todd, and William Antholis. "A Changing Climate: The Road Ahead for the United States." *Washington Quarterly* 31, 1 (Winter 2007–2008), 175–187.

Victor, David G. *Climate Change: Debating America's Options*. New York: Council on Foreign Relations, 2004.

Zweig, David, and Bi Jianhai. "China's Global Hunt for Energy." *Foreign Affairs* 84, 5 (September/October 2005), 18–24.

Looking Ahead

American national security is in a transition that began with the end of the Cold War, was jolted by the events of 9/11, and continues to be buffeted by external traumas from terrorists to developing world internal conflicts (DWICs) and the vicissitudes of US politics. The rise of and campaign against the Islamic State (IS) remains the most visible manifestation of this volatility. There is no consensus within the United States about the strategic and tactical responses the country should adopt toward individual crises and the overall environment, a condition magnified by the Trump presidency. The parameters of the resulting debate can be viewed along a continuum of levels of US activism that help frame possible and likely outcomes.

The United States continues to founder to reach a national security strategy and policy consensus in a rapidly changing environment, the nature and hostility of which are of debatable seriousness. International events are traumatic depending on perceptions of the national security environment by different figures with different perspectives on international issues. Periods of change are always unpredictable to some extent, partly because of uncertainties and imponderables about the new environment, the predilections of policymakers, and the mood of the American public both about the experience they are leaving behind and the prospects for the future.

The background of the current transition, of course, is the ongoing but fading reaction to the terrorist attacks of September 11, 2001. The national security environment has been "highlighted" by major concerns that remain part of the national context. The reaction to the attacks in terms of a "war" on terror and the active pursuit of Al Qaeda (AQ) and later the Islamic State have been the most basic of these responses. The assassination of Osama bin Laden in Pakistan in May 2011 punctuated the dismantling of the original AQ leadership, and while remnants of both its leaders and followers remain at large, the threat they pose is clearly of a lesser order. They have, of course, been replaced by other threats that will remain a problem of greater or lesser importance as time passes.

Other responses to 9/11 were ultimately more controversial, arguably less successful, and possibly more consequential in framing the ways the past environment shapes how the future is viewed. The American war in Iraq is over, but that country struggles to reach postwar normalcy, and it is not clear how their internal disagreements—which the United States certainly contributed to—will be resolved or whether their resolution will be an outcome in which the United States can take pride. IS, after all, drew much of its strength from the Sunni regions of Iraq. In Afghanistan, American active participation continues, and the future prospects for governance in that far-off land remain sufficiently opaque that it is hard to predict which American objectives will have been attained when the United States leaves. Both adventures have left a bad taste on the American palate.

Domestic factors also affect the transition. The largest influence is the enormous hyper-partisanship within the American body politic that has been accentuated by the unconventional, sometimes erratic foreign policy actions of President Trump. The sharp division of Americans along partisan, ideological lines has become the underlying cause of both a caustic national dialogue and a primary barrier to governmental action. Political moderation and the willingness to compromise have given way to ideological rigidity. In the current atmosphere, ideological purity often trumps the politics of policy reconciliation, and the result is to make it virtually impossible to reach agreed-upon grounds for policy outcomes. This problem is most pronounced on domestic matters, but it extends to national security.

The policy debate must take place within these parameters, which are further influenced by some new realities that have emerged from the recent past and that help shape consideration of future concerns in the national security area. One is the basic nature of modern armed conflict captured in the idea of asymmetrical warfare. Traditional Eurocentric models of war simply do not clearly apply where rejection of the rules of traditional war is seen as a way to alter the balance of power and take the advantage away from the traditional warrior and toward his or her asymmetrical counterpart. This form of adaptation is particularly present in the DWICs that are the major venue within which war is now conducted and where the United States is likely to find its most inviting opportunities to use force in the future. These frustrations and difficulties also detract from the popularity and support for these conflicts.

The most apparent past analogy with which to compare the current situation is the post-Vietnam experience. The bases of commonality are American extrication from what was in retrospect a classic asymmetrical war (the term *asymmetrical* was, of course, not in vogue at the time, even though Vietnam was the model for its introduction) that ended poorly from an American viewpoint. In the postwar phase after American combat presence ended, all American objectives based in a noncommunist outcome failed to be realized. Instead, the war had the effect of contributing to a crippling economic inflation in the United States and was part of the erosion of American faith in the political system, along with the Watergate scandal that brought down the Nixon administration. A more ominous comparison may be in length and cost: Americans are still paying some of the costs of Vietnam in terms of long-term medical and psychological bills for veterans of that conflict. That bill will be even higher for Iraq and Afghanistan veterans.

The analogy between Vietnam and the present is based in the similarity of the Iraq and Afghanistan Wars to the conflict in Southeast Asia. This analogy holds more closely in Afghanistan in terms of the war's dynamics. Afghanistan has always been an asymmetrical war, whereas the reaction to the American occupation in Iraq became asymmetrical during the occupation. In both cases, the United States was unable to achieve its objectives through the application of military force. Unlike Vietnam, the ultimate results in Iraq and Afghanistan have not been as stark, at least not yet.

The tendency to draw analogies from Vietnam to the future depends to a large degree on what one feels about the reaction in the 1970s. The clarion call of the early 1970s was "no more Vietnams," and while it took a decade or more to figure out exactly what that meant, it included a reluctance to invoke and project American military force aggressively into ongoing developing world instabilities. Those who believe the Vietnam analogy applies to the contemporary environment tend also to be less expansive and activist about the expeditionary use of force generally; those who argue the analogy does not hold generally want a more robust military orientation toward the future. Since 2013, this divide could be seen in differing views about what the United States should do about the carnage in Syria and the controversy over the Iranian nuclear weapons program. In 2016, it was reflected in attitudes about what to do about IS. The absence of overt American military participation in either situation may be an implicit response to how the United States will deal with future DWICs.

There are no "correct" solutions to the debate about the future direction or content of American national security policy. Rather, there are honest differences of opinion and perspective about what directions the United States can and should take to pursue its national security interests in the future, how factors included in previous chapters can be applied to clarifying that problem, and the role of institutionalized volatility in American politics. The rest of this chapter is devoted to an attempt to raise and explicate some of those choices.

EXPLORING THE FUTURE

Just how much adjustment to basic American national security policy is necessary and prudent for the country in the face of the structure of problems it faces in the world? Have American basic interests, including those vital interests that have historically been the trigger for invoking force, changed fundamentally, or have they not? Has the structure of threats to those interests changed in a more uncertain world of variegated challenges ranging from turmoil surrounding American relations with traditional friends and adversaries to global warming? Is there a new pattern of threats in the environment to which the United States must respond, and what risks are entailed for the United States in its various kinds and degrees of response to those emerging threats? Does the pattern of contemporary American response correspond well to the world as it is emerging? To what extent does the Trump unilateralist approach improve or distract from the traditional American view of the world, and do those changes improve the American security position in the international environment?

All these are fundamental questions on which there is and will continue to be basic disagreement in a national security environment and policy toward it that is in flux. To try to make some sense of the parameters of the problems, the discussion will proceed through three steps. The first is an examination of the major variables—the unknowns—in which the debate must be couched. The second is the basic policy framework and limits that exist to deal with an uncertain future. The third is a continuum of models around which one can group policy preferences toward that future.

Variables in the Environment

Among the beguiling characteristics of uncertainty about the future are the variable influences that might affect that future environment. American planners, for instance, have been caught off-guard on many occasions about events and factors that emerged and for which they hardly had planned or could have planned. American national security planners in the early 1970s had scarcely considered the prospect of the downfall of the shah of Iran and thus had not planned or prepared for that exigency, but that event fundamentally changed the nature and direction of US policy in the region. In turn, the impact was enormous and a source of many of the country's problems in the region today. One view of that impact is explored in Amplification 14.1.

AMPLIFICATION 14.1

Unforeseen Consequences: The Fall of the Shah and Al Qaeda

A major effect of the fall of the shah of Iran in 1979 and his replacement by a rabidly anti-American regime in Tehran was that the United States no longer

(continued)

had a faithful deputy in the oil-rich Persian/Arabian Gulf to ensure peace and tranquility in the region and the free flow of oil to the West. The shah's bitterly anti-American successors quickly renounced that arrangement. The question became who would succeed Iran as the guarantor of the continuing flow of oil through the Straits of Hormuz to the West. The answer was the United States, which became a major military presence, setting off a sequence of unforeseen consequences.

Two other unpredicted events occurred in 1979. In Iraq, an obscure Iraqi Army officer by the name of Saddam Hussein seized and consolidated power in his country to Iran's west. To its east, the Soviet Union invaded Afghanistan. The Soviet invasion prompted a regional jihad in the form of both indigenous and foreign fighters (mujahidin) who came to the aid of the Afghans to expel the Soviet infidels. Among those outsiders were the core of what would become AQ under the leadership of Osama bin Laden. Hussein decided to gain regional favor in the Sunni Arab world by invading Shiite and Persian Iran in 1980. The dominos of unforeseen consequences were ready to begin falling.

The Iran-Iraq War and the Soviet occupation of Afghanistan both ended by the conclusion of the 1980s but left residues. After the Iran-Iraq War ended in 1988, Hussein turned to his former benefactors like Saudi Arabia and Kuwait for assistance in recovery from the war, and he was rebuffed. The invasion of Kuwait followed both as revenge and as an attempt to gain the resources he needed. With Iraq poised on the Saudi border, the question was whether the Saudi Arabians could defend themselves in the event Iraq continued south toward the Saudi oil fields. The answer was that without outside help, they could not. Among the candidates to fill the void were the Americans and bin Laden, who volunteered to reform the mujahidin he helped recruit to defend the kingdom. The Saudis rejected bin Laden and chose instead the Americans, who flooded into the holy land of Islam.

The link was established. When bin Laden announced his intentions against the United States in the mid-1990s, a staple among his points was the "desecration" of the "holy lands" that an American presence in the Saudi kingdom entailed. This was the direct result of the American decision to replace Iran as the guarantor of the oil; the Iraqi decision to invade Iran, which placed Iraq in the position of needing relief after the war; and in turn the Saudi decision that alienated the terrorist leader (one of his other goals was to overthrow the Saudi monarchy). A causal string can thus be drawn between the fall of the shah and the terrorism threat that dominated American national security in the 2000s.

One can, of course, dispute the causal chain involved in this analogy. The point is not its literal accuracy but to point out that unforeseen variables can and do arise that complicate and upset planning for the future. Provision for the unforeseen must always be part of planning. ■

It is difficult to anticipate every development that might affect the relevant future and unanticipated events in the national security environment that might affect national security, but one can proceed with at least a partial list of variables in the current mix. Three will be explored: the continuing degree of partisanship and gridlock within the American political system; changes and continuities in the environment of national security threats; and the degree to which the Iraq and Afghanistan experiences affect American national mood toward national security activism (memory).

Domestic Political Hyper-partisanship and Gridlock The condition of enormous ideological antipathy and rancor between political elements and individuals within the United States manifests itself as fundamental disagreement across the board on policy and has produced public policy gridlock. The trend has been building for some time. Its roots go back well before the turn of the millennium as ideological liberals and conservatives—notably the ideologically pure wings of both political parties—have come to dominate the moderate middle that prevails in periods of greater agreement.

The result of the current political deadlock has been the virtual inability of the branches of the federal government and political parties to agree on policy matters, including those affecting national security. The budgetary process is the most obvious example. Budgets provide resources that allow the government to respond to political needs, and the absence of fruitful budget agreements between the political parties and the executive and legislative branches reflects a deeper disagreement about *what* to fund. National security is not exempt from this phenomenon or immune from its consequences. The February 2018 budget deal that effectively suspended the sequester provided extra defense funds that President Trump promised would increase American military strength. He also proposed an expensive military parade in Washington that the services did not want because it would absorb some of those funds. Democrats screamed in opposition. Republicans were mostly silent. Gridlock ruled.

The current level of animosity exaggerates differences on national security matters that exist even when the divide is not as great as it currently is. Historically, the Democratic Party's liberal internationalist propensity has manifested itself in a political preference for a less militarized, more cooperative foreign policy, although the Democrats led the country into two of the largest wars since 1945, the conflicts in Korea and Vietnam. The more conservative GOP, on the other hand, has been more philosophically unilateralist and more willing to threaten or resort to military solutions to foreign policy problems; the ascendancy of the neoconservatives during the George W. Bush administration is a sort of caricature of this tendency. The approach of Trump accentuates that unilateralism in two fundamental ways: his willingness to approach national security problems like North Korea and Russia unilaterally and his confrontation with allies over commitments to NATO (North Atlantic Treaty Organization) and economic isolationism in the form of unilaterally imposed tariffs and attacks on symbols of globalization like NAFTA (North American Free Trade Agreement).

These national security differences become entangled in the current debate about defense participation in the developing world and about what should be learned from the Iraq and Afghanistan experiences. From the extreme wings of each party, there are diametrically opposed views of what or if the lessons of these forays should apply to national security, including spending. The right wing of the GOP wants large cuts in federal spending everywhere *but* defense spending. The left wing of the Democratic Party advocates large cuts in defense along with tax increases (primarily for the wealthy) to minimize cuts in social spending. Most moderate observers argue that the sensible policy path lies between these extremes (some tax increases, less extreme cuts in defense), but such advocacies are currently drowned out in the hyper-partisan cacophony.

What will cause this partisanship to relent? It is scant comfort that historically such periods have been cyclical and that the pendulum will somehow eventually swing back to greater cooperation and bipartisanship in the long run. For the moment, two things could bring about a dramatic change. One would be public revulsion with the current situation that causes the political center to rise electorally and vanquish the extremes. The 2018 off-year election offered a preview of the battle for the "soul" of each party, but the interparty competition was affected by the overall division surrounding support or opposition to the president generally. The 2020 election cycle may (or may not) provide a more accurate indication about trends—whether a relaxation of partisanship is beginning to occur.

The other event would be a national security crisis so traumatic that it would galvanize public support behind government and create functionality in government along the way. The ominous rise of Soviet communism and the onset of the Cold War were so dangerous and all-encompassing that this cemented support for over twenty years until dissent over its application in Vietnam fractured the consensus. The initial reaction to the terrorist attacks of September 11 was to create a broad consensus, but the underlying context of the partisan division in the country was so deep that consensus did not endure or extend to other parts of the political agenda.

It is not clear what will break the current domestic political impasse, but as long as it exists, it will continue to infect all other political aspects of the future. It certainly affects and impedes decisive action on the economy, and it also has probable effects both on how changes in the national security environment are interpreted and on the lessons and legacies of the national security experiences of the past decade.

Changes in the National Security Environment Risk management, reduction, and ideally elimination are the goals of national security policy. The nature of dealing with the international environment makes attaining these goals difficult. Most of the challenges result from activities by foreigners over whose actions one does not have total control. These actions are not entirely predictable, despite considerable efforts by the intelligence community to make them so. Worst-case analysis thinking dictates the simplest way to deal with uncertainty is to prepare for every possible threat that can emerge and thus be ready to negate it. The result of such an approach would be to reduce risk as close as possible to zero; it would also overtax resources.

The logic underlying an attempt to deal with all possible threats is the core of "worst case analysis." This construct is a product of Cold War planning. It holds that if one prepares for the worst things that could happen (the "worst case"), one will be able to manage both that situation and lesser dangers (the "lesser included cases"). This logic assumes that these lesser cases will be similar enough to the worst case that worst-case planning will encompass solutions to lesser cases (e.g., if one prepares for a major conventional war, one in the process develops the capability to handle a smaller conventional war). If lesser contingencies are fundamentally dissimilar to the worst case (e.g., preparing for a conventional war but encountering an unconventional, asymmetrical opponent), the logic can fail. In that case, worst-case analysis must be applied to multiple possible worst cases to be inclusive.

Something like worst-case analysis is the natural proclivity of the national security professional, whose charge is to protect the country from all possible threats. It is reinforced by the potentially catastrophic consequences of being unprepared for a contingency that does arise, ultimately including defeat in war. Thus, there is a built-in bias to prepare for everything. The approach is inherently conservative because it tends to resist changes to policies and capabilities that have apparently been successful and that could always arise again in the future.

Pursuing the worst-case approach is both very expensive and very political (the two factors are, of course, not mutually exclusive). A comprehensive approach to worst-case preparation requires very robust forces capable of dealing successfully with multiple, and sometimes very different, situations. The logic of the worst case inevitably calls for more rather than less comprehensive preparation, and this is always going to entail maximum expense: defense "on the cheap" will not do.

Worst-case analysis is also highly political. First, preparing for the worst case implies expending large amounts of money for things like procurement of weapons systems and large numbers of forces on bases around the country and the world. All this activity means federal resources are pumped into select communities and states, and the congressional representatives where this spending occurs tend to become protective of those funds and thus sympathetic to the purposes for which they were developed. One would, for example, expect the House member representing Pascagoula, Mississippi, to favor naval procurement at least partly because that community houses a major naval shipbuilding facility. Second, the existence of the worst-case possibility becomes a patriotic banner than can be used to demonstrate one's desire to protect the country. Those who seek limitations in defense expenditures may be accused of potentially exposing the country to grievous dangers.

The worst-case approach is workable when the threat is particularly dire and agreed upon as such and when a concomitant sacrifice to protect the country will be undertaken by virtually everyone, as it was during the Cold War that spawned the approach. Such a consensus is clearly missing in the present situation. There certainly are challenges in the national security environment, but relatively few of these are so threatening to basic American security as to warrant an application of worst-case planning and preparation. IS posed a threat, but it was simply not equivalent to the Soviet communist threat that clearly mandated a high level of sacrifice during the last century.

Retention of the worst-case planning model also flies in the face of other influences on future planning. The condition of hyper-partisan-induced gridlock may militate against changes in thinking about dealing with future threats, but the combination of a constrained economic environment and post-Iraq and post-Afghanistan War weariness also restrains support for defense spending.

Is moving away from comprehensive worst-case preparation wise or prudent in the contemporary threat environment? The basic rationale for devoting scarce resources to national security is to protect the national population and territory from physical harm to the greatest extent possible, and since the price of miscalculation—notably under-calculation—can be catastrophic, the tendency is to err on the side of overestimation and overly robust preparation. But what if the country is simply unwilling to support such an approach in view of other priorities? In that case, is it necessary to rethink the contingencies—the worst cases—for which it will and will not prepare, in the process accepting the notion that some risks may be involved in the calculation. The *Challenge!* box explores these possibilities.

CHALLENGE!

Contemporary Worst Cases: The Democratic People's Republic of Korea (DPRK)?

If one begins from the premise (admittedly not universally accepted) that the United States cannot afford to provide resources for national security based on the kind of comprehensive worst-case planning that dominated the past, for what kinds of worst cases should or must it prepare and thus commit its resources? Security, after all, has a psychological as well as a purely physical base, and another way to ask the question is what makes Americans feel safe, and thus what must be done to ensure that feeling of safety?

The assessment includes at least two calculations. One of these is an analysis of the threat environment. What threats face the United States? Which are the most dangerous (most likely to cause problems)? Which are the deadliest (have the most harmful effects on the United States if they are carried out)? Are the most dangerous and deadliest threats the same, or are some threats more dangerous but less deadly and vice versa? In the latter cases, which are the most important to devote resources to counter? In other words, what kind of threats could be subjected to worst-case analysis and its consequences? In what order of priority should they be placed?

The ongoing conflict with the DPRK over the North Korean nuclear weapons program illustrates the dilemma. In a purely physical sense, the DPRK's attainment of a nuclear capability that can reach and destroy targets in the continental United States (CONUS, or the forty-eight contiguous states) represents the most significant new existential threat of the new century. Given the catastrophe such an attack would represent, it is the clearest new worst case for which to prepare.

But what should the United States do? Previous national security efforts did not stifle the DPRK developmental effort (acquisition deterrence failed), so what can the national security community do to make sure a North Korean attack does not occur (employment deterrence)? There are two broad approaches: "denuclearization" and deterrence. The "denuclearizers" argue the only way to be sure the DPRK does not attack is for them to give up their arsenal. Opponents counter that this has never occurred before and suggest adequate incentives have not been offered to the DPRK to make them seriously consider disarming. Why should they? Moreover, the DPRK knows an attack on

(continued)

CONUS would be suicidal. The other approach is deterrence: acknowledging the DPRK capability and convincing them to become members of the deterrence system.

The problem is there is disagreement about what to do and how to do it. President Trump has opted for direct head of state summitry as the best approach, but critics are skeptical of the results and the prospects. The ongoing confrontation has a Damoclean flavor (it is a delicate balance that could go bad), and so it clearly represents a real or potential worst case. How to overcome it in a way that satisfies all relevant actors remains one of America's most important issues. ■

Memory The way the country thinks about and reacts to the future environment is influenced to some degree by prior successes or failures. The national security paradigm has been obsessed with 9/11-based terrorism has been tainted by its application to Iraq and Afghanistan. Terrorism remains a potent force, but it is different than it was in 2001. IS and other offshoots of AQ are not the same as the bin Laden–led AQ of a decade ago and probably require paradigmatic adjustments. The unsuccessful efforts in Iraq and Afghanistan represent American incursions into the complex, difficult dynamics of DWICs, a problem with which the country clearly must come to grips.

The entreaties and controversies about Iraq and Afghanistan encompass at least two of the dimensions discussed in earlier chapters. Militarily, the clear lesson is that some form of asymmetrical warfare will, along with terrorism, be the dominant type of opposition the United States will likely face for the foreseeable future. In some places, the problems will comingle, as in the struggle with IS. The lessons of Iraq and Afghanistan clearly show that adopting unconventional means does in fact level the playing field for underdogs to provide at least the chance of success. The Iraq example is particularly clear: Saddam Hussein's army could not compete head to head with the Americans, and so after a token resistance, it quit the field. Hussein was no longer part of the equation, but the resistance that emerged around 2004 was decidedly asymmetrical in nature. IS in some important ways built on that model and adopted much of this approach—unsurprisingly. In the Kurdish *pesh merga*, IS encountered a force better at unconventional war than it was. The Afghans have never had an effective conventional national armed force, and so the contest with the Taliban has been fought the way the Afghans have always fought, which has been asymmetrically when faced with a symmetrical force. One can, of course, argue how well the American armed forces have acquitted themselves in either or both conflicts. One can scarcely deny that the opposition has done better than it would have had it fought in the preferred American manner. Future potential American opponents cannot help but take notice. The American military realizes this fact and is trying to incorporate it into future planning, but it is a bitter and unwelcome pill reluctantly swallowed.

The other part of the memory has to be that in modern warfare, military outcomes are not the sole measure of success. Military forces may be able to stop fighting by their presence (peace imposition), but the process of enforcing, maintaining, keeping, and stabilizing that peace falls under the general categories of development and state building. These efforts are both expensive and their success problematic: the fact that a successful outcome in both Iraq and Afghanistan remains beyond grasp is testimony to the length and difficulty of that process. Whether the American public is willing to accept and embrace the added expense of developmental imperatives is certainly not a given and is indeed a question rarely even raised. At the same time, it is difficult to project positive outcomes to future conflicts in which military and developmental successes do not go hand in hand.

Policies and Effects

The ancient Greek philosopher Heraclitus, who lived around 500 BCE, believed the world is in a state of constant change, and he is most famously remembered for his assertion that one can never step into the same river twice because the water in the stream at any one point in time is not the same water as it was at any previous time or will be at any future point. Policy may not be in a state of constant Heraclitean change, but the set of policies that surrounds national security (or any other policy area) and the assessment of its future environment are constantly being bombarded by different policy influences, only some of which are predictable.

It is feckless to try to list and examine all of even the fairly near term outside influences that will have an effect on future national security orientations, but it is possible to single out some that are clearly on the horizon as examples. Two will be identified that have already been touched upon. The first, fiscal constraints and their likely impacts on future defense budgets, can be brought into great clarity. The other, energy independence, has also been raised, but its direct impact on national security has been less fully incorporated into a discussion on national security thinking.

Fiscal Responsibility and Budgetary Implications Fiscal responsibility became a political shibboleth of essentially all political factions after the Great Recession of 2008. It was a battle waged on several levels: at the philosophical level of how extensive a role government should play in American life, and at another level of the appropriate role of the government in those aspects of national life. At the bottom line, it was a debate over the size of government and what government should do. The philosophical aspects of this debate continue to congeal over what the central and peripheral roles of government should be, and at the heart of that debate is the centrality of national security to governmental purpose.

The broad contours of this debate are by now well established rhetorically and in terms of the hyper-partisan political debate. Attempting to strip away the most inflammatory epithets the two sides heap upon one another, the basic differences boil down to which of the Declaration of Independence's assertions about citizen rights—life, liberty, and the pursuit of happiness—are the province of governmental action and which should be left to individual pursuit independent of government action or restriction. Those with a positive, liberal/progressive view of the government's role tend to maintain an active place for government in promoting happiness, which generally translates into opportunities and certain basic conditions of existence that can, in their view, only fully be met by government. Those with a more restrictive, conservative view tend to argue that the basic role of government is to ensure maximum citizen liberty to pursue their individual goals and that the role of the government should be to create and enforce conditions that maximize individual ability to pursue individual ends. The liberal view necessarily results in a larger government that takes on more responsibilities and thus must claim greater resources in that pursuit. Their basic underlying argument is that if government does not do some basic things, no one will or access to them will not be available to all citizens equally. Governmental minimalists deny or seek to restrict the reach of this inclusiveness.

Almost everyone does agree that a prime role—some would say *the* prime role—of government is to provide for the common safety (the protection of life). This agreement creates the consensus on which support for national security and spending on its behalf are based. The basic premise that only the government can provide for the common defense is essentially unchallenged, but not all its premises and implications are. There is, for instance, currently considerable disagreement over the territorial and other boundaries of national security. A restrictive view of the national security mandate suggests it extends only to items directly involved in the sanctity of American territory, a position taken by libertarians like Rand Paul and, to a lesser extent, President Trump. More expansive views suggest it extends to the promotion of American interest beyond that border and necessitates more international cooperation to attain.

These philosophical disagreements have direct policy implications. One effect of the Great Recession was to create a spike in government deficit spending due to decreased government revenue and increased expenditures to stimulate recovery. That spike in spending, unaccompanied by additional revenues from taxes, was added to national security sources of deficit spending like the wars in Iraq and Afghanistan as a contributor to the ballooning national debt. The Trump administration has not shown great interest in deficit or debt reduction. Its major economic achievement has been the 2017 tax cut, which reduced government revenues without specific provisions for cutting spending. The rationale has been that the tax cuts would stimulate economic growth that will create additional wealth that can be taxed to provide enough revenue to compensate for tax dollars lost due to lower tax rates. It is an old idea the validity of which is not universally accepted.

At some point, an honest movement toward deficit and debt reduction will almost certainly arise, and the question is how it will affect national security. How does national security policy escape the current malaise so it can be considered solely on its own merits? One extreme solution is to exempt national security funding from the budget exercise, as some conservatives prefer. If this solution prevails, there would be virtually no funding impact on the national security policy area, and all cuts would have to be absorbed by some combination of "revenue enhancements" (taxes) and cuts to other governmental spending, prominently including entitlement programs. At the other extreme, national security spending would be a major component of the cuts used to reduce deficits, as the 2013 sequester dictates. How catastrophic the impact would be to actual defense budgets would depend on whether budget restraints came exclusively from cuts in spending (the conservative preference) or some combination of taxes and program cuts (the liberal preference). In either case, national security concerns would be both beneficiaries and victims. Exempting defense budgets would entail cuts in social programs, which many in the defense sector enjoy, and including defense in budget-cutting processes would prune current budgets and limit capabilities that can be applied to risk management.

If some renewed spirit of bipartisanship emerges in the near term (admittedly not very likely), the actual level of participation will be somewhere between those extremes. This probably means that cuts will be accomplished through a combination of program reductions and new revenues, that the pace of reduction will be stretched over some time, and that both defense and non-defense programs will face less severe but real sacrifices, as will taxpayers. Conceptually, this approach is not dissimilar to the reasoning underlying the thrust of the sequester.

Energy Independence   The notion that the United States should move to free itself from dependence on foreign energy sources—mostly petroleum—has become a possible reality in the past few years. If the trend continues to grow, it will have both national security origins and consequences. There are numerous, differently motivated American groups supporting a movement away from dependence on foreign energy sources. Environmentalists, for instance, see the issue as an argument for developing more fully domestic, renewable, nonpolluting sources of energy (solar, wind, etc.), while representatives of various industries from which domestic supplies would come (the coal, natural gas, and petroleum industries, for example) see it as a way not only to increase national independence but also to enhance their own economic profitability. National security enthusiasts see it as one way to reduce levels of commitment to protect vulnerable sources of energy in unstable parts of the world, especially the Persian/Arabian Gulf littoral.

The movement toward energy independence has become theoretically possible for two basic reasons: the rise in costs of foreign energy sources that encourage economic exploitation of domestic energy sources like shale oil and gas and the maturation and application of exploiting shale energy at competitive prices. Energy dependence on foreign sources—notably the Middle East—has been a national security and economic albatross, compromising foreign and national security policy in the world's most volatile region and contributing to American balance-of-payment deficits. A very aggressive and determined policy of American energy independence could break this cycle of dependence by severing the tether that oil dependence has created for American foreign and national security policy. As this author has argued elsewhere (see *The Middle East, Oil, and the American National Security Policy*), it could loosen or break altogether the stranglehold countries like Saudi Arabia have over US Middle East policy. At the same time, making the United States a net energy exporter has major international economic benefits in both balance of payments and economic leverage areas.

A policy aggressively promoting movement toward energy independence thus has major implications for national security. The most obvious area is the Middle East, and particularly the Persian Gulf littoral from which so much of the world's petroleum is extracted. Roughly 20 percent of the world's and 10 percent of the United States' petroleum has traditionally passed through the narrow Straits of Hormuz, for instance. The straits have been a major source of contention with Iran, whose coastline washes its eastern side and most of the Persian/Arabian Gulf, adding a potentially explosive aspect to American-Iranian relations and a potential spark for a wider shooting aspect of that confrontation. American secure access to regional oil is the major reason the United States maintains a major naval presence in the Gulf in the form of at least one carrier battle group (CVBG) at virtually all times. That need would virtually disappear were America no longer in need of personal access to oil from the region.

The change can, of course, be overblown. A movement toward energy independence does not necessarily mean the United States can simply leave the region entirely. There are, after all, regimes in the region (e.g., Saudi Arabia) that rely heavily on American protection from the Iranians and one another, and an American withdrawal could leave those countries much more vulnerable to pressure than they are now. Saudi insulation from criticism for its indirect support of IS through contributions by its citizens is one clear example. At the same time, critical American allies do rely on

Middle Eastern oil and do not share the American luxury of shale-based energy independence as a short-term possibility. These countries, mostly in Europe, would suddenly find their security of access endangered by a precipitous American withdrawal. Moreover, oil producers like Saudi Arabia would suddenly find themselves in need of new customers for their oil and potential new partners to protect them, a role that countries like China would be more than happy to fulfill. It would certainly not be in American interests to see a much-widened presence of China, or possibly even Russia, in the region if the United States left behind a vacuum.

The point of the example, of course, is that energy independence opens new vistas for American policy. Extreme changes are by no means automatically dictated, but more subtle changes in relationships are possible. Under current circumstances, the American ability to stand independently in the Persian Gulf region is unquestionably compromised and limited by continued dependence on petroleum from the region, a limit that regional states with whom the United States must deal are clearly aware. Knowing, on the other hand, that the United States does not itself absolutely need to protect energy resource decreases the leverage states in the region have on this country. Saudi Arabia is the most obviously affected state. Its oil-based relationship with the United States has allowed the Saudis a level of influence that a loosening of US oil dependency undercuts. The Saudis realize this.

These policy examples are only exemplary, but they suggest there are forces in the international environment that can militate toward a change in American national security policy in this period when the dominance of the terrorism-centered paradigm for framing defense problems and responses is not so great. This leads to a final consideration of the possible ways in which an approach to an altered policy orientation might be implemented.

National Security Policy Models

There are always powerful forces that resist change in the policy realm, particularly when the changes being contemplated are fundamental and far-reaching. The present period is no exception. The hyper-partisan gridlock that currently paralyzes the policy community is certainly a prominent barrier wherein the "horse" of policy desirability and the "wagon" of funding are effectively reversed: budgeting paralysis precludes serious policy adjustment. Policymakers in the national security area are basically conservative, and this often translates into a resistance to changes in "tried and true" ways of doing things crafted to cope with a very different environment. The current national security structure has a sizable resource commitment to conceptualizing national security—and especially military—matters in conventional ways, and the political structure that must authorize changes or continuities is driven by many factors, including monies sunk into and self-interest in the way things have been. The forces that produce inertia are by no means trivial.

The current dysfunction inhibits creative thinking by relegating national security to the status of a sideshow in the circus that is ongoing American politics. The question of strategy, however, also has philosophical roots that predispose proponents to favor basic national security strategies compatible with their fundamental beliefs. Through most of recent US history, the dominant philosophical position has been realism, which was discussed extensively in Chapter 2. No one explicitly rejects realism as the underlying basis of national security policy, but its implications have been indirectly assaulted, notably in advocacies of employing force where American vital interests are not unambiguously involved (e.g., the neoconservatives of the early 2000s). Whether realism should be the basis of a new national security paradigm is raised in Amplification 14.2.

AMPLIFICATION 14.2

Is Realism Too Restrictive a Paradigm?

At the operational level, there are three basic dictates of realism as it was captured in the Cold War realist paradigm and that would be the centerpiece of a return to a national security strategy grounded explicitly in realism. The three principles are that force should only be contemplated when vital interests are clearly at stake, that American force be used only as a last resort when all other means of achieving vital interests have failed, and that there should be a reasonable chance that force can achieve the goals for which it is invoked. President Obama espoused these principles to limit American military interventions during his two terms. President Trump has not articulated a coherent view of his views on the subject. Each of these principles has come under some level of scrutiny and questioning in recent years.

The restriction on contemplating force only when vital interests are at stake has been criticized, notably by the neoconservatives who were prominent advisors during the George W. Bush administration, as being too restrictive—in effect raising the bar too high in situations where force could be used effectively to achieve other American interests that did not clearly reflect American vital interests. This criticism has some validity in that most of the opportunities for employing American force are in DWICs, one of the characteristics of which is that these conflicts arguably do not raise vital American concerns. A strict interpretation of vitality, for instance, would have made the American decision to invade Iraq much more difficult to sustain after claims about the Iraqis could not be demonstrated (e.g., weapons of mass destruction programs and ties to terrorism).

The enjoinder only to use force as a last resort has historical bases and has generally been the way most Americans felt about risking American blood. Former secretary of defense Robert Gates, in a December 2015 article, captured this sentiment, saying it has been an American tradition to keep its leaders "restrained from foreign adventures and from using force as a first option rather than a last resort." The pull-and-tug of policy debates over whether to use American ground forces in the fight against IS reflects the debate over this principle and the "triumph" of strict realist principles.

The third principle is of more recent vintage and reflects the questionable outcomes of some recent American military excursions. One can debate whether the failure of the United States to achieve its goals in places like Iraq, Afghanistan, or Vietnam was the result of an inadequate or overly restrained control of American forces, but it is also possible that the reason for failure was that the mission was impossible in the first place. This is particularly true of DWICs. In internal wars, the ability of outsiders to act decisively is limited, and the recourse to asymmetrical techniques makes them difficult to prosecute, leaving Robert Kaplan to conclude that "the United States has limited ability to determine the outcome of many conflicts, despite being a superpower."

In contemporary world affairs, a national security strategy based in realism suggests considerable restraint in the use of American force to solve world problems. On the face of it, this may seem an odd conclusion since realism has historically been associated with a defense of the sovereign state system and military force to enforce that sovereignty. In the contemporary environment, where most violence and instability is internal or emanating from non-state actors, the conclusion is the opposite. Is realism the realistic approach for the environment in which we exist? What do you think? ■

How can we think about the changes that might be contemplated in the post-Iraq and post-Afghanistan period for American national security policy? One way to look at that problem is to borrow the basic organizational tool devised to conceptualize the war/peace spectrum (peacekeeping) in Chapter 12, with levels of American national security activism as the dominant basis of the paradigm. This basic relationship is captured in Figure 14.1.

The key element in defining the various points along the spectrum is the extent to which the United States conceives of using force to deal with different world situations to try to create outcomes favorable to American

High Activism----------------Restrained Activism----------------Isolationism

FIGURE 14.1
US National Security Activism Options

interests. It is thus a measure of the predilection to view employing the military instrument of power to promote American national security. As such, it presupposes some determination about when force should be contemplated, such as applying the realist criteria of vitality, last resort, and likely outcomes.

The spectrum moves from an extreme where the military instrument and its application is used or threatened in many instances to the other extreme where military activism is considered inappropriate except in the event of direct and demonstrable assaults on primary American values, such as the sanctity of American territory (survival interests, in language introduced in Chapter 2). For most purposes, these extremes can be thought of as "ideal types" that represent pure orientations toward the use of force that people rarely hold. Hardly anyone thinks a military response is appropriate for all situations, and equally, very few think the military option is never applicable. Between these two extreme points is a broad range of possibilities. This description of a continuum with discrete end points and a broad, changing center represents a major point of similarity between this analogy and the war/peace continuum in Chapter 12. The major dissimilarity is that points along the activism spectrum represent policy preferences rather than points of progress along the path from war to peace.

At least three sets of factors have some effect on where individuals and groups fit on this spectrum and what policy preferences and options they prefer toward different situations. The first of these is the predilection that different people have toward various solutions to threats to American interests. It is largely a question about orientations toward one or another of the instruments of political power: when a problem arises, to what part of the "arsenal" of policy instruments does the individual policymaker gravitate? In all real situations, there will be some consideration of all possibilities, from the most cooperative to the most militant, but policy predilections affect what individuals see as best approaches. To some extent, these differences are institutionalized within the American system: the State Department, for instance, has an institutional mandate to promote diplomatic solutions and thus more automatically searches for political and economic incentives and penalties to solve problems, whereas the Department of Defense is similarly likely to explore (if not necessarily to advocate) military solutions.

The second factor is the more general philosophical orientation one has toward the American role in the world: to what degree should the

United States act to influence what goes on in the world around it? The historical preference of the United States toward the international system has been largely reactive: until World War II, the United States neither wanted nor was required to be a major shaper of the international system. After the war, the emergence of the United States as virtually the only counterweight to expansionist Soviet communism thrust the United States into a leadership role. Opposition to American activism has philosophical roots in questions about the role and extent of government in promoting or protecting American values: opposition to American international military activism, for instance, flows naturally from minimalist conceptions of the role of government generally, whereas activism implies a greater role for government.

The third factor reflects an assessment of environmental influences. The points that dominate vary in some measure based upon world conditions. The immediate post-9/11 period, for instance, was one of maximum activism, providing the platform from which the wars in Iraq and Afghanistan emerged. In that environment of national rage, the hostility of the international environment largely overrode any suggestions of restraint from memories about precedents like Vietnam, and even the growing sense of political partisanship and paralysis were overcome in the patriotic outpouring of support for pursuing goals consciously tied to revenge for the September 11 attacks.

Conditions in the 2010s have been more ambivalent. The militant activism of the immediate post-9/11 period created the improved conditions that American policymakers hoped for at the time, and the result has been to raise questions about the policy of activism in places like the Middle East, a position President Trump appears to share. Syria is a particularly significant marker, where the forty-fifth president has essentially maintained that the outcome is a local, internal problem, and certainly not an American imperative to shape.

The *high activism* end of the scale (what Sapolsky, Gholz, and Talmadge and others call *primacist* to indicate a belief in American primacy in the world) has come into especially intense question. Within the American tradition, this position has rarely been expressed in overtly militarist terms, such as the advocacy of evangelical applications of force as the primary tool of American policy. The period of "manifest destiny" as the United States spread across the American West may be an exception, especially from the vantage point of those Native American tribes who were subjugated by the US Army in the process. Rather, high activism in the American experience must be considered as a more restrained predilection toward a universal view of the utility of force to solve American national security problems. It represents a tendency to consider the utility of force earlier, rather than later, in the consideration of how the United States ought to respond to different challenges—force as less than a last resort. Even this predilection has come into question in an international environment in which there is considerable systemic volatility but in which American vital interests are often not clearly engaged or threatened.

The closest example of advocacy for the high activism position in the contemporary environment is probably reserved for the remnants of the neoconservatives, people like John Bolton. This philosophy is evangelical and idealist in its advocacy of political democracy as a palliative to instability and insecurity and in its willingness to consider the use of military force to promote or even install democracy in places where it does not currently exist. The clearest evidence of the application of this philosophical predisposition was the attempted "conversion by the sword" of Iraq from the authoritarian rule of Saddam Hussein in the 2003 invasion, an action advocated, planned, and largely implemented by the neoconservatives who dominated national security discussions within the George W. Bush administration. Open advocacy of this position has receded markedly since the neoconservatives were displaced from policy positions in 2009 with the election of Democratic president Obama.

Although he was not a neoconservative himself, the late senator John McCain of Arizona was as close a beacon of the high activism position as could be found in the current political landscape. His advocacy of the application of American military means manifested itself in his support for more aggressive American actions in Libya in 2011 and in his continuing advocacy of similar policies toward the rule of Bashar al-Assad in Syria, where he led calls for the United States to provide military assistance to the rebels and against IS.

The other end of the spectrum, *isolationism*, has attracted a small and curious combination of supporters. The core assumption of this position is that the United States should only contemplate and employ American military forces in situations of clear and unambiguous threat directly to the United States and should, as a rule, neither think about nor use that force for expeditionary purposes not intimately tied to a direct assault on this country. The odd combination of supporters for this position includes libertarians on the political right and antimilitary radicals on the political left. The libertarians, of whom maverick GOP senator Rand Paul has been the most visible symbol, argue the basis of noninvolvement in the affairs of other states on constitutional grounds. Paul, for instance, argues a very limited interpretation of the constitutional intention for government activism, maintaining that the government's sole legitimate role is protecting the liberty of individuals from compromise by government. This protection includes the need to protect that liberty from outside threats, but he and his followers argue that such threats should be assessed narrowly in a way that leads to something like a severe interpretation of using force only when the most vital interests, those bordering on national survival, are engaged. Applications to contingencies that are less dire represent prostitutions of the concept of defense and infringements on the liberty of those who are forced to carry out such adventures.

The libertarians are joined by the generally pacifist, antiwar left in adopting the isolationist banner. The reasons are, of course, different. Pacifists tend to couch their opposition to using force in moral terms about the rectitude of imposing one's will forcefully on others. While many in the antiwar camp do not oppose a large welfare role for the government, they are also suspicious of the application of force as representing a self-interested "plot" on the part of members of what President Dwight D. Eisenhower (by no means an isolationist or antimilitary) deemed the "military-industrial complex." For many, humanitarian intervention represents a limited exception to this opposition.

Between these extremes is the position of *restrained activism*. It covers the broad gamut from high activism to isolationism, with numerous permutations that are more or less enthusiastic about the employment of force and that reflect a greater or lesser belief in the utility of force in specific situations.

If high activism answers the question "when should force be considered?" positively (most or all the time) and isolationism answers the same question negatively (hardly any of the time), restrained activists answer the same question more ambivalently (some of the time). This position recognizes that force is always a possible tool to be used in specific situations; it is an option "that remains on the table," but it may represent an option about which the policymaker has greater or lesser enthusiasm in a given situation. The position is politically centrist, seeking to reconcile the enthusiasm and reluctance of both extremes over the use of force. This includes the assessment of many of the variables considered earlier in this chapter.

To some extent, virtually all real situations and reactions to them fall within the range of restrained activist responses. For a country with as much military power as the United States, employing force is always a possibility both the United States and those opposing it must consider. Indeed, knowing that the American military option is available becomes part of the entire dynamic of many international conflict events, including the calculation of whether to precipitate a crisis given possible American responses. These reactions in turn reflect different assessments of the level of interests involved in any situation, whether other options have been exhausted, and whether force is efficacious. People who believe in restrained activism are likely to be more open-minded about each of these criteria than those at the extremes: high activists are likely to maintain force is always useful while isolationists maintain it hardly ever is.

The restrained activist position may be better understood by examples that exemplify different contemporary situations and responses across the spectrum. Three are offered here: American actions toward Libya in 2011, the assassination of Osama bin Laden in 2011, and current militant

Russian expansionism. In each of these instances, the extreme positions were rejected: the United States did not go (or has not gone) to war in any of these crises, but neither has it responded passively.

The case of Libya demonstrates the self-imposition of restraint. When the Libyan uprising against Muammar Gaddafi broke out as part of the Arab Spring of 2011, there was little overt American response. As the rebellion grew and the brutality of the regime against its opponents became more intense, pressure began to mount on the United States for some kind of response. From the high-activist end of the spectrum, there were calls for direct American military intervention, generally in the form of protection of the rebels through implementation of a no-fly zone that would keep Libyan government air forces from bombing them and allow the United States and its allies to attack Libyan ground forces. From the other end of the spectrum were calls counseling inaction on the grounds either that intervention was not in American interests or that it was unlawful and unwise.

The Obama administration chose an intermediate ground within the restrained activist part of the spectrum. It condemned Libyan brutality against its own people, and it helped organize and support a coalition of NATO allies, notably the French and Italians, in erecting and enforcing a no-fly zone. The French and Italians were more logical direct participants than the Americans on grounds of physical proximity to Libya, historical relationships (Libya was ruled by Italy between the World Wars and Britain and France after World War II), and greater interests (both countries are heavily dependent on Libyan oil, and most of their refineries are only configured to process the "sweet"—low-sulfur content—oil Libya produces). Given these circumstances and heavy American personal military involvement in Iraq and Afghanistan, the United States chose instead to "lead from behind," a restrained form of response.

The execution of bin Laden represents a more overt but still restrained form of applying force and one that seems likely to be a precedent for the future. When it learned that the Saudi terrorist was living virtually openly in the Pakistani city of Abbottabad and that the Pakistani government had no apparent plans to arrest him and turn him over to the United States, the Obama administration authorized a covert operation. Central Intelligence Agency (CIA) operational intelligence and planning were given to the Navy SEALs (Sea, Air, and Land Teams) to execute, and the result was a surgical strike that resulted in the killing of bin Laden. This form of military action had long been favored by elements within the administration and probably will serve as the model for controlling terrorist threats in the future. The option includes both the use of special operations forces (SOFs) and air options. It represents a military option, but one that is limited in what it can accomplish and in duration, expense, and length of commitment.

The example of American reaction to Russian expansionist moves in the Crimea and Eastern Ukraine represents the closest case of ambivalence about the propriety of responses within the middle option. When Russia moved into and annexed Crimea in 2014, the United States adopted a classically internationalist, restrained activism response, condemning the action, organizing international disapproval, and imposing sanctions on the Russians. When Russia upped the ante by providing military assistance to ethnic Russians in Eastern Ukraine seeking to break away from the Ukraine and become part of Russia, the Obama administration responded with additional sanctions and the limited provision of arms to aid the Ukrainian regime.

The reaction at the time and later illustrates the political peril of the middle ground. High activists like McCain argued the response was too weak and tepid in its military aspects and that a much stronger response in east Ukraine was necessary to protect American interests from the voracious Russians. Since his 2016 election, Trump has implicitly swung to the isolationist, pacifistic extreme, attempting to influence the Russians through highly personalized interactions with Putin and avoiding criticism of Russian expansionism. At the end of 2018, the result of applying these approaches was a major de-escalation of overt Russian expansionist activity in Ukraine and their retention of Crimea.

The choices about levels of restraint in the future will, of course, be affected by numerous other variables as well. Domestic political influences, including those driven by budgetary concerns, will militate toward the isolationist end of the spectrum, whereas the critical nature of some crises may nudge the country in the direction of greater activism. One outcome of the debate will be either to facilitate the development of a new national security strategy paradigm or to leave the country in its current strategic limbo of ad hoc responses to national security challenges as they arise.

CONCLUSION: ASSESSING THE FUTURE

In the end, the discussion returns to the observations with which the book began. It was asserted there that the United States was at one of its periodic national security policy crossroads. The reasons for this situation are both domestic and international. Domestically, the American political system is paralyzed by a hyper-partisan atmosphere in which the resulting inability to reach compromise solutions to complex problems has led to a debilitating policy gridlock. Few fundamental decisions get made in this atmosphere. Gridlock, however, means there is virtually no agreement on how to approach and try to solve the problems the country faces toward countries like China, the DPRK, and Russia and the tragic situations in places like Syria and Rohingya. This partisan deadlock has been made worse by the erratic behavior of the Trump White House in foreign affairs. Reduction on spending for national security is one candidate to help alleviate the situation, thereby ensnaring national security in a more fundamental American policy disagreement of which national security is not otherwise intrinsically a part. Internationally, the environment sends mixed messages. When crises ranging from Iranian nuclear weapons prospects to dealing with IS arise, policy pronouncements from the presidential administration are routinely met with denunciations from other Americans of opposing political persuasion, and they are instant, reflexive, and entirely predictable. What are American adversaries to think about what the United States will do in any given situation? Inconstancy appears to many foreign leaders to be the only constant in dealing with the Americans.

There are no easy answers or outcomes to the resulting debate over national security policy. High levels of American national security activism represented by inflated military employment have traditionally been followed by some level of respite, and the US military has benefited from a period of relatively lesser physical deployment to reinvigorate and refurbish itself, but potential situations that could be answered with American military forces remain on the international radar. The current domestic environment requires that one ask what future activism the United States government can agree to pursue in different situations and places. The recent experience in Iraq and Afghanistan requires asking what the United States might be getting itself into, whether it is willing or able to take on all the commitments that its intrusion may require both on the battlefield and in the postwar peace that ensues, and whether success can be reasonably assured under any circumstances.

None of these questions have easy answers. Indeed, the introductory chapter concluded by admitting that, in this situation of uncertainty, there are more questions than there are answers, and the same applies to the conclusion. This volume has tried to present and provide some analytical framework for thinking about the national security future. Assessing that future and arriving at sensible, defensible policy positions remains a work in progress that is itself subject to the vicissitudes of not always foreseeable influences.

STUDY/DISCUSSION QUESTIONS

1. What does it mean to say that the United States is "entering one of its periodic national security transitions"? What factors are creating the need for and influencing that transition? How do these factors contrast with the immediate post-9/11 environment?
2. What variables in the contemporary national security environment affect planning for the transition period in American national security policy? Describe each and its effects. How are they interactive?
3. What current policies and policy areas have an obvious impact on national security planning? Describe the influence of each. Are there other policy areas you think should be added to the list in the text? What are they?

4. Describe the spectrum of policy action models available to cope with the evolving national security environment in terms of the policy content and directions each proposes. Why is the general approach of restrained activism the most politically attractive alternative?
5. A return to a strategy based in realism is one possible outcome to the policy debate. On what premises would such a strategy be based? Would it work? Why or why not?
6. Based on your understanding of the relevant variables and forces that are at play, what kinds of general policy directions do you believe are most appropriate for the United States for the balance of the 2010s? Why?

SELECTED BIBLIOGRAPHY

Bacevich, Andrew J. "Even If We Defeat the Islamic State, We'll Still Lose the Bigger War." *Washington Post* (online), (October 3, 2014).

———. *Washington Rules: America's Path to Permanent War*. New York: Henry Holt and Company, 2010.

Betts, Richard K. "Pick Your Battles: Ending America's Permanent State of War." *Foreign Affairs* 93, 6 (November/December 2014), 15–24.

Chart Book: The Legacy of the Great Recession. New York: Center on Budget and Policy Priorities (online), (February 8, 2012).

Chua, Amy. "Tribal World: Identity Is All." *Foreign Affairs* 94, 4 (July/August 2018), 25–33.

Clausewitz, Carl von. *On War*. Rev. ed. Translated and edited by Michael Howard and Peter Paret. Princeton, NJ: Princeton University Press, 1984.

Cronin, Audrey Kurth, and James M. Ludes (eds.). *Modern Terrorism: Elements of a Grand Strategy*. Washington, DC: Georgetown University Press, 2004.

Deudmey, Daniel, and G. John Ikenberry. "Liberal World: The Resilient Order." *Foreign Affairs* 97, 4 (July/August 2018), 16–24.

Drew, Dennis M., and Donald M. Snow. *Making Strategy for the Twenty-First Century: An Introduction to National Security Processes and Problems*. Montgomery, AL: Air University Press, 2006.

Farrow, Ronan. *War on Peace: The End of Diplomacy and the Decline of American Influence*. New York: W. W. Norton, 2018.

Fishel, John T. *American National Security Policy: Authorities, Institutions, and Cases*. Lanham, MD: Rowman & Littlefield, 2017.

Gates, Robert M. "The Kind of President We Need." *Washington Post* (online), (December 3, 2015).

———. *Memoirs of a Secretary at War*. New York: Knopf, 2014.

George, Roger, Harvey Rishikoff, and Brent Scowcroft (eds.). *The National Security Enterprise: Navigating the Labyrinth*. 2nd ed. Washington, DC: Georgetown University Press, 2017.

Grusky, David N., Bruce Western, and Christopher Wimer (eds.). *The Great Recession*. New York: Russell Sage Foundation, 2011.

Jarmon, Jack. *The New Era in U.S. National Security: An Introduction to Emerging Threats and Challenges*. Lanham, MD: Rowman & Littlefield, 2014.

Jisi, Wang, et al. "Did America Get China Wrong? The Engagement Debate." *Foreign Affairs* 97, 4 (July/August 2018), 183–195.

Kaplan, Robert D. "The Art of Avoiding War." *The Atlantic* 313, 5 (June 2015), 32–33.

Kessler, Ronald. *The Trump White House: Changing the Rules of the Game*. New York: Crown Forum, 2018.

Kimmage, Michael. "The People's Authoritarian: How Russian Society Created Putin." *Foreign Affairs* 97, 4 (July/August 2018), 176–182.

Kotkin, Stephen. "Realist World: The Players Change, but the Game Remains." *Foreign Affairs* 97, 4 (July/August 2018), 10–15.

Meacham, Jon. *The Soul of America: The Battle for Our Better Angels*. New York: Random House, 2018.

Pinker, Steven. *The Better Angels of Our Nature: Why Violence Has Declined*. New York: Penguin Books, 2012.

Preble, Christopher A., and John Mueller. *A Dangerous World: Threat Perception and U.S. National Security*. Washington, DC: CATO Institute, 2014.

Reveron, Derek S., and Nikolas Gvosdev. *The Oxford Handbook of U.S. National Security*. Oxford, UK: Oxford University Press, 2018.

Sapolsky, Harvey M., Eugene Gholz, and Caitlin Talmadge. *U.S. Defense Policies: The Origins of Security Policy*. New York: Routledge, 2009.

Snow, Donald M. *Cases in U.S. National Security: Concepts and Processes*. Lanham, MD: Rowman & Littlefield, 2019.

———. *The Middle East, Oil, and the American National Security Policy: Intractable Conflicts, Impossible Solutions*. Lanham, MD: Rowman and Littlefield, 2016.

Stoessinger, John G. *Why Nations Go to War*. 11th ed. Belmont, CA: Wadsworth Publishing, 2010.

Suri, Jeremi, and Benjamin Valentino. *Sustainable Security: Rethinking American National Security Strategy*. Oxford, UK: Oxford University Press, 2016.

The United States Army and Marine Corps Counterinsurgency Manual: U.S. Army Field Manual 3–24, Marine Corps Warfighting Publication 3–33.5. Chicago, IL: University of Chicago Press, 2006.

Woodward, Bob. *Fear: Trump in the White House*. New York: Simon and Schuster, 2018.

INDEX

Note: Page numbers in italics indicate a figure and page numbers in bold indicate a table on the corresponding page.